PRINCE
Freya

3

STORY AND ART BY
KEIKO ISHIHARA

3
CONTENTS

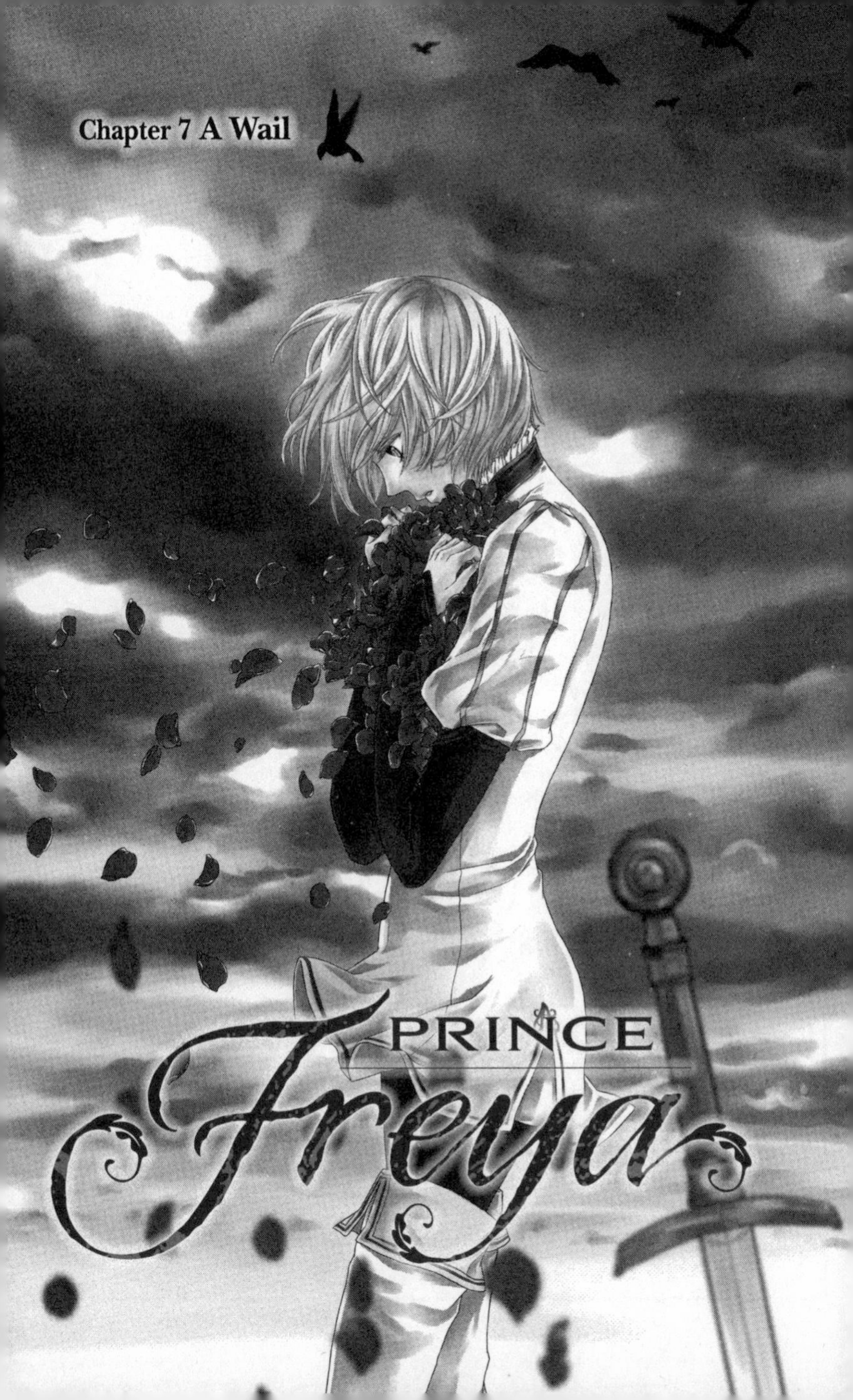
Chapter 7 A Wail
PRINCE
Freya

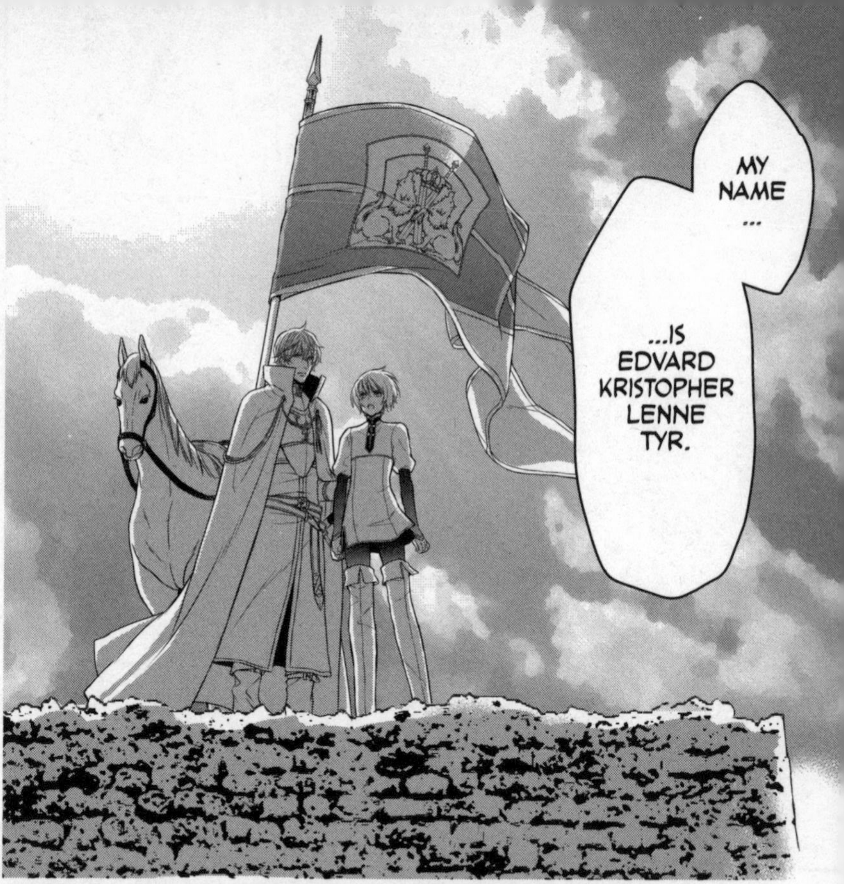
MY NAME ...
...IS EDVARD KRISTOPHER LENNE TYR.
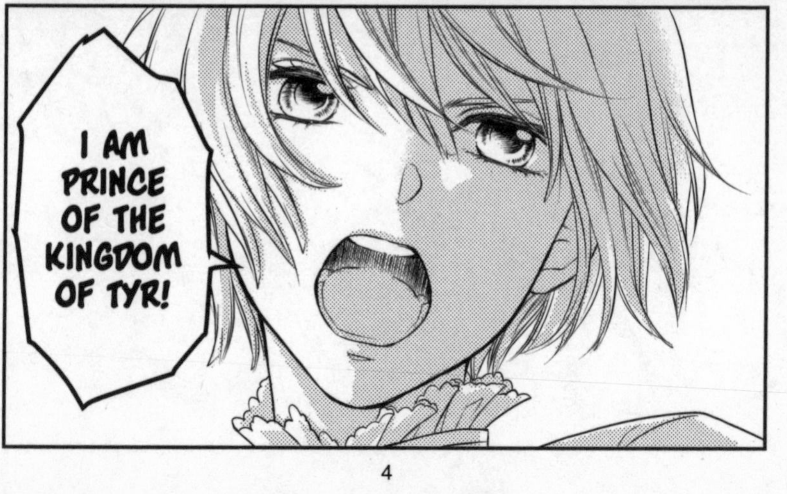
I AM PRINCE OF THE KINGDOM OF TYR!

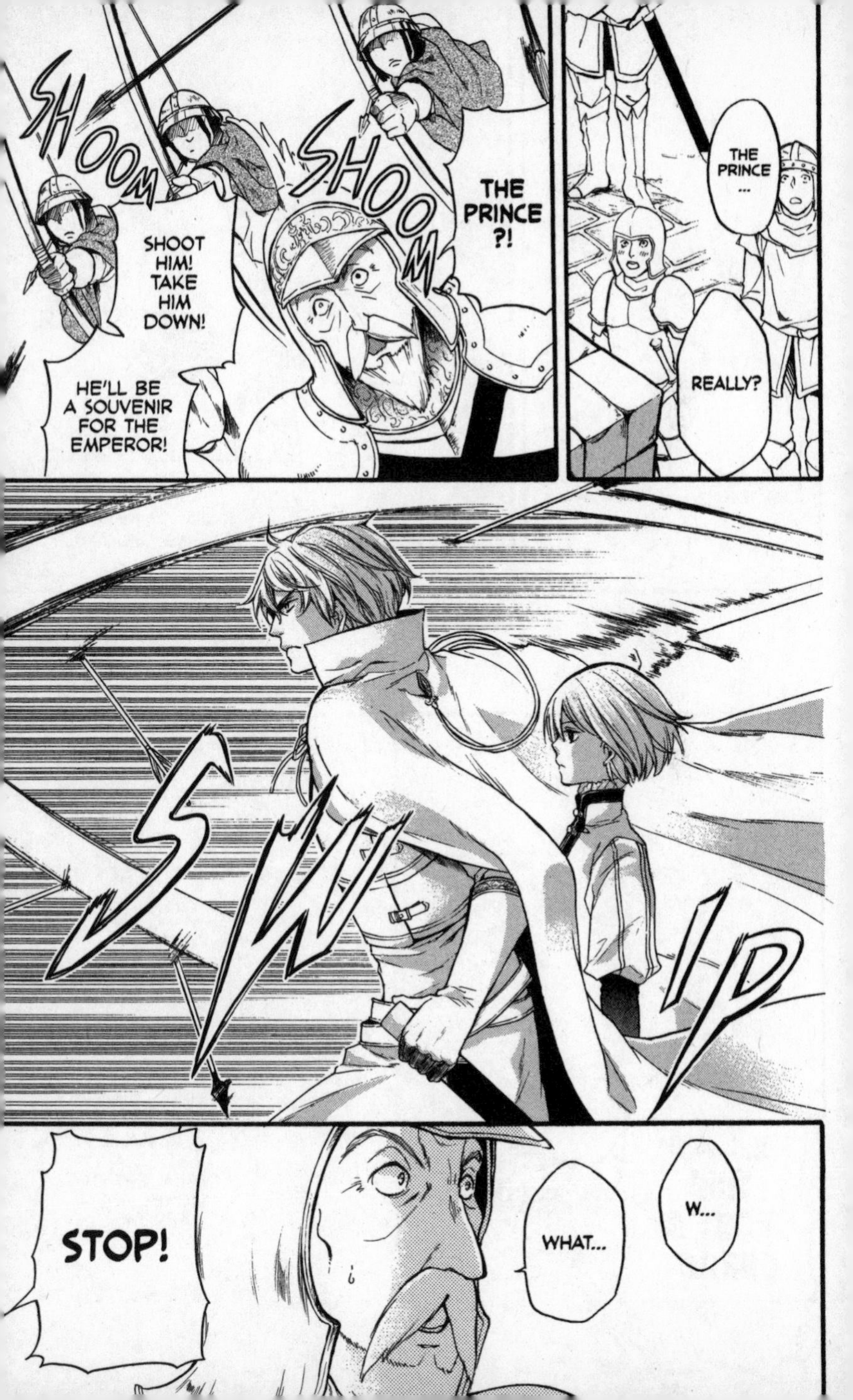
THE PRINCE ...
REALLY?
THE PRINCE ?!
SHOOM
SHOOM
SHOOT HIM! TAKE HIM DOWN!
HE'LL BE A SOUVENIR FOR THE EMPEROR!
SWIP
W...
WHAT...
STOP!

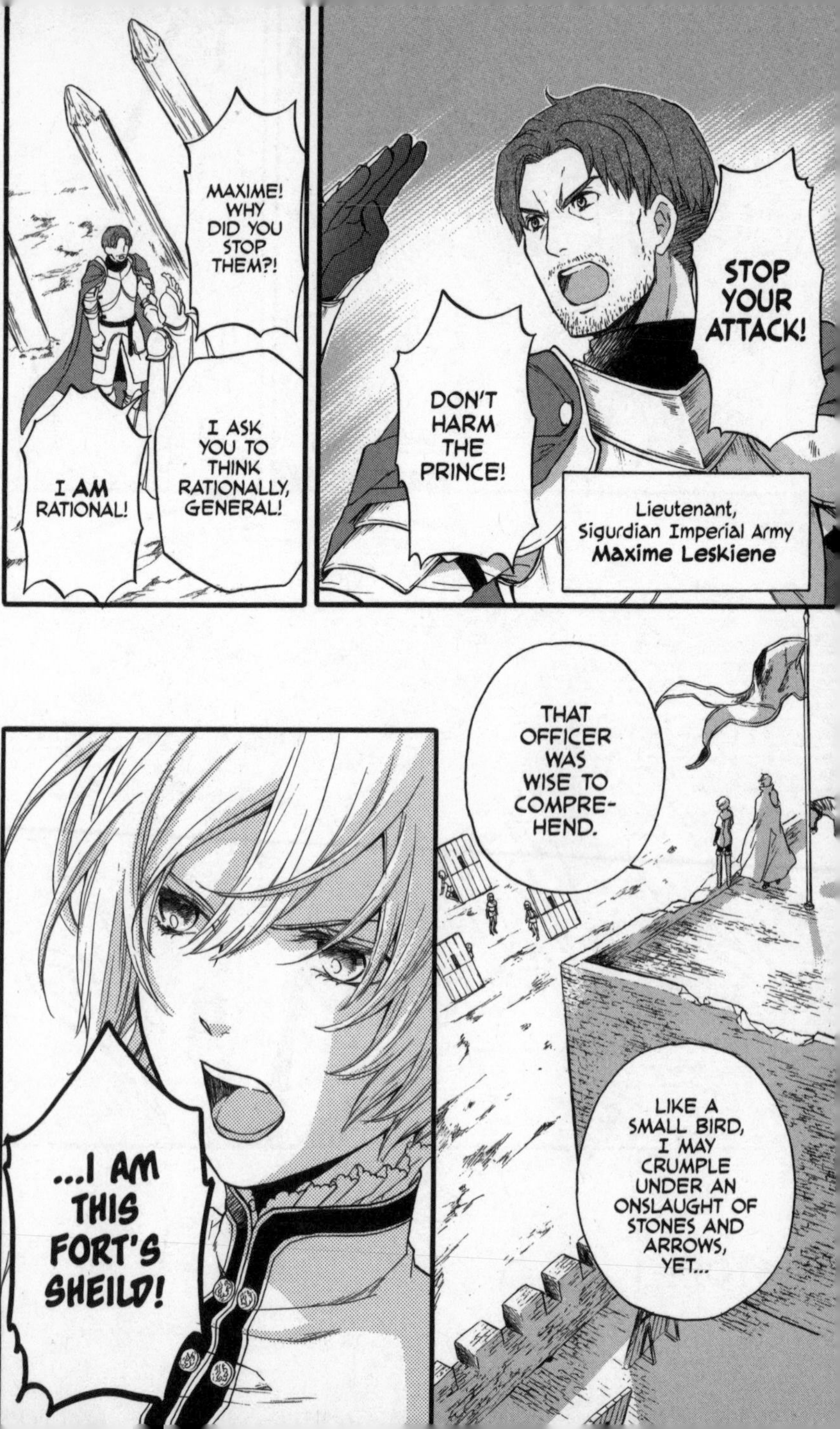
STOP YOUR ATTACK!
DON'T HARM THE PRINCE!
Lieutenant, Sigurdian Imperial Army Maxime Leskiene
MAXIME! WHY DID YOU STOP THEM?!
I ASK YOU TO THINK RATIONALLY, GENERAL!
I AM RATIONAL!
THAT OFFICER WAS WISE TO COMPREHEND.
LIKE A SMALL BIRD, I MAY CRUMPLE UNDER AN ONSLAUGHT OF STONES AND ARROWS, YET...
...I AM THIS FORT'S SHEILD!

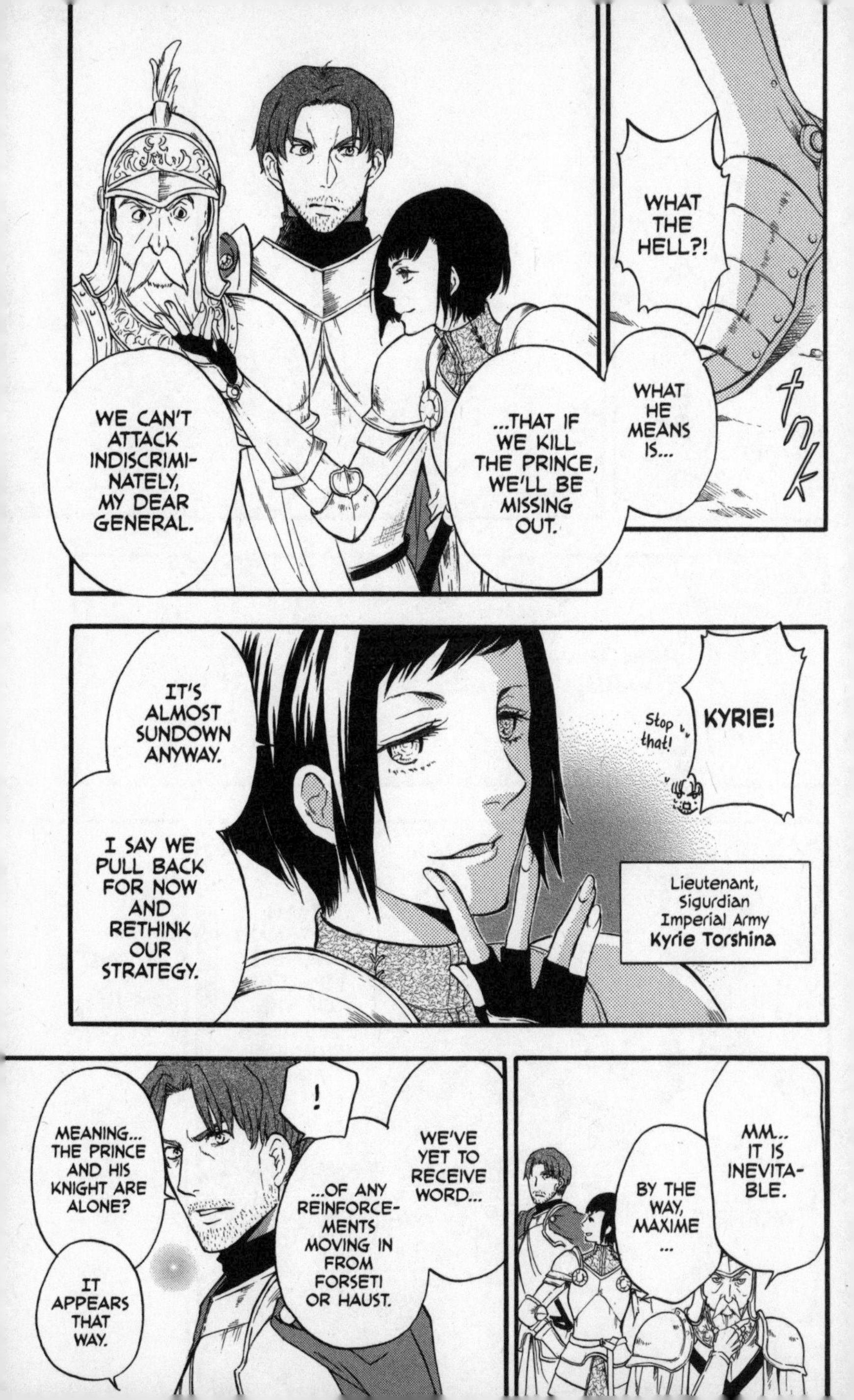
WHAT THE HELL?!
WHAT HE MEANS IS...
...THAT IF WE KILL THE PRINCE, WE'LL BE MISSING OUT.
WE CAN'T ATTACK INDISCRIMINATELY, MY DEAR GENERAL.
KYRIE!
Stop that!
IT'S ALMOST SUNDOWN ANYWAY.
I SAY WE PULL BACK FOR NOW AND RETHINK OUR STRATEGY.
Lieutenant, Sigurdian Imperial Army
Kyrie Torshina
MM.. IT IS INEVITABLE.
BY THE WAY, MAXIME ...
WE'VE YET TO RECEIVE WORD...
...OF ANY REINFORCEMENTS MOVING IN FROM FORSETI OR HAUST.
!
MEANING... THE PRINCE AND HIS KNIGHT ARE ALONE?
IT APPEARS THAT WAY.

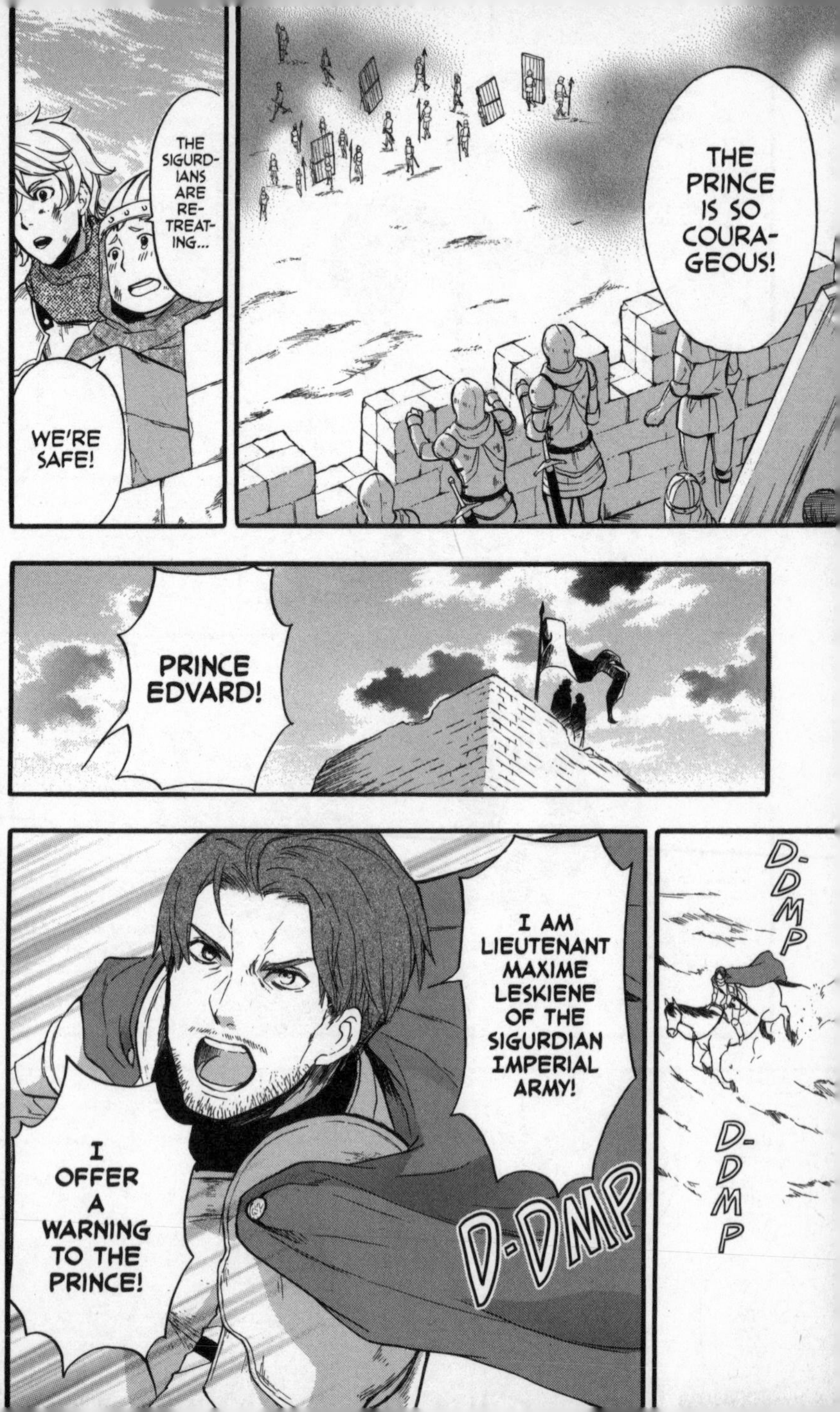
THE PRINCE IS SO COURAGEOUS!
THE SIGURDIANS ARE RETREATING...
WE'RE SAFE!
PRINCE EDVARD!
D-DDMP
D-DDMP
I AM LIEUTENANT MAXIME LESKIENE OF THE SIGURDIAN IMPERIAL ARMY!
D-DMP
I OFFER A WARNING TO THE PRINCE!

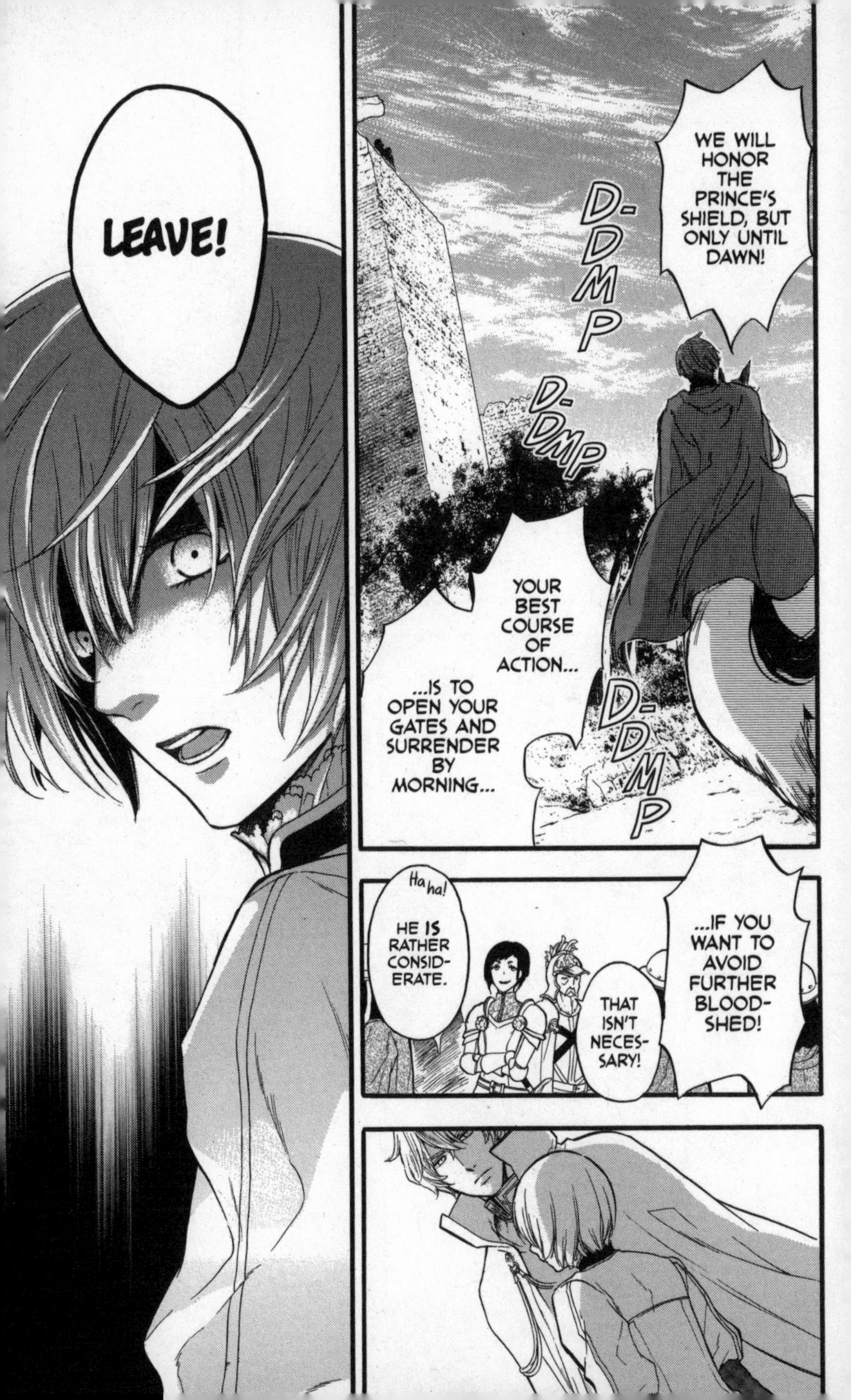
WE WILL HONOR THE PRINCE'S SHIELD, BUT ONLY UNTIL DAWN!
D-DMP
D-DMP
YOUR BEST COURSE OF ACTION...
...IS TO OPEN YOUR GATES AND SURRENDER BY MORNING...
D-DMP
...IF YOU WANT TO AVOID FURTHER BLOOD-SHED!
THAT ISN'T NECES-SARY!
Ha ha!
HE IS RATHER CONSID-ERATE.
LEAVE!

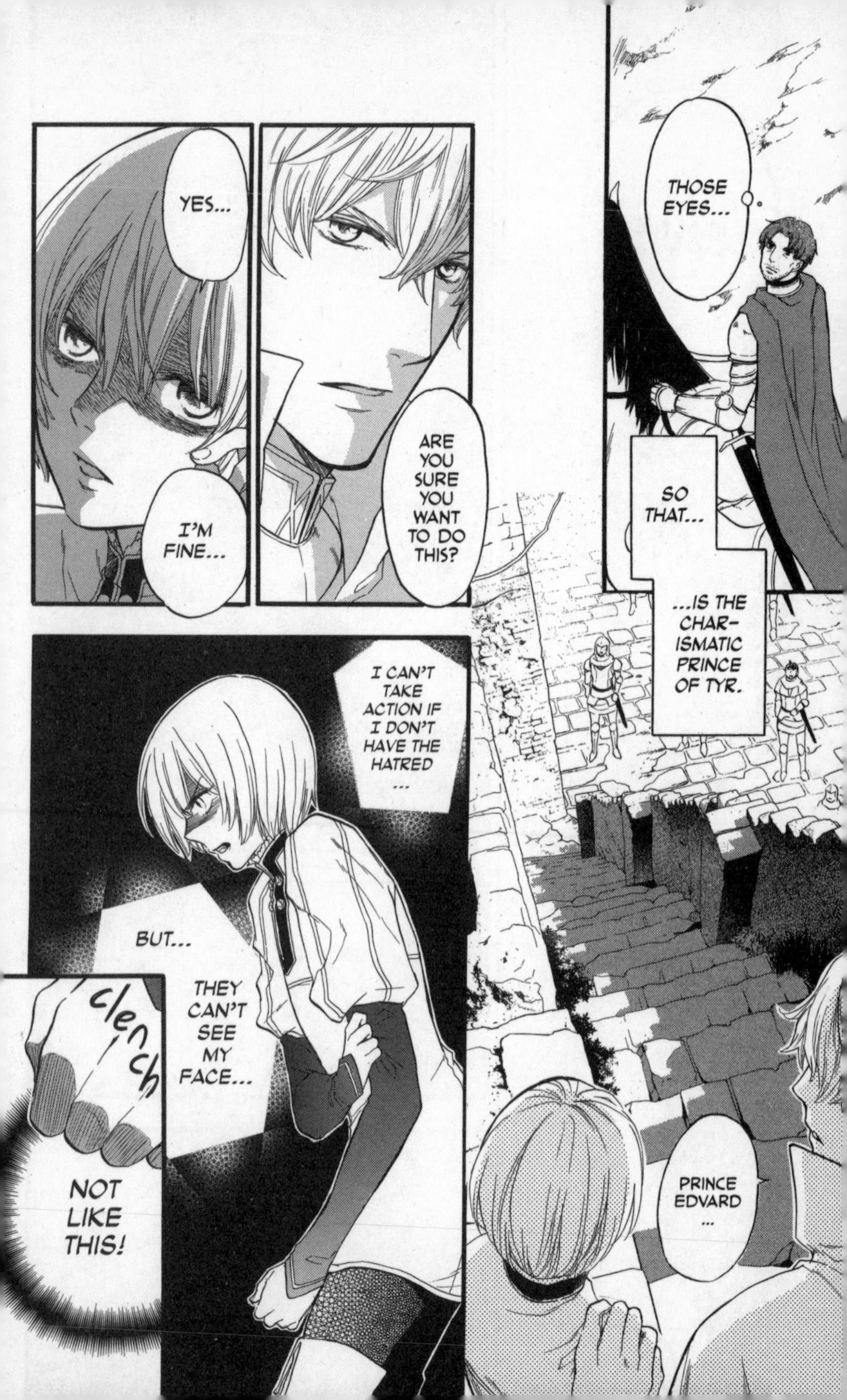
THOSE EYES...
SO THAT...
...IS THE CHARISMATIC PRINCE OF TYR.
PRINCE EDVARD...
ARE YOU SURE YOU WANT TO DO THIS?
YES...
I'M FINE...
I CAN'T TAKE ACTION IF I DON'T HAVE THE HATRED...
BUT...
THEY CAN'T SEE MY FACE...
clench
NOT LIKE THIS!

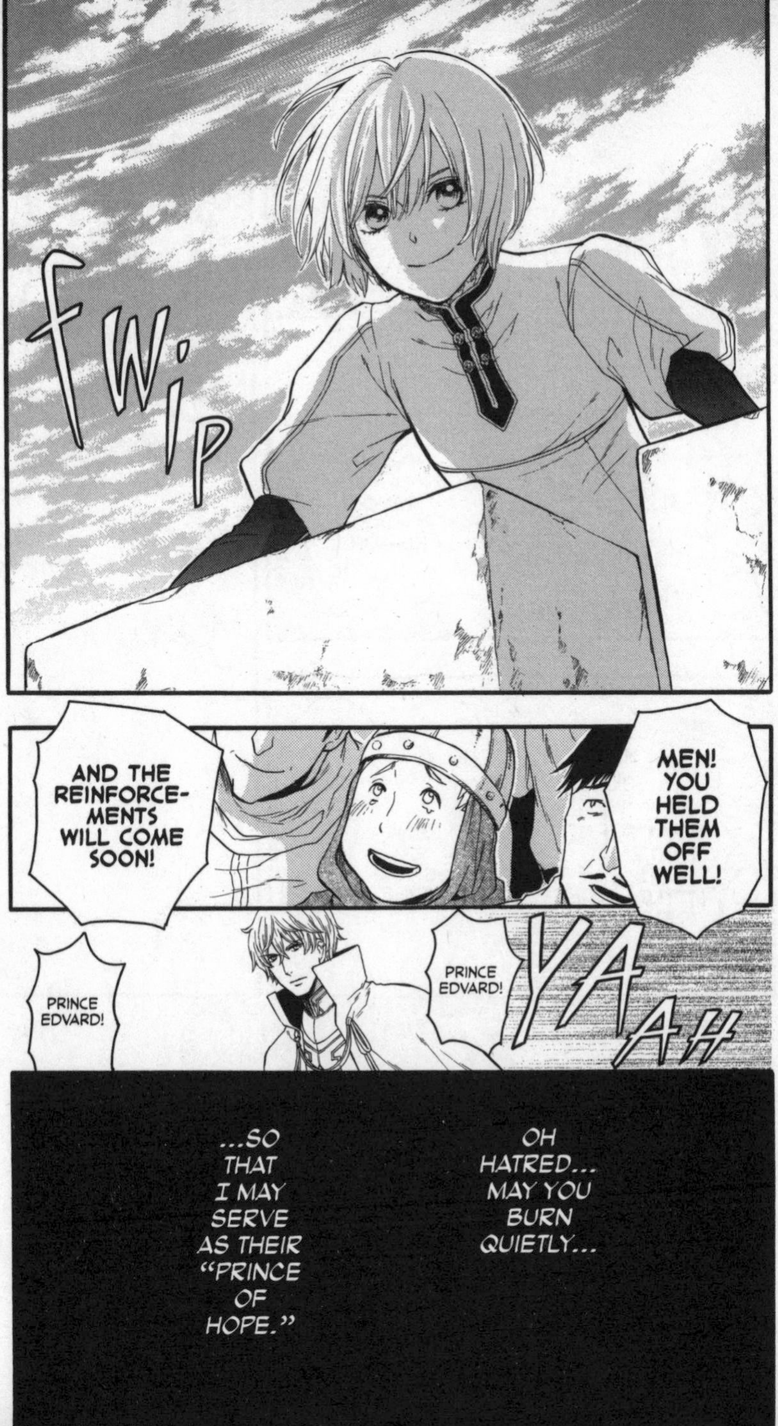
FWIP
MEN! YOU HELD THEM OFF WELL!
AND THE REINFORCEMENTS WILL COME SOON!
YAAH
PRINCE EDVARD!
PRINCE EDVARD!
OH HATRED... MAY YOU BURN QUIETLY...
...SO THAT I MAY SERVE AS THEIR "PRINCE OF HOPE."

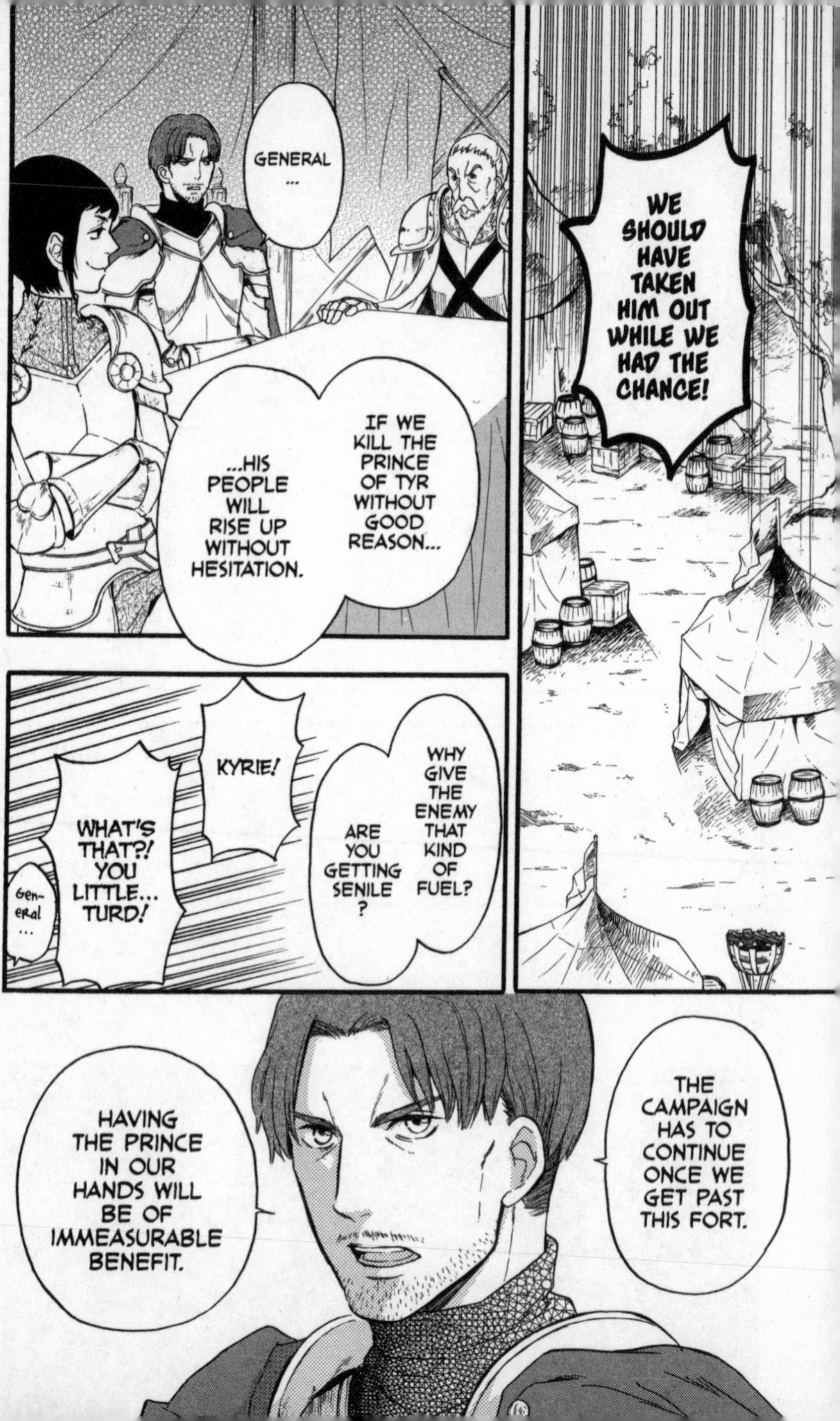
WE SHOULD HAVE TAKEN HIM OUT WHILE WE HAD THE CHANCE!
GENERAL ...
IF WE KILL THE PRINCE OF TYR WITHOUT GOOD REASON...
...HIS PEOPLE WILL RISE UP WITHOUT HESITATION.
WHY GIVE THE ENEMY THAT KIND OF FUEL?
ARE YOU GETTING SENILE?
KYRIE!
WHAT'S THAT?! YOU LITTLE... TURD!
General ...
THE CAMPAIGN HAS TO CONTINUE ONCE WE GET PAST THIS FORT.
HAVING THE PRINCE IN OUR HANDS WILL BE OF IMMEASURABLE BENEFIT.

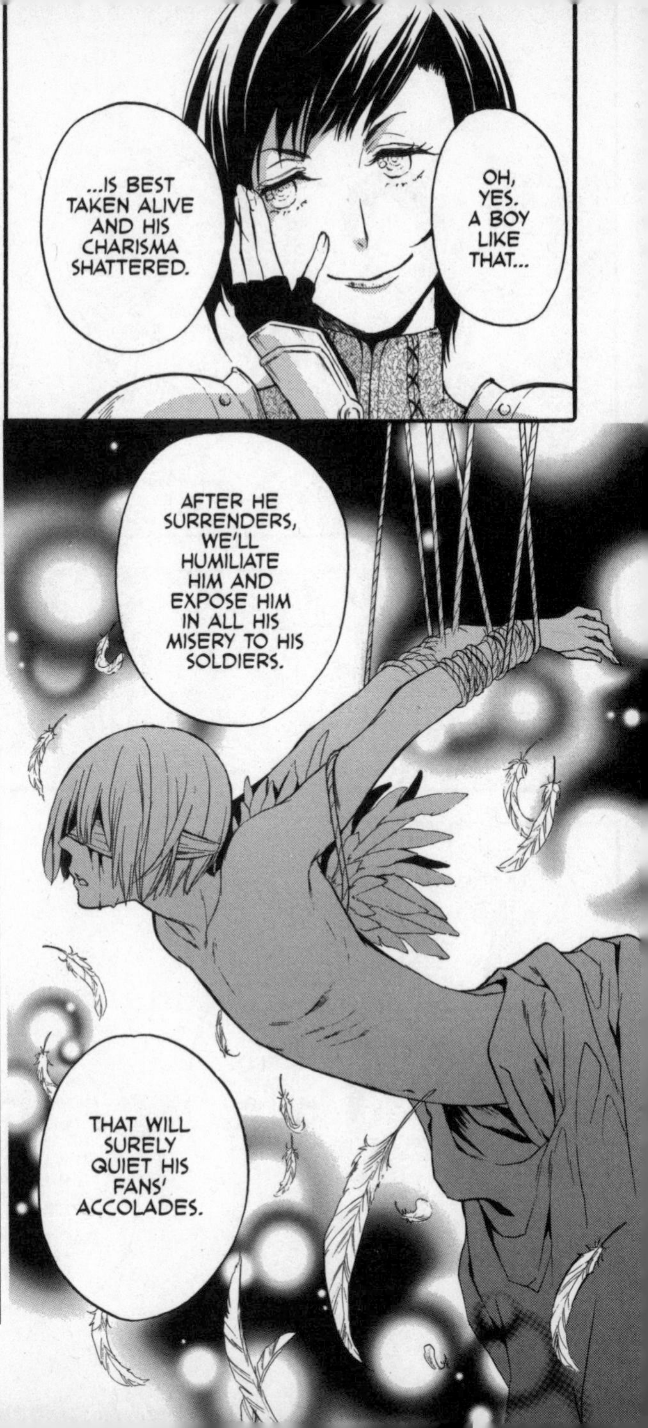
OH, YES. A BOY LIKE THAT...
...IS BEST TAKEN ALIVE AND HIS CHARISMA SHATTERED.
AFTER HE SURRENDERS, WE'LL HUMILIATE HIM AND EXPOSE HIM IN ALL HIS MISERY TO HIS SOLDIERS.
THAT WILL SURELY QUIET HIS FANS' ACCOLADES.

Thank you for picking up a copy of *Prince Freya*, volume 3!

I'm truly happy to have made it to the third volume and to dove right in.

In this volume, Freya and her companions face difficult challenges again...

I hope you root for them as they grit their teeth and fight through the hardships.

And with that, I hope you keep reading until the end.

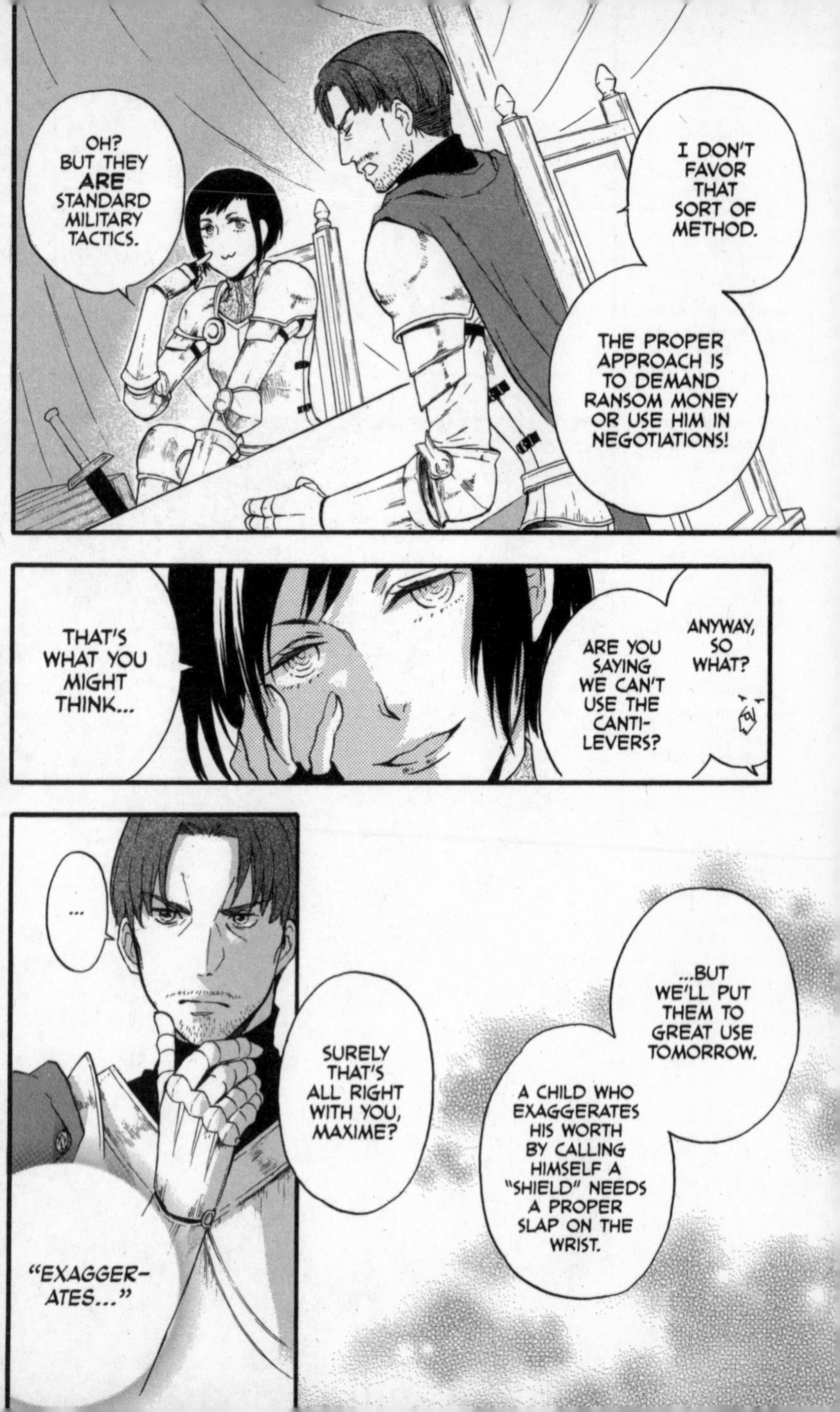
I DON'T FAVOR THAT SORT OF METHOD.
THE PROPER APPROACH IS TO DEMAND RANSOM MONEY OR USE HIM IN NEGOTIATIONS!
OH? BUT THEY **ARE** STANDARD MILITARY TACTICS.
ANYWAY, SO WHAT?
ARE YOU SAYING WE CAN'T USE THE CANTI-LEVERS?
THAT'S WHAT YOU MIGHT THINK...
...BUT WE'LL PUT THEM TO GREAT USE TOMORROW.
A CHILD WHO EXAGGERATES HIS WORTH BY CALLING HIMSELF A "SHIELD" NEEDS A PROPER SLAP ON THE WRIST.
SURELY THAT'S ALL RIGHT WITH YOU, MAXIME?
...
"EXAGGER-ATES..."

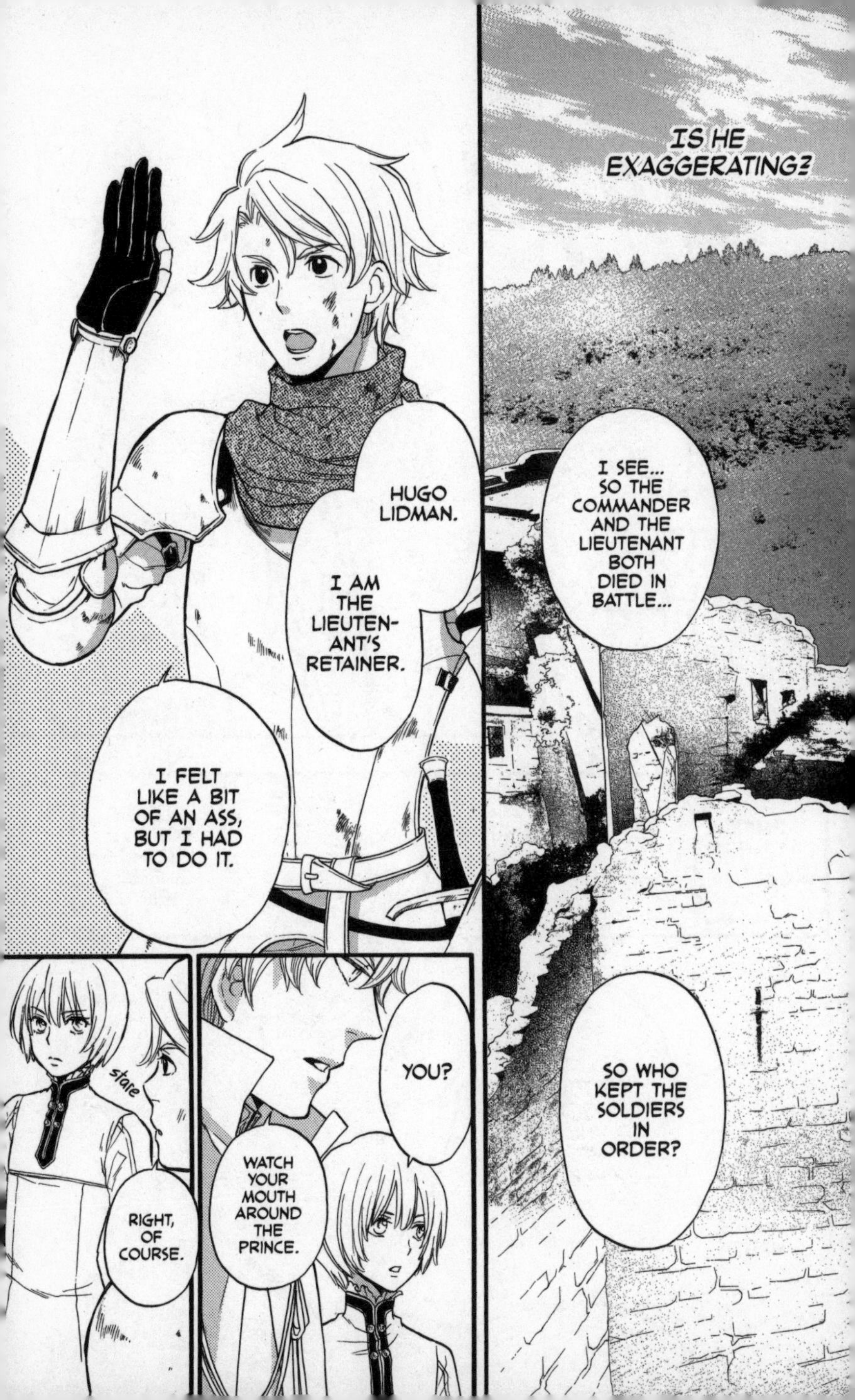
IS HE EXAGGERATING?
I SEE... SO THE COMMANDER AND THE LIEUTENANT BOTH DIED IN BATTLE...
SO WHO KEPT THE SOLDIERS IN ORDER?
HUGO LIDMAN.
I AM THE LIEUTEN-ANT'S RETAINER.
I FELT LIKE A BIT OF AN ASS, BUT I HAD TO DO IT.
YOU?
WATCH YOUR MOUTH AROUND THE PRINCE.
stare
RIGHT, OF COURSE.

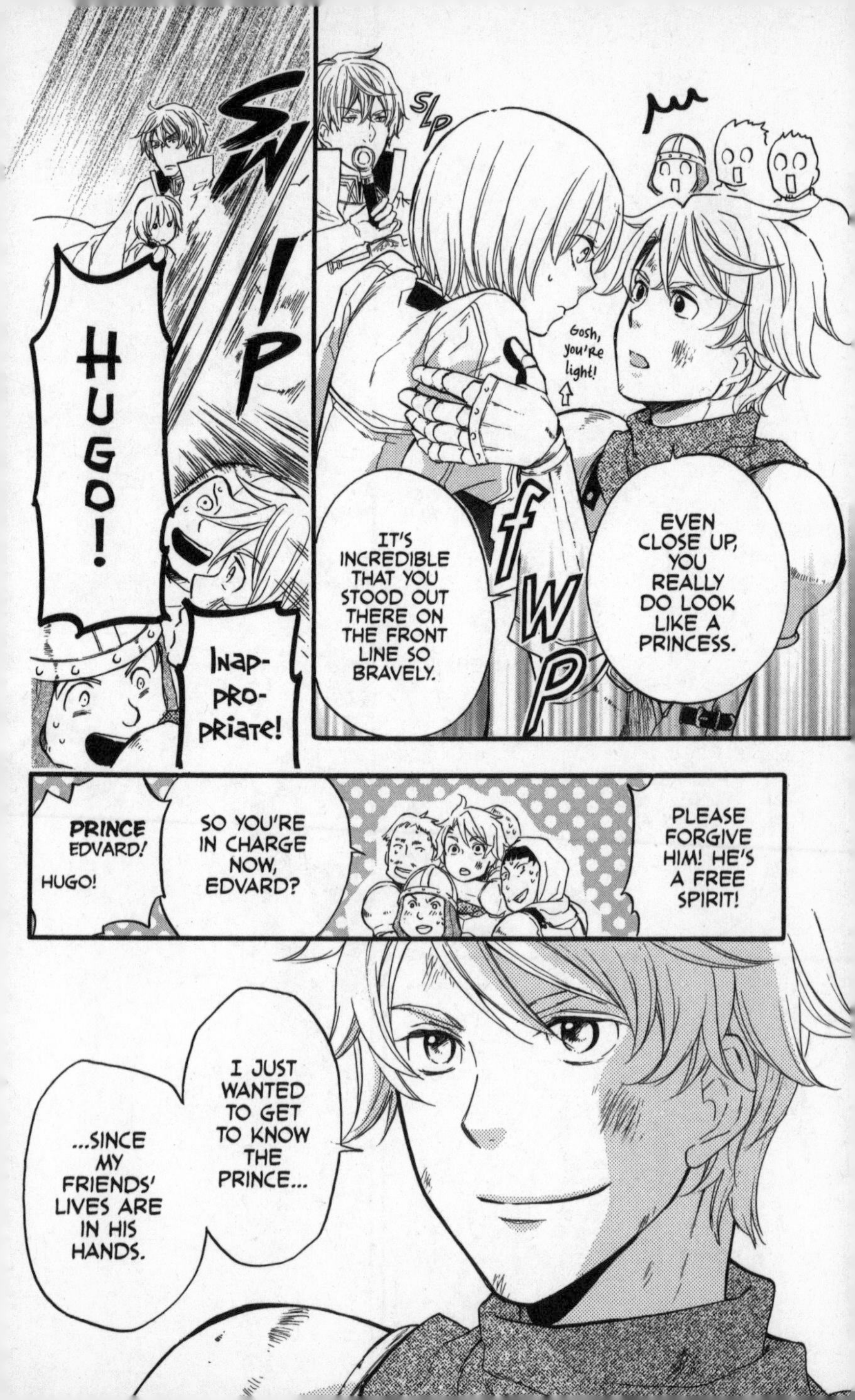
SLP
Gosh, you're light!
EVEN CLOSE UP, YOU REALLY DO LOOK LIKE A PRINCESS.
fwp
IT'S INCREDIBLE THAT YOU STOOD OUT THERE ON THE FRONT LINE SO BRAVELY.
SWIP
HUGO!
Inap-pro-priate!
PLEASE FORGIVE HIM! HE'S A FREE SPIRIT!
SO YOU'RE IN CHARGE NOW, EDVARD?
PRINCE EDVARD!
HUGO!
I JUST WANTED TO GET TO KNOW THE PRINCE...
...SINCE MY FRIENDS' LIVES ARE IN HIS HANDS.

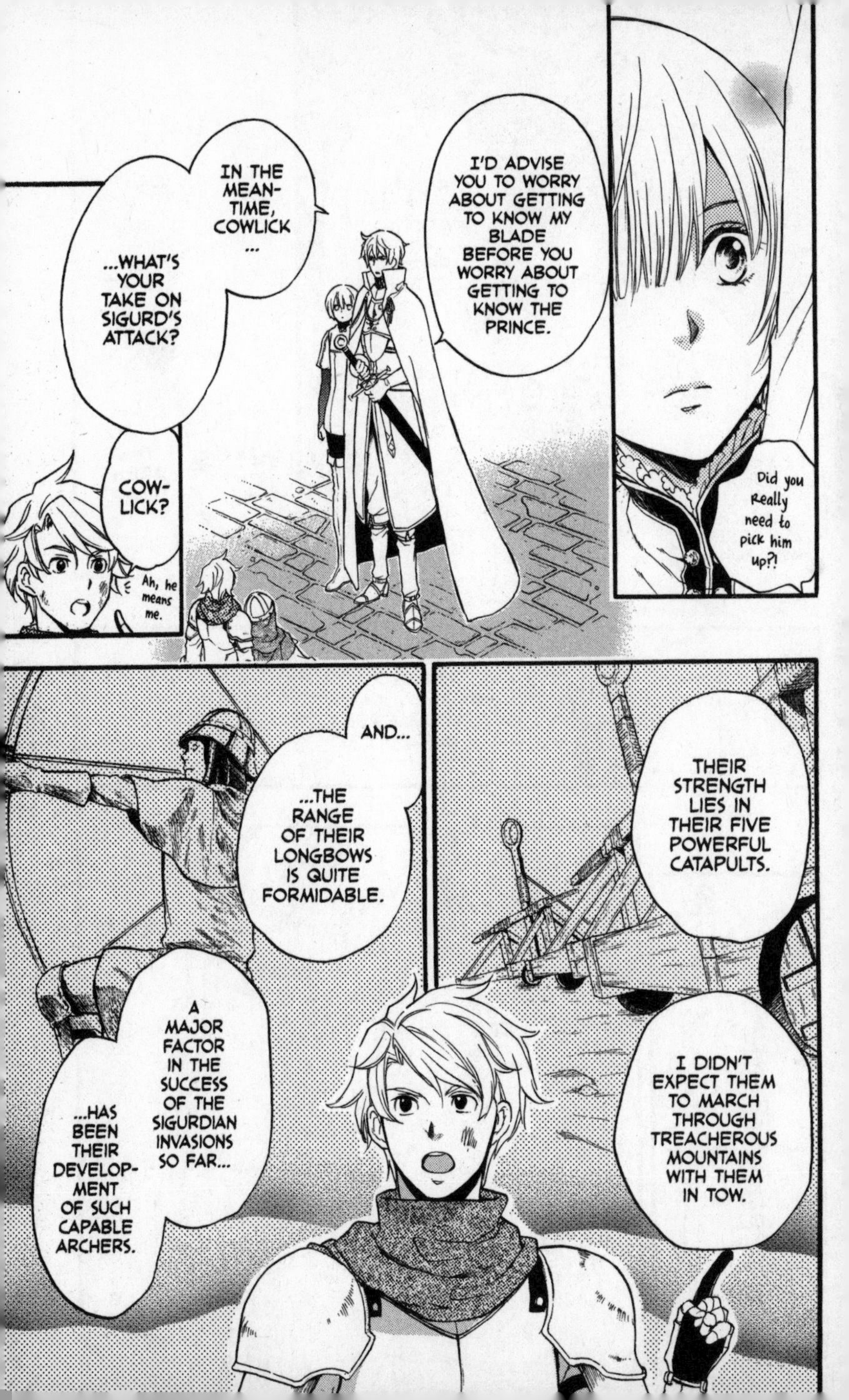
Did you Really need to pick him up?!
I'D ADVISE YOU TO WORRY ABOUT GETTING TO KNOW MY BLADE BEFORE YOU WORRY ABOUT GETTING TO KNOW THE PRINCE.
IN THE MEAN-TIME, COWLICK ...
...WHAT'S YOUR TAKE ON SIGURD'S ATTACK?
COW-LICK?
Ah, he means me.
THEIR STRENGTH LIES IN THEIR FIVE POWERFUL CATAPULTS.
I DIDN'T EXPECT THEM TO MARCH THROUGH TREACHEROUS MOUNTAINS WITH THEM IN TOW.
AND...
...THE RANGE OF THEIR LONGBOWS IS QUITE FORMIDABLE.
A MAJOR FACTOR IN THE SUCCESS OF THE SIGURDIAN INVASIONS SO FAR...
...HAS BEEN THEIR DEVELOP-MENT OF SUCH CAPABLE ARCHERS.

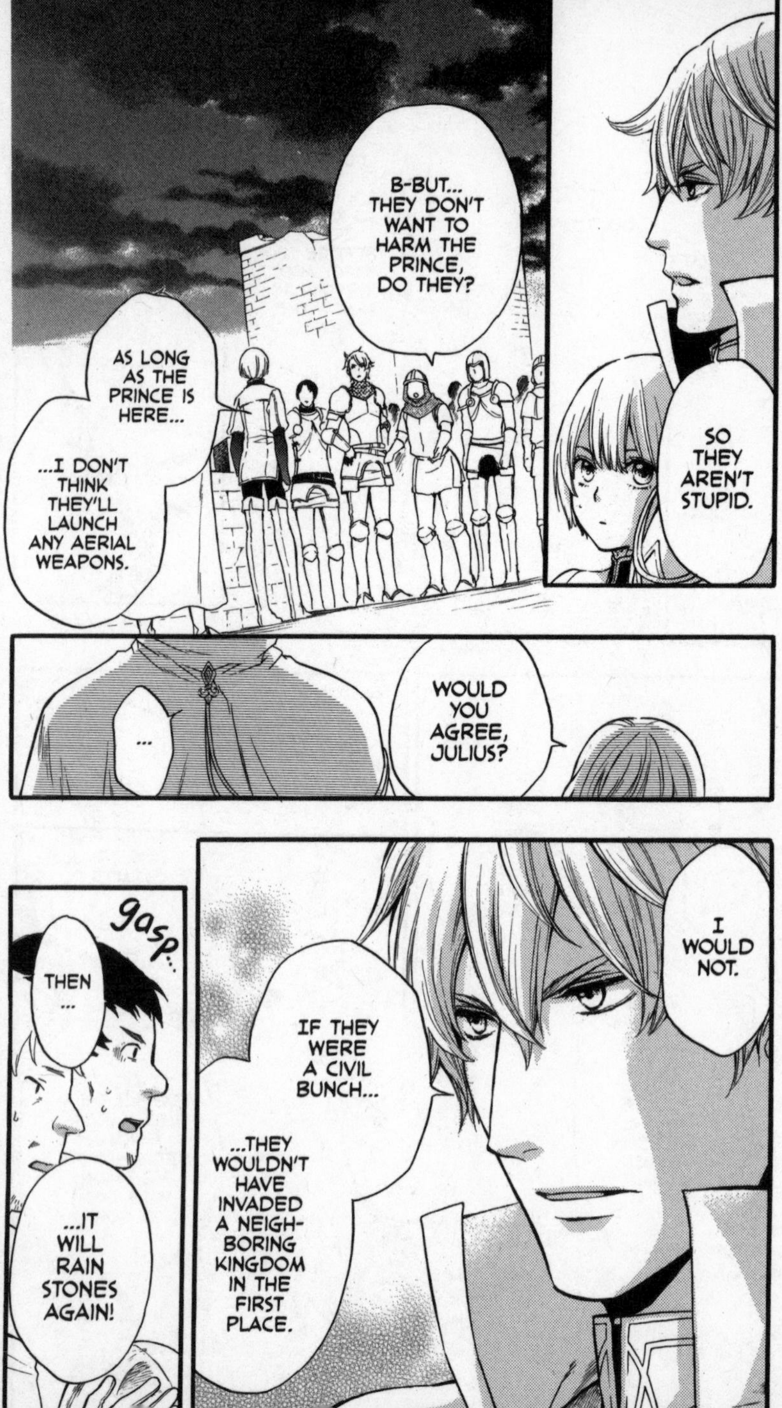
SO THEY AREN'T STUPID.
B-BUT... THEY DON'T WANT TO HARM THE PRINCE, DO THEY?
AS LONG AS THE PRINCE IS HERE...
...I DON'T THINK THEY'LL LAUNCH ANY AERIAL WEAPONS.
WOULD YOU AGREE, JULIUS?
...
I WOULD NOT.
IF THEY WERE A CIVIL BUNCH...
...THEY WOULDN'T HAVE INVADED A NEIGHBORING KINGDOM IN THE FIRST PLACE.
gasp...
THEN...
...IT WILL RAIN STONES AGAIN!

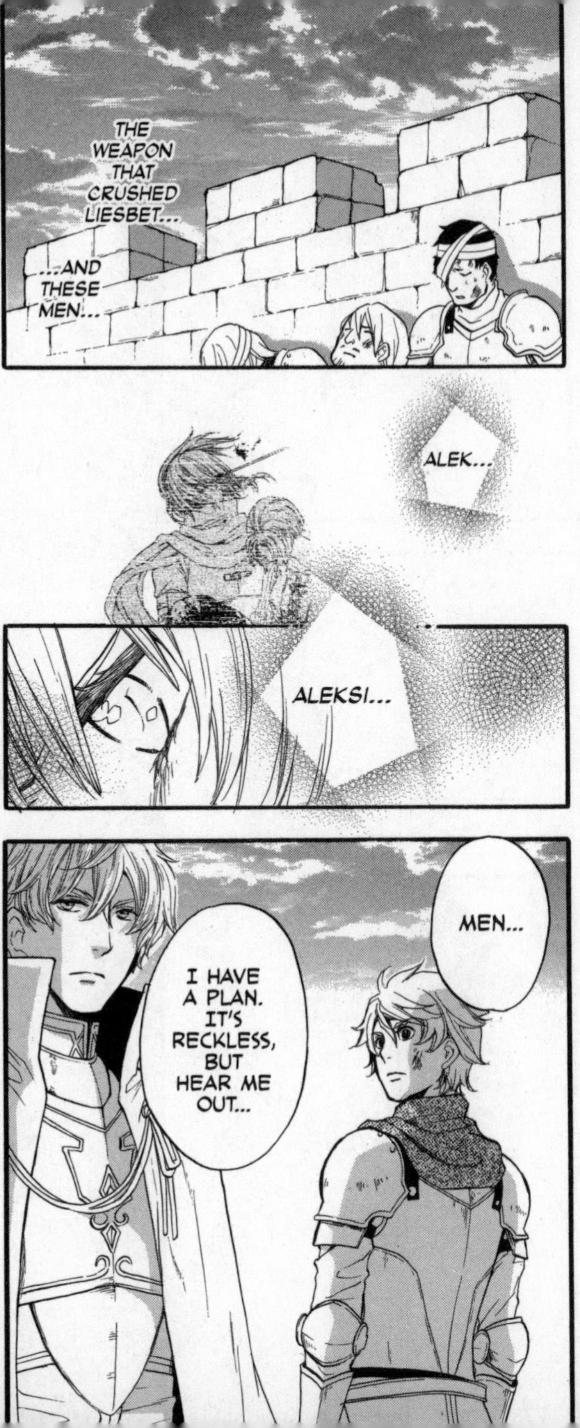
THE WEAPON THAT CRUSHED LIESBET...
...AND THESE MEN...
ALEK...
ALEKSI...
MEN...
I HAVE A PLAN. IT'S RECKLESS, BUT HEAR ME OUT...

Hugo

He's a happy soldier who takes pride in his unruly hair.

He comes off as someone who doesn't know how to read a room, but he actually pays quite close attention to the people around him. He was the life of the party at the fort.

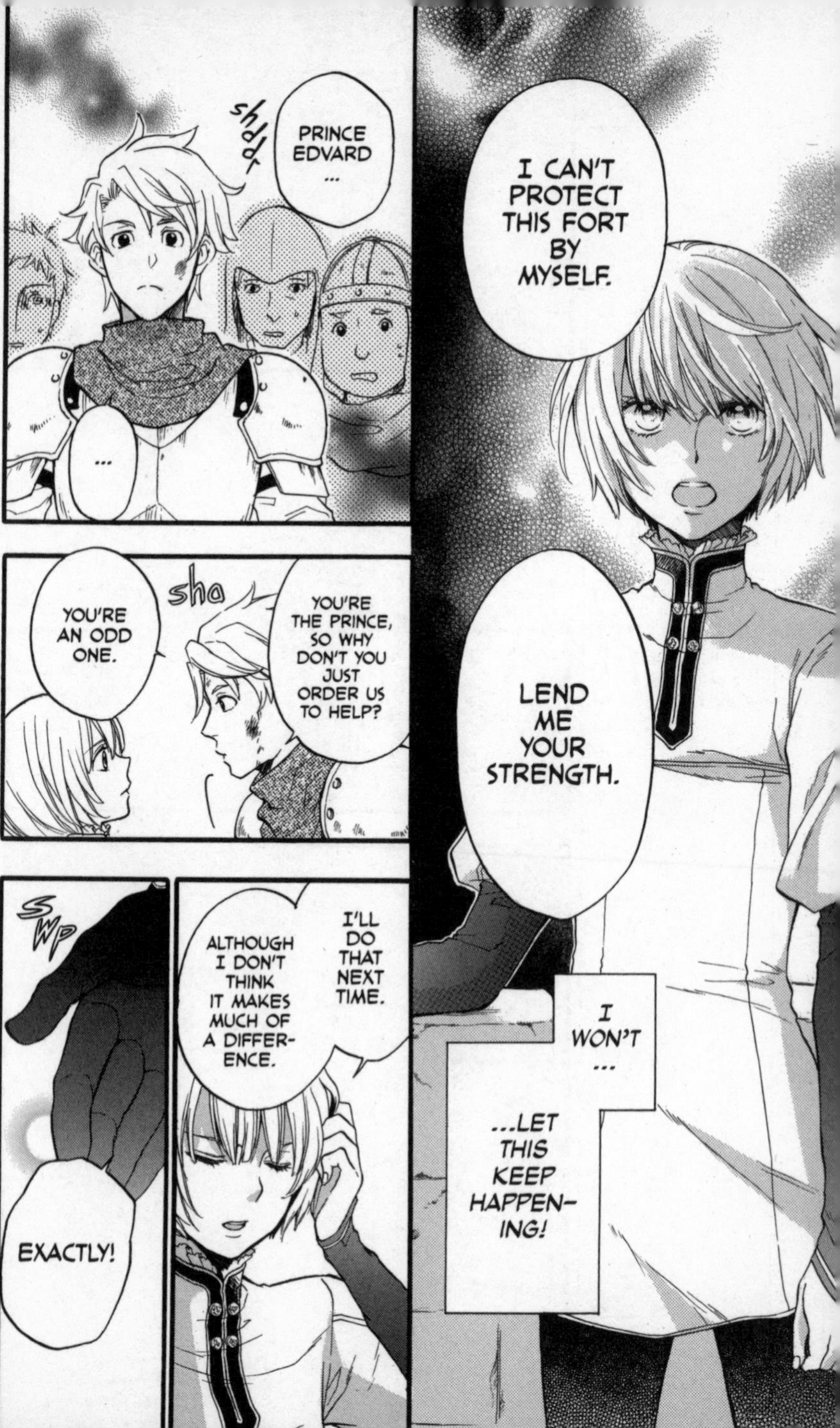
I CAN'T PROTECT THIS FORT BY MYSELF.
LEND ME YOUR STRENGTH.
I WON'T ...
...LET THIS KEEP HAPPEN-ING!
shdd
PRINCE EDVARD ...
...
YOU'RE THE PRINCE, SO WHY DON'T YOU JUST ORDER US TO HELP?
sha
YOU'RE AN ODD ONE.
I'LL DO THAT NEXT TIME.
ALTHOUGH I DON'T THINK IT MAKES MUCH OF A DIFFER-ENCE.
SWP
EXACTLY!

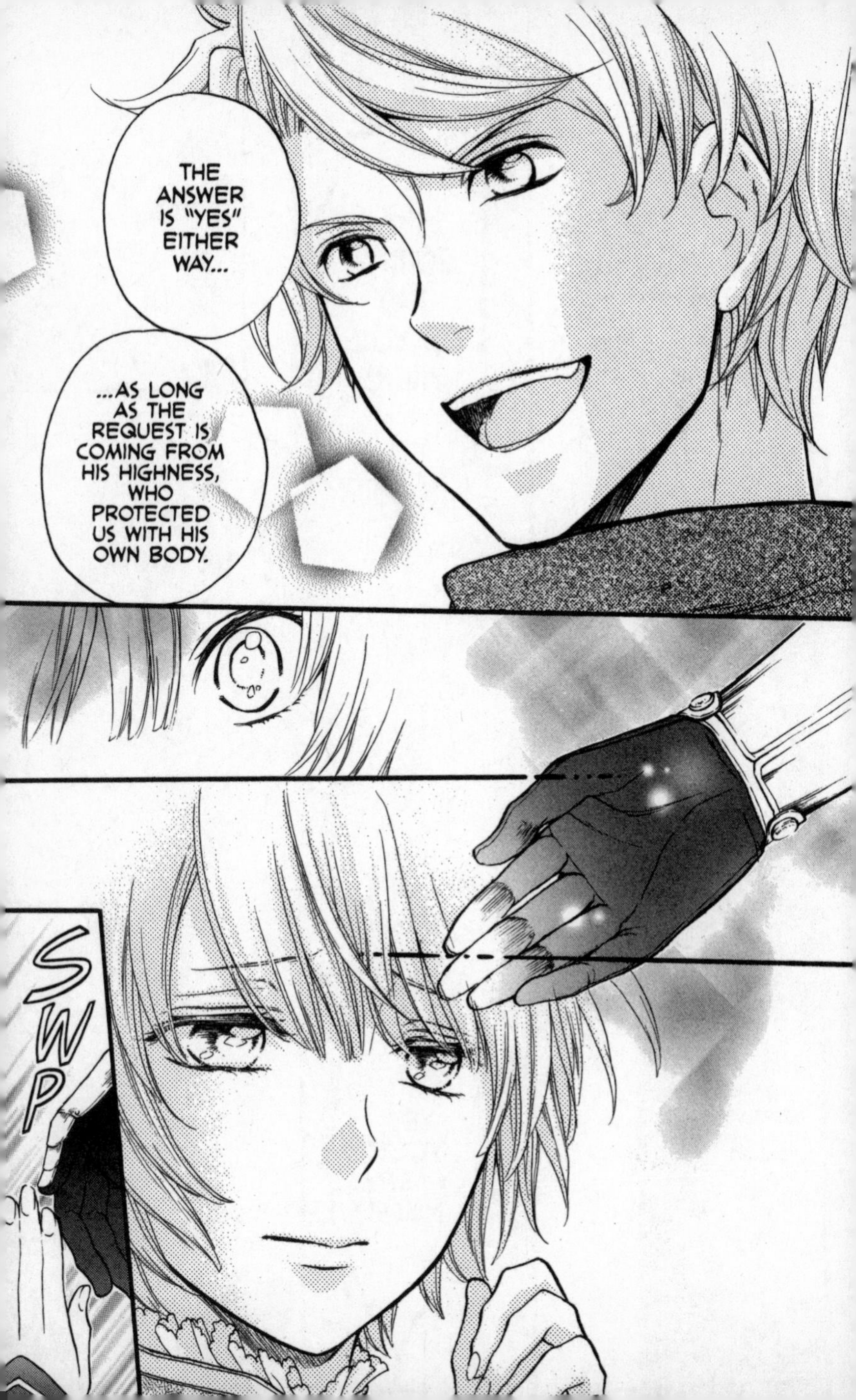
THE ANSWER IS "YES" EITHER WAY...
...AS LONG AS THE REQUEST IS COMING FROM HIS HIGHNESS, WHO PROTECTED US WITH HIS OWN BODY.
SWP

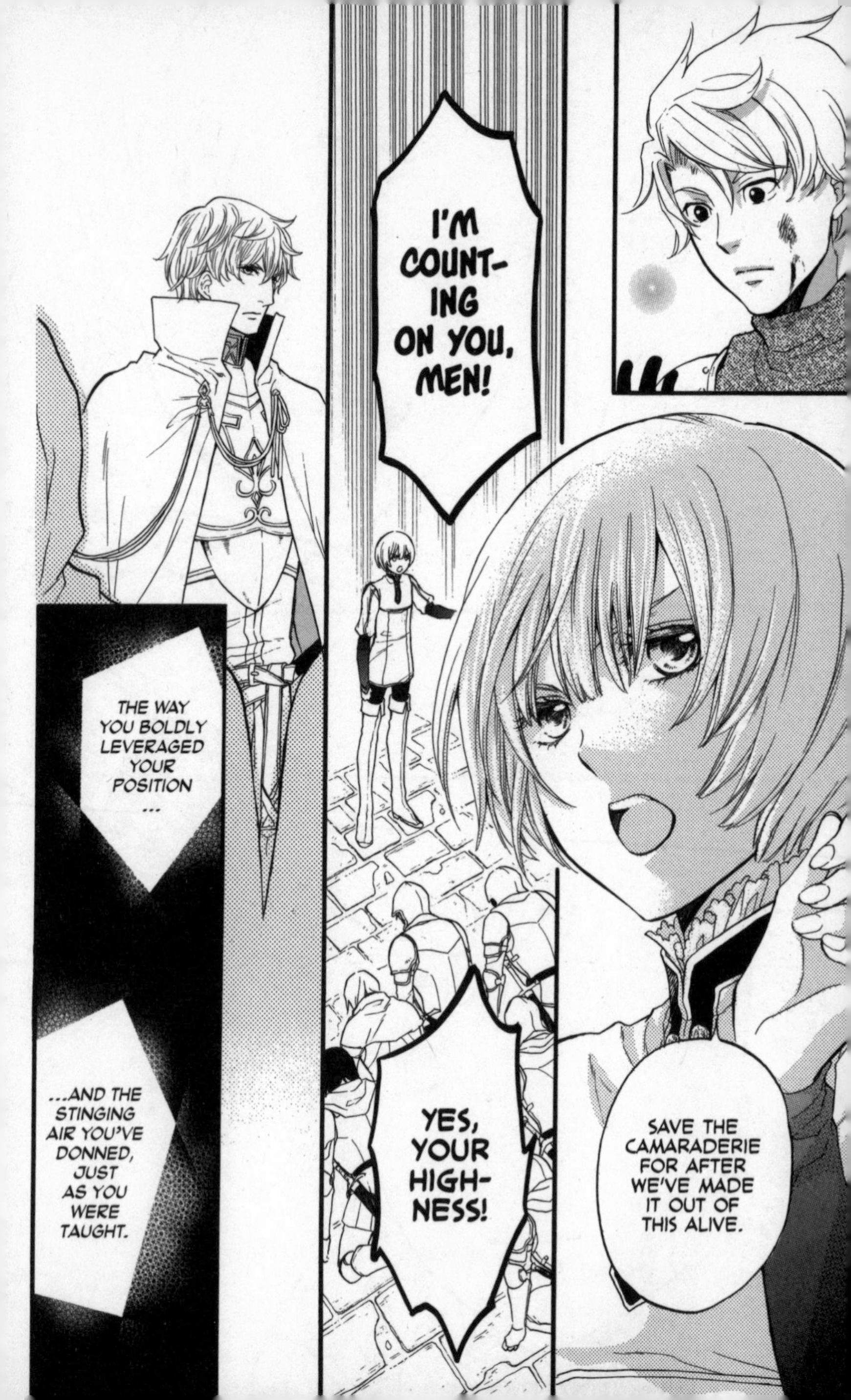
SAVE THE CAMARADERIE FOR AFTER WE'VE MADE IT OUT OF THIS ALIVE.
I'M COUNTING ON YOU, MEN!
YES, YOUR HIGHNESS!
THE WAY YOU BOLDLY LEVERAGED YOUR POSITION ...
...AND THE STINGING AIR YOU'VE DONNED, JUST AS YOU WERE TAUGHT.

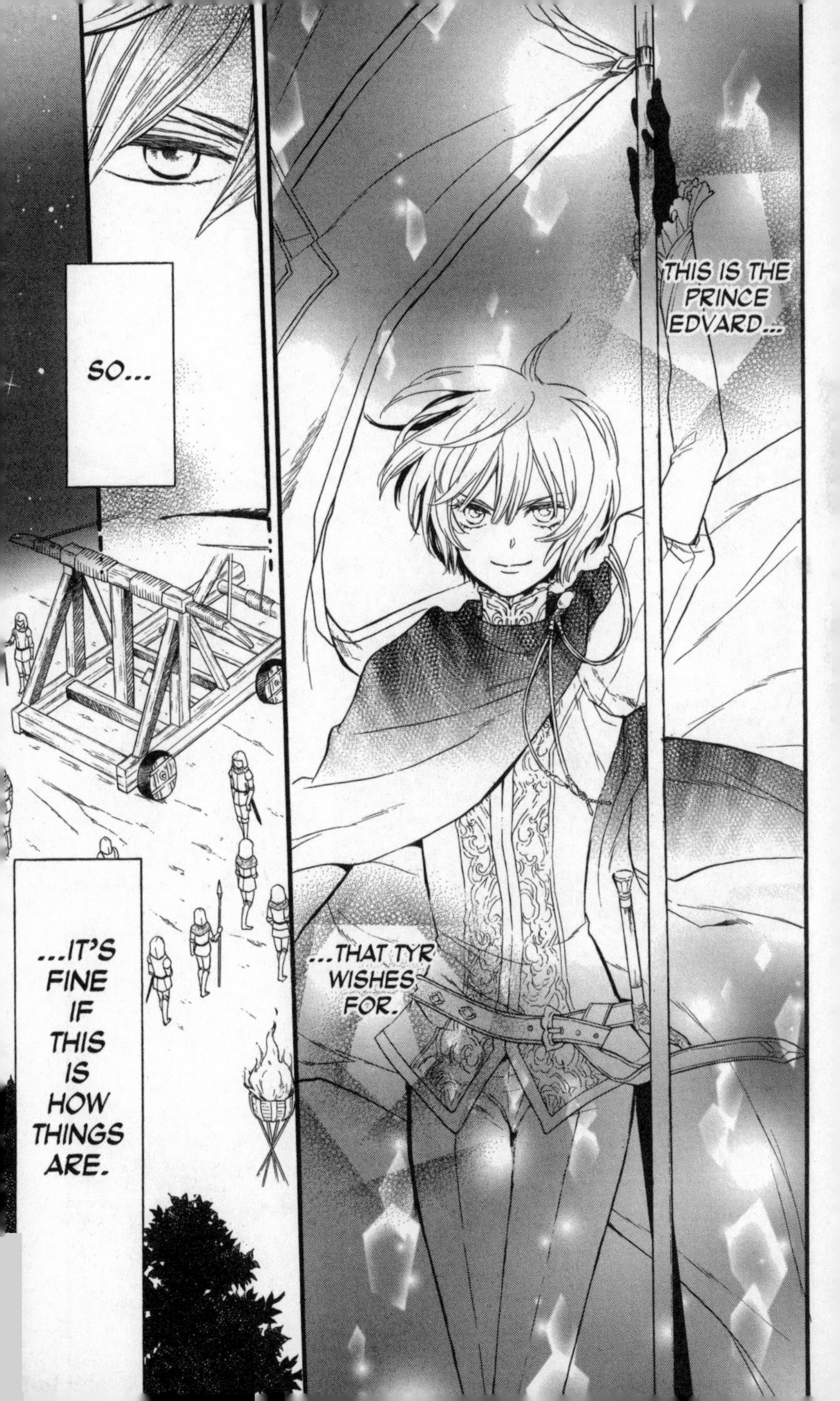
THIS IS THE PRINCE EDVARD...
...THAT TYR WISHES FOR.
SO...
...IT'S FINE IF THIS IS HOW THINGS ARE.

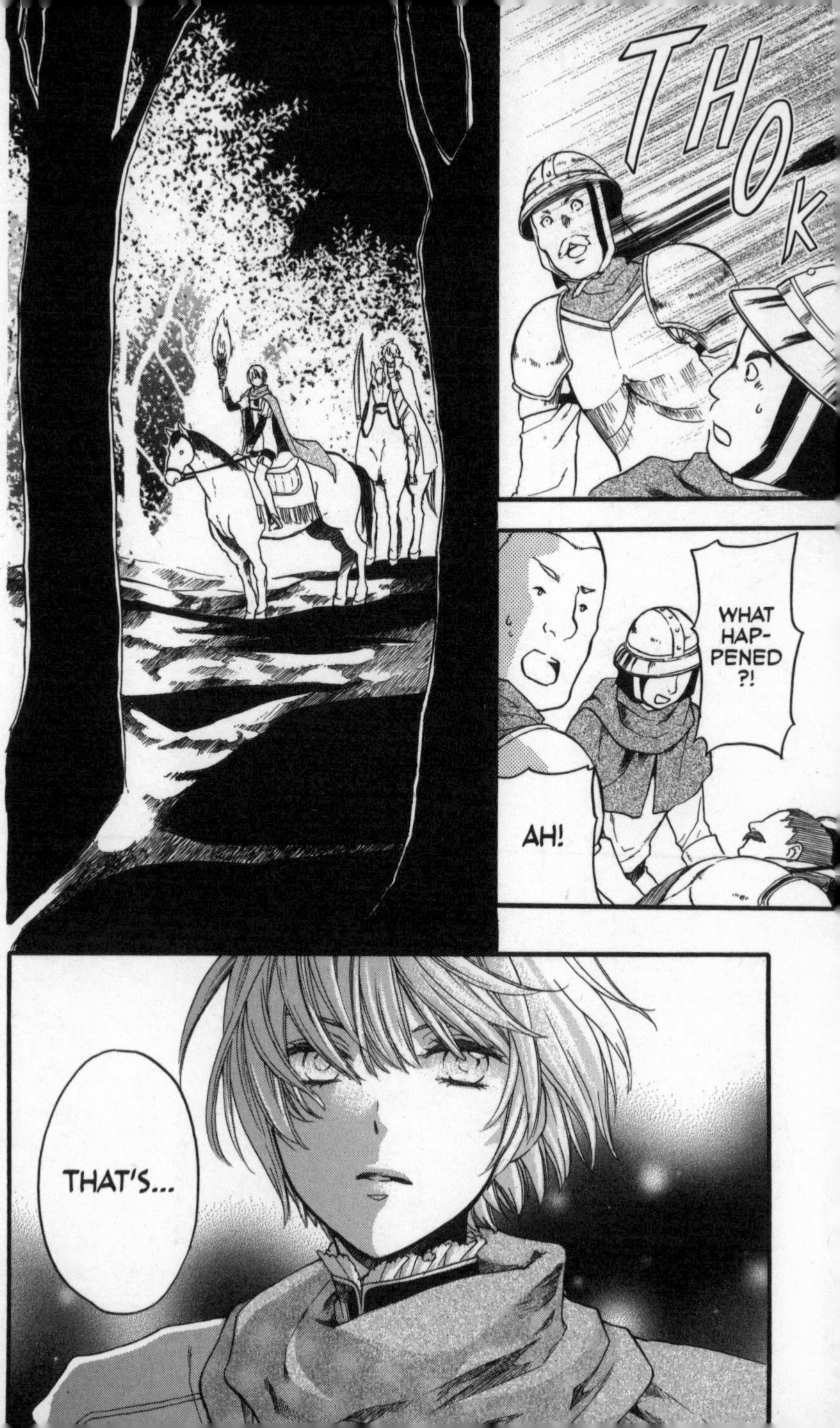
THOK
WHAT HAP-PENED?!
AH!
THAT'S...

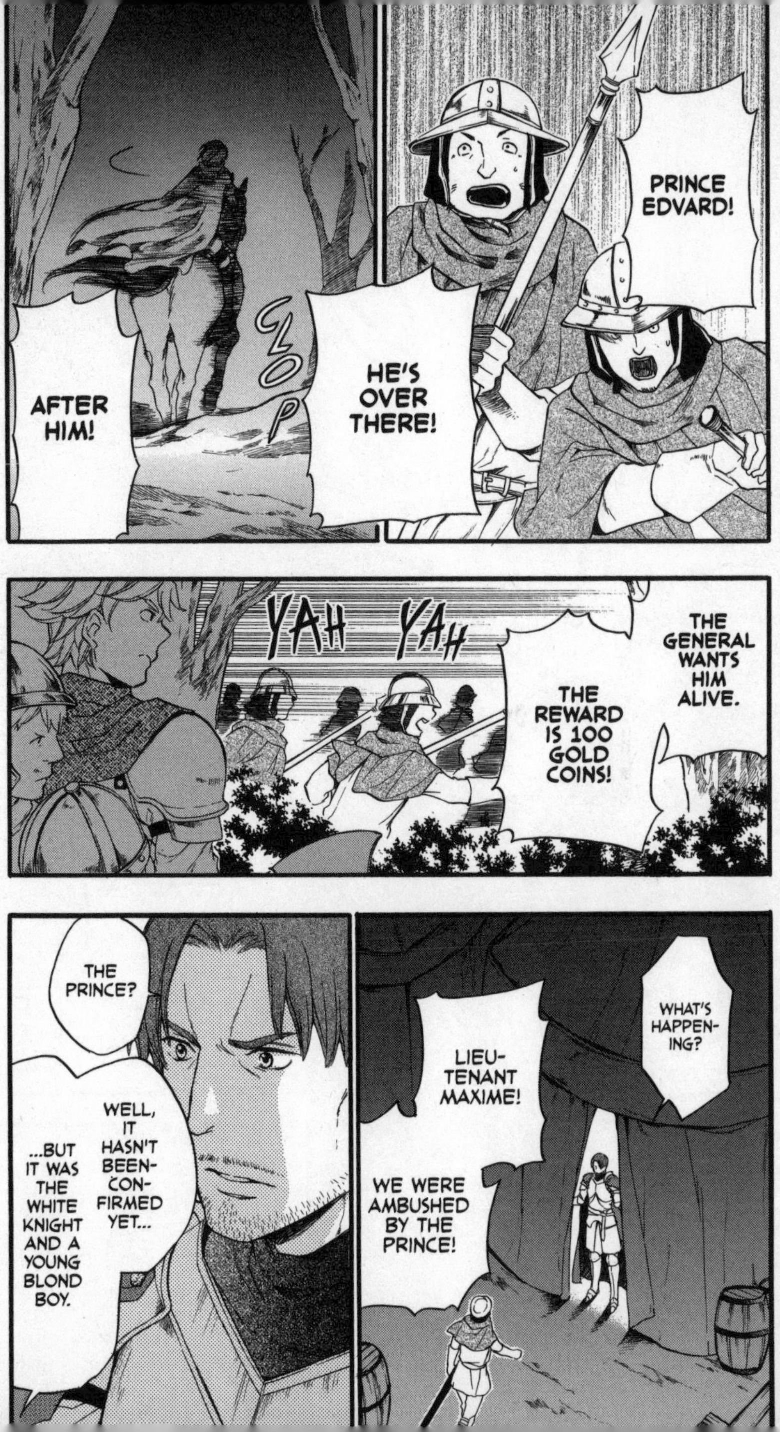
PRINCE EDVARD!
HE'S OVER THERE!
CLOP
AFTER HIM!
YAH YAH
THE GENERAL WANTS HIM ALIVE.
THE REWARD IS 100 GOLD COINS!
WHAT'S HAPPENING?
LIEUTENANT MAXIME!
WE WERE AMBUSHED BY THE PRINCE!
THE PRINCE?
WELL, IT HASN'T BEEN CONFIRMED YET...
...BUT IT WAS THE WHITE KNIGHT AND A YOUNG BLOND BOY.

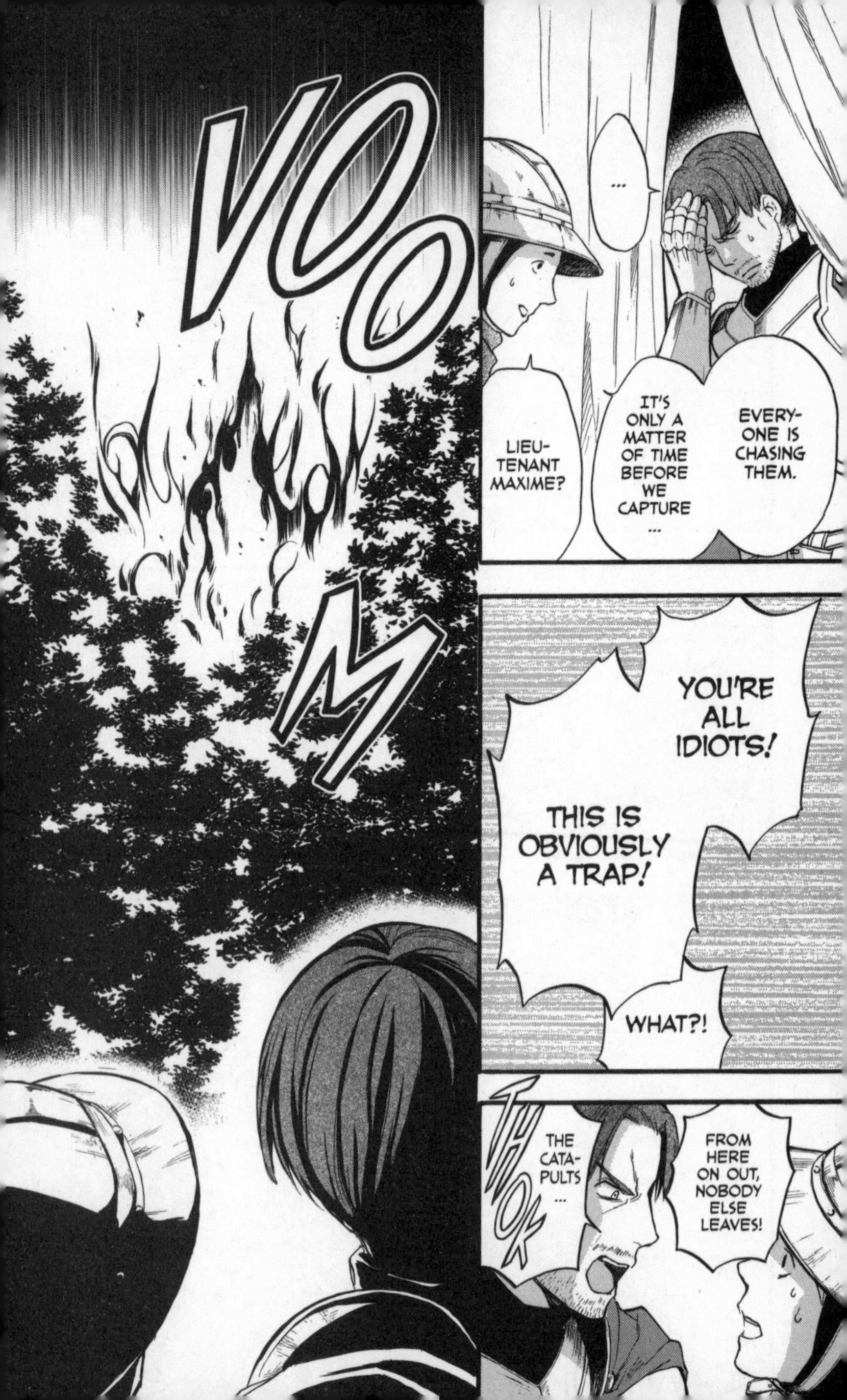
...
EVERYONE IS CHASING THEM.
IT'S ONLY A MATTER OF TIME BEFORE WE CAPTURE ...
LIEUTENANT MAXIME?
YOU'RE ALL IDIOTS!
THIS IS OBVIOUSLY A TRAP!
WHAT?!
FROM HERE ON OUT, NOBODY ELSE LEAVES!
THE CATAPULTS ...
THOK
VOOM

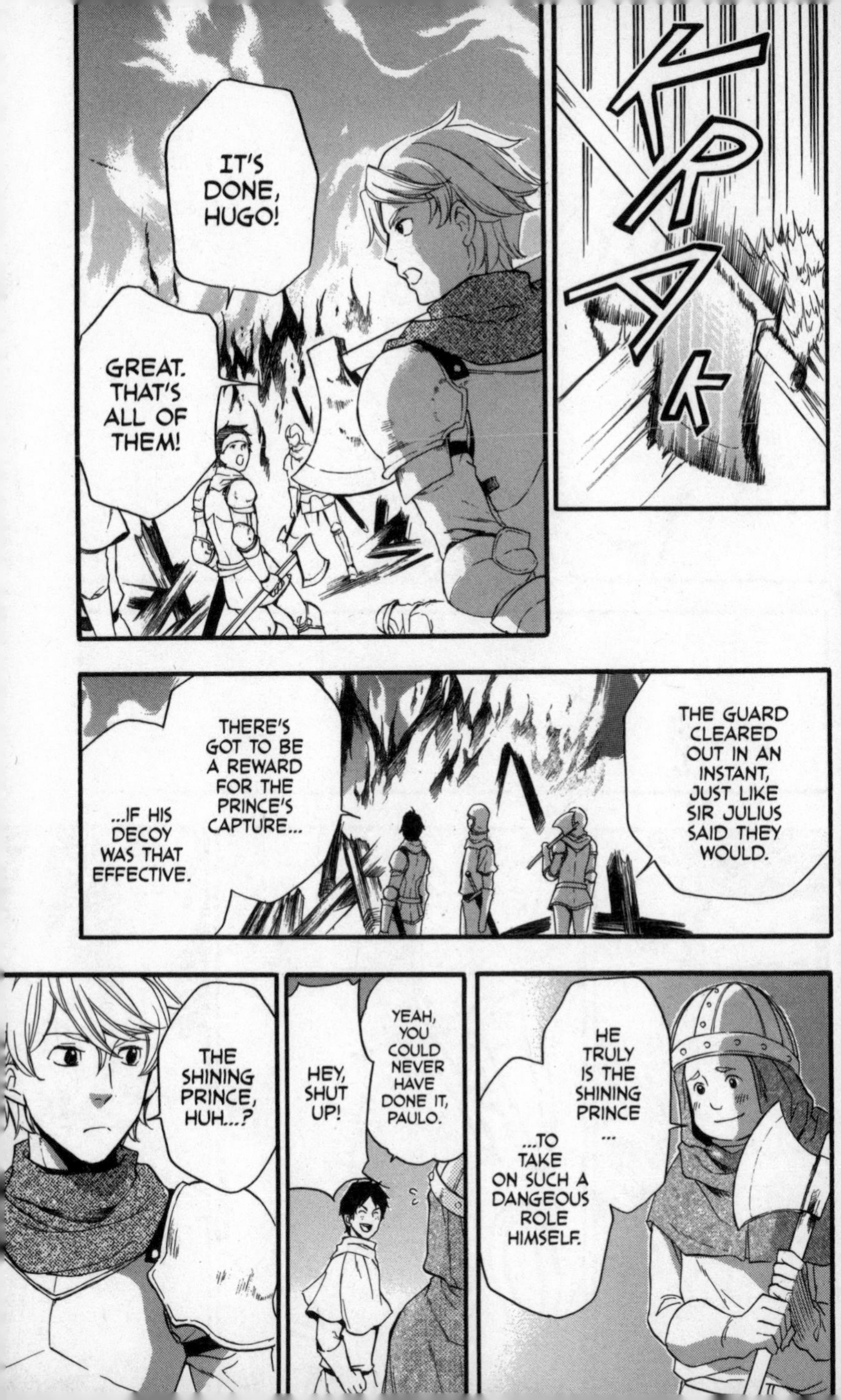
KRAK
IT'S DONE, HUGO!
GREAT. THAT'S ALL OF THEM!
THE GUARD CLEARED OUT IN AN INSTANT, JUST LIKE SIR JULIUS SAID THEY WOULD.
THERE'S GOT TO BE A REWARD FOR THE PRINCE'S CAPTURE...
...IF HIS DECOY WAS THAT EFFECTIVE.
HE TRULY IS THE SHINING PRINCE...
...TO TAKE ON SUCH A DANGEOUS ROLE HIMSELF.
YEAH, YOU COULD NEVER HAVE DONE IT, PAULO.
HEY, SHUT UP!
THE SHINING PRINCE, HUH...?

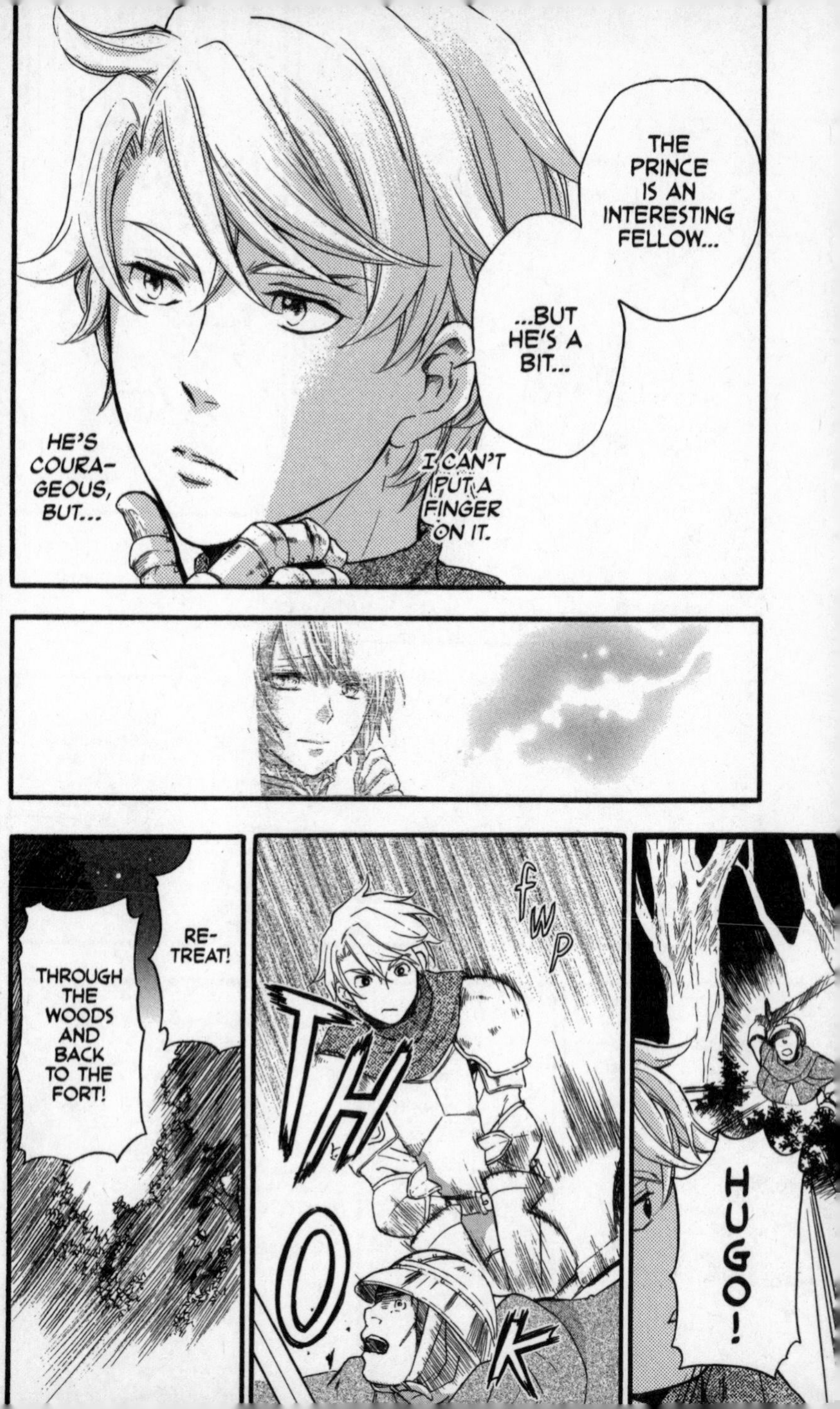
THE PRINCE IS AN INTERESTING FELLOW...
...BUT HE'S A BIT...
I CAN'T PUT A FINGER ON IT.
HE'S COURAGEOUS, BUT...
HUGO!
fwp
THOK
RE-TREAT!
THROUGH THE WOODS AND BACK TO THE FORT!

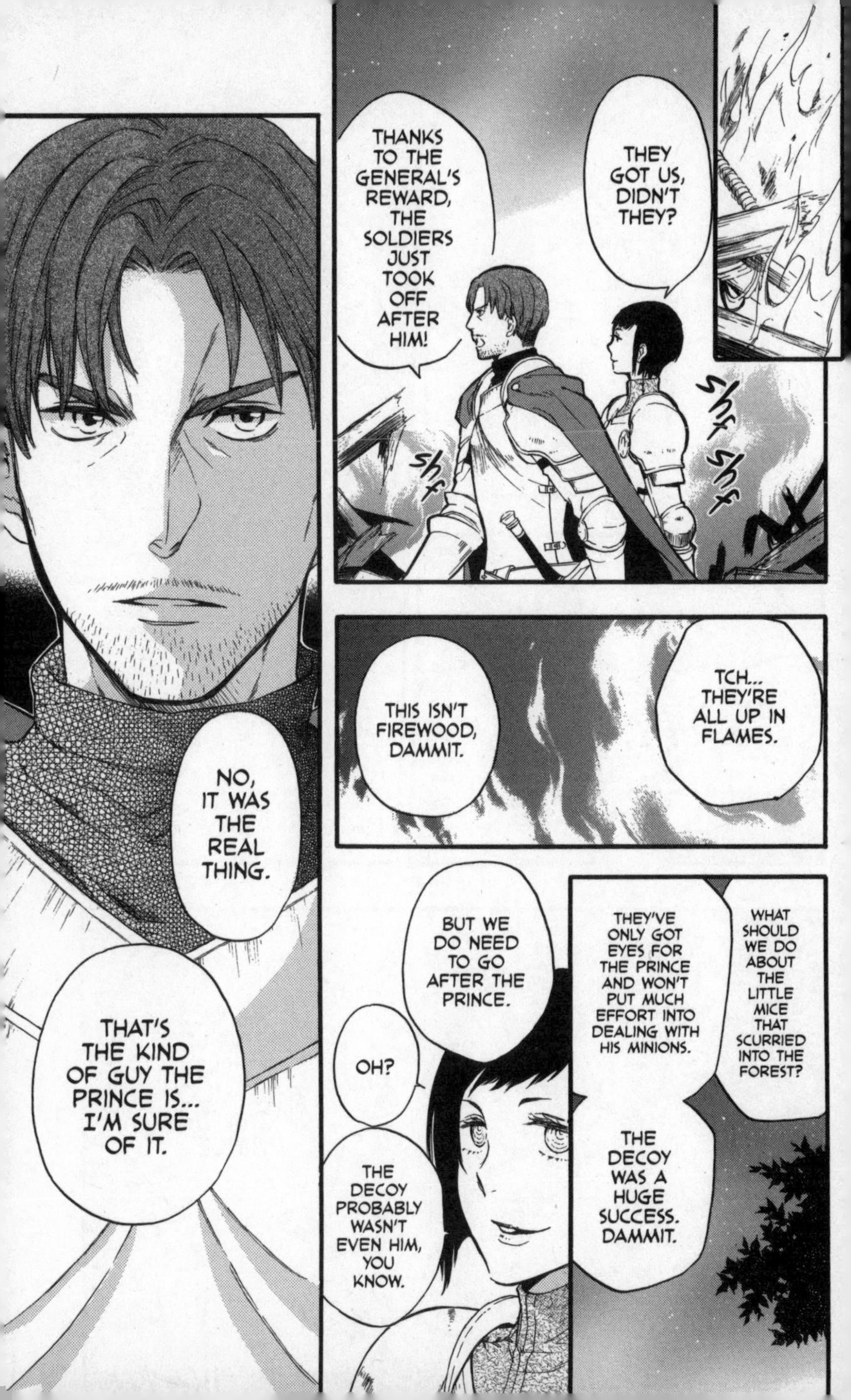
THEY GOT US, DIDN'T THEY?
THANKS TO THE GENERAL'S REWARD, THE SOLDIERS JUST TOOK OFF AFTER HIM!
shf shf
shf
TCH... THEY'RE ALL UP IN FLAMES.
THIS ISN'T FIREWOOD, DAMMIT.
WHAT SHOULD WE DO ABOUT THE LITTLE MICE THAT SCURRIED INTO THE FOREST?
THEY'VE ONLY GOT EYES FOR THE PRINCE AND WON'T PUT MUCH EFFORT INTO DEALING WITH HIS MINIONS.
BUT WE DO NEED TO GO AFTER THE PRINCE.
THE DECOY WAS A HUGE SUCCESS. DAMMIT.
OH?
THE DECOY PROBABLY WASN'T EVEN HIM, YOU KNOW.
NO, IT WAS THE REAL THING.
THAT'S THE KIND OF GUY THE PRINCE IS... I'M SURE OF IT.

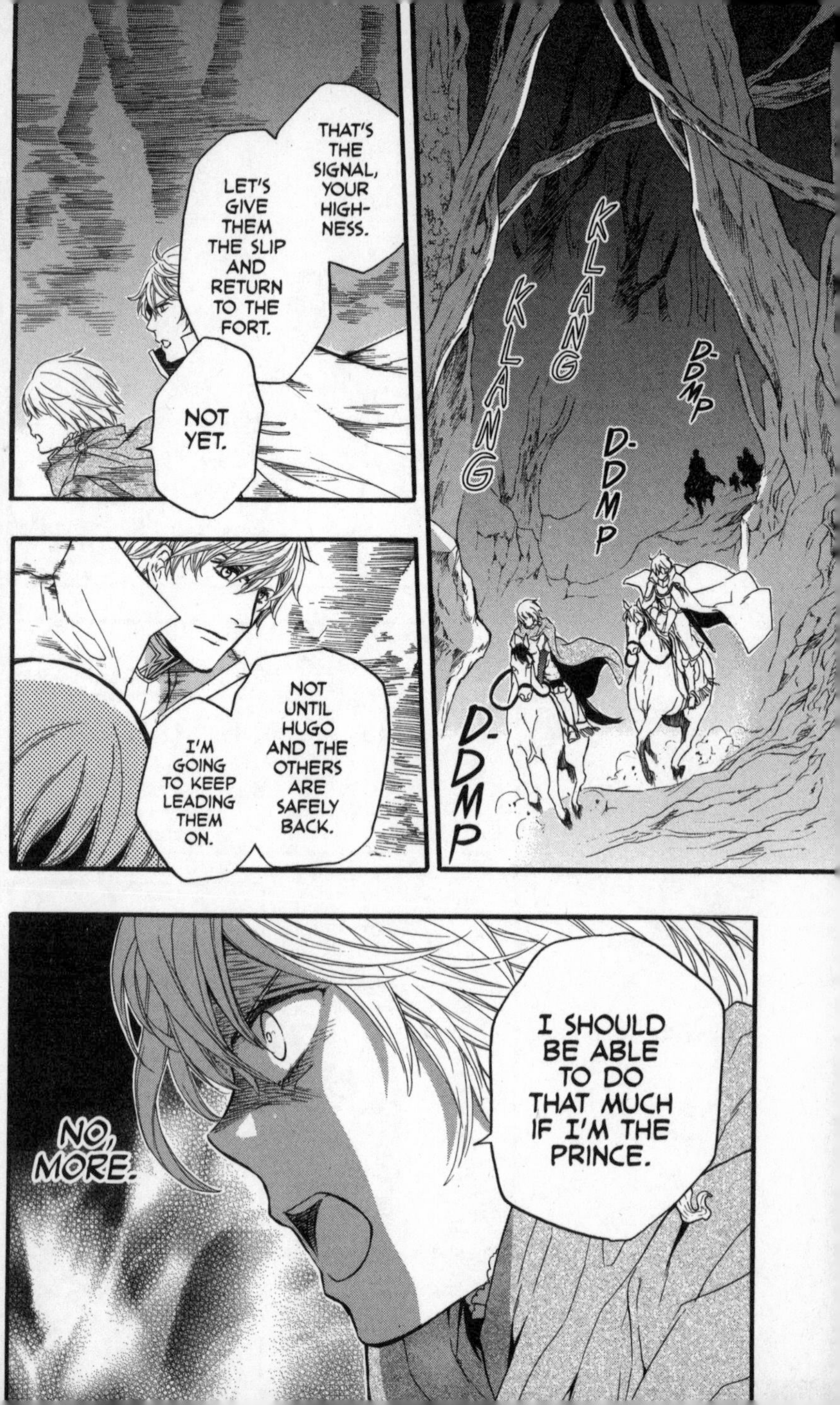
KLANG
KLANG
D-DMP
D-DMP
D-DMP
THAT'S THE SIGNAL, YOUR HIGHNESS.
LET'S GIVE THEM THE SLIP AND RETURN TO THE FORT.
NOT YET.
NOT UNTIL HUGO AND THE OTHERS ARE SAFELY BACK.
I'M GOING TO KEEP LEADING THEM ON.
I SHOULD BE ABLE TO DO THAT MUCH IF I'M THE PRINCE.
NO, MORE.

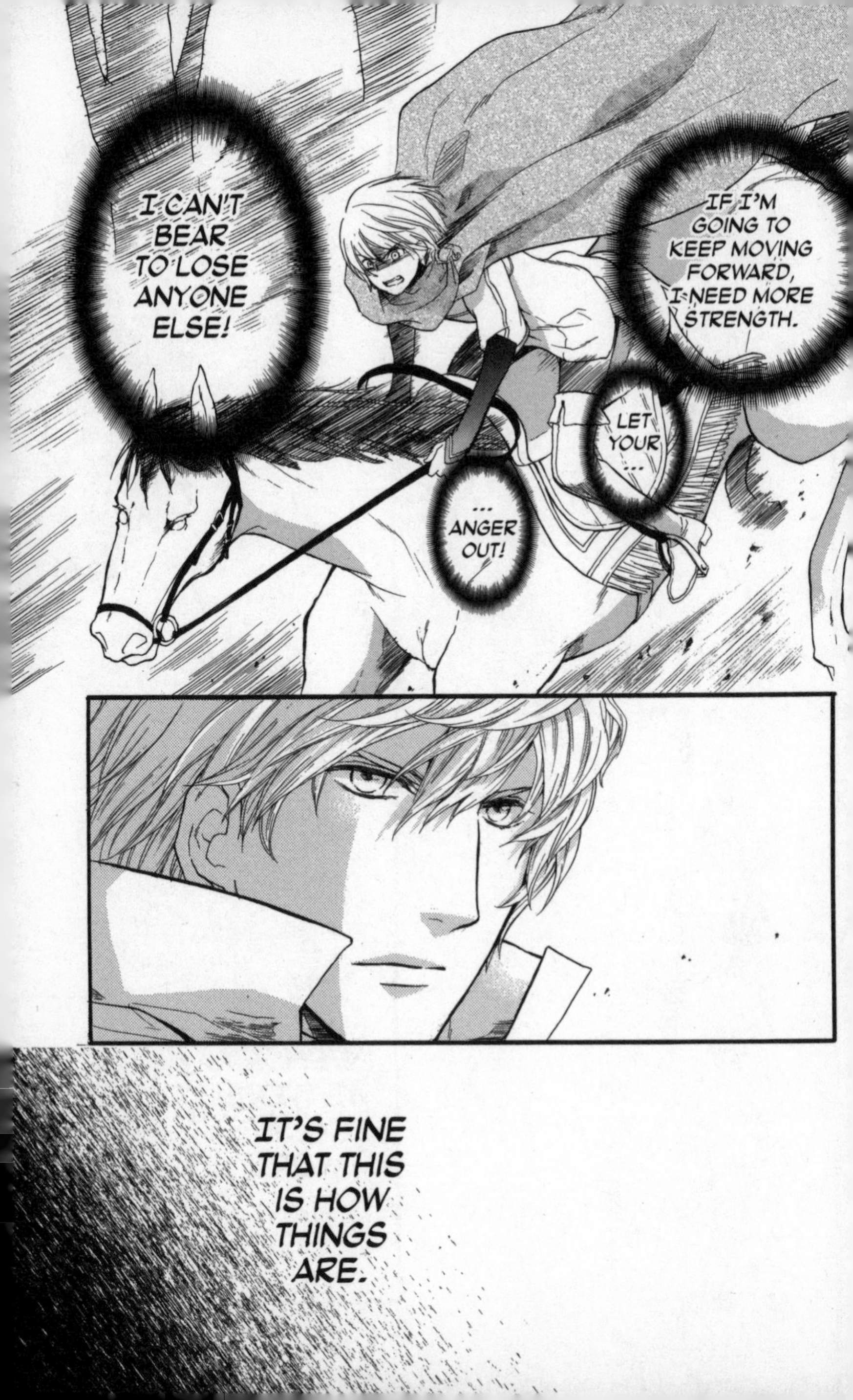
IF I'M GOING TO KEEP MOVING FORWARD, I NEED MORE STRENGTH.
I CAN'T BEAR TO LOSE ANYONE ELSE!
LET YOUR...
...ANGER OUT!
IT'S FINE THAT THIS IS HOW THINGS ARE.

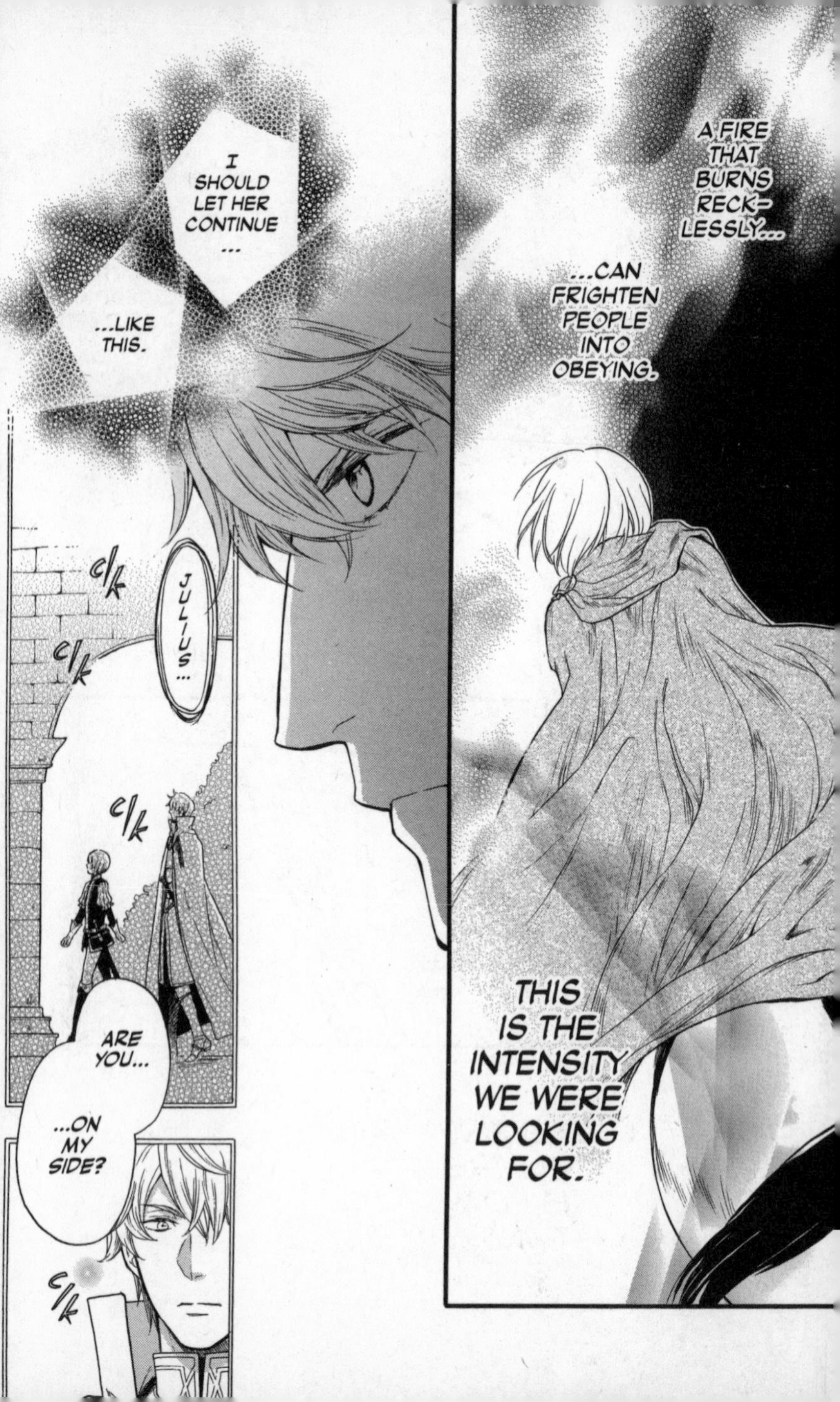
A FIRE THAT BURNS RECK-LESSLY...
...CAN FRIGHTEN PEOPLE INTO OBEYING.
THIS IS THE INTENSITY WE WERE LOOKING FOR.
I SHOULD LET HER CONTINUE...
...LIKE THIS.
JULIUS...
C/K
C/K
C/K
ARE YOU...
...ON MY SIDE?
C/K

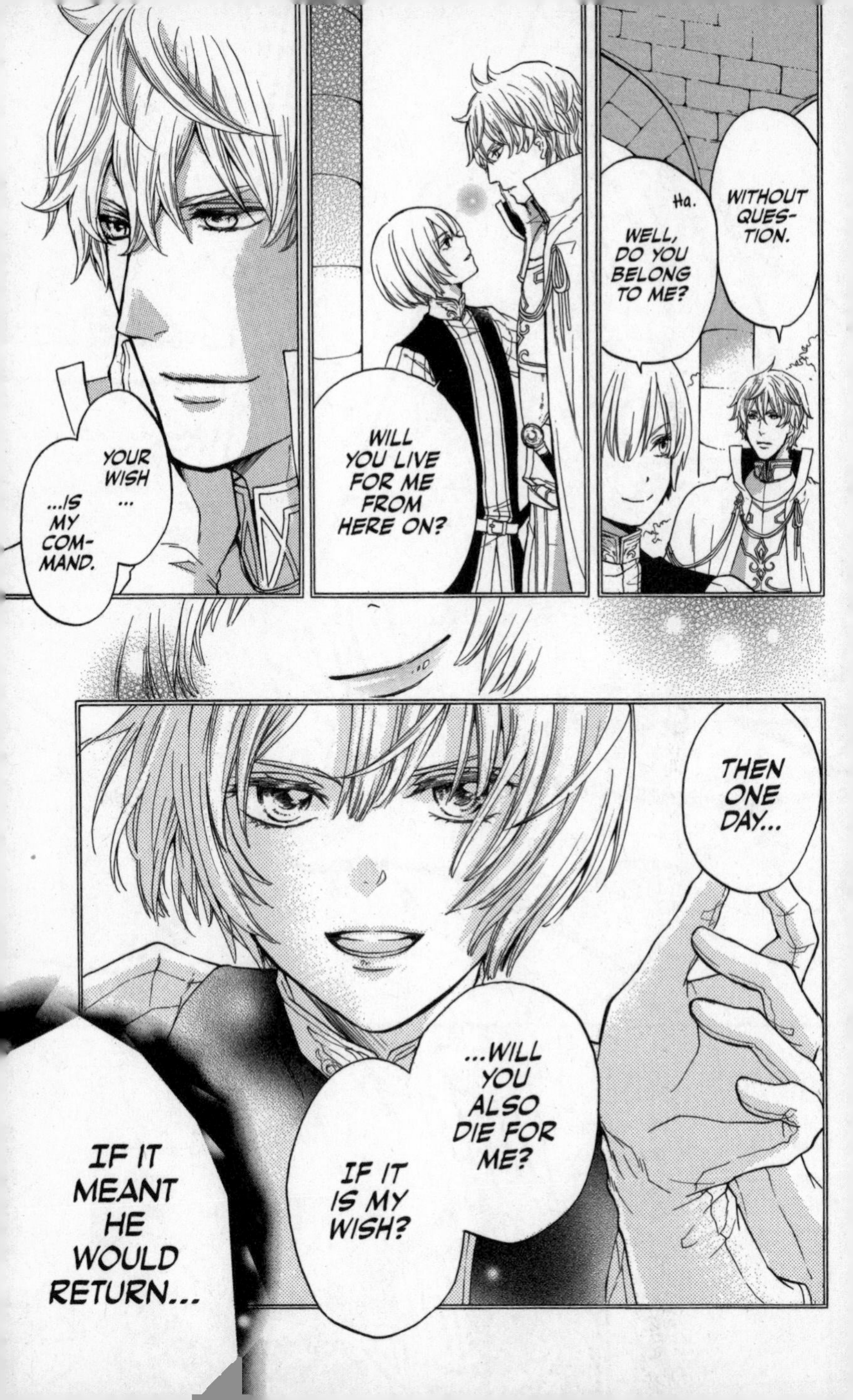
WITHOUT QUES-TION.
Ha. WELL, DO YOU BELONG TO ME?
WILL YOU LIVE FOR ME FROM HERE ON?
YOUR WISH ... ...IS MY COM-MAND.
THEN ONE DAY...
...WILL YOU ALSO DIE FOR ME?
IF IT IS MY WISH?
IF IT MEANT HE WOULD RETURN...

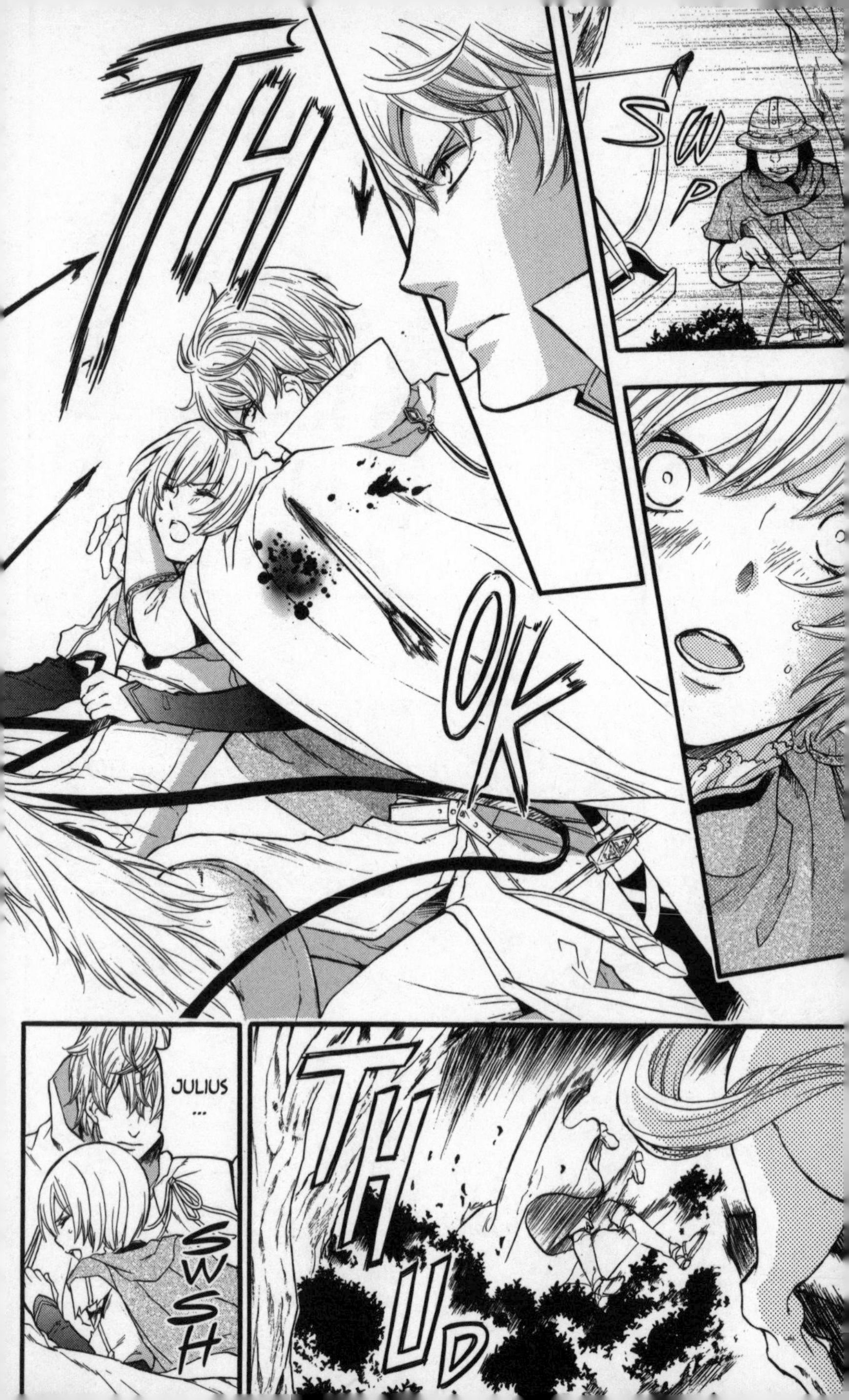
SWP
THOK
THUD
JULIUS
...
SWSH

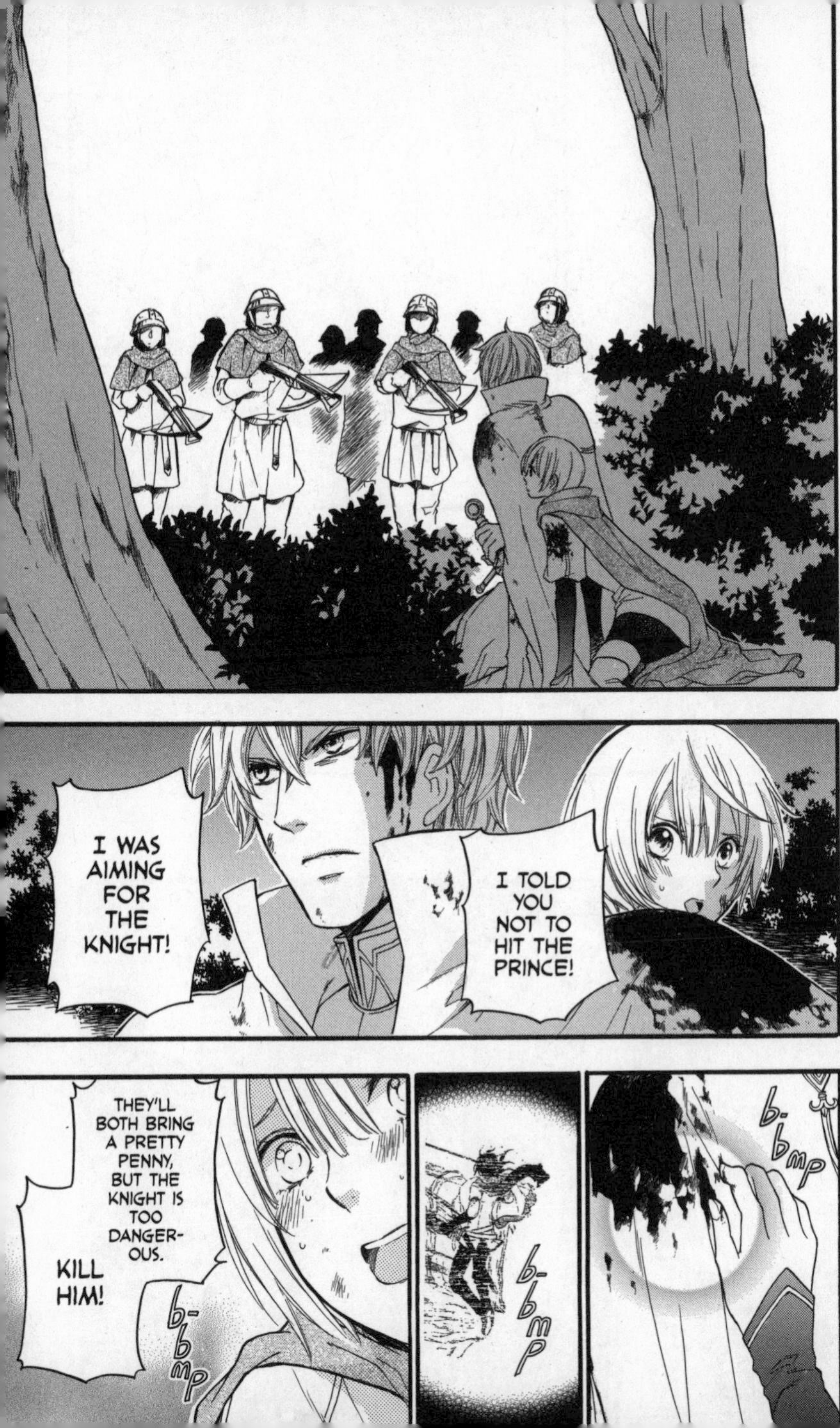
I TOLD YOU NOT TO HIT THE PRINCE!
I WAS AIMING FOR THE KNIGHT!
b-bmp
b-bmp
THEY'LL BOTH BRING A PRETTY PENNY, BUT THE KNIGHT IS TOO DANGEROUS.
KILL HIM!
b-bmp

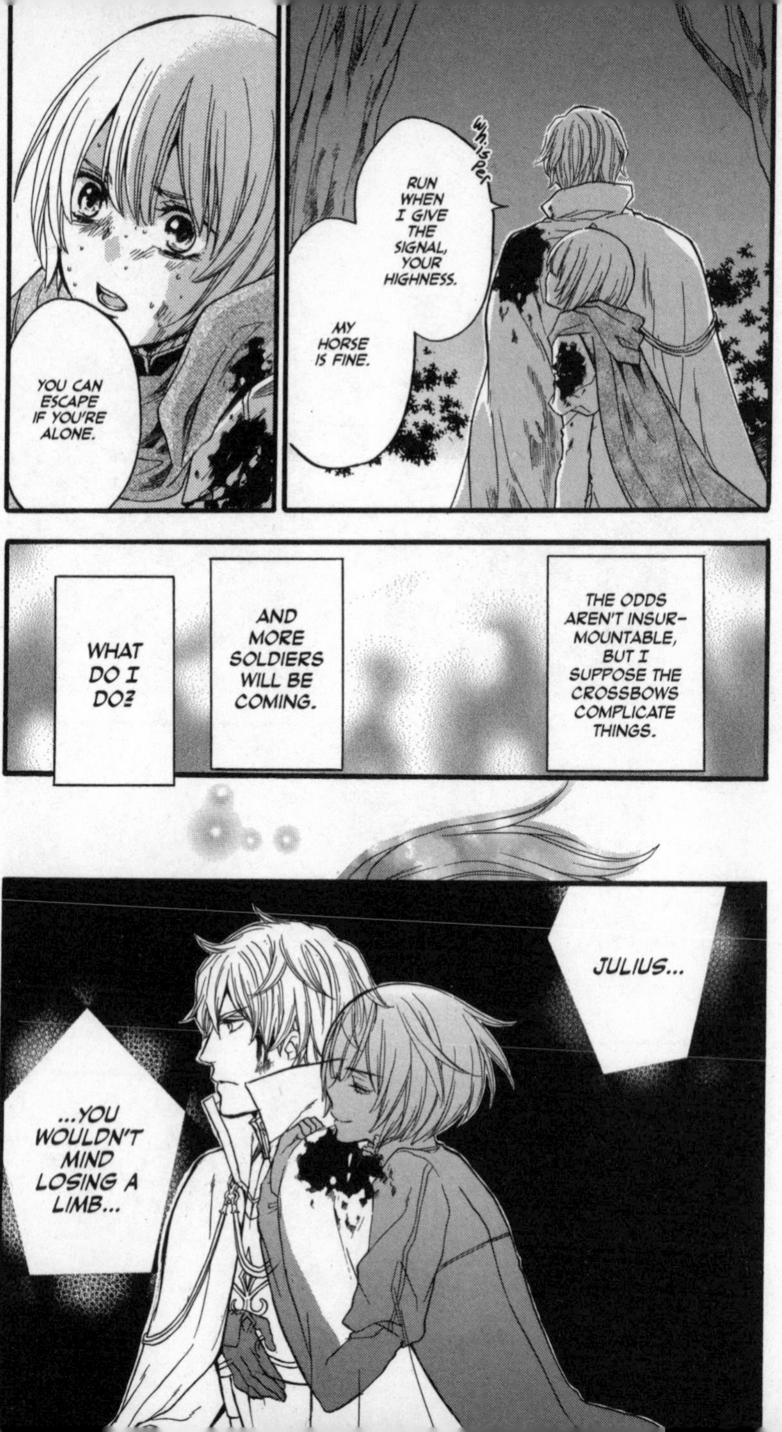
whisper
RUN WHEN I GIVE THE SIGNAL, YOUR HIGHNESS.
MY HORSE IS FINE.
YOU CAN ESCAPE IF YOU'RE ALONE.
THE ODDS AREN'T INSUR-MOUNTABLE, BUT I SUPPOSE THE CROSSBOWS COMPLICATE THINGS.
AND MORE SOLDIERS WILL BE COMING.
WHAT DO I DO?
JULIUS...
...YOU WOULDN'T MIND LOSING A LIMB...

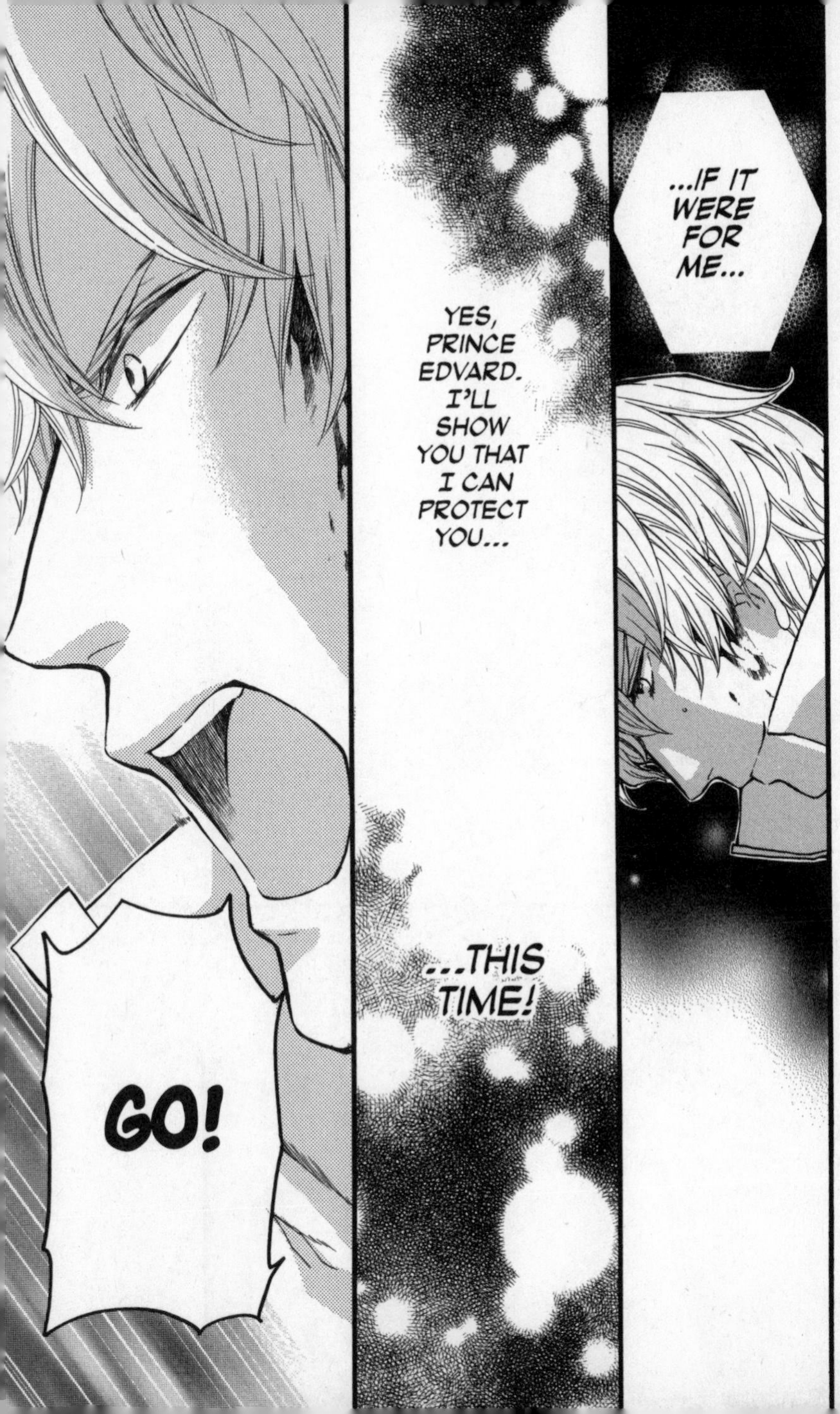
...IF IT WERE FOR ME...
YES, PRINCE EDVARD. I'LL SHOW YOU THAT I CAN PROTECT YOU...
...THIS TIME!
GO!

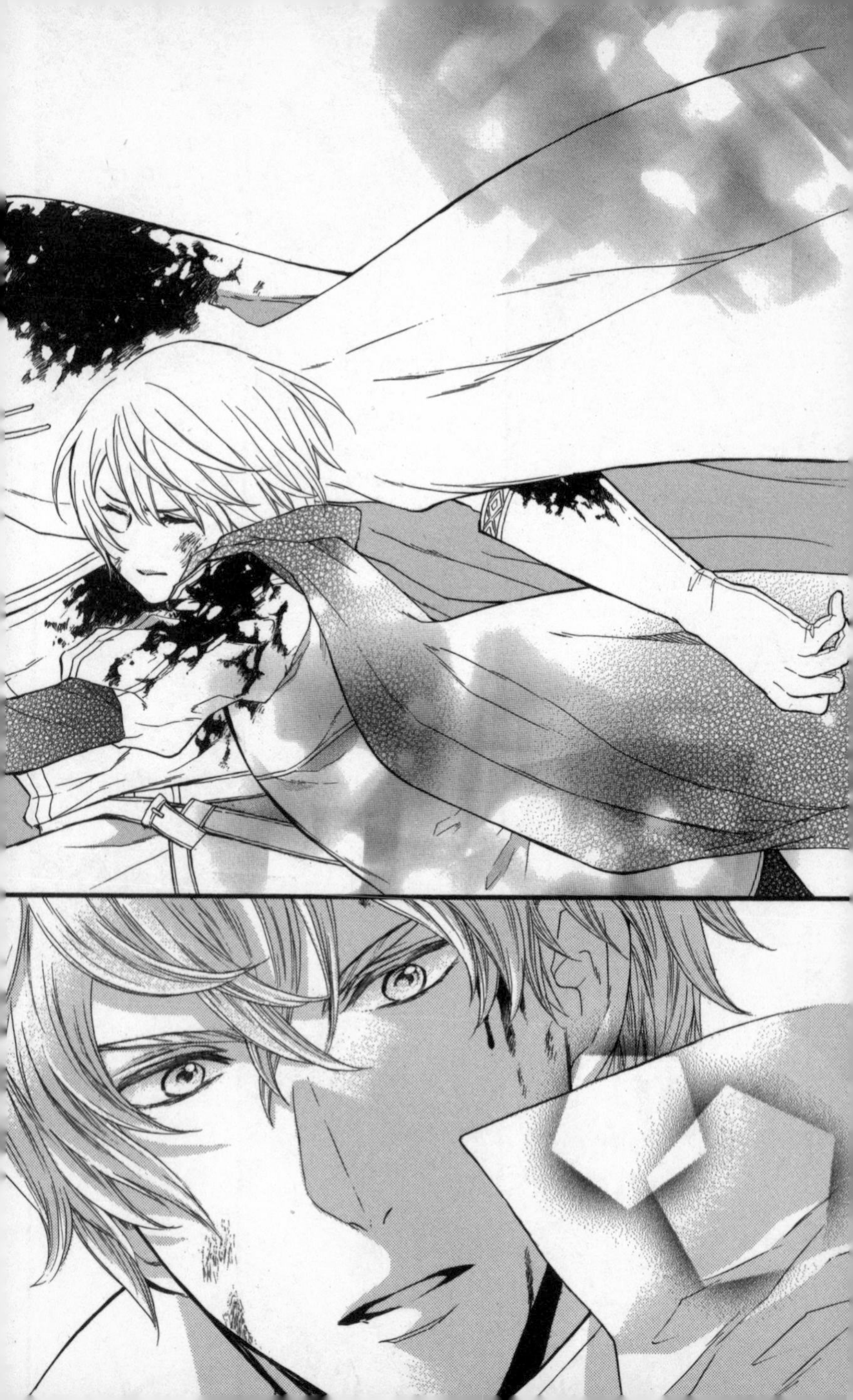

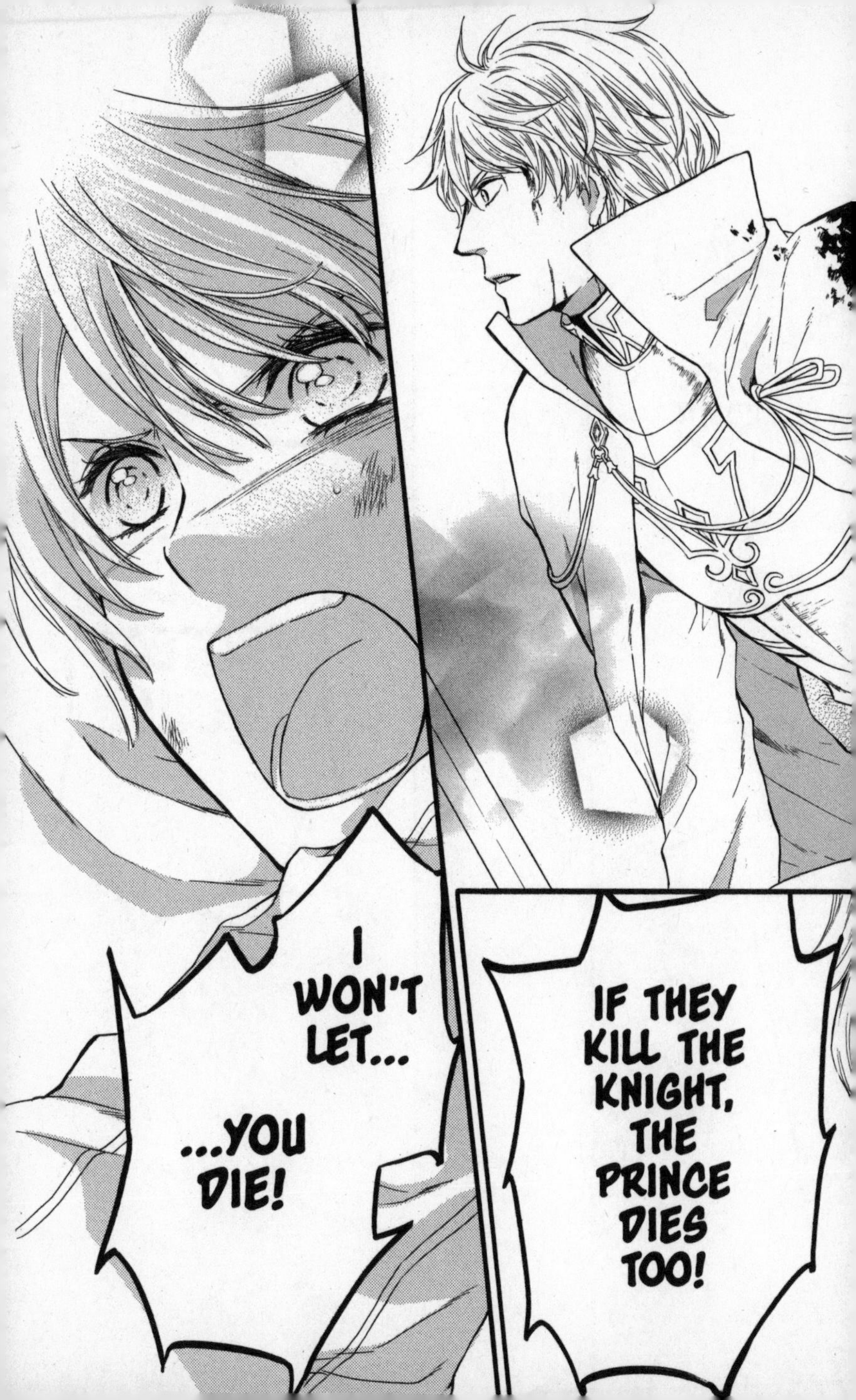
IF THEY KILL THE KNIGHT, THE PRINCE DIES TOO!
I WON'T LET...
...YOU DIE!

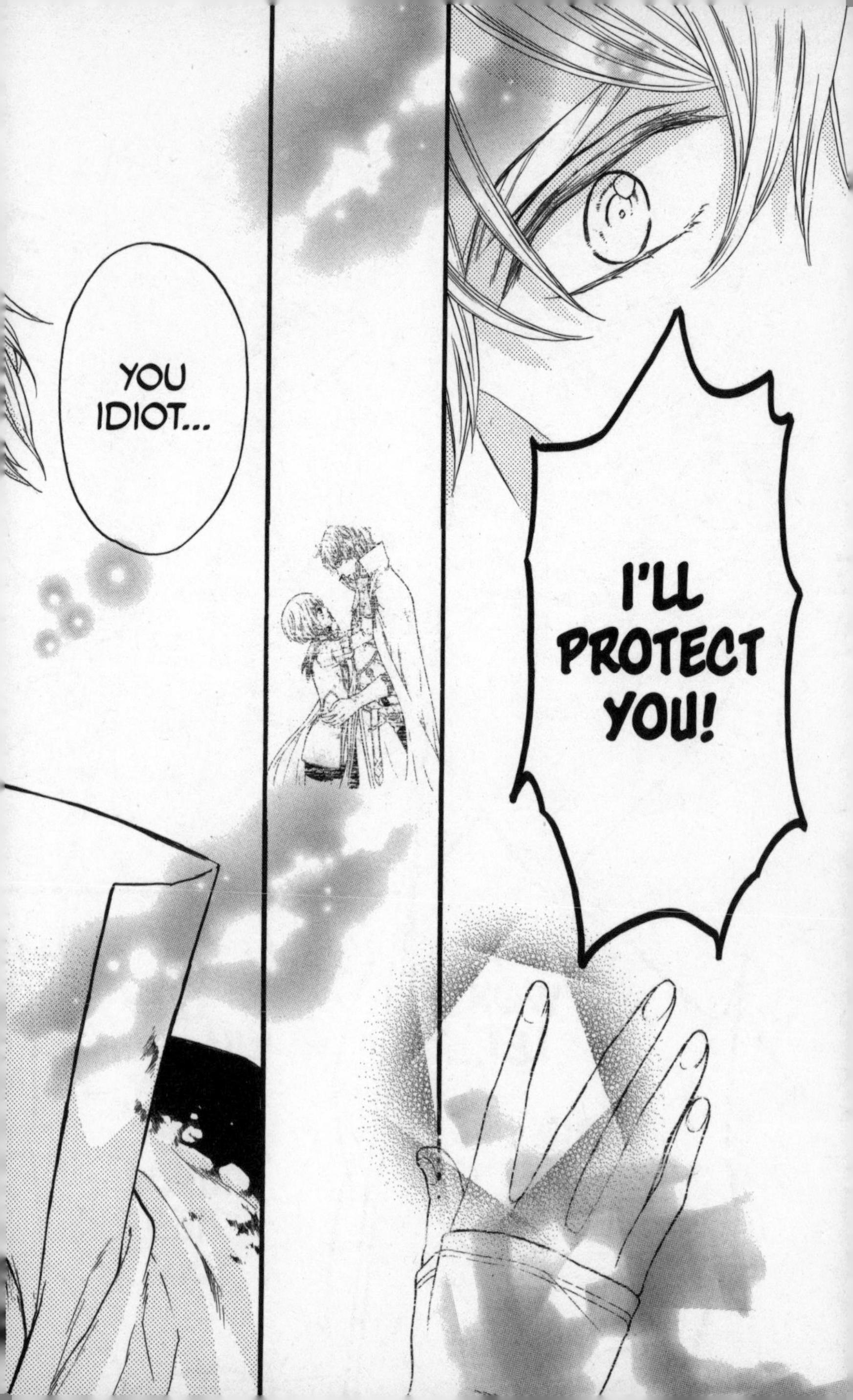
I'LL PROTECT YOU!
YOU IDIOT...

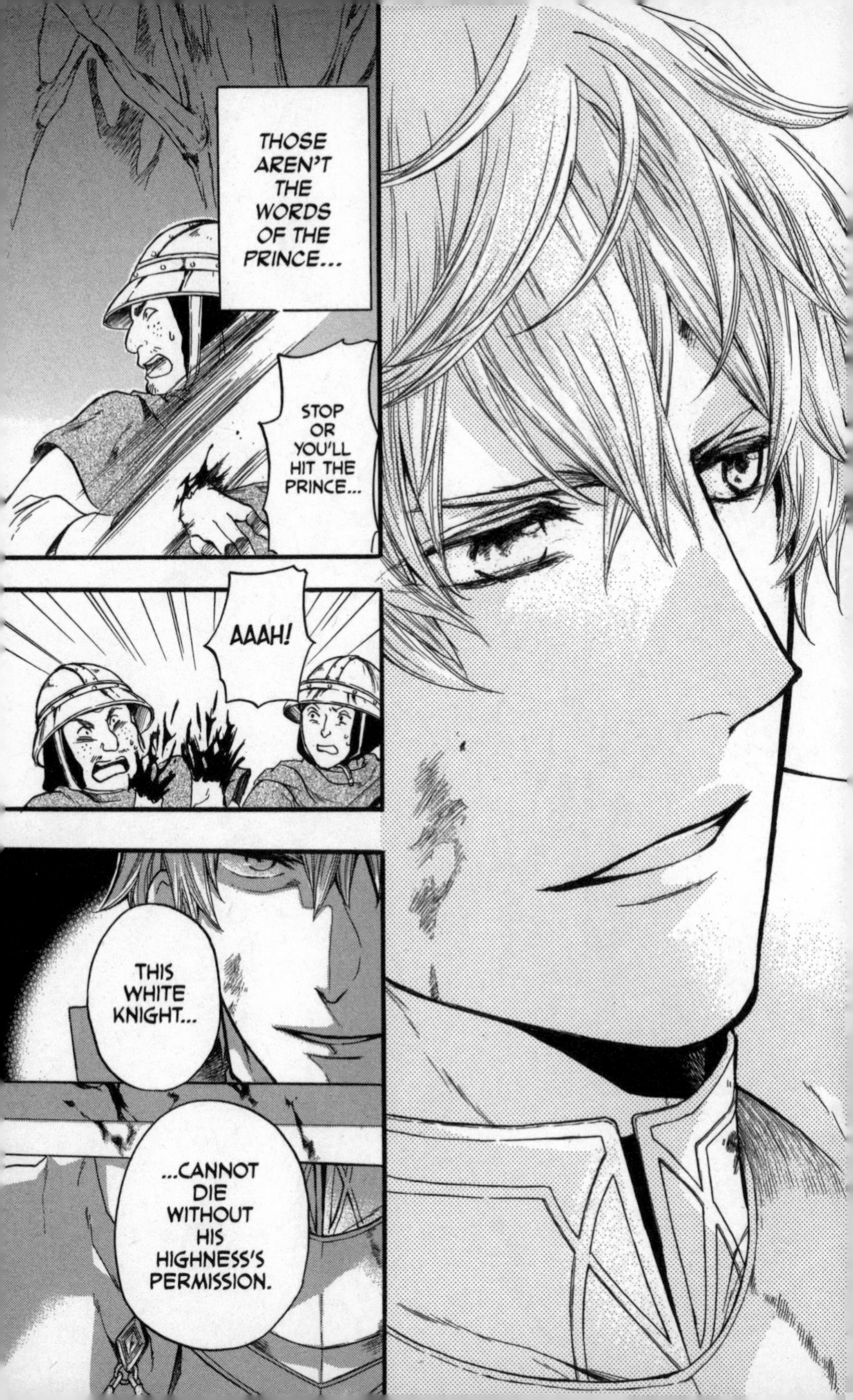
THOSE AREN'T THE WORDS OF THE PRINCE...
STOP OR YOU'LL HIT THE PRINCE...
AAAH!
THIS WHITE KNIGHT...
...CANNOT DIE WITHOUT HIS HIGHNESS'S PERMISSION.

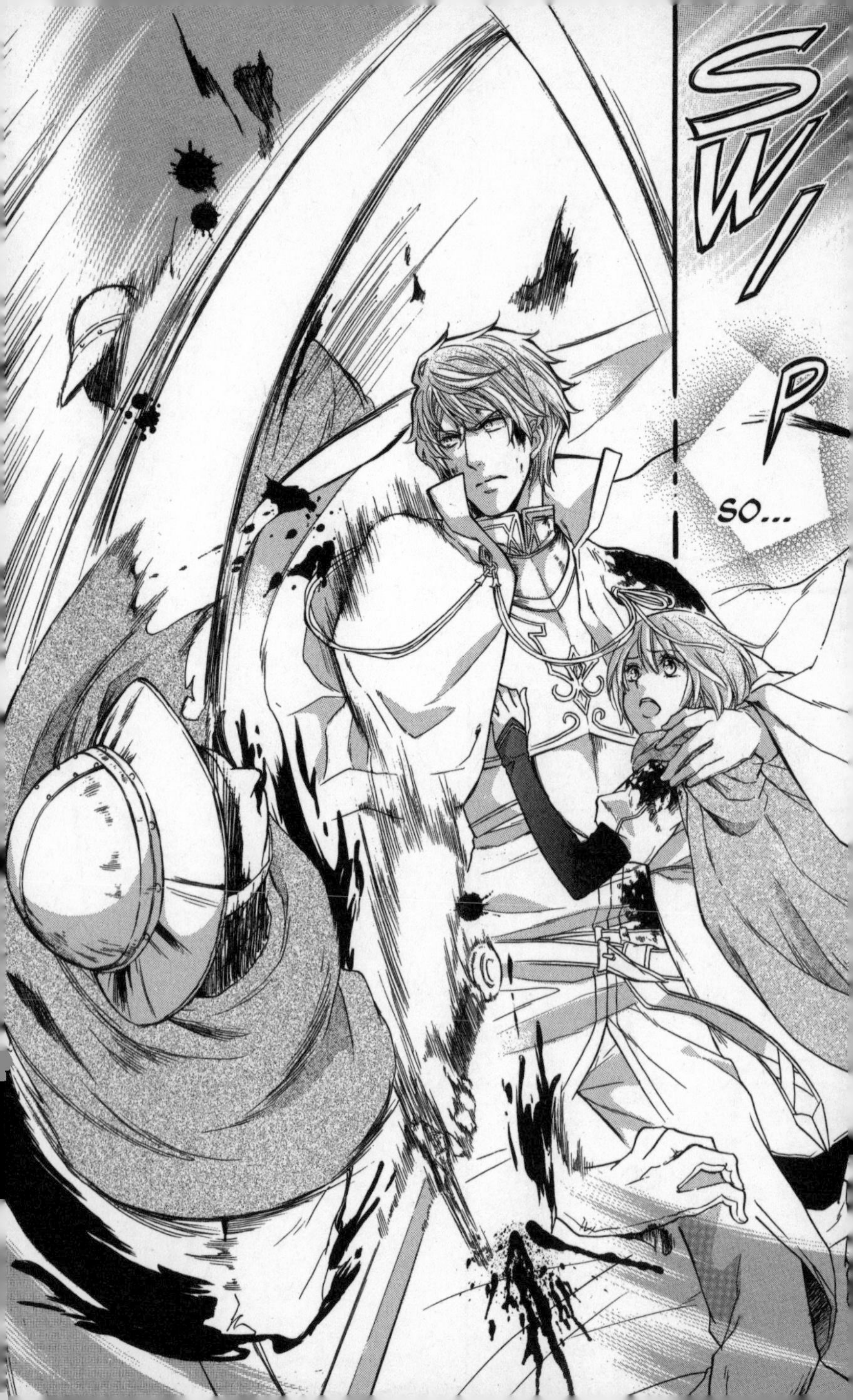
SWIP
SO...

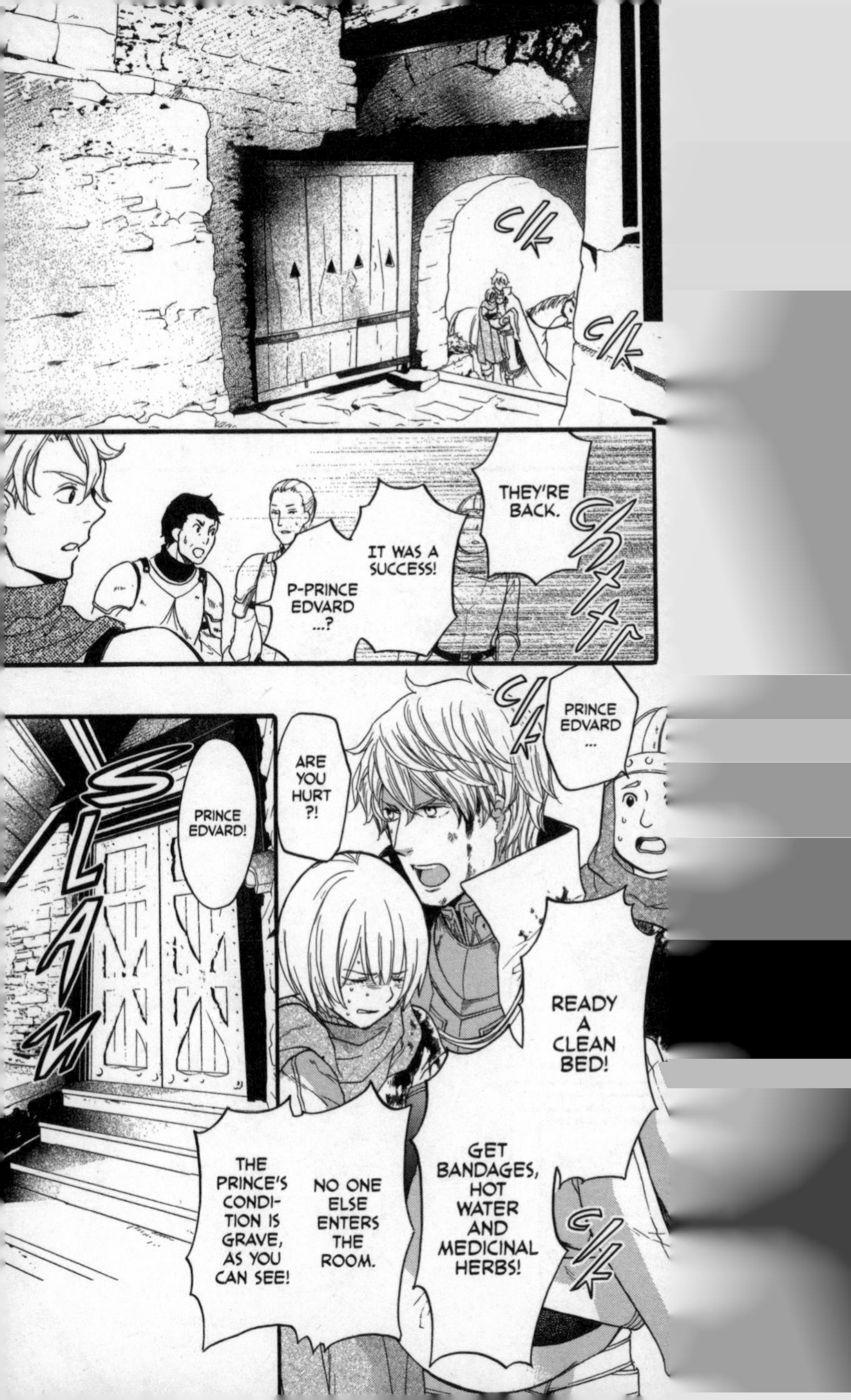
CLK
CLK
THEY'RE BACK.
IT WAS A SUCCESS!
P-PRINCE EDVARD ...?
CLK
PRINCE EDVARD ...
ARE YOU HURT ?!
PRINCE EDVARD!
SLAM
READY A CLEAN BED!
GET BANDAGES, HOT WATER AND MEDICINAL HERBS!
CLK
NO ONE ELSE ENTERS THE ROOM.
THE PRINCE'S CONDI-TION IS GRAVE, AS YOU CAN SEE!

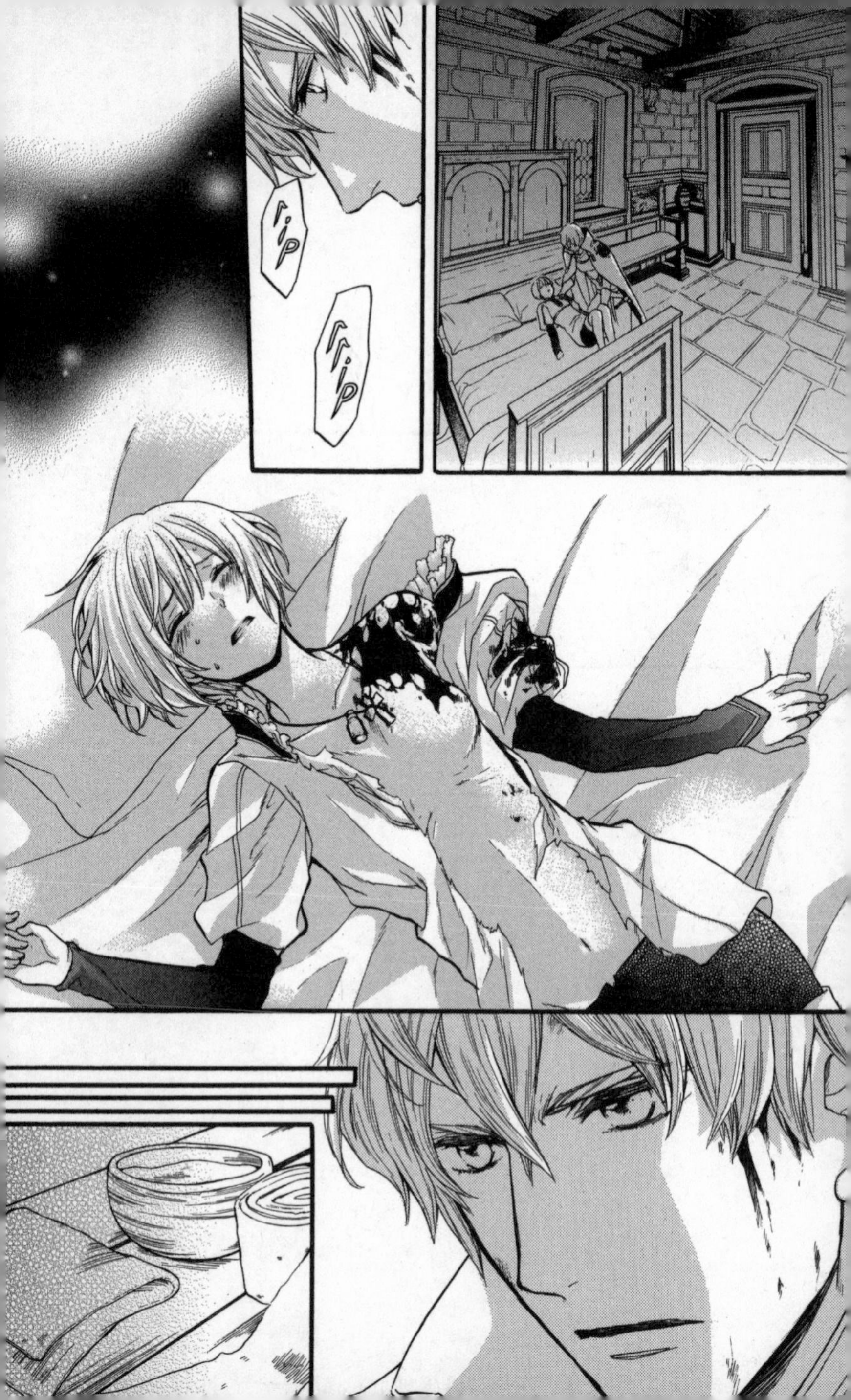
rip
rrip

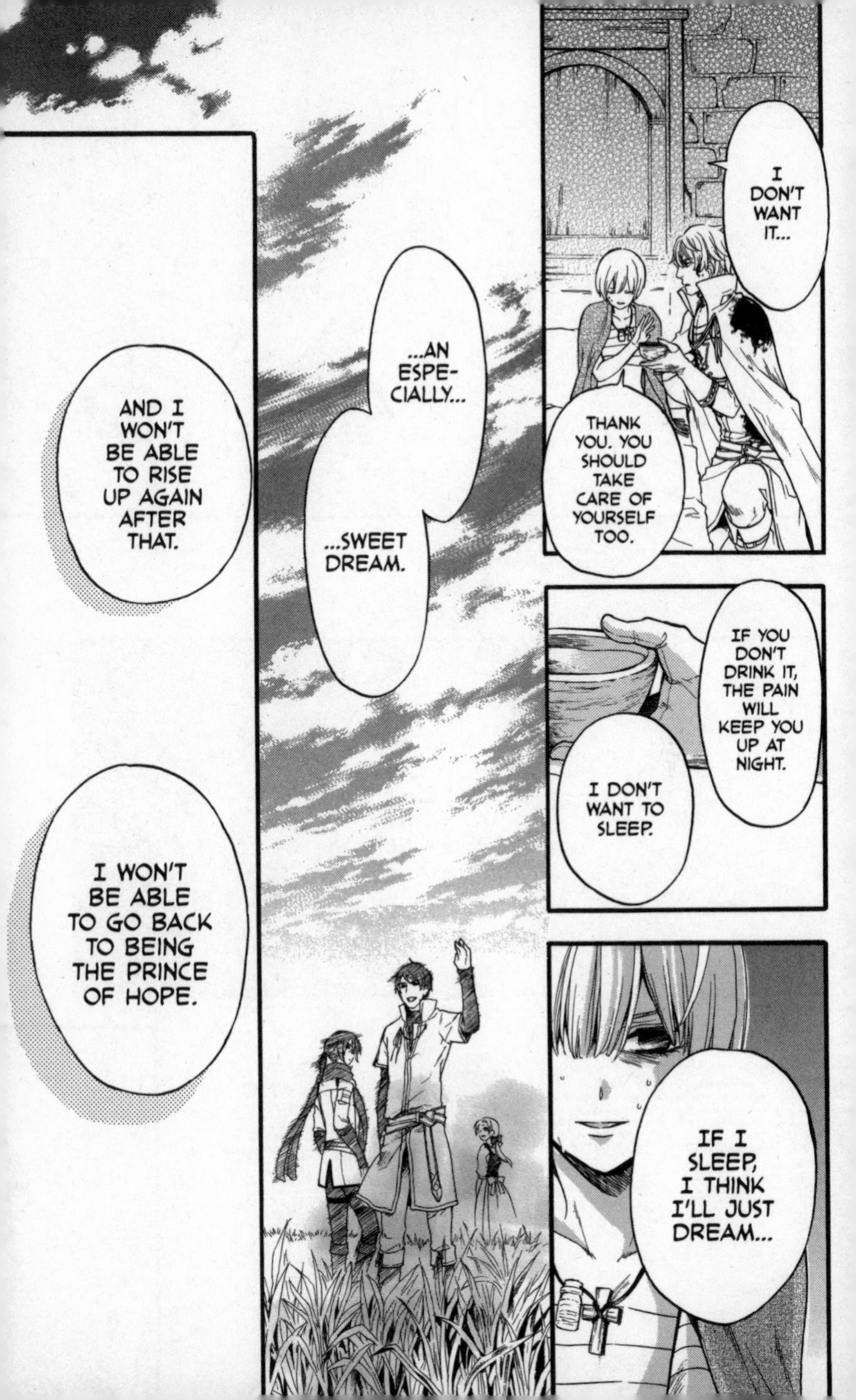
I DON'T WANT IT...
THANK YOU. YOU SHOULD TAKE CARE OF YOURSELF TOO.
IF YOU DON'T DRINK IT, THE PAIN WILL KEEP YOU UP AT NIGHT.
I DON'T WANT TO SLEEP.
IF I SLEEP, I THINK I'LL JUST DREAM...
...AN ESPE-CIALLY...
...SWEET DREAM.
AND I WON'T BE ABLE TO RISE UP AGAIN AFTER THAT.
I WON'T BE ABLE TO GO BACK TO BEING THE PRINCE OF HOPE.

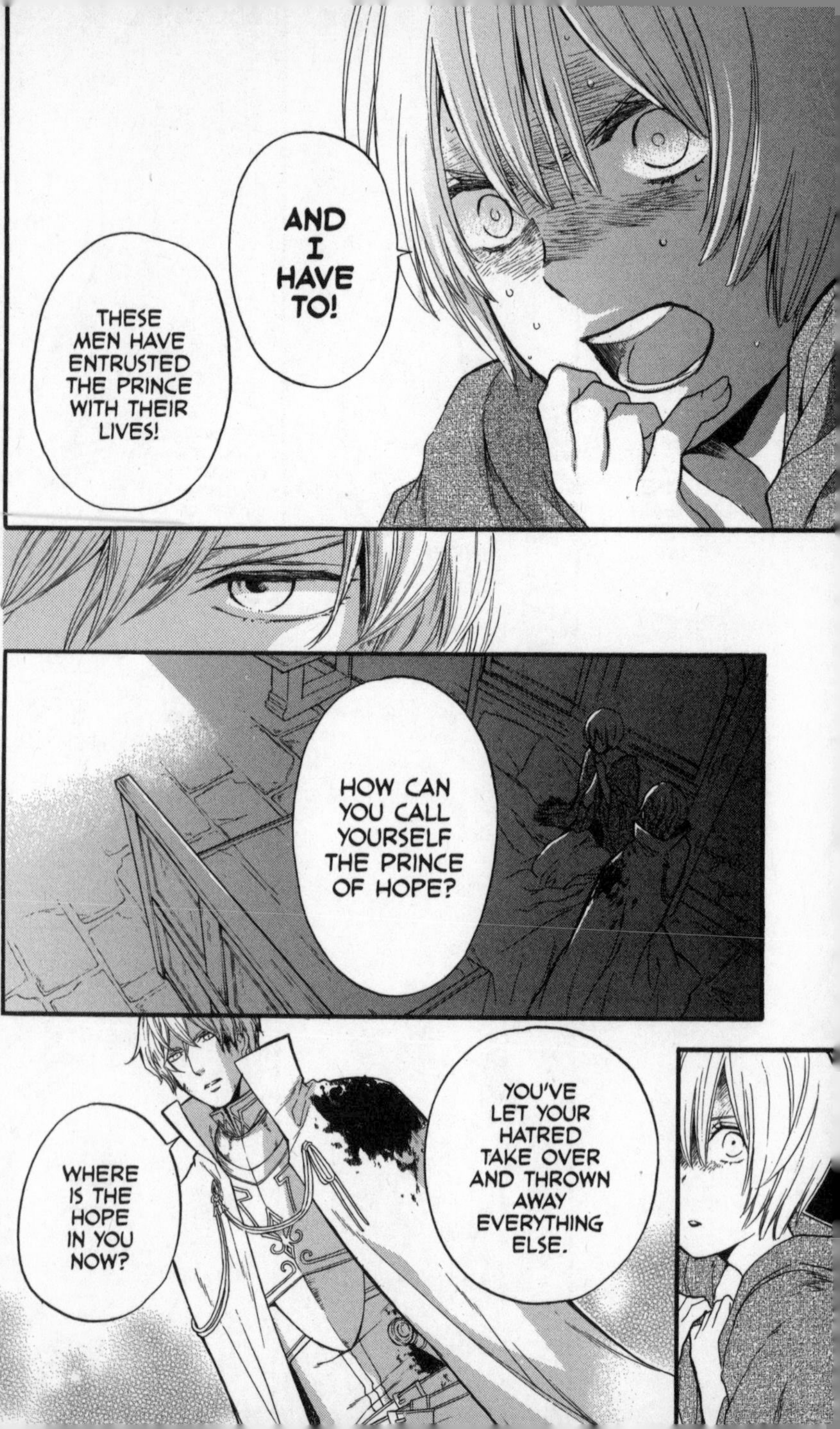
AND I HAVE TO!
THESE MEN HAVE ENTRUSTED THE PRINCE WITH THEIR LIVES!
HOW CAN YOU CALL YOURSELF THE PRINCE OF HOPE?
YOU'VE LET YOUR HATRED TAKE OVER AND THROWN AWAY EVERYTHING ELSE.
WHERE IS THE HOPE IN YOU NOW?

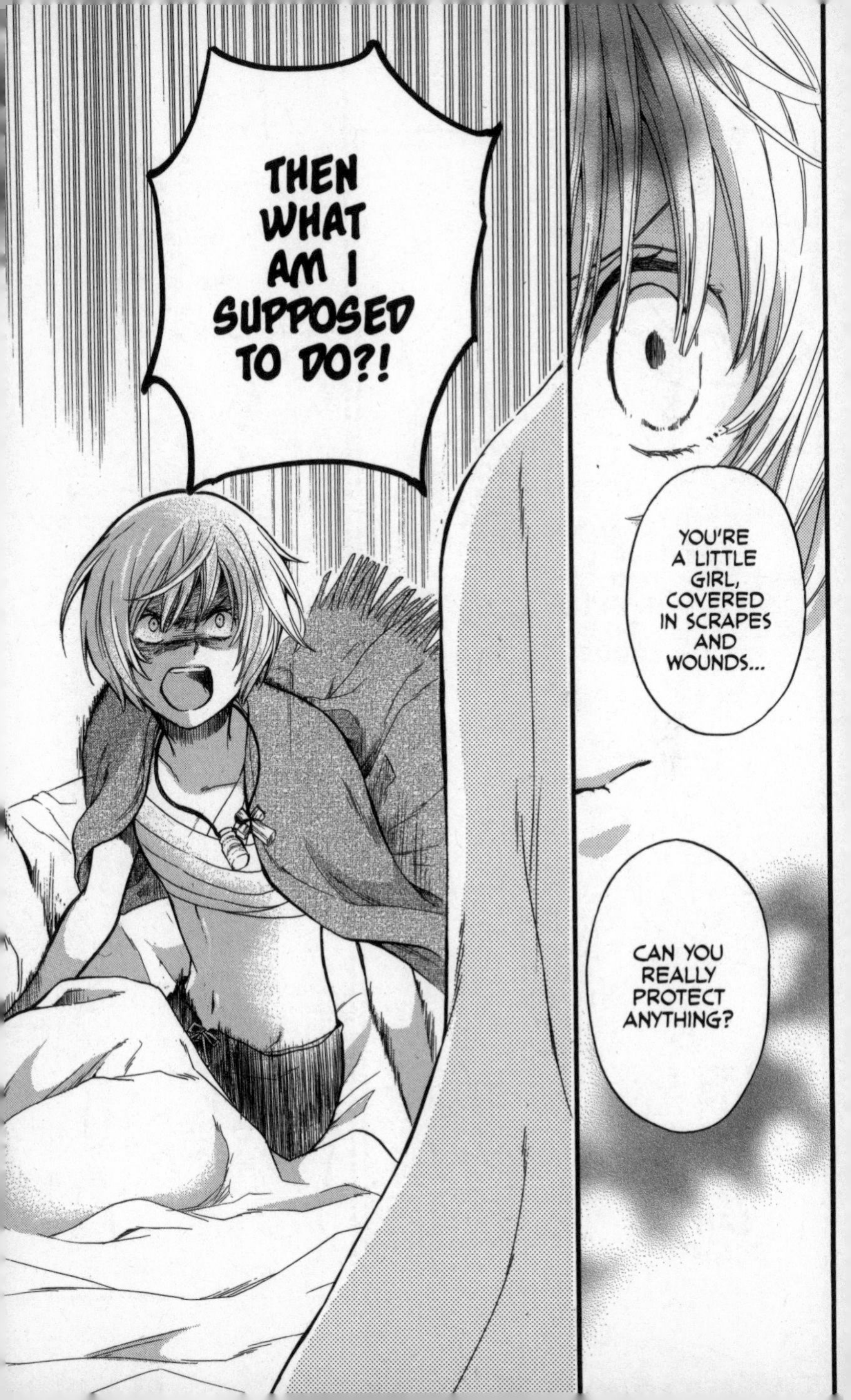
YOU'RE A LITTLE GIRL, COVERED IN SCRAPES AND WOUNDS...
CAN YOU REALLY PROTECT ANYTHING?
THEN WHAT AM I SUPPOSED TO DO?!

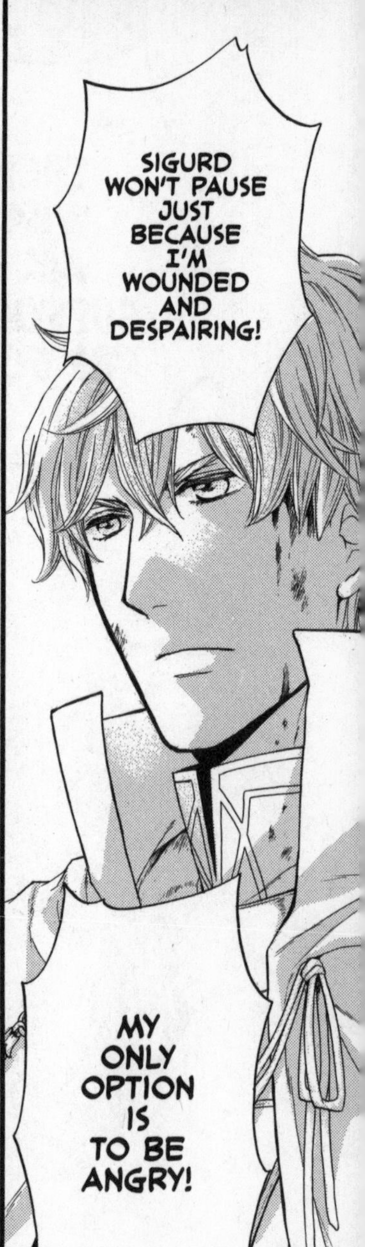
SIGURD WON'T PAUSE JUST BECAUSE I'M WOUNDED AND DESPAIRING!
MY ONLY OPTION IS TO BE ANGRY!

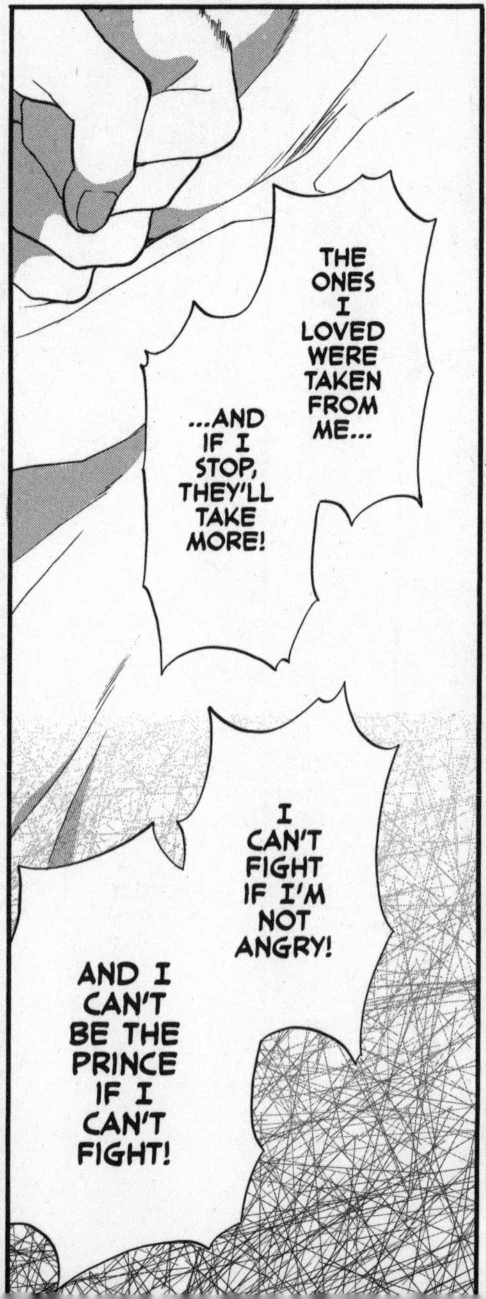
THE ONES I LOVED WERE TAKEN FROM ME...
...AND IF I STOP, THEY'LL TAKE MORE!
I CAN'T FIGHT IF I'M NOT ANGRY!
AND I CAN'T BE THE PRINCE IF I CAN'T FIGHT!

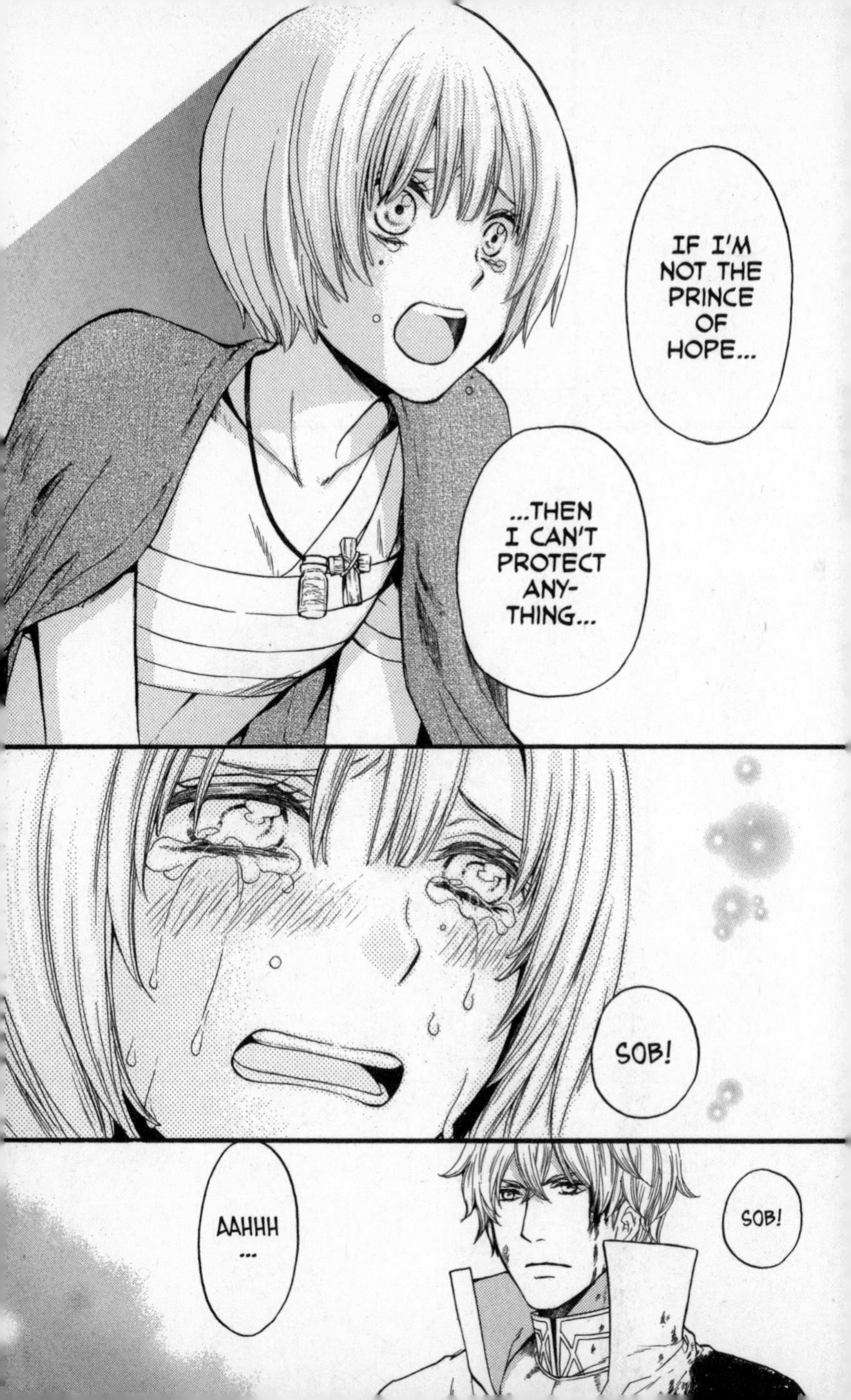
IF I'M NOT THE PRINCE OF HOPE...
...THEN I CAN'T PROTECT ANY-THING...
SOB!
SOB!
AAHHH ...

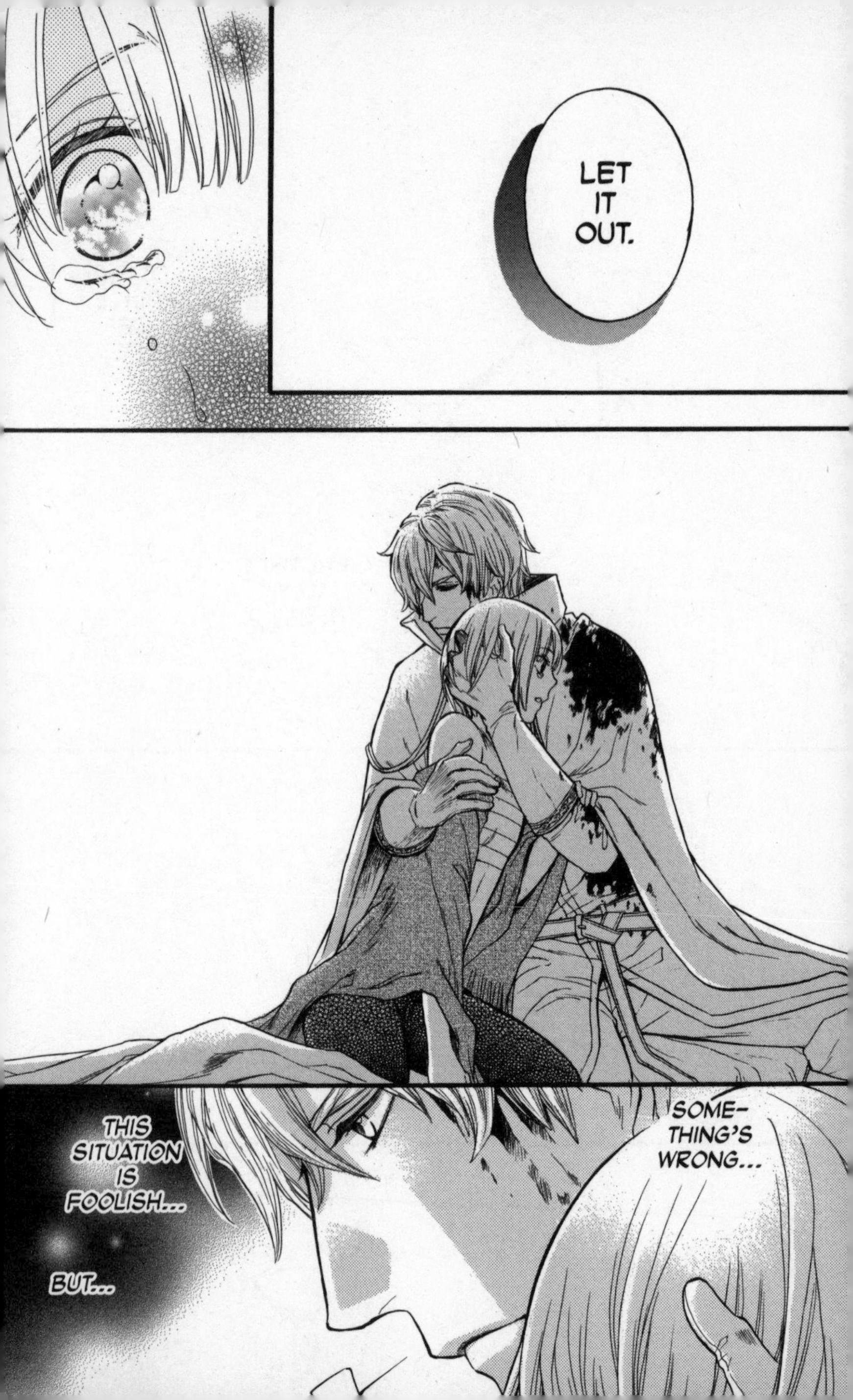
LET IT OUT.
SOME-THING'S WRONG...
THIS SITUATION IS FOOLISH...
BUT...

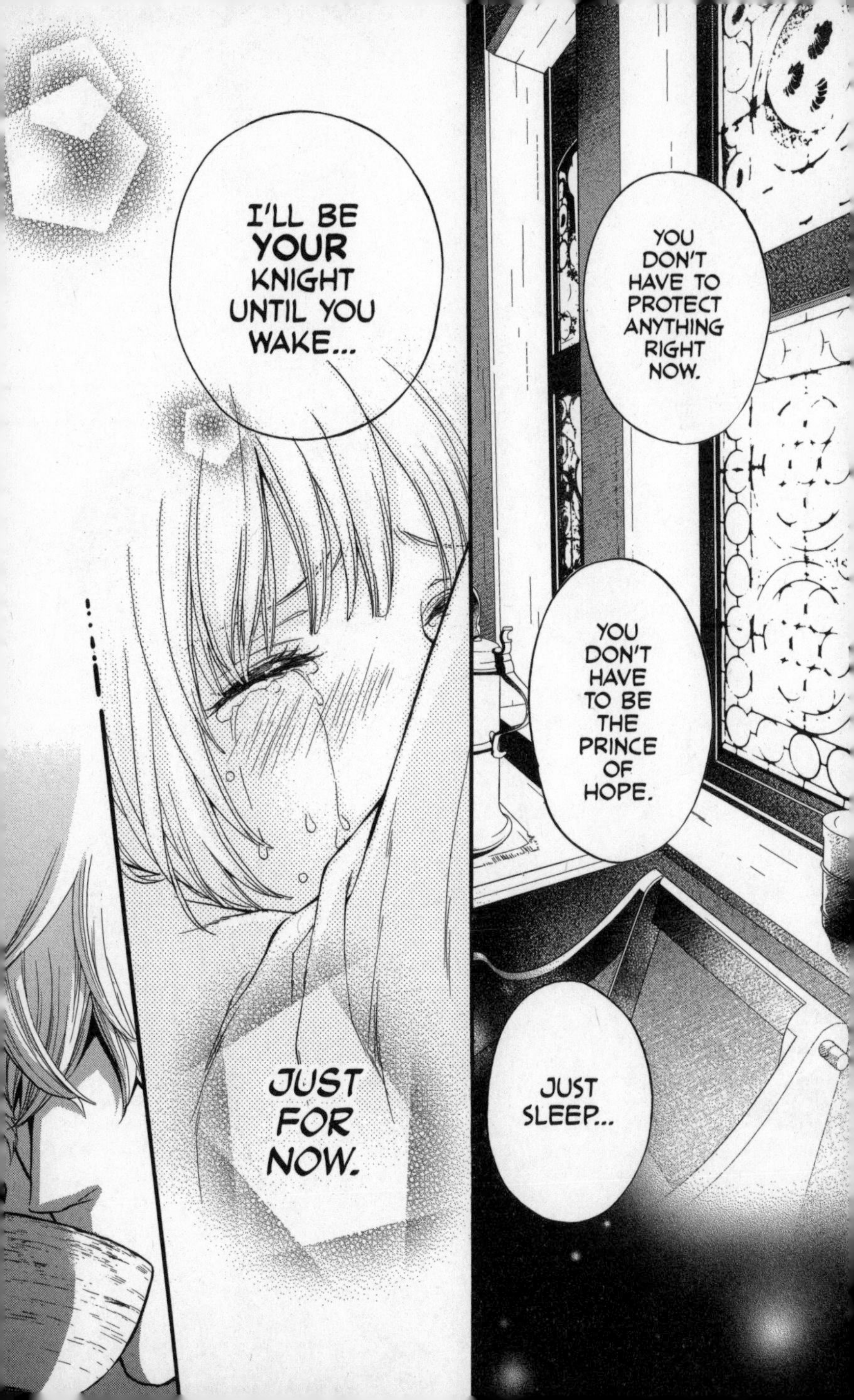
YOU DON'T HAVE TO PROTECT ANYTHING RIGHT NOW.
YOU DON'T HAVE TO BE THE PRINCE OF HOPE.
JUST SLEEP...
I'LL BE YOUR KNIGHT UNTIL YOU WAKE...
JUST FOR NOW.

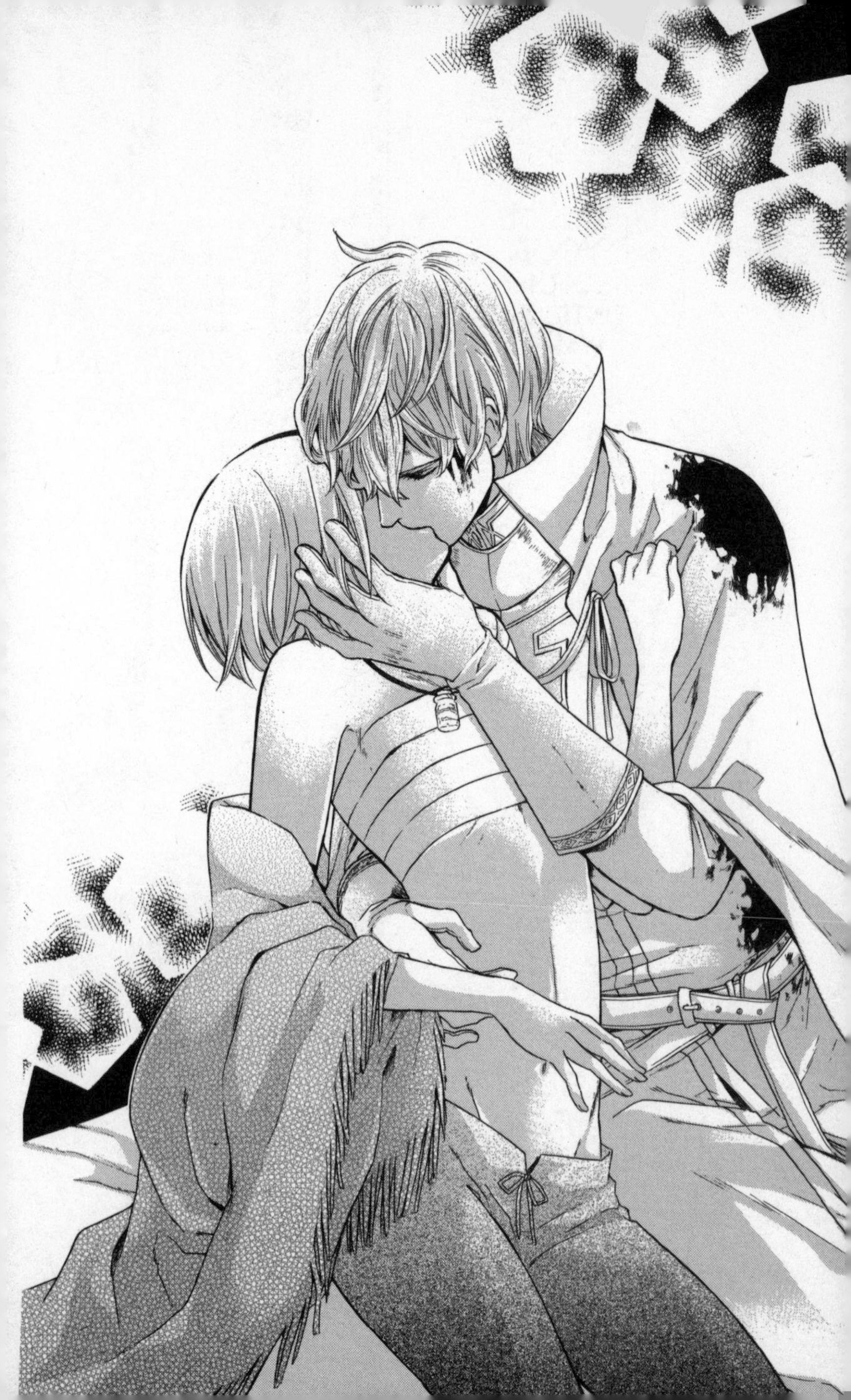

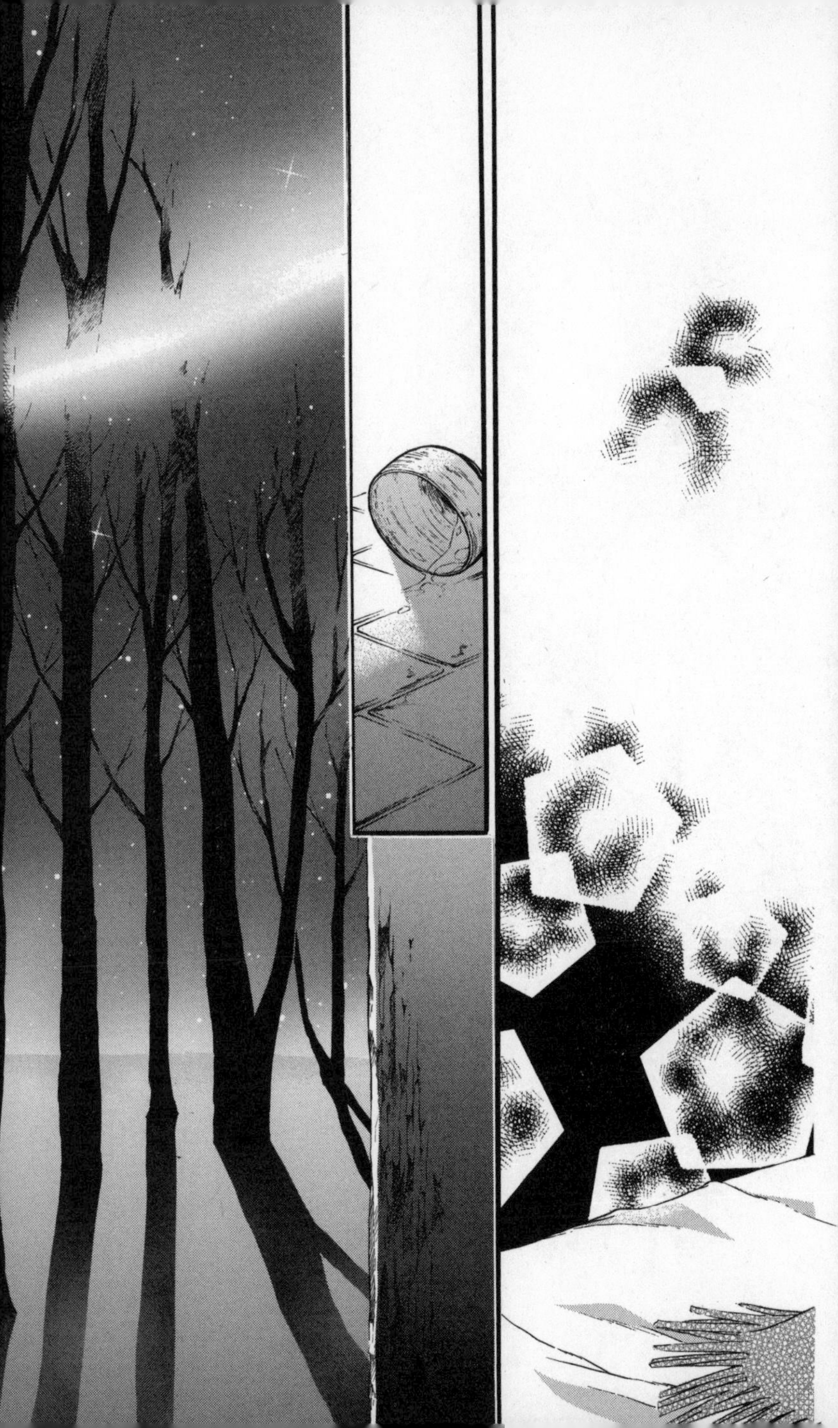

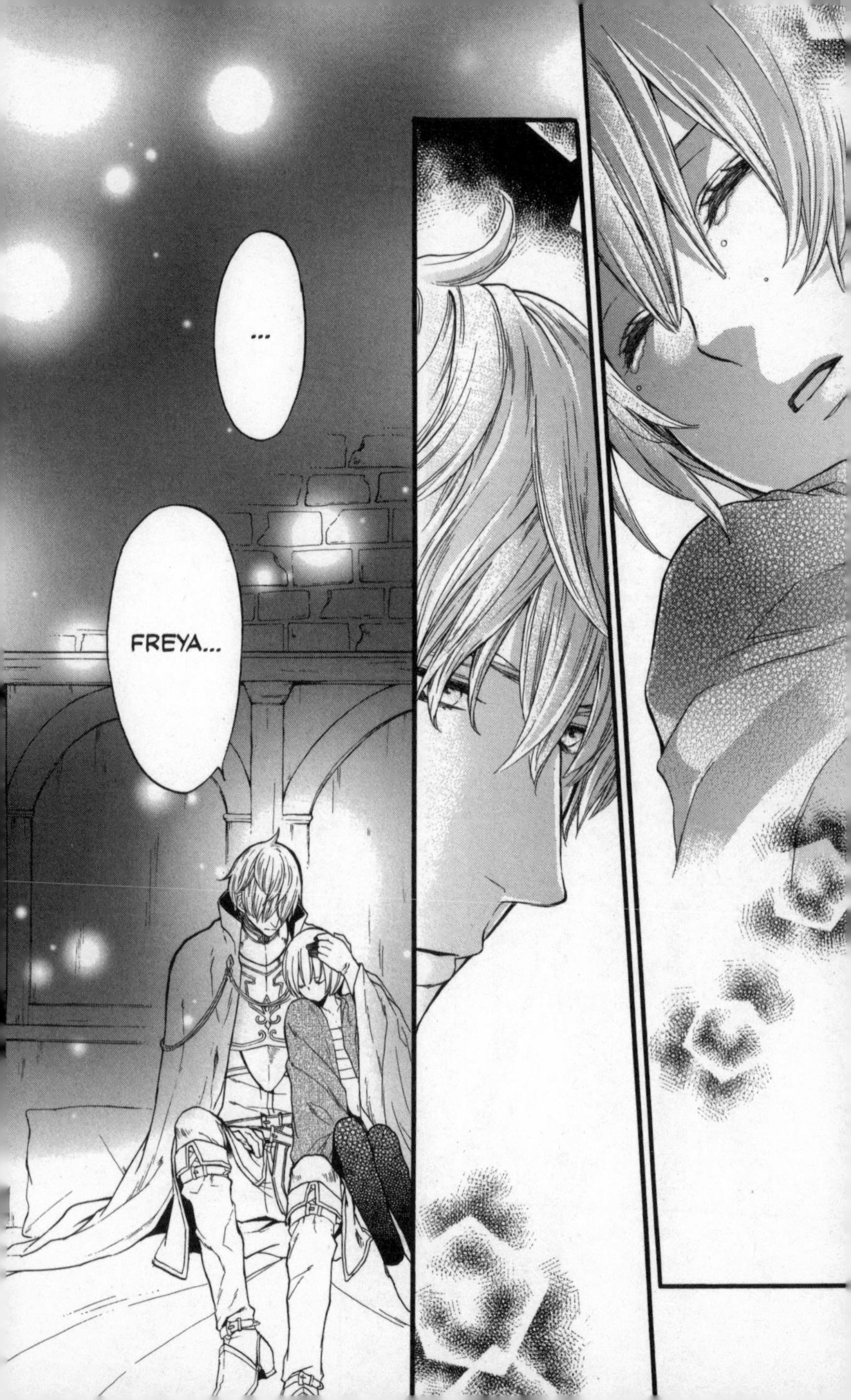
...
FREYA...

PRINCE

Freya

Chapter 8 The Shining Prince, Part 1

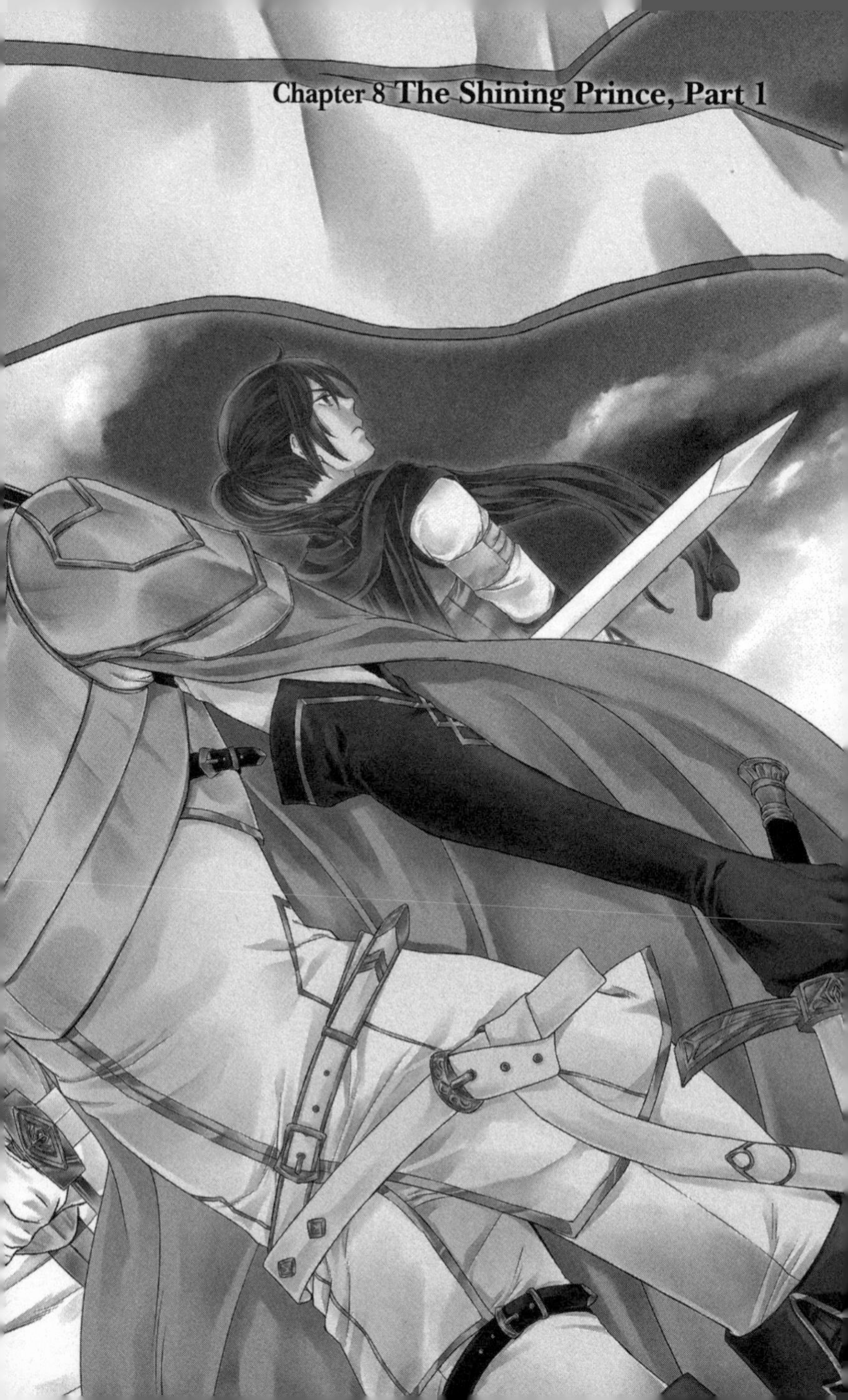

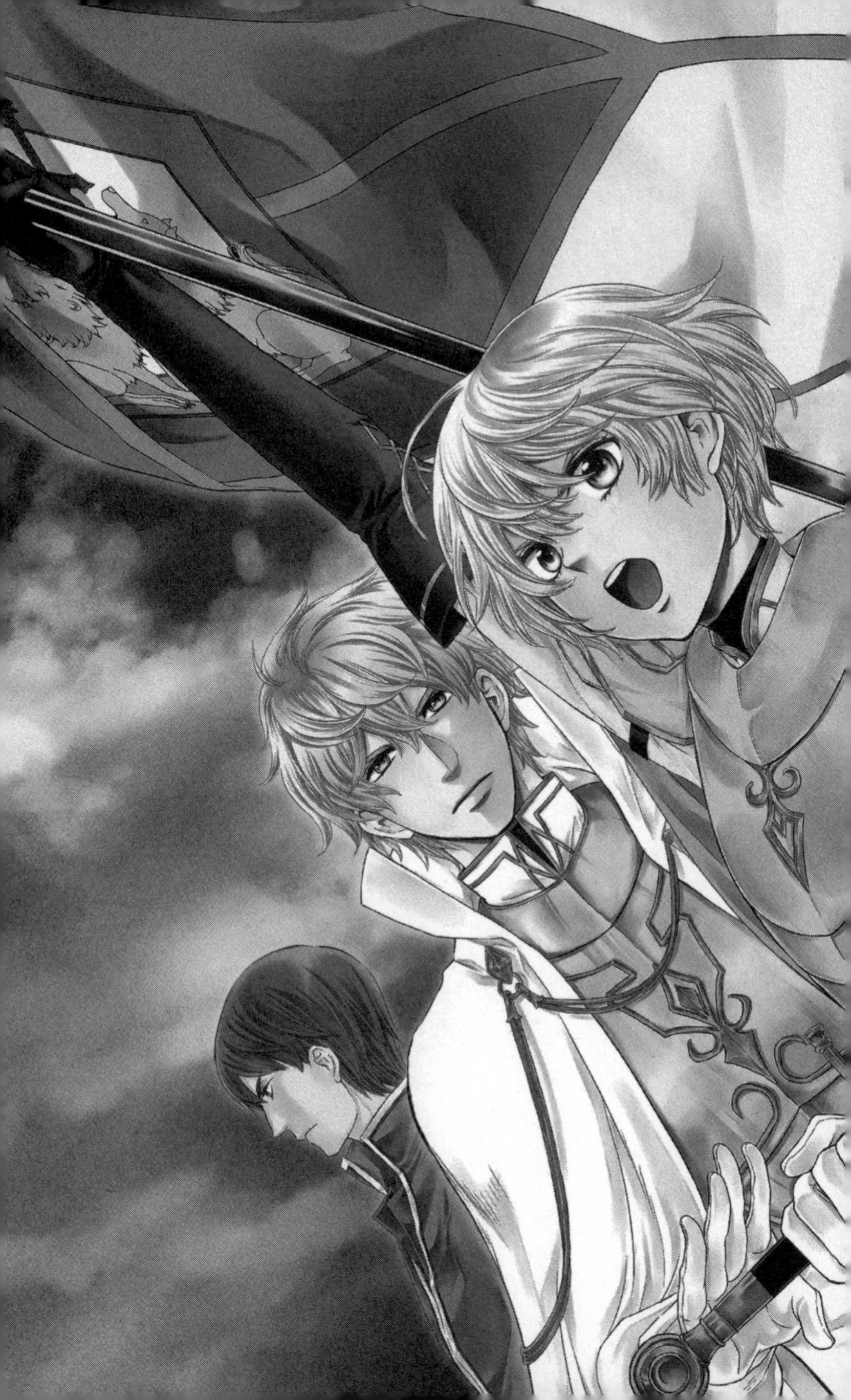

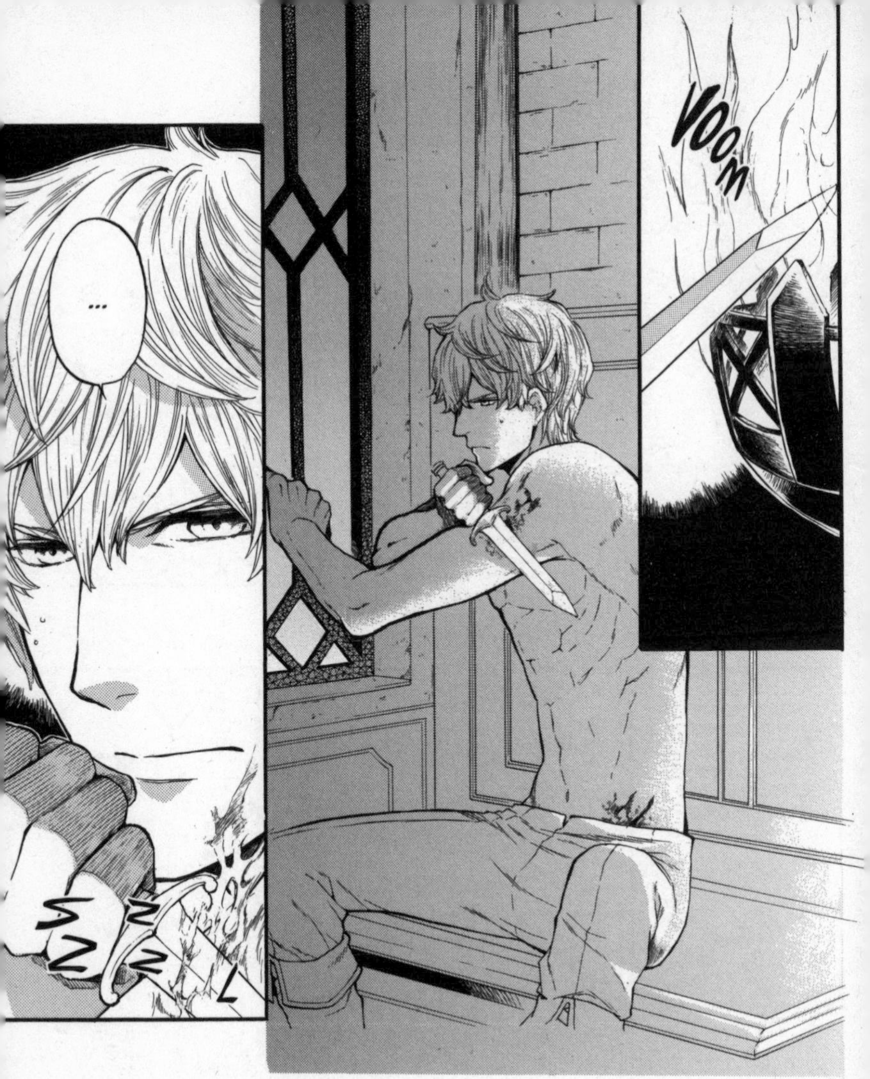
VOOM
...
SZZZZL

PRINCE
Freya

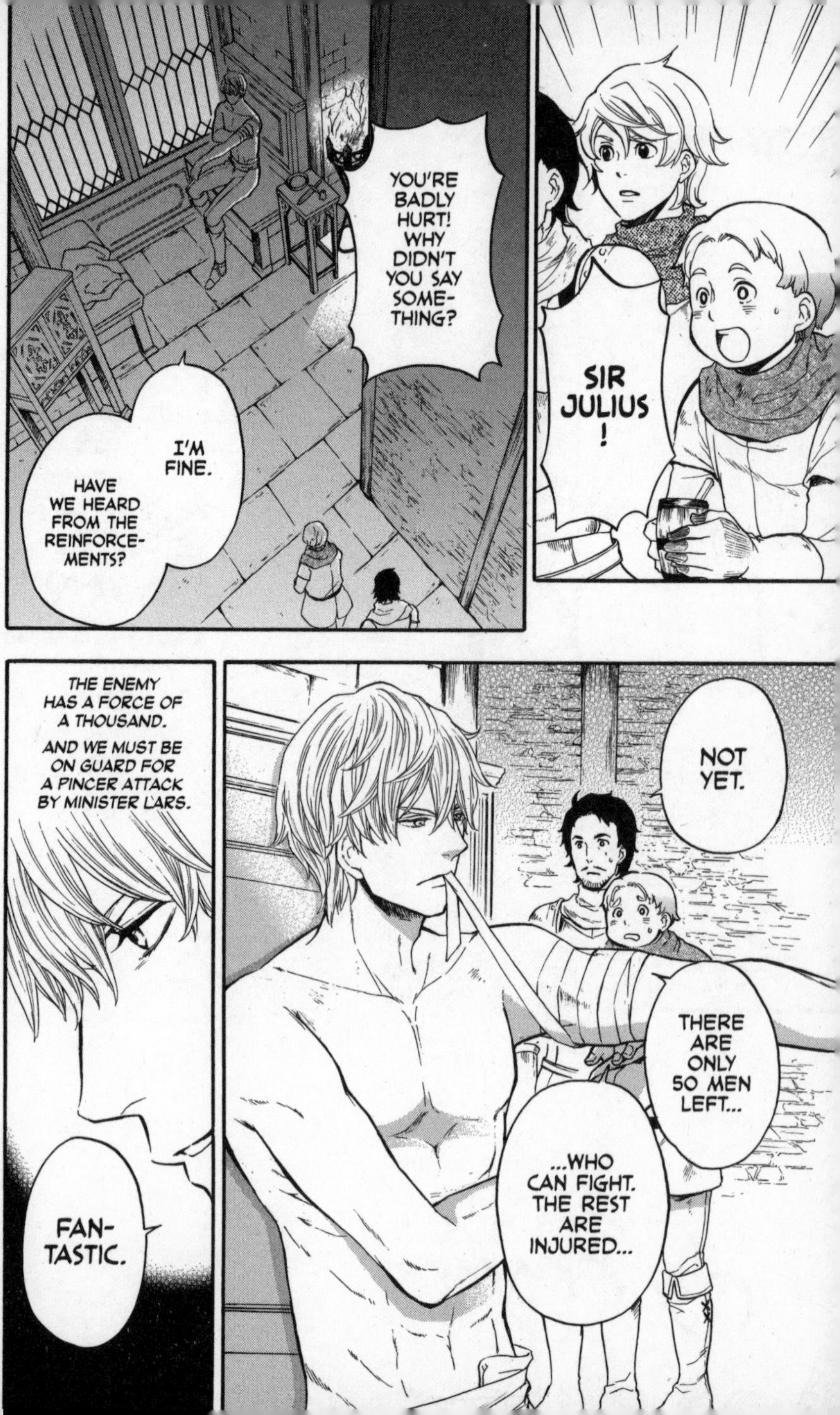
SIR JULIUS!
YOU'RE BADLY HURT! WHY DIDN'T YOU SAY SOME-THING?
I'M FINE.
HAVE WE HEARD FROM THE REINFORCE-MENTS?
NOT YET.
THERE ARE ONLY 50 MEN LEFT...
...WHO CAN FIGHT. THE REST ARE INJURED...
THE ENEMY HAS A FORCE OF A THOUSAND.
AND WE MUST BE ON GUARD FOR A PINCER ATTACK BY MINISTER LARS.
FAN-TASTIC.

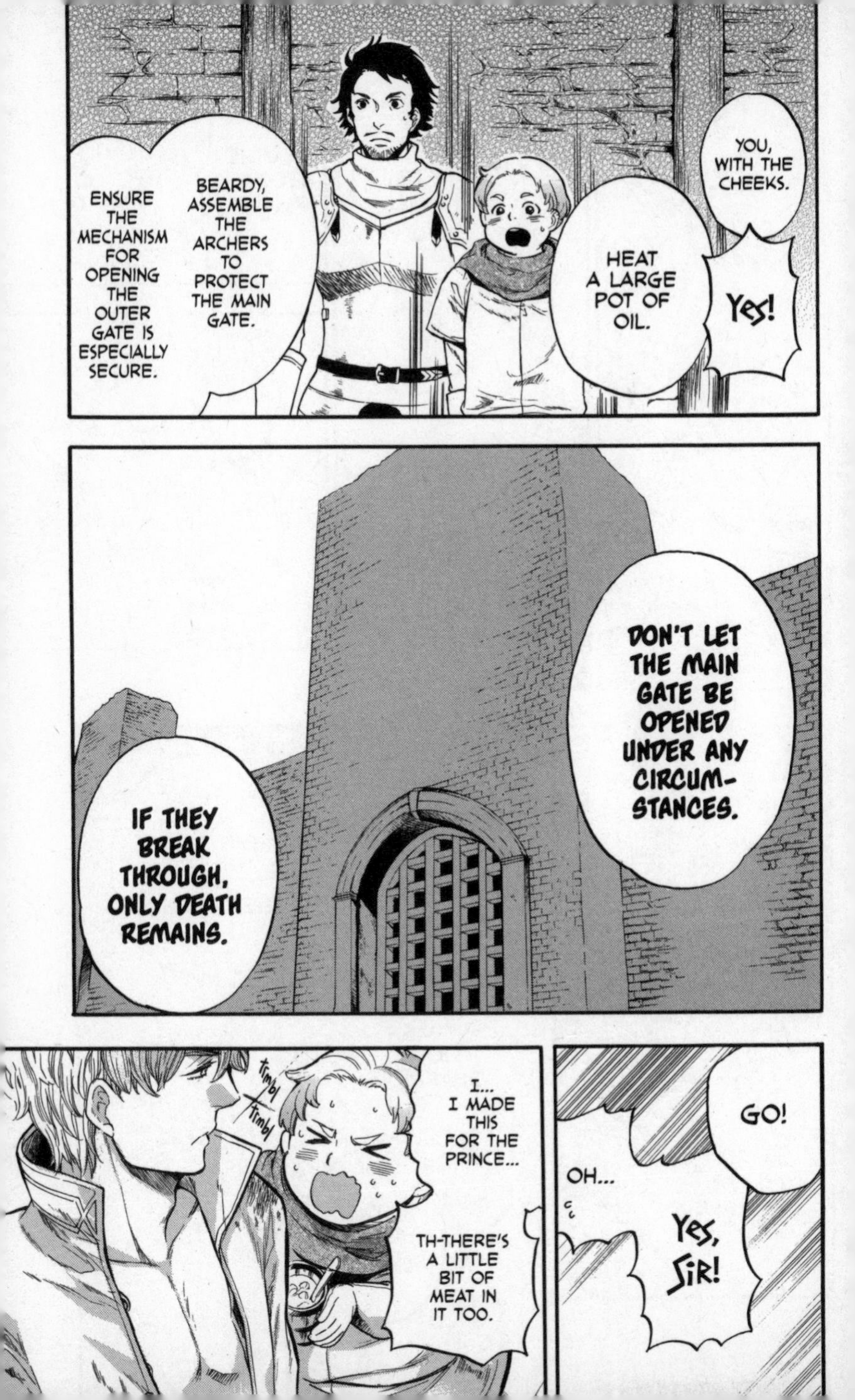
YOU, WITH THE CHEEKS.
HEAT A LARGE POT OF OIL.
Yes!
BEARDY, ASSEMBLE THE ARCHERS TO PROTECT THE MAIN GATE.
ENSURE THE MECHANISM FOR OPENING THE OUTER GATE IS ESPECIALLY SECURE.
DON'T LET THE MAIN GATE BE OPENED UNDER ANY CIRCUM-STANCES.
IF THEY BREAK THROUGH, ONLY DEATH REMAINS.
GO!
Yes, Sir!
OH...
I... I MADE THIS FOR THE PRINCE...
TH-THERE'S A LITTLE BIT OF MEAT IN IT TOO.
trmbl trmbl

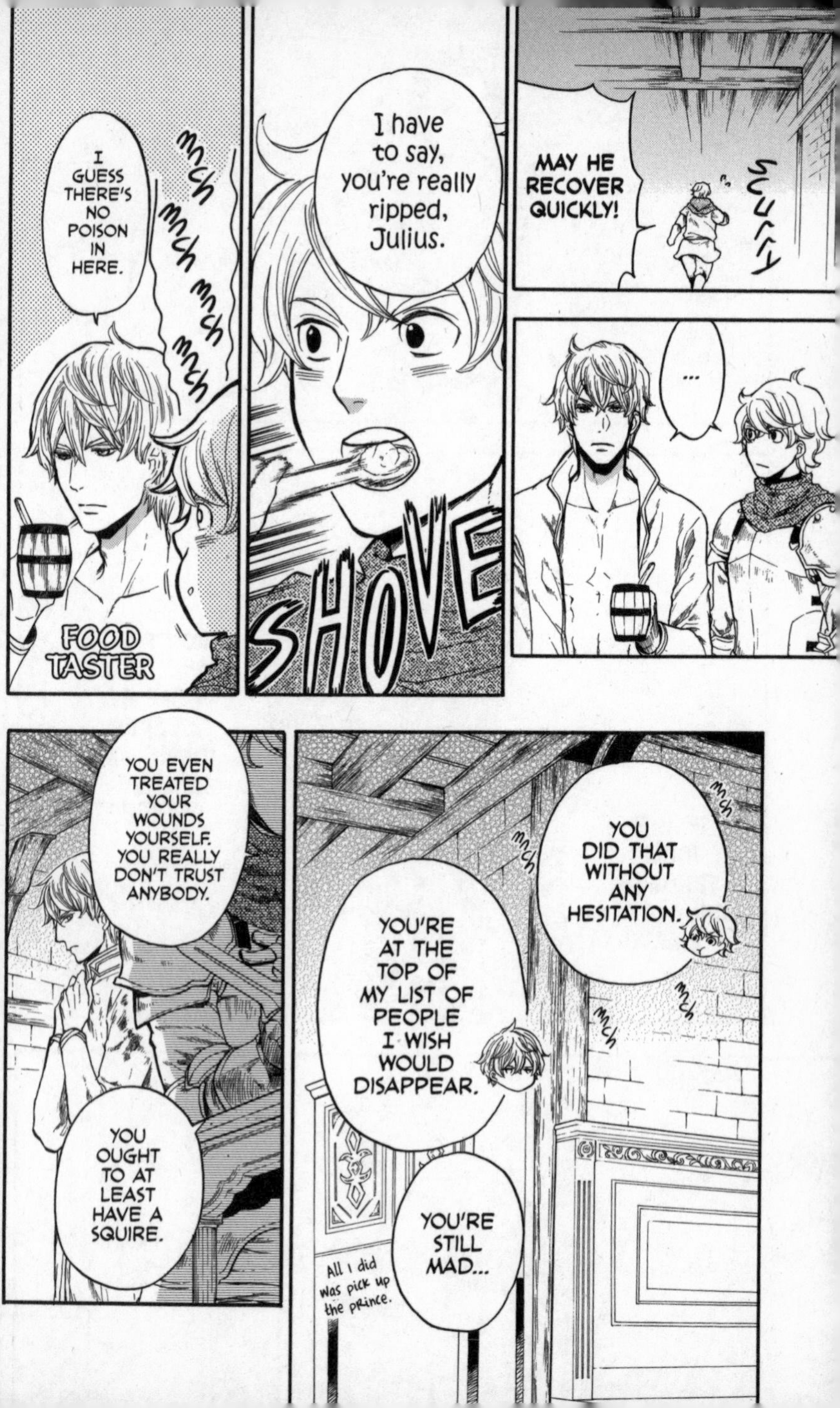
MAY HE RECOVER QUICKLY!
SCURRY
...
I have to say, you're really ripped, Julius.
SHOVE
I GUESS THERE'S NO POISON IN HERE.
mch mch mch mch mch
FOOD TASTER
YOU DID THAT WITHOUT ANY HESITATION.
mch mch mch mch
YOU'RE AT THE TOP OF MY LIST OF PEOPLE I WISH WOULD DISAPPEAR.
YOU'RE STILL MAD...
All I did was pick up the prince.
YOU EVEN TREATED YOUR WOUNDS YOURSELF. YOU REALLY DON'T TRUST ANYBODY.
YOU OUGHT TO AT LEAST HAVE A SQUIRE.

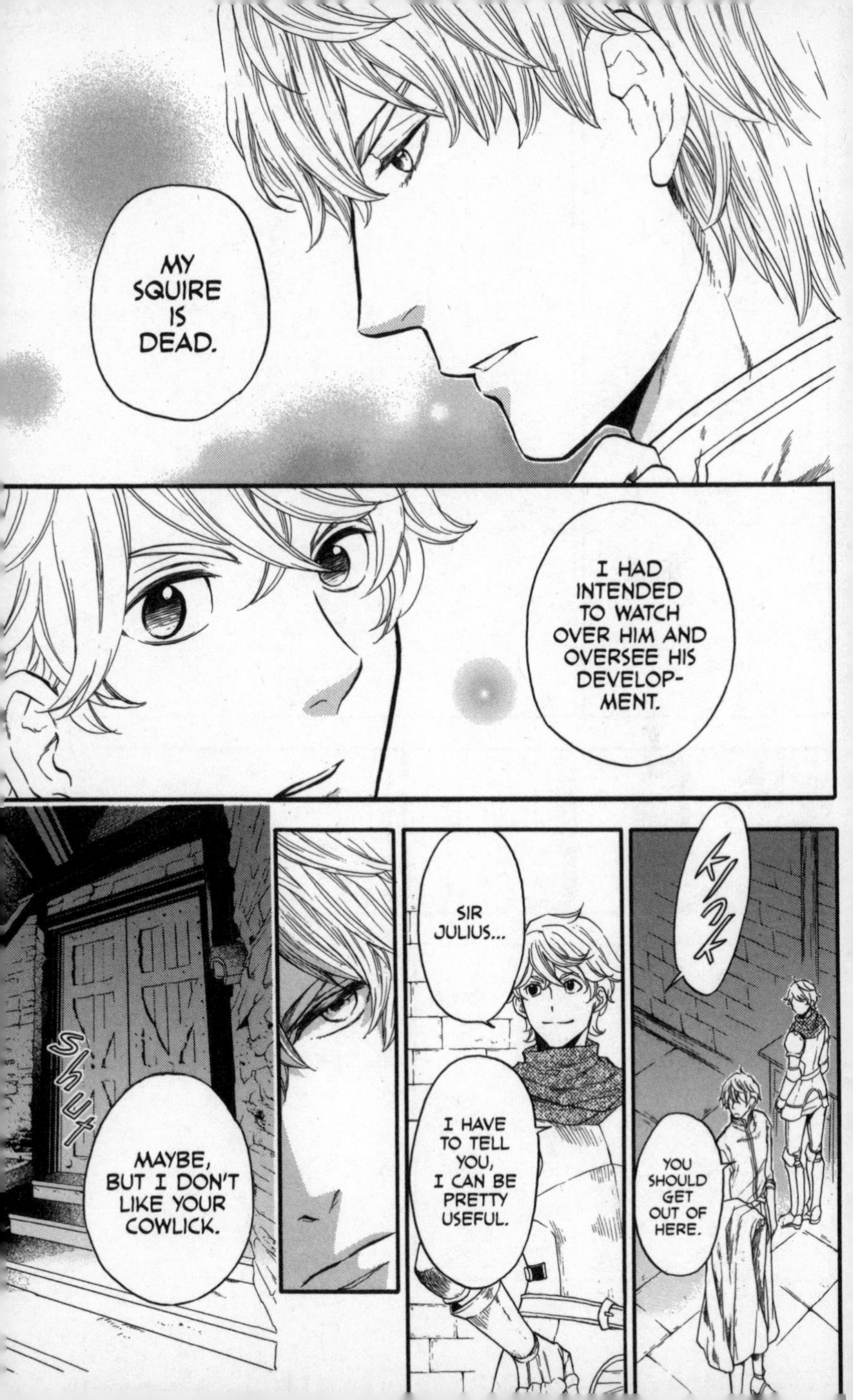
MY SQUIRE IS DEAD.
I HAD INTENDED TO WATCH OVER HIM AND OVERSEE HIS DEVELOP-MENT.
KLIK
YOU SHOULD GET OUT OF HERE.
SIR JULIUS...
I HAVE TO TELL YOU, I CAN BE PRETTY USEFUL.
SHUT
MAYBE, BUT I DON'T LIKE YOUR COWLICK.

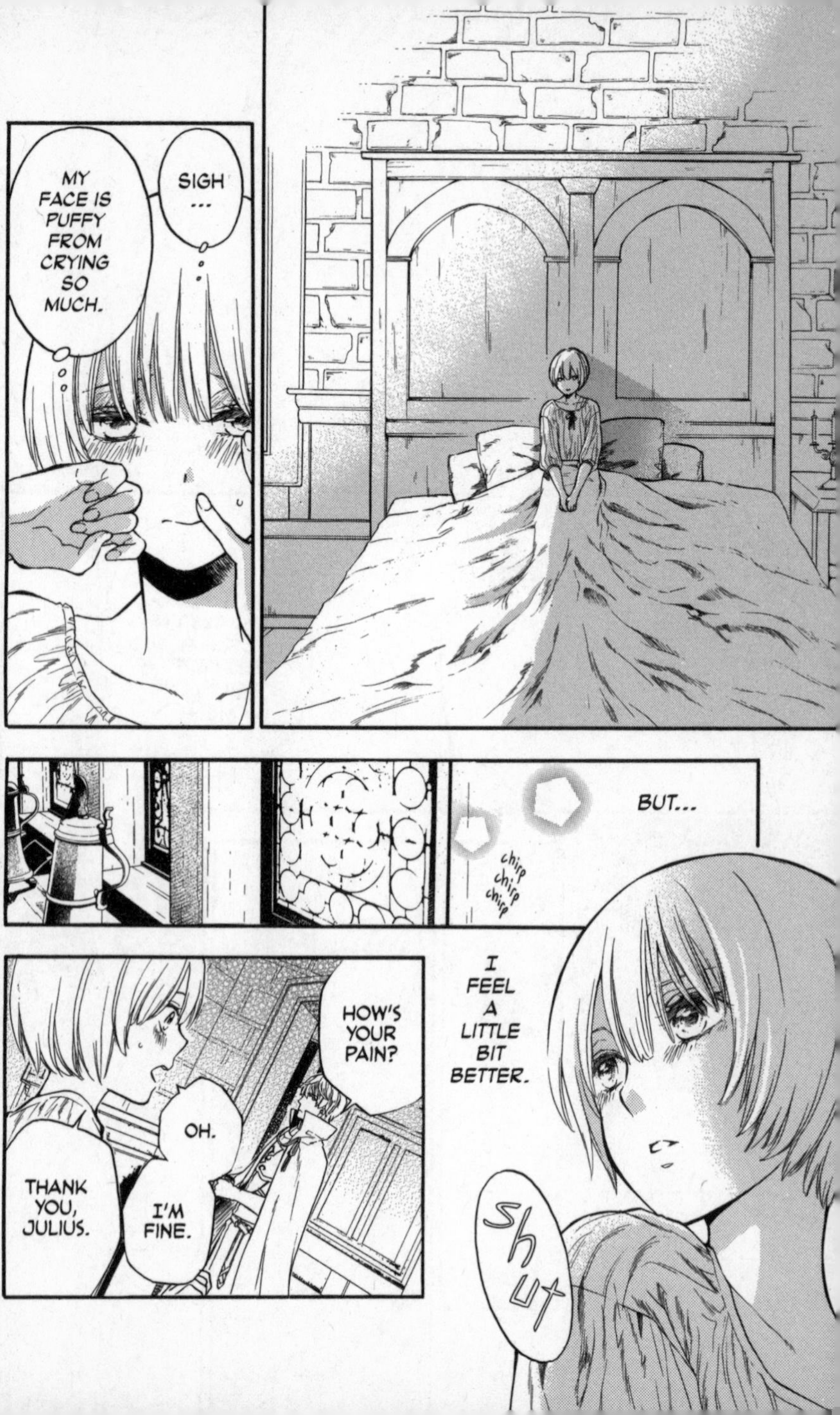
SIGH...
MY FACE IS PUFFY FROM CRYING SO MUCH.
BUT...
chirp chirp chirp
I FEEL A LITTLE BIT BETTER.
Shut
HOW'S YOUR PAIN?
OH.
I'M FINE.
THANK YOU, JULIUS.

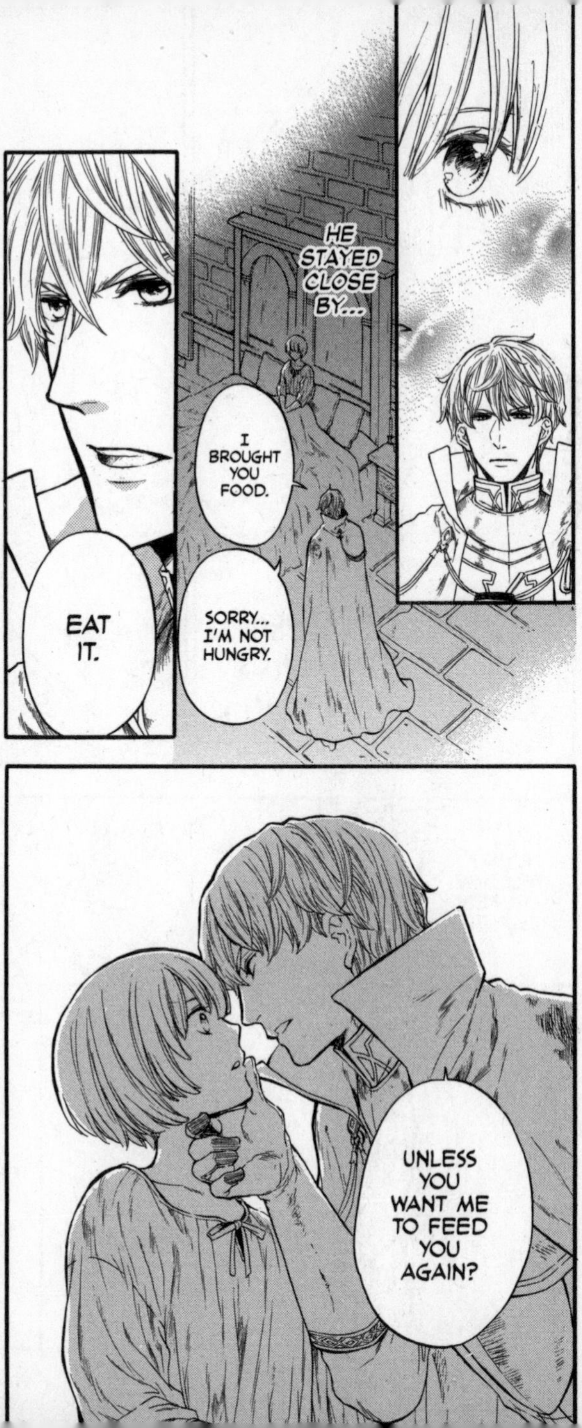

HE STAYED CLOSE BY...
I BROUGHT YOU FOOD.
SORRY... I'M NOT HUNGRY.
EAT IT.
UNLESS YOU WANT ME TO FEED YOU AGAIN?

Maxime and Kyrie

A pair of lieutenants in the Sigurdian Army.

Maxime is a great swordsman on the battlefield, but sadly he doesn't have much luck with the ladies.

Kyrie is a sadist who finds humor in her partner's shortcomings.

General

I never reveal his name, but there isn't a deep reason for that.

He's rather self-centered and causes a lot of problems for others.

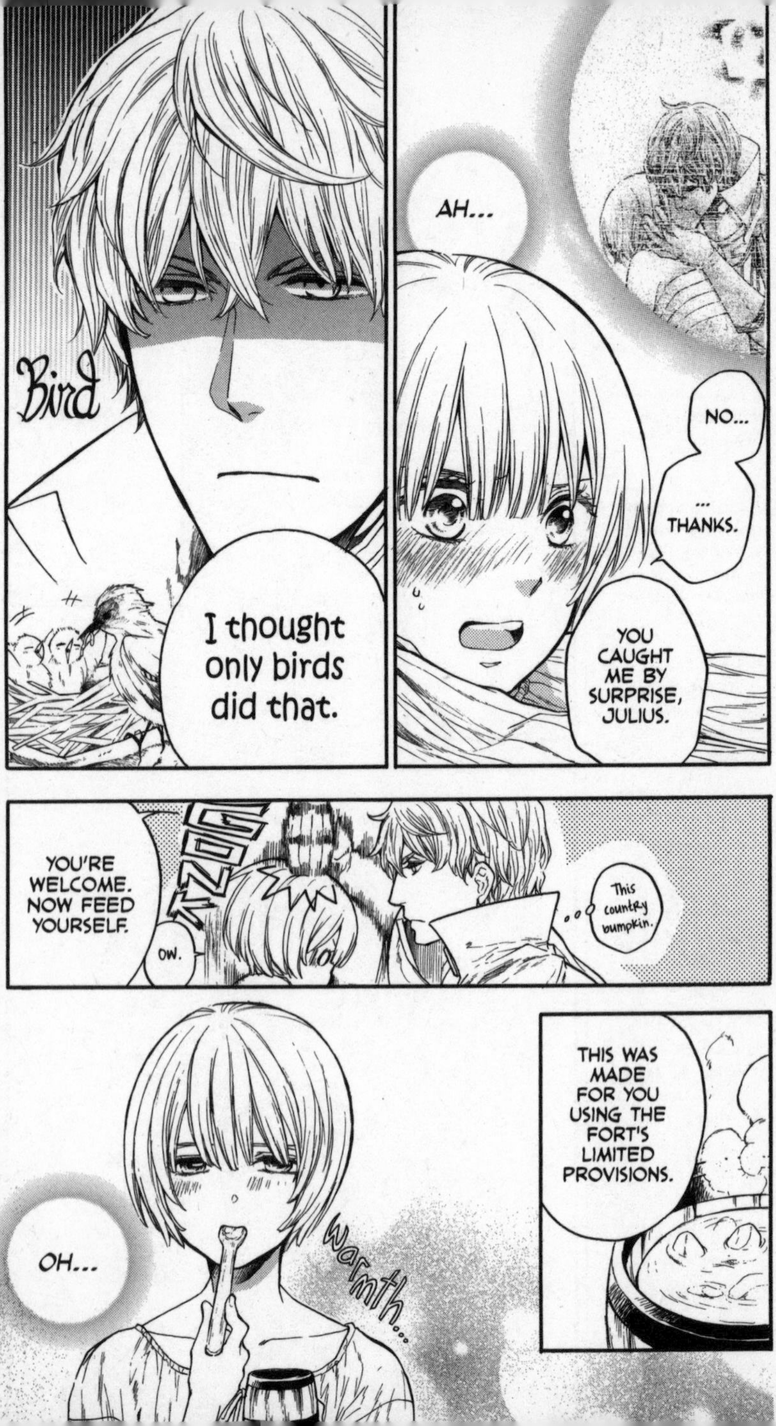
AH...
NO...
...THANKS.
YOU CAUGHT ME BY SURPRISE, JULIUS.
Bird
I thought only birds did that.
YOU'RE WELCOME. NOW FEED YOURSELF.
OW.
This country bumpkin.
THIS WAS MADE FOR YOU USING THE FORT'S LIMITED PROVISIONS.
OH...
warmth...

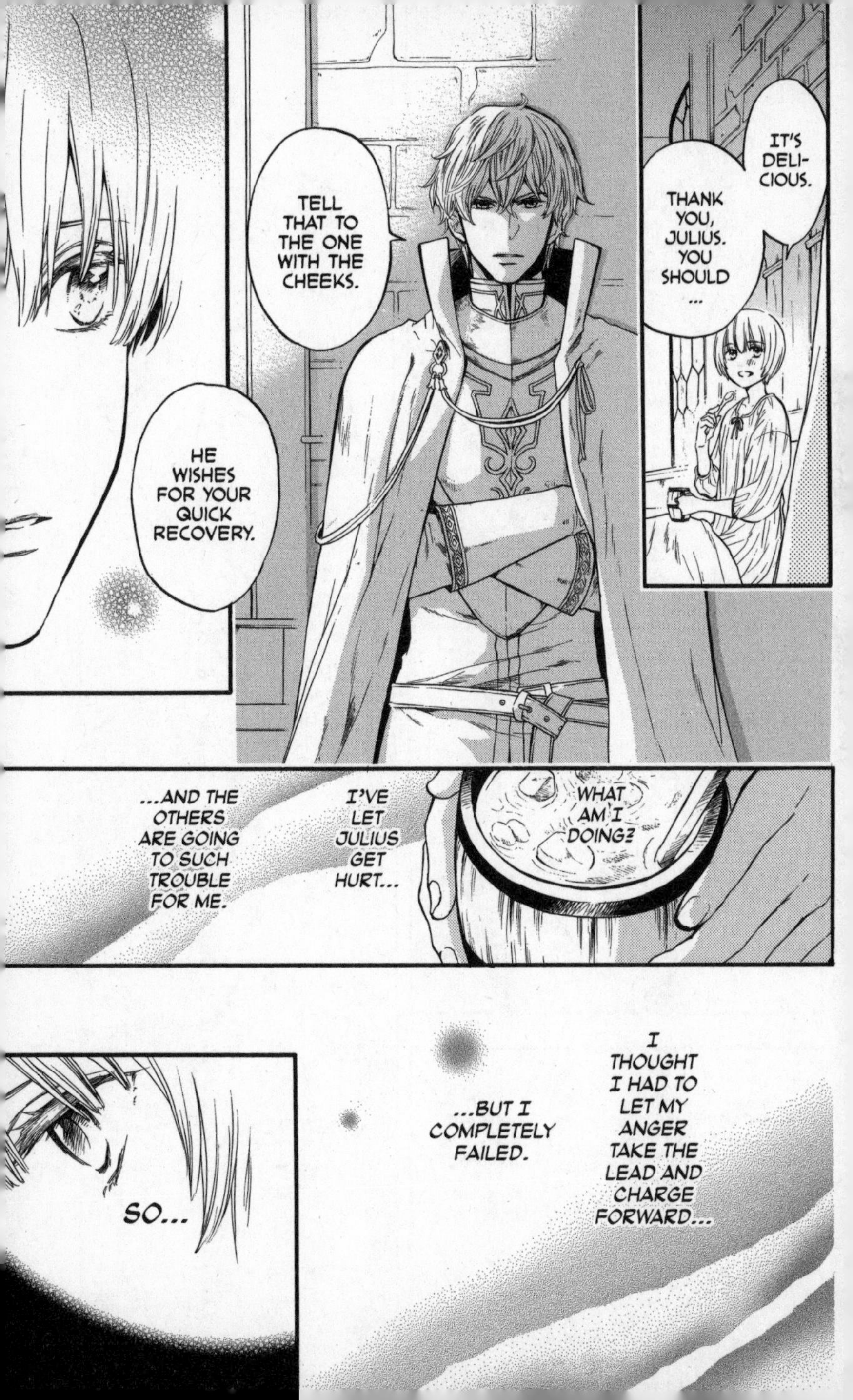
IT'S DELICIOUS.
THANK YOU, JULIUS. YOU SHOULD ...
TELL THAT TO THE ONE WITH THE CHEEKS.
HE WISHES FOR YOUR QUICK RECOVERY.
WHAT AM I DOING?
I'VE LET JULIUS GET HURT...
...AND THE OTHERS ARE GOING TO SUCH TROUBLE FOR ME.
I THOUGHT I HAD TO LET MY ANGER TAKE THE LEAD AND CHARGE FORWARD...
...BUT I COMPLETELY FAILED.
SO...

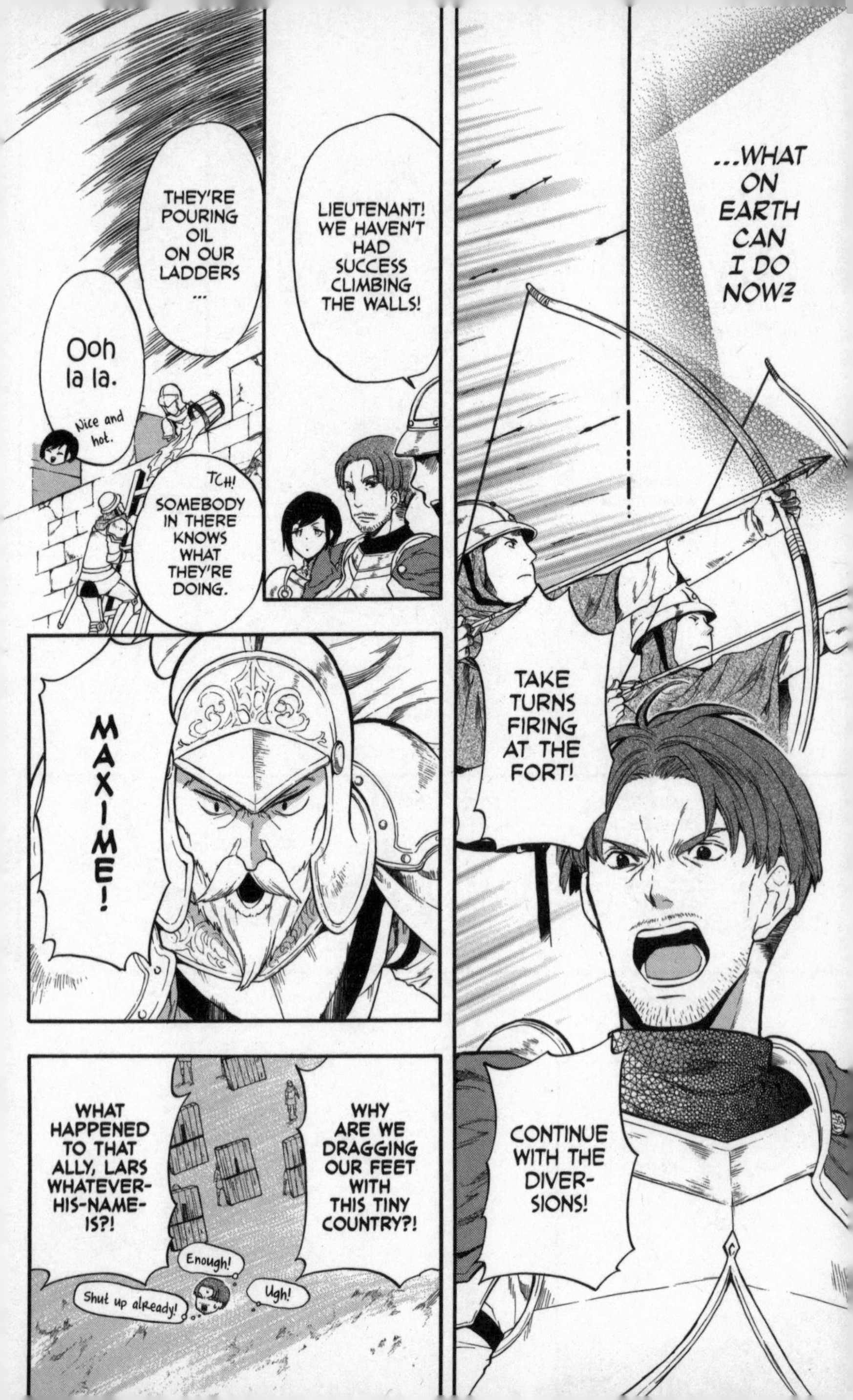
...WHAT ON EARTH CAN I DO NOW?
TAKE TURNS FIRING AT THE FORT!
CONTINUE WITH THE DIVER-SIONS!
LIEUTENANT! WE HAVEN'T HAD SUCCESS CLIMBING THE WALLS!
THEY'RE POURING OIL ON OUR LADDERS ...
Ooh la la.
Nice and hot.
TCH!
SOMEBODY IN THERE KNOWS WHAT THEY'RE DOING.
MAXIME!
WHY ARE WE DRAGGING OUR FEET WITH THIS TINY COUNTRY?!
WHAT HAPPENED TO THAT ALLY, LARS WHATEVER-HIS-NAME-IS?!
Enough!
Ugh!
Shut up already!

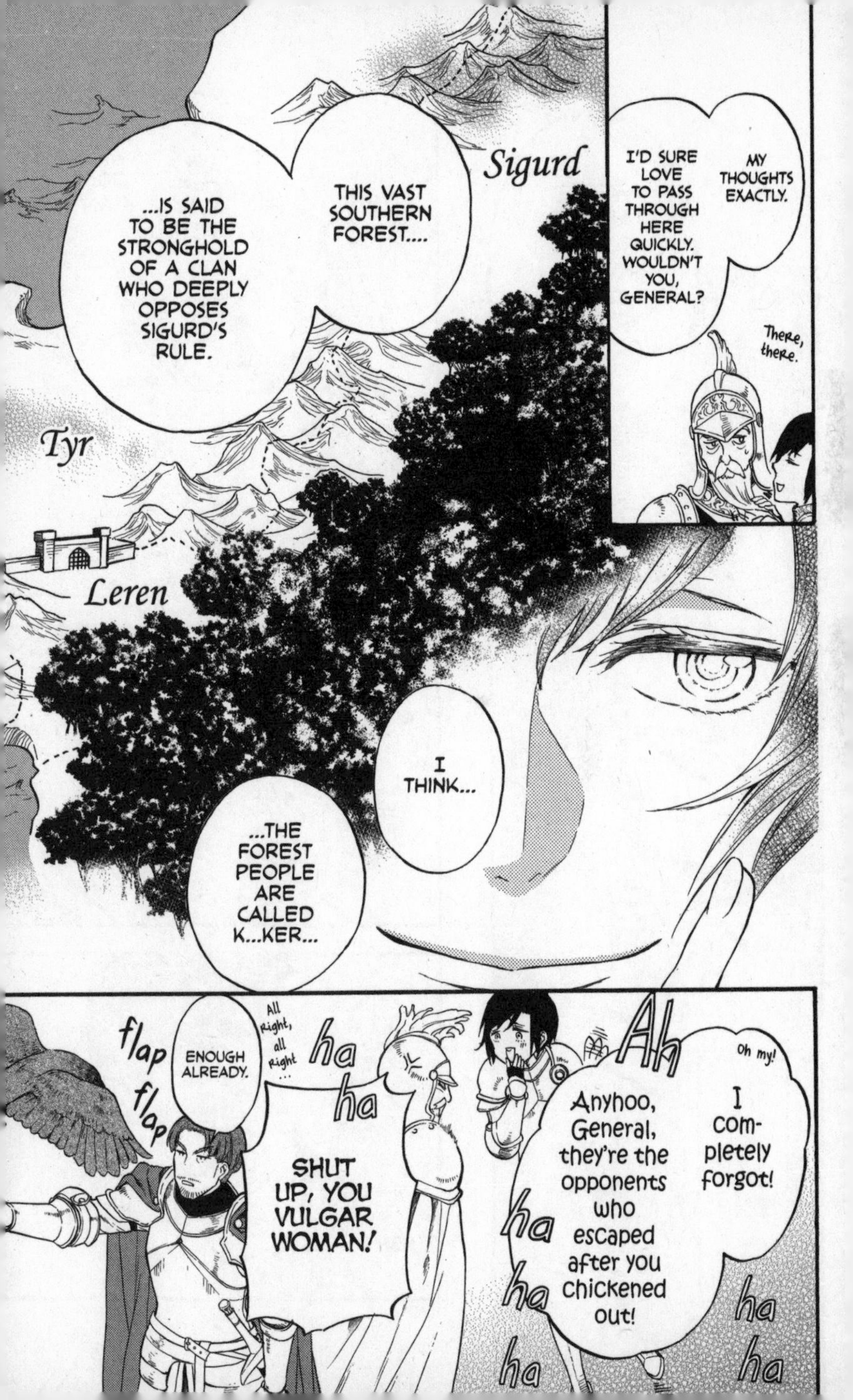
MY THOUGHTS EXACTLY.
I'D SURE LOVE TO PASS THROUGH HERE QUICKLY. WOULDN'T YOU, GENERAL?
There, there.
THIS VAST SOUTHERN FOREST....
...IS SAID TO BE THE STRONGHOLD OF A CLAN WHO DEEPLY OPPOSES SIGURD'S RULE.
Sigurd
Tyr
Leren
I THINK...
...THE FOREST PEOPLE ARE CALLED K...KER...
Oh my!
I com-pletely forgot!
Ah
Anyhoo, General, they're the opponents who escaped after you chickened out!
ha ha ha ha ha ha
SHUT UP, YOU VULGAR WOMAN!
ha ha
All right, all right...
ENOUGH ALREADY.
flap flap

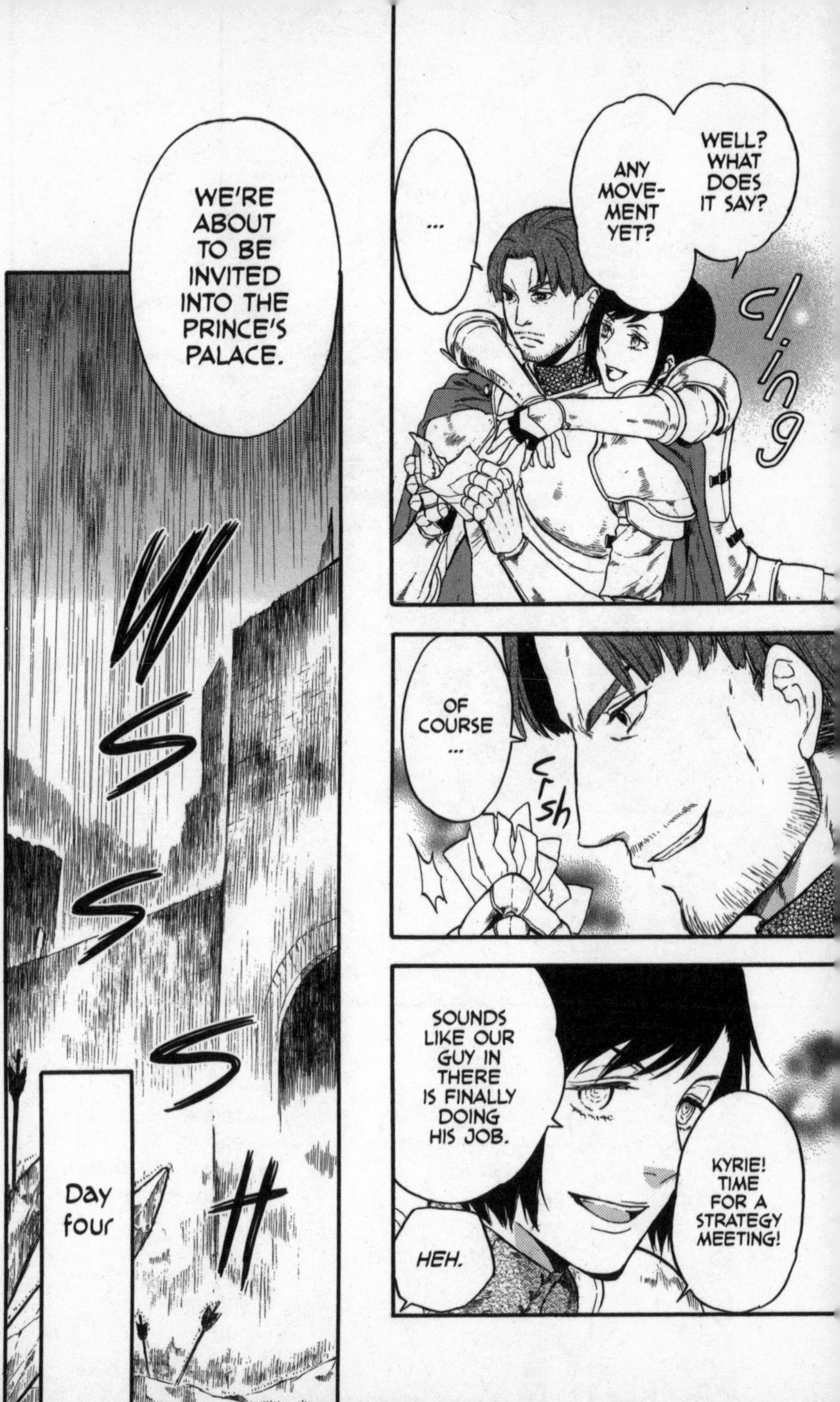
WELL? WHAT DOES IT SAY?
cling
ANY MOVE-MENT YET?
...
OF COURSE ...
crsh
KYRIE! TIME FOR A STRATEGY MEETING!
SOUNDS LIKE OUR GUY IN THERE IS FINALLY DOING HIS JOB.
HEH.
WE'RE ABOUT TO BE INVITED INTO THE PRINCE'S PALACE.
WSSSH
Day four

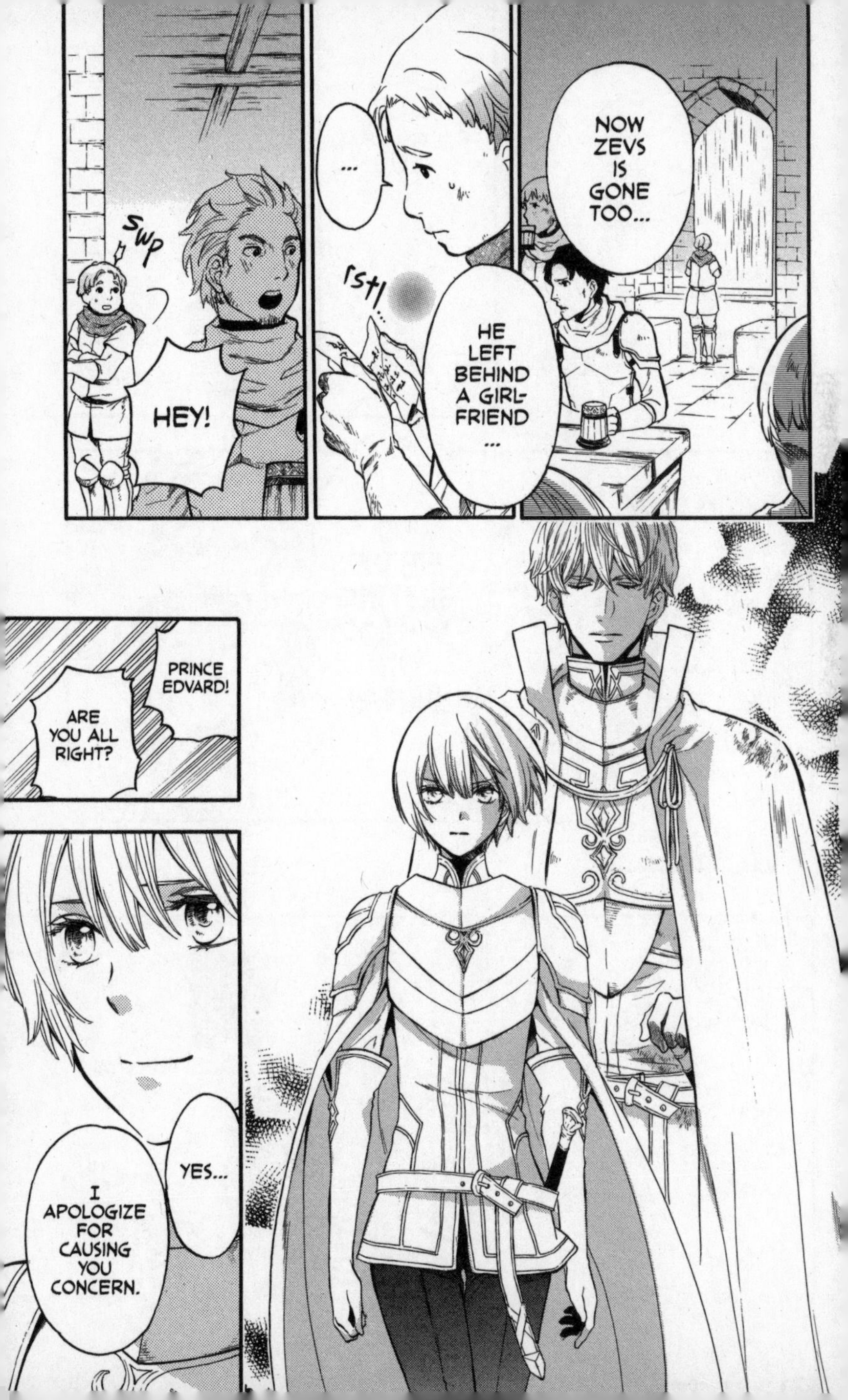
NOW ZEVS IS GONE TOO...
...
rst!
HE LEFT BEHIND A GIRL-FRIEND...
SWP
HEY!
PRINCE EDVARD!
ARE YOU ALL RIGHT?
YES...
I APOLOGIZE FOR CAUSING YOU CONCERN.

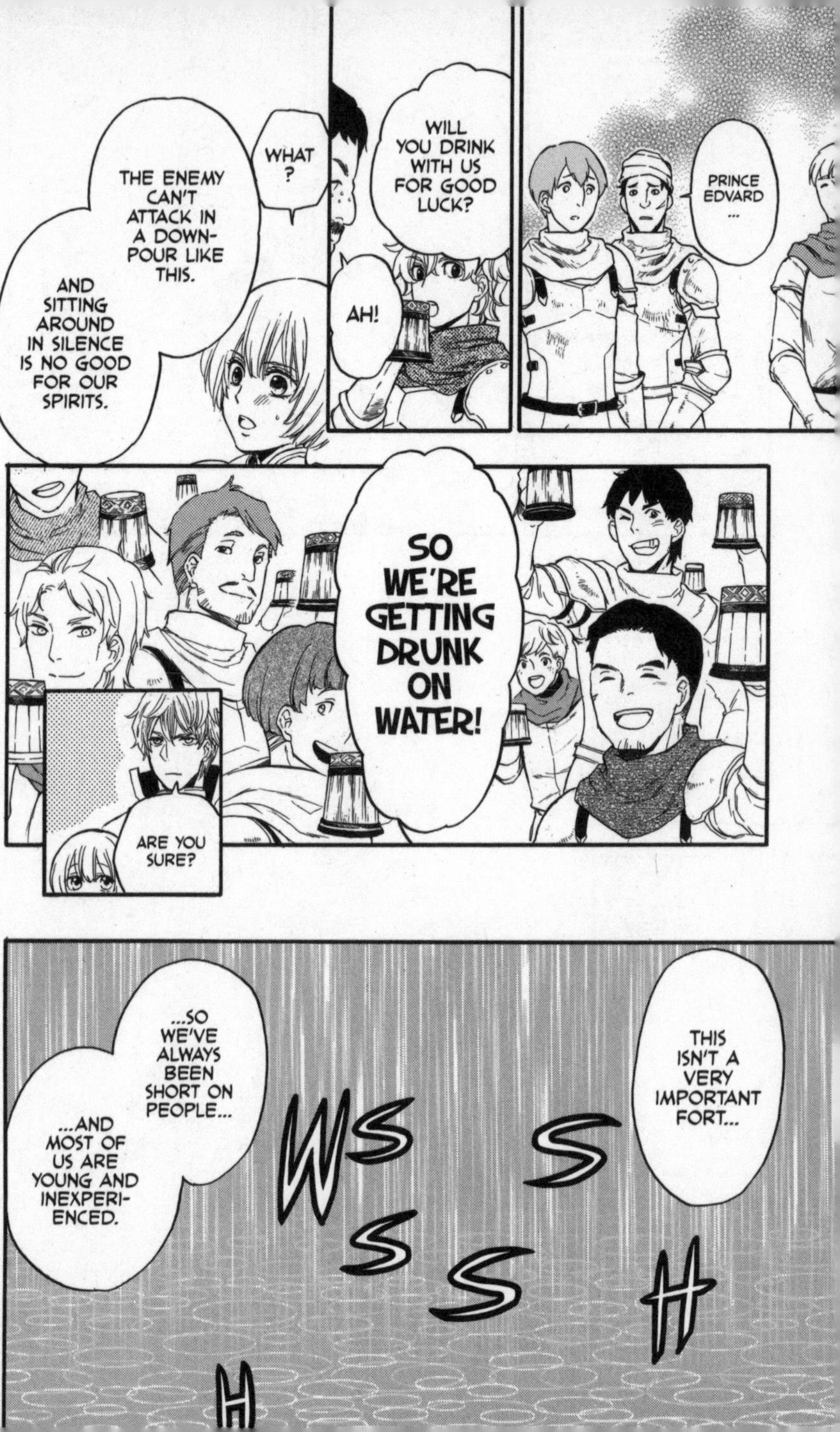

PRINCE EDVARD ...
WILL YOU DRINK WITH US FOR GOOD LUCK?
AH!
WHAT?
THE ENEMY CAN'T ATTACK IN A DOWNPOUR LIKE THIS.
AND SITTING AROUND IN SILENCE IS NO GOOD FOR OUR SPIRITS.
SO WE'RE GETTING DRUNK ON WATER!
ARE YOU SURE?
THIS ISN'T A VERY IMPORTANT FORT...
WSSSSHH
...SO WE'VE ALWAYS BEEN SHORT ON PEOPLE...
...AND MOST OF US ARE YOUNG AND INEXPERIENCED.

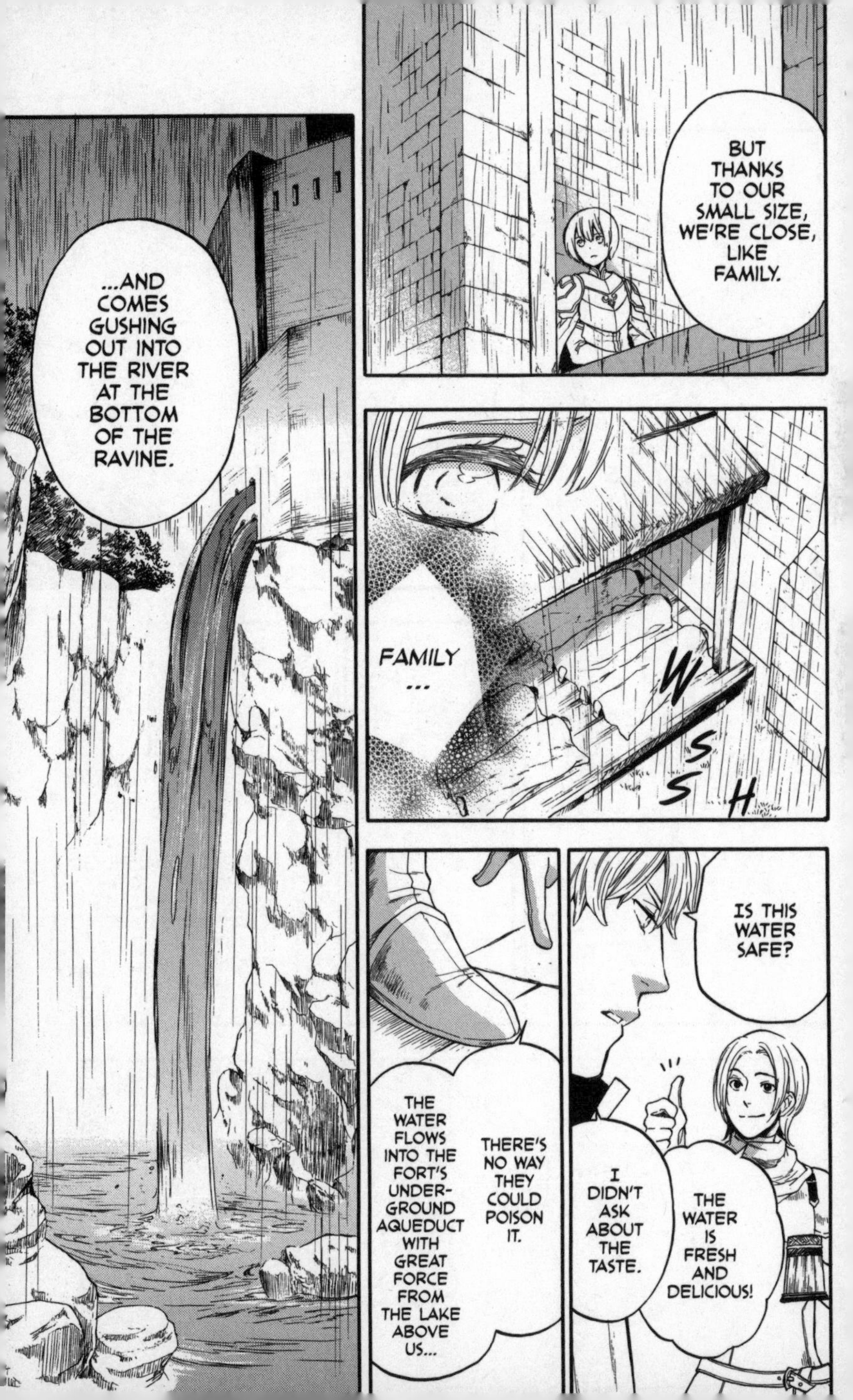
BUT THANKS TO OUR SMALL SIZE, WE'RE CLOSE, LIKE FAMILY.
FAMILY...
WSSH
IS THIS WATER SAFE?
THE WATER IS FRESH AND DELICIOUS!
I DIDN'T ASK ABOUT THE TASTE.
THERE'S NO WAY THEY COULD POISON IT.
THE WATER FLOWS INTO THE FORT'S UNDER-GROUND AQUEDUCT WITH GREAT FORCE FROM THE LAKE ABOVE US...
...AND COMES GUSHING OUT INTO THE RIVER AT THE BOTTOM OF THE RAVINE.

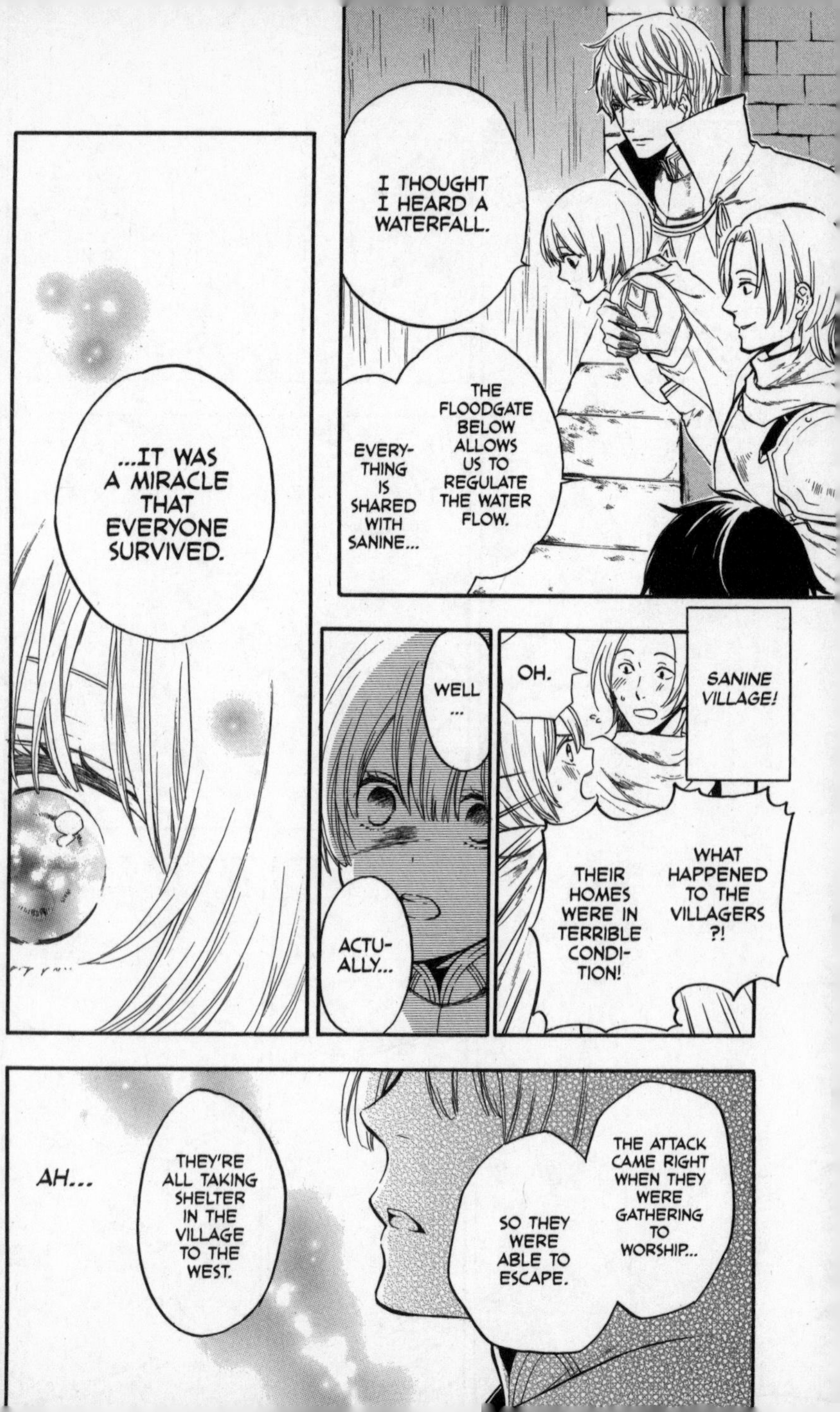
I THOUGHT I HEARD A WATERFALL.
THE FLOODGATE BELOW ALLOWS US TO REGULATE THE WATER FLOW.
EVERYTHING IS SHARED WITH SANINE...
SANINE VILLAGE!
OH.
WHAT HAPPENED TO THE VILLAGERS?!
THEIR HOMES WERE IN TERRIBLE CONDITION!
WELL...
ACTUALLY...
...IT WAS A MIRACLE THAT EVERYONE SURVIVED.
THE ATTACK CAME RIGHT WHEN THEY WERE GATHERING TO WORSHIP...
SO THEY WERE ABLE TO ESCAPE.
THEY'RE ALL TAKING SHELTER IN THE VILLAGE TO THE WEST.
AH...

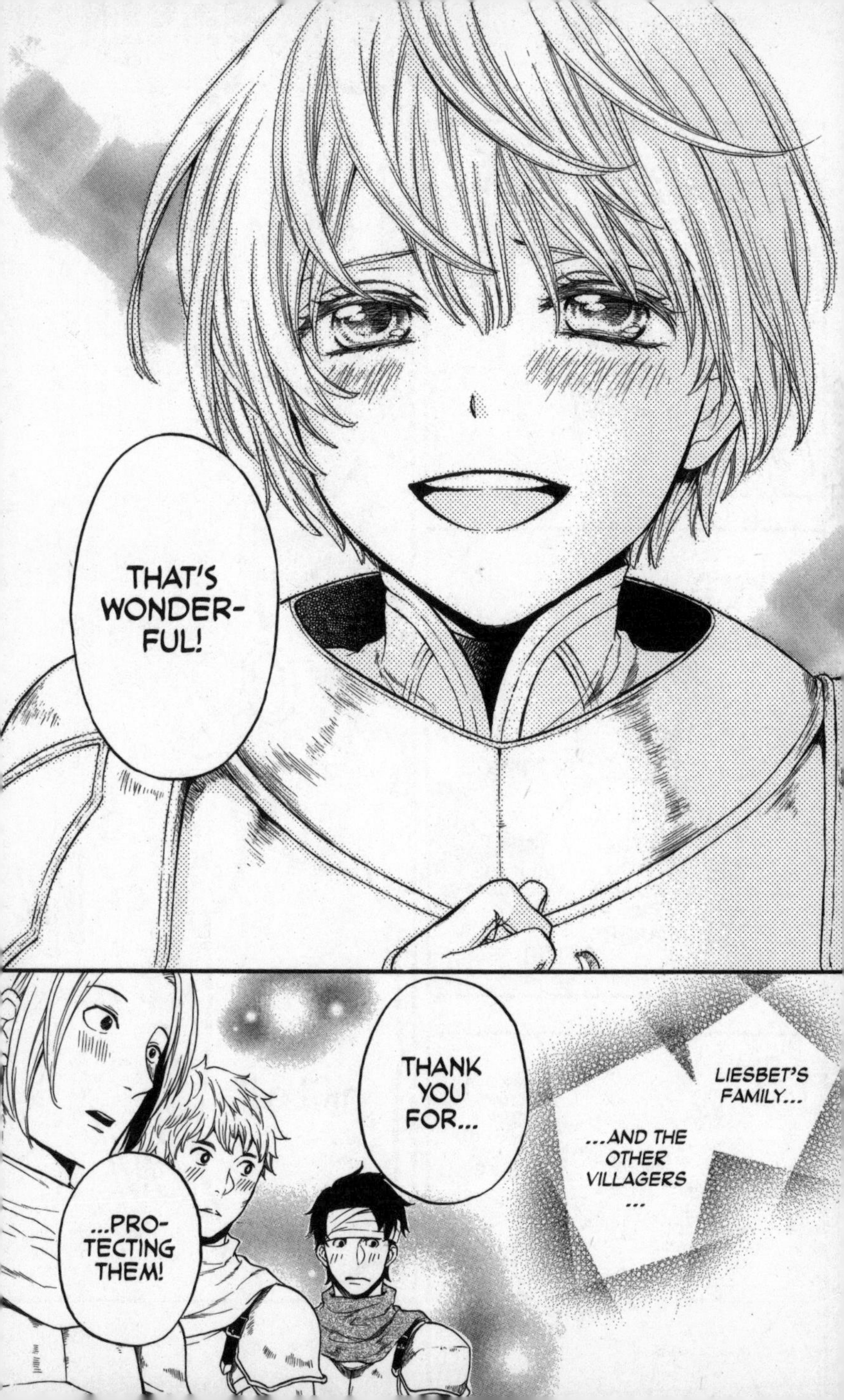
THAT'S WONDER-FUL!
LIESBET'S FAMILY...
...AND THE OTHER VILLAGERS ...
THANK YOU FOR...
...PRO-TECTING THEM!

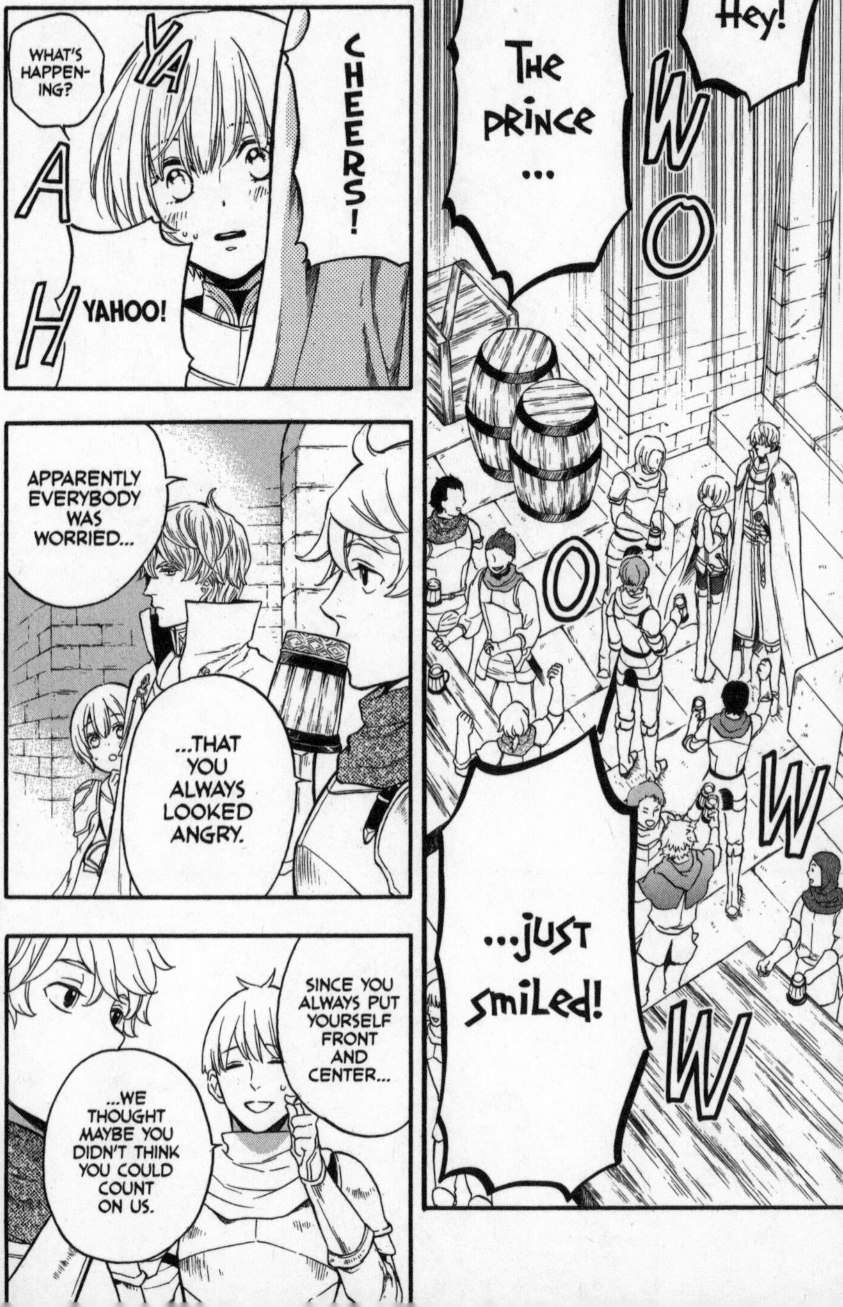
Hey!
The prince...
WOOO
...just smiled!
WW
CHEERS!
YA
WHAT'S HAPPENING?
AH
YAHOO!
APPARENTLY EVERYBODY WAS WORRIED...
...THAT YOU ALWAYS LOOKED ANGRY.
SINCE YOU ALWAYS PUT YOURSELF FRONT AND CENTER...
...WE THOUGHT MAYBE YOU DIDN'T THINK YOU COULD COUNT ON US.

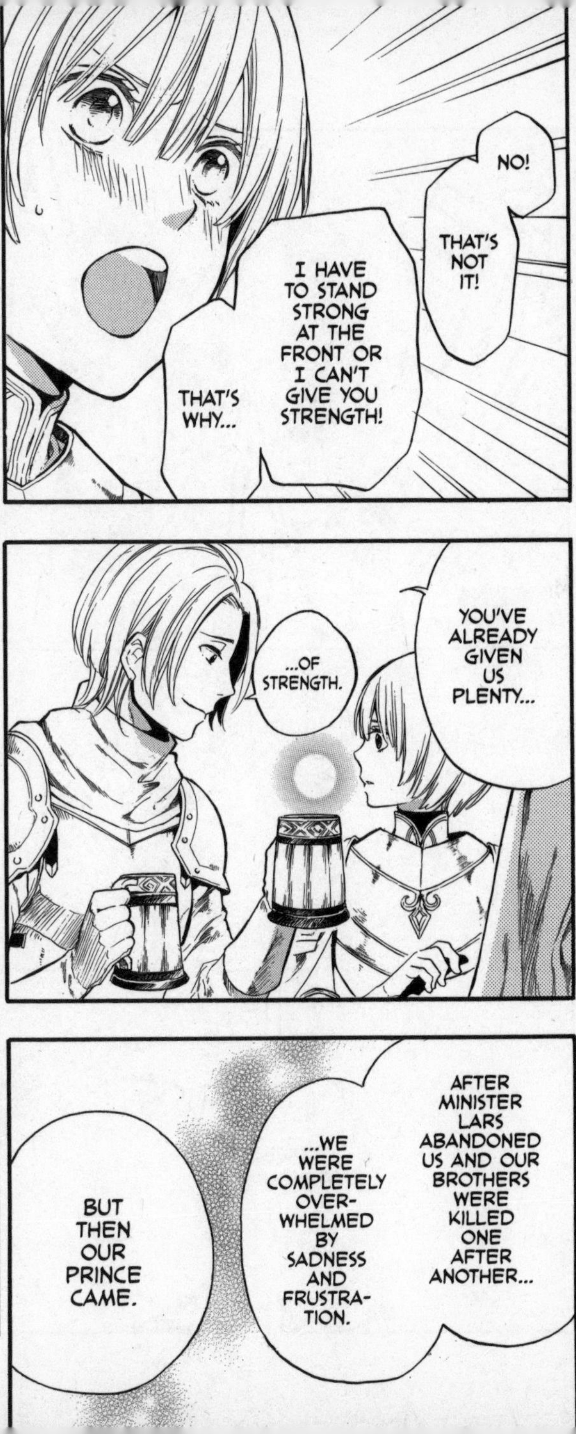
NO!
THAT'S NOT IT!
I HAVE TO STAND STRONG AT THE FRONT OR I CAN'T GIVE YOU STRENGTH!
THAT'S WHY...
YOU'VE ALREADY GIVEN US PLENTY...
...OF STRENGTH.
AFTER MINISTER LARS ABANDONED US AND OUR BROTHERS WERE KILLED ONE AFTER ANOTHER...
...WE WERE COMPLETELY OVER-WHELMED BY SADNESS AND FRUSTRA-TION.
BUT THEN OUR PRINCE CAME.

Thank you for reading along this far.

I'll do my best with volume 4 as well.
I do hope you enjoy it!

Assistants:
Sadayuki Amehara
Ryo Sakimiya
Miyuki Tsutsui
Pochiko
Misaya Morifuji

Special thanks to:
U.
Shiho
K.Y.

My editors

Everybody involved in the making of the comic book.

My family.

My readers.

Thank you very much.

石原ケイコ
Keiko Ishihara

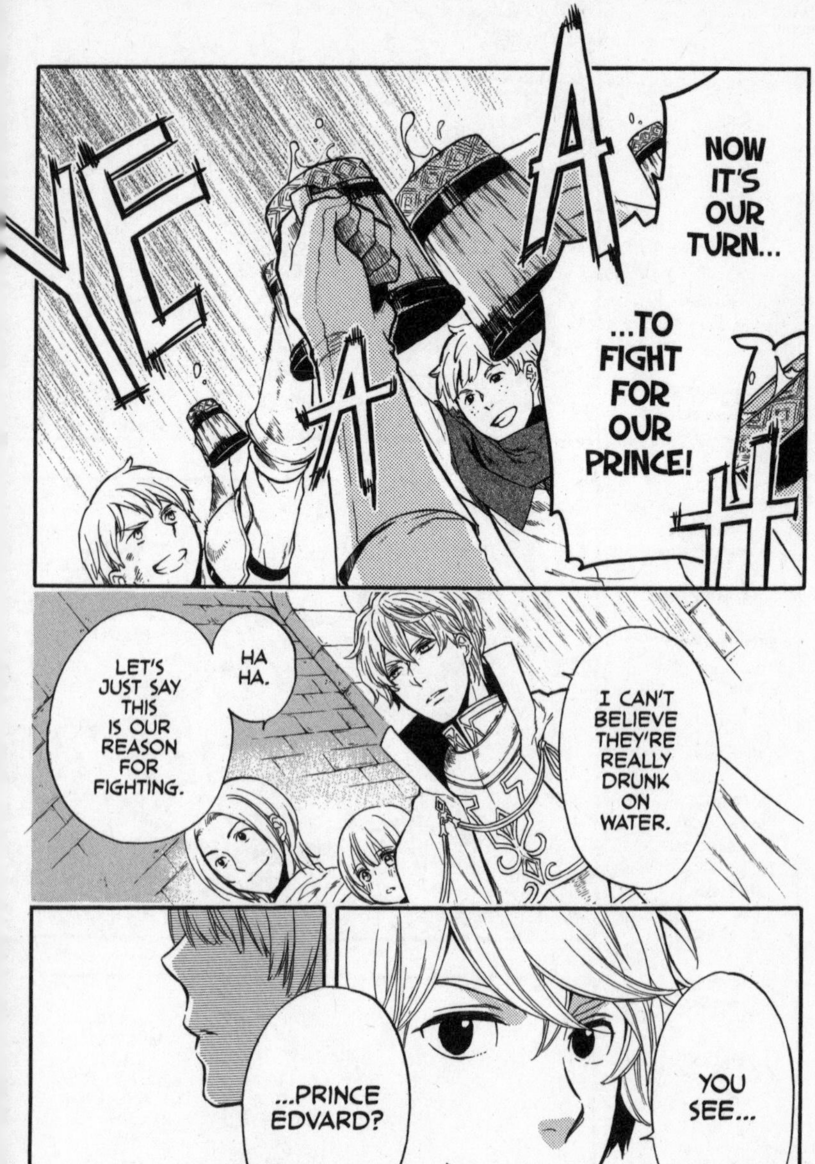
NOW IT'S OUR TURN...
...TO FIGHT FOR OUR PRINCE!
YEAAH
I CAN'T BELIEVE THEY'RE REALLY DRUNK ON WATER.
HA HA.
LET'S JUST SAY THIS IS OUR REASON FOR FIGHTING.
YOU SEE...
...PRINCE EDVARD?

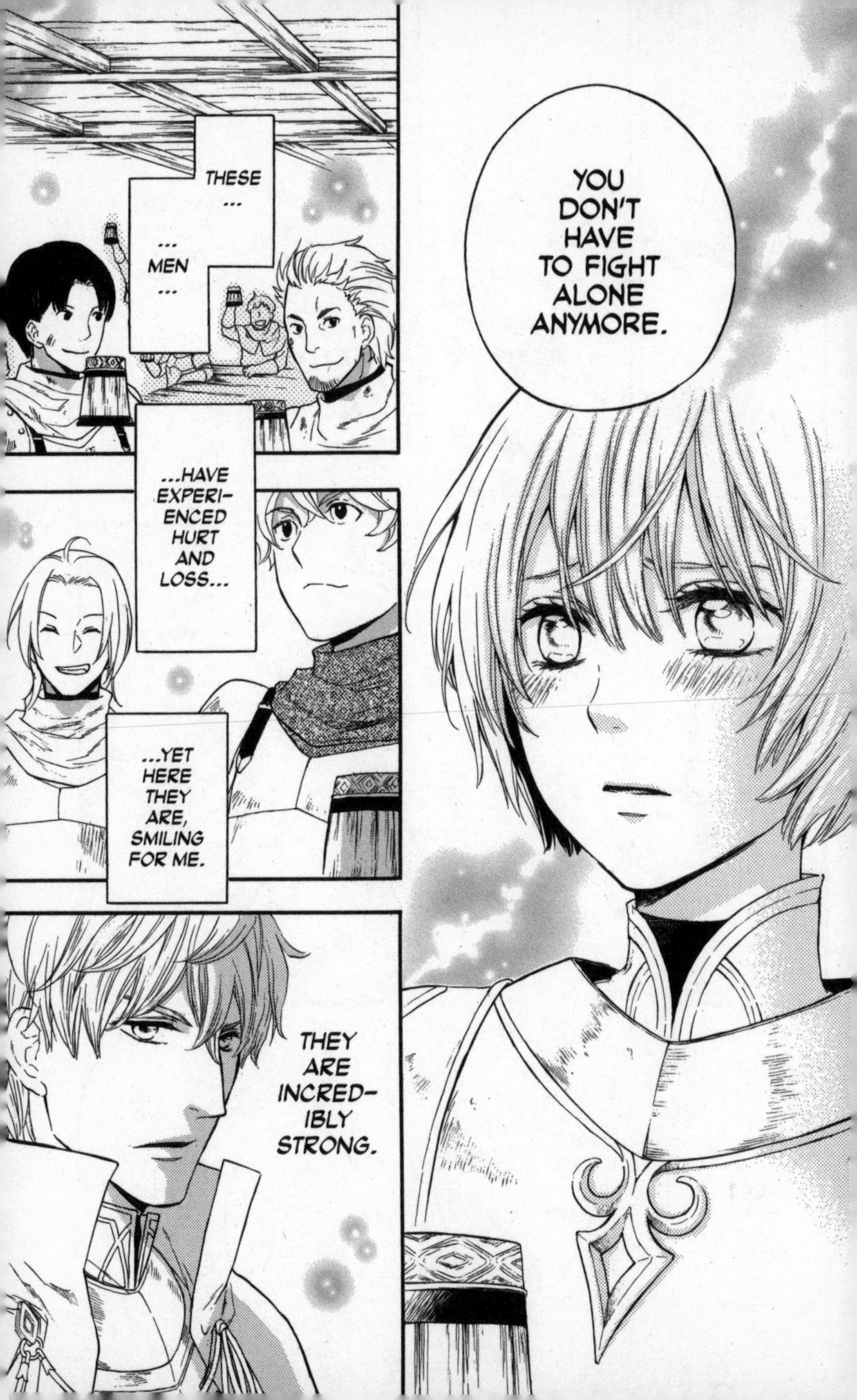
YOU DON'T HAVE TO FIGHT ALONE ANYMORE.
THESE...
...MEN...
...HAVE EXPERIENCED HURT AND LOSS...
...YET HERE THEY ARE, SMILING FOR ME.
THEY ARE INCREDIBLY STRONG.

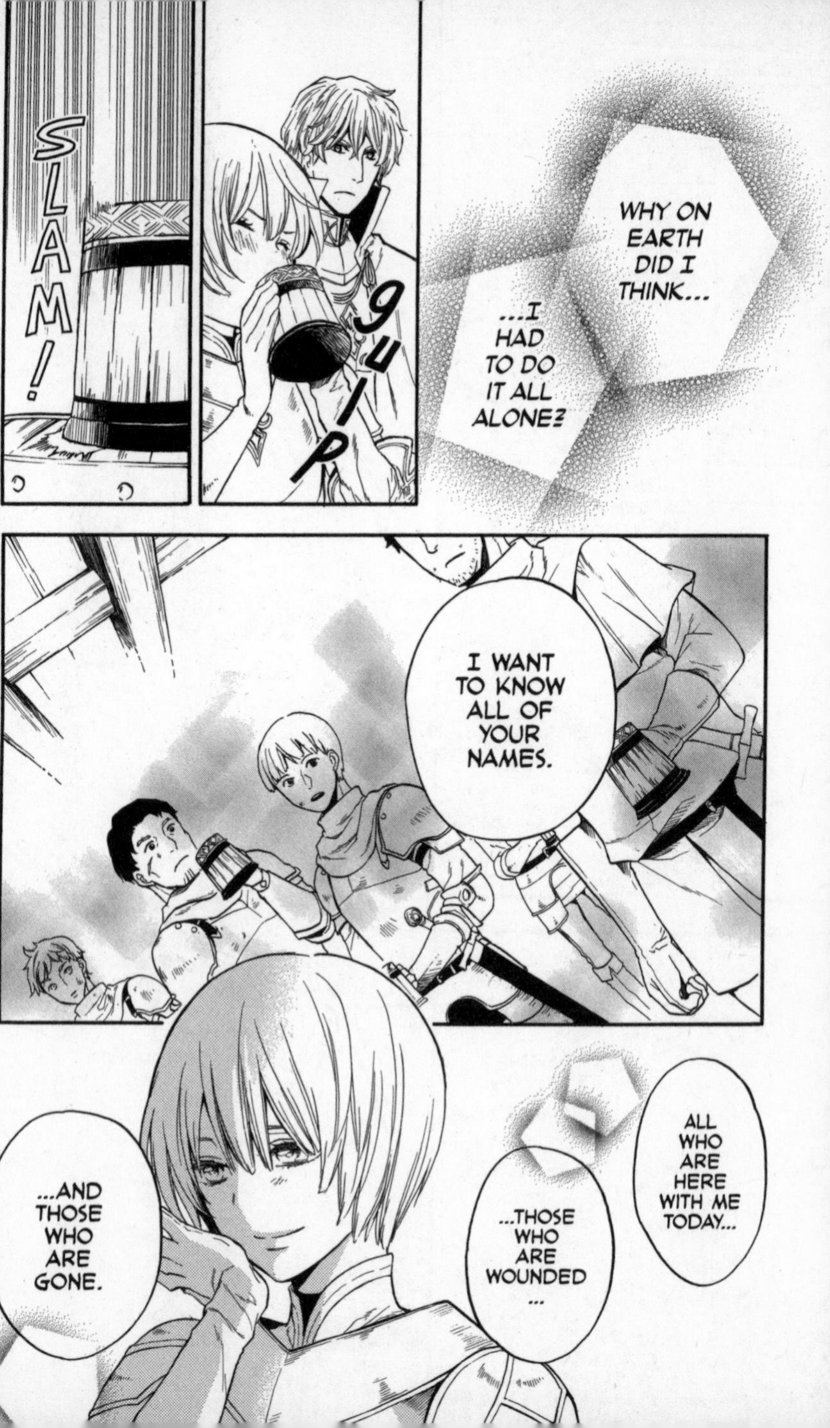
WHY ON EARTH DID I THINK...
...I HAD TO DO IT ALL ALONE?
GULP
SLAM!
I WANT TO KNOW ALL OF YOUR NAMES.
ALL WHO ARE HERE WITH ME TODAY...
...THOSE WHO ARE WOUNDED...
...AND THOSE WHO ARE GONE.

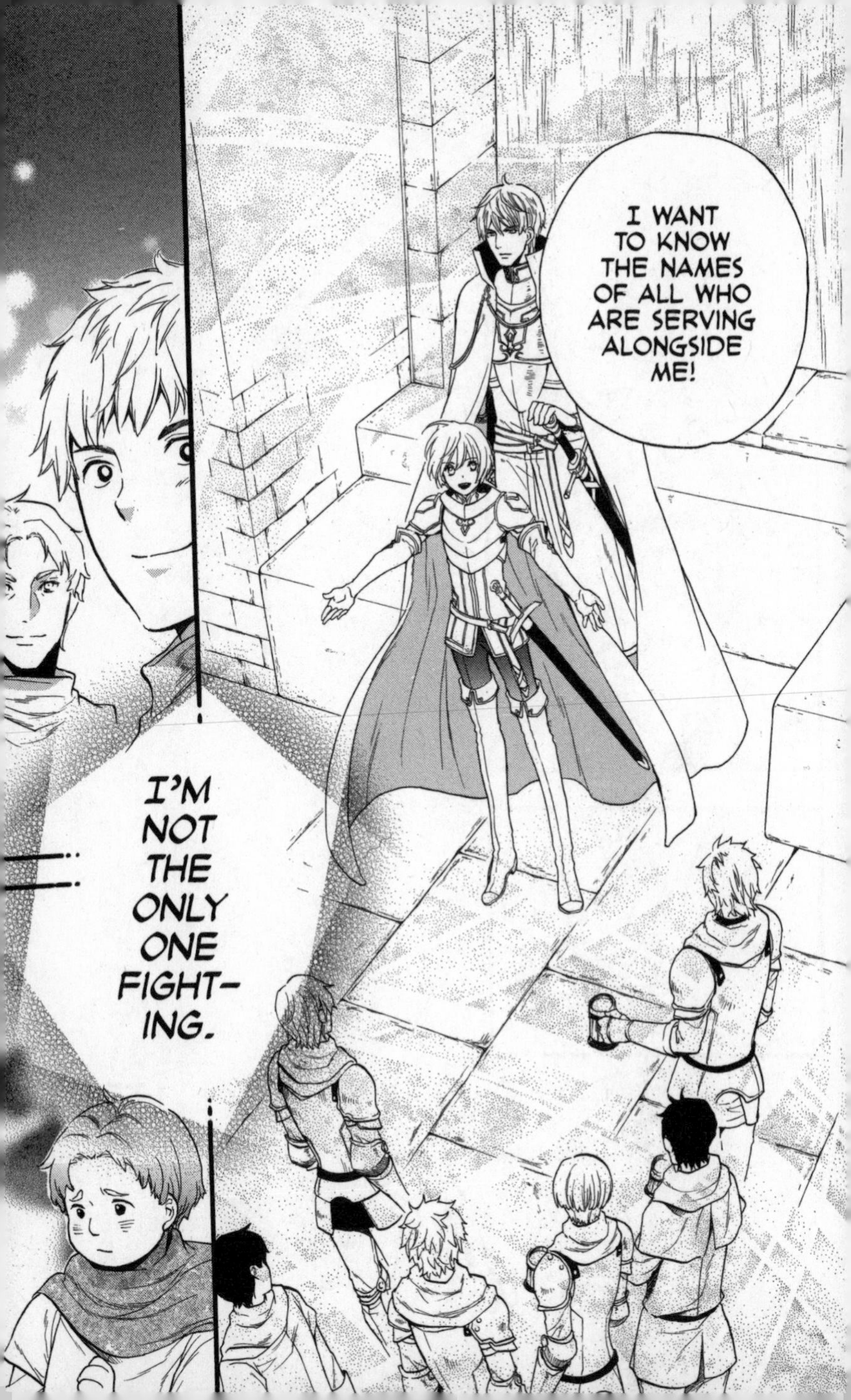
I WANT TO KNOW THE NAMES OF ALL WHO ARE SERVING ALONGSIDE ME!
I'M NOT THE ONLY ONE FIGHTING.

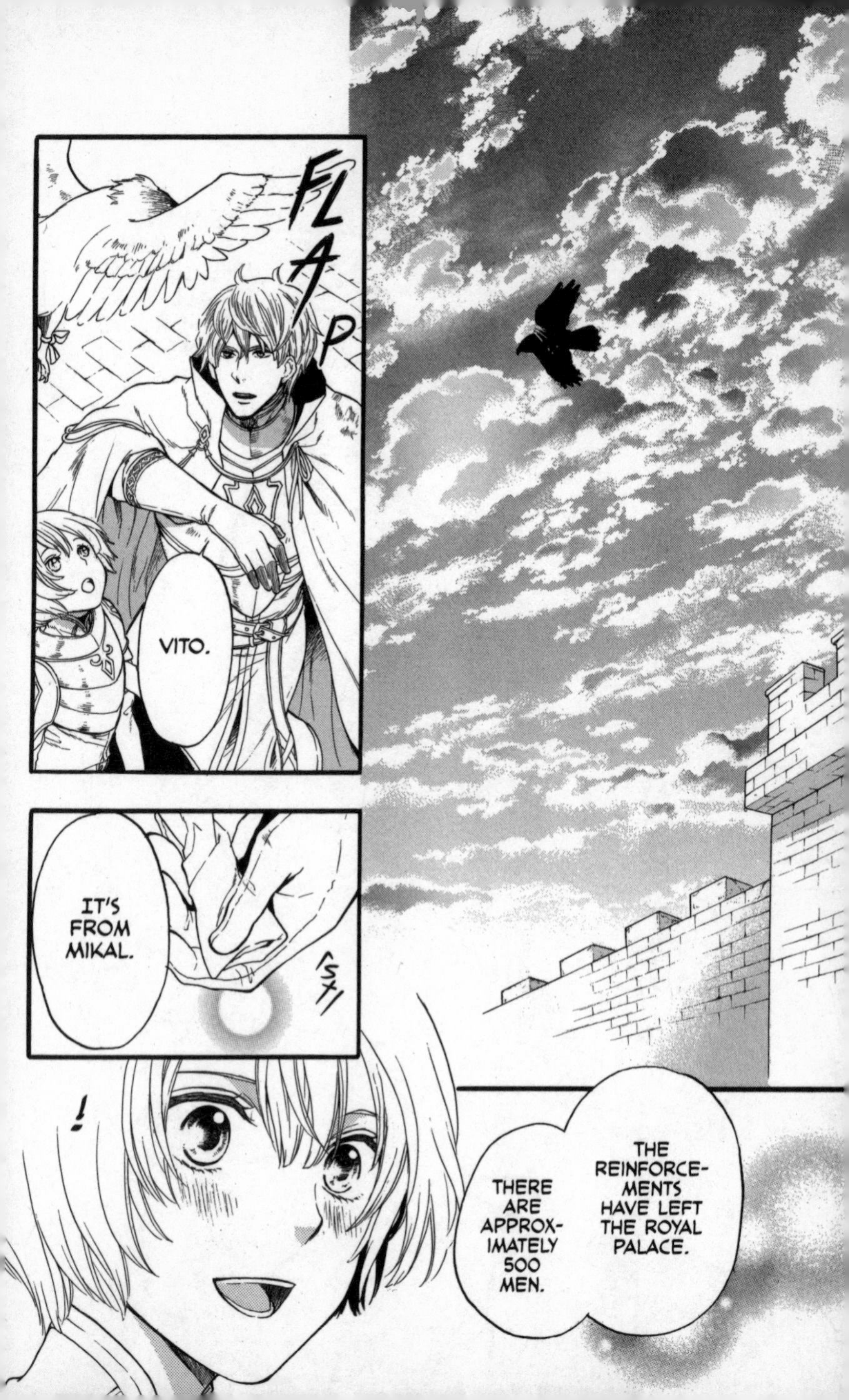
FLAP
VITO.
IT'S FROM MIKAL.
!
THE REINFORCEMENTS HAVE LEFT THE ROYAL PALACE.
THERE ARE APPROXIMATELY 500 MEN.

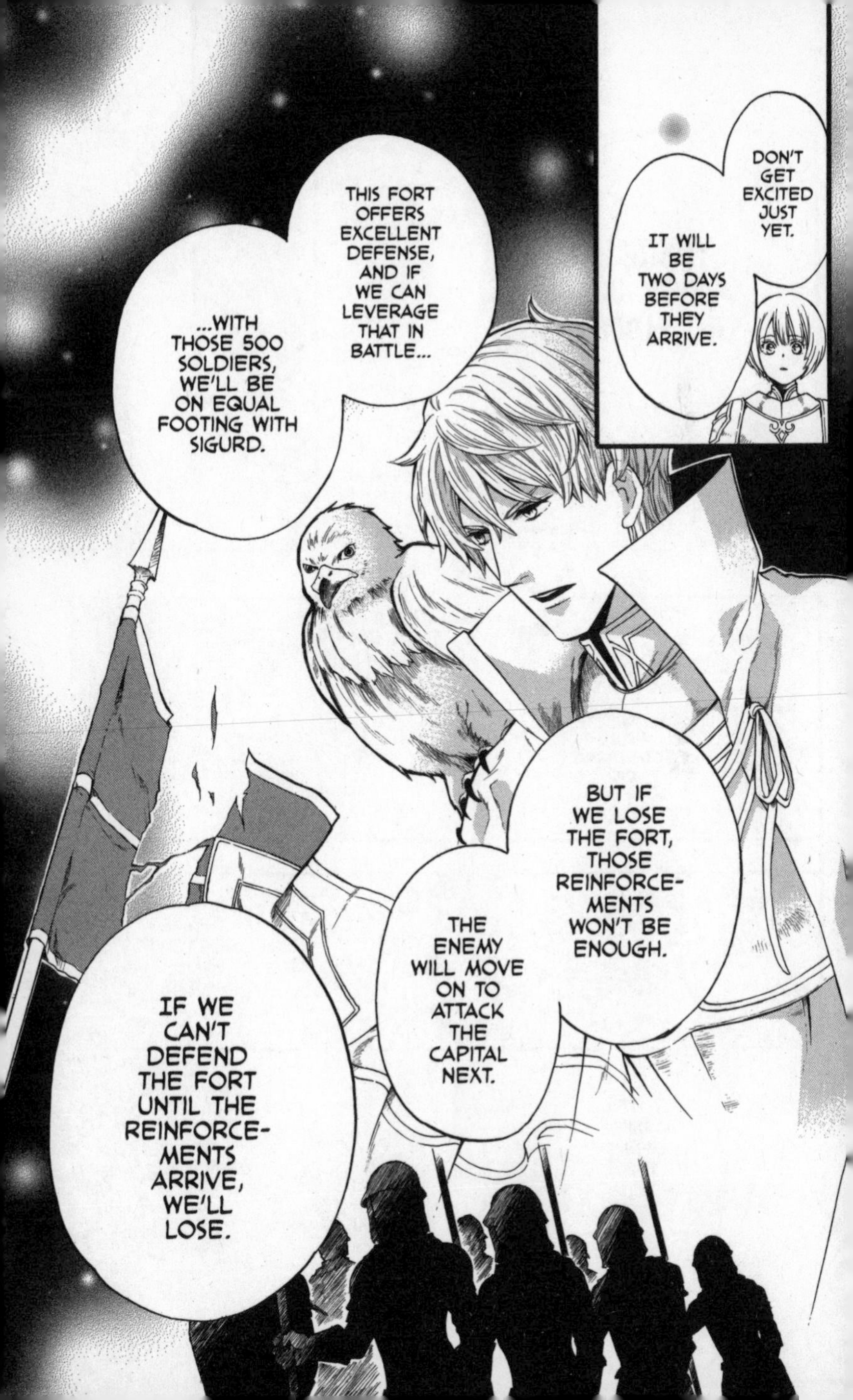
DON'T GET EXCITED JUST YET.
IT WILL BE TWO DAYS BEFORE THEY ARRIVE.
THIS FORT OFFERS EXCELLENT DEFENSE, AND IF WE CAN LEVERAGE THAT IN BATTLE...
...WITH THOSE 500 SOLDIERS, WE'LL BE ON EQUAL FOOTING WITH SIGURD.
BUT IF WE LOSE THE FORT, THOSE REINFORCE-MENTS WON'T BE ENOUGH.
THE ENEMY WILL MOVE ON TO ATTACK THE CAPITAL NEXT.
IF WE CAN'T DEFEND THE FORT UNTIL THE REINFORCE-MENTS ARRIVE, WE'LL LOSE.

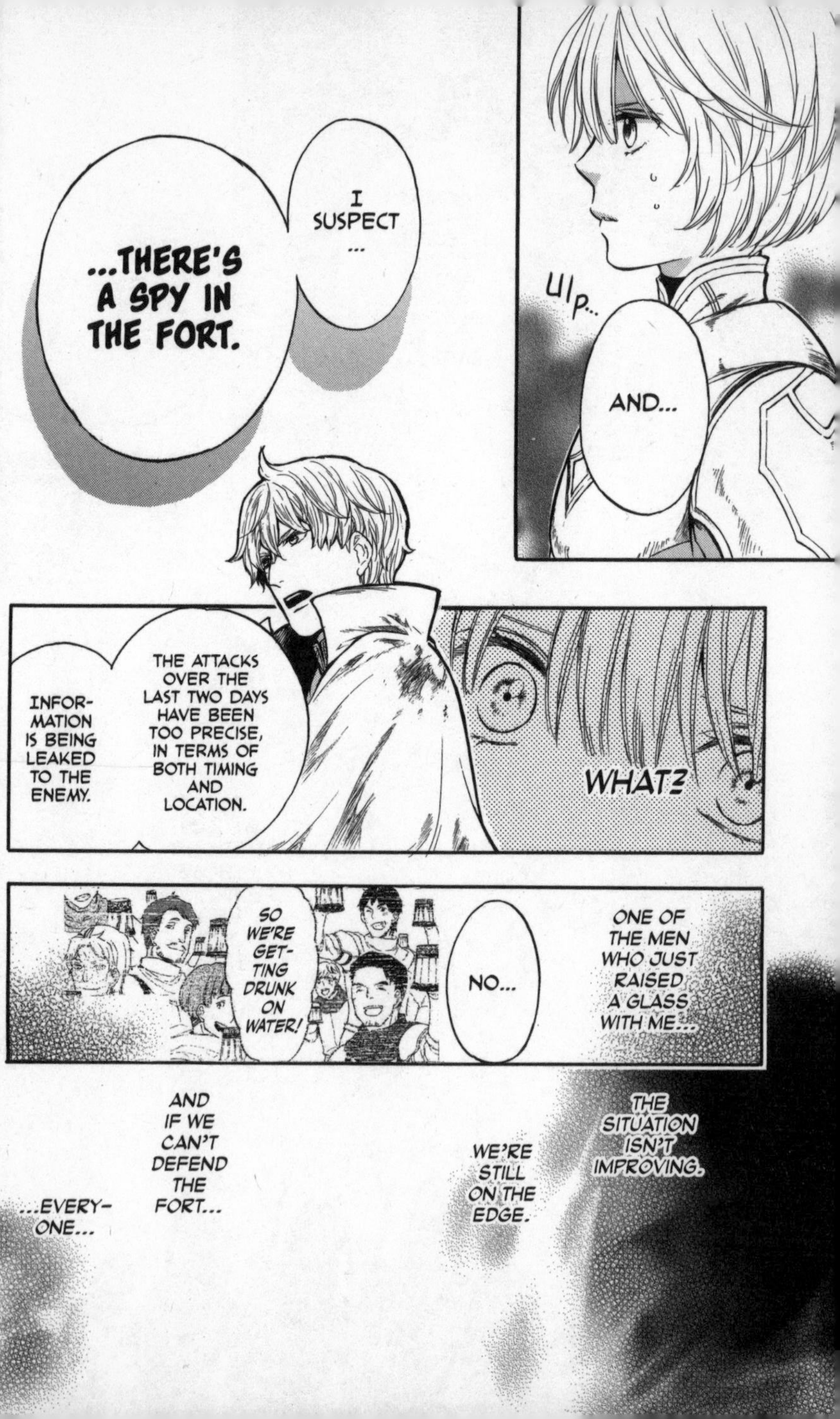
Ulp...
AND...
I SUSPECT ...
...THERE'S A SPY IN THE FORT.
WHAT?
THE ATTACKS OVER THE LAST TWO DAYS HAVE BEEN TOO PRECISE, IN TERMS OF BOTH TIMING AND LOCATION.
INFORMATION IS BEING LEAKED TO THE ENEMY.
ONE OF THE MEN WHO JUST RAISED A GLASS WITH ME...
NO...
SO WE'RE GETTING DRUNK ON WATER!
THE SITUATION ISN'T IMPROVING.
WE'RE STILL ON THE EDGE.
AND IF WE CAN'T DEFEND THE FORT...
...EVERYONE...

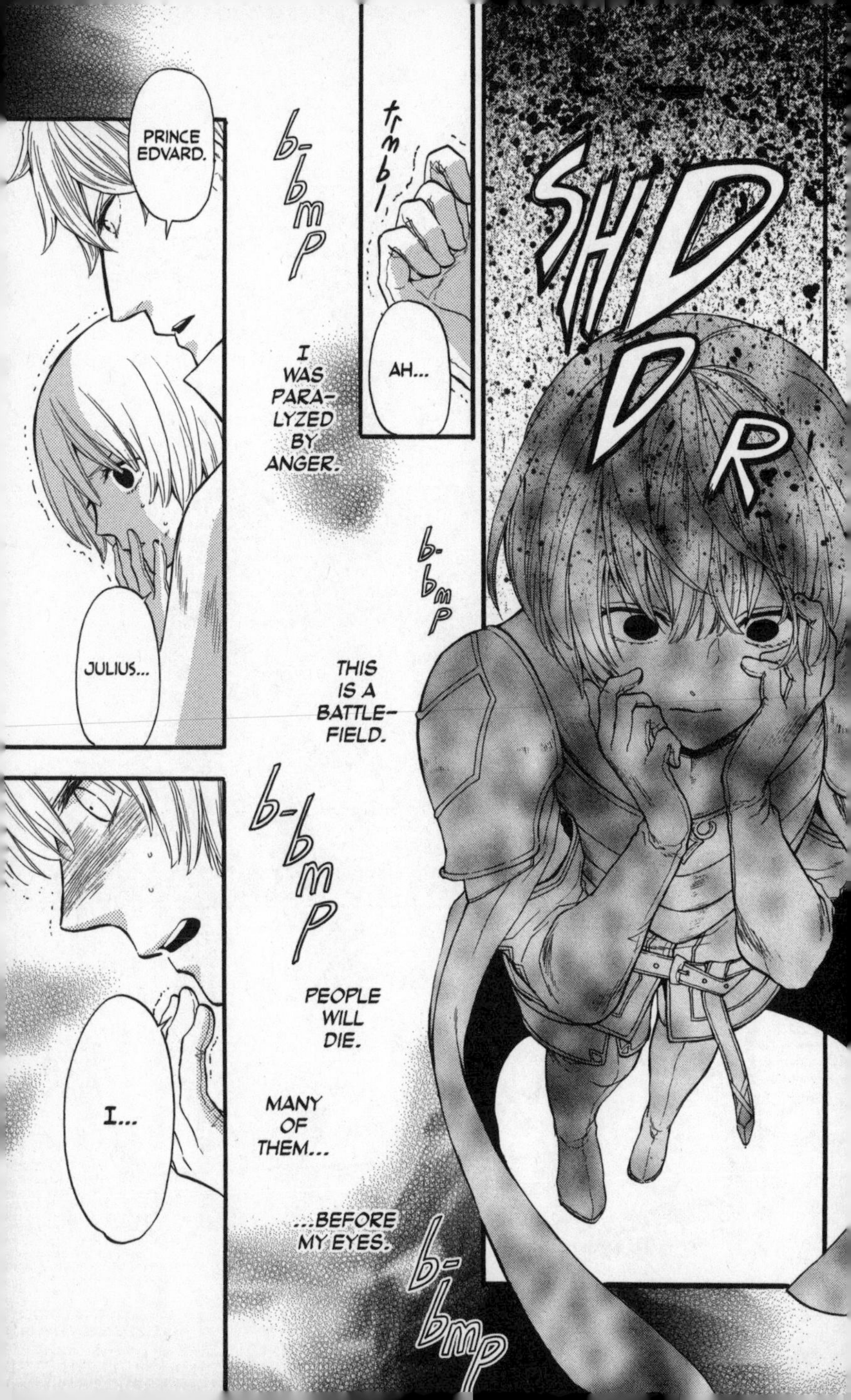
SHDDR
trmbl
AH...
b-bmp
I WAS PARALYZED BY ANGER.
b-bmp
THIS IS A BATTLEFIELD.
b-bmp
PEOPLE WILL DIE.
MANY OF THEM...
...BEFORE MY EYES.
b-bmp
PRINCE EDVARD.
JULIUS...
I...

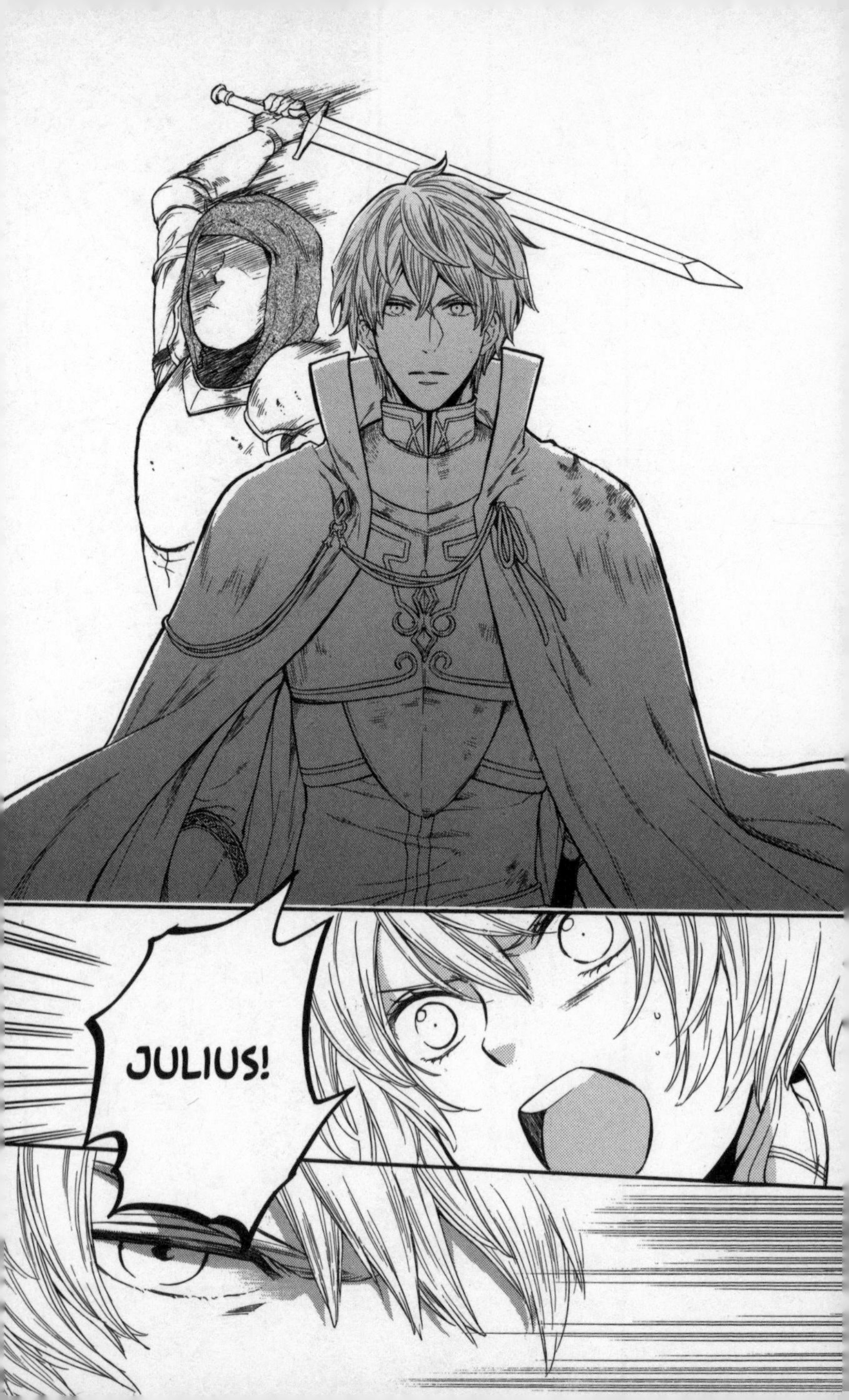
JULIUS!

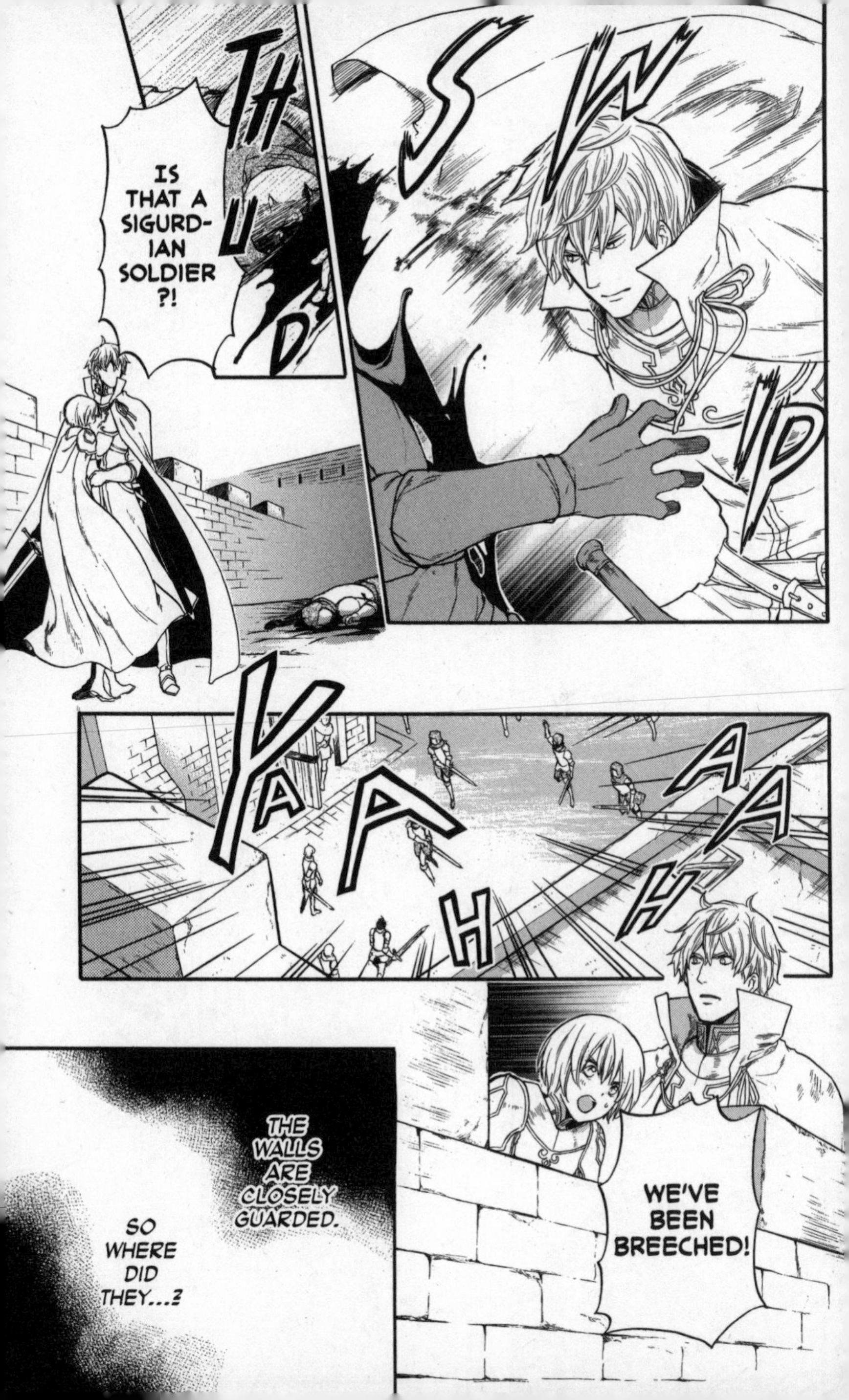
SWIP
THUD
IS THAT A SIGURD-IAN SOLDIER?!
YAAH
AAH
WE'VE BEEN BREECHED!
THE WALLS ARE CLOSELY GUARDED.
SO WHERE DID THEY...?

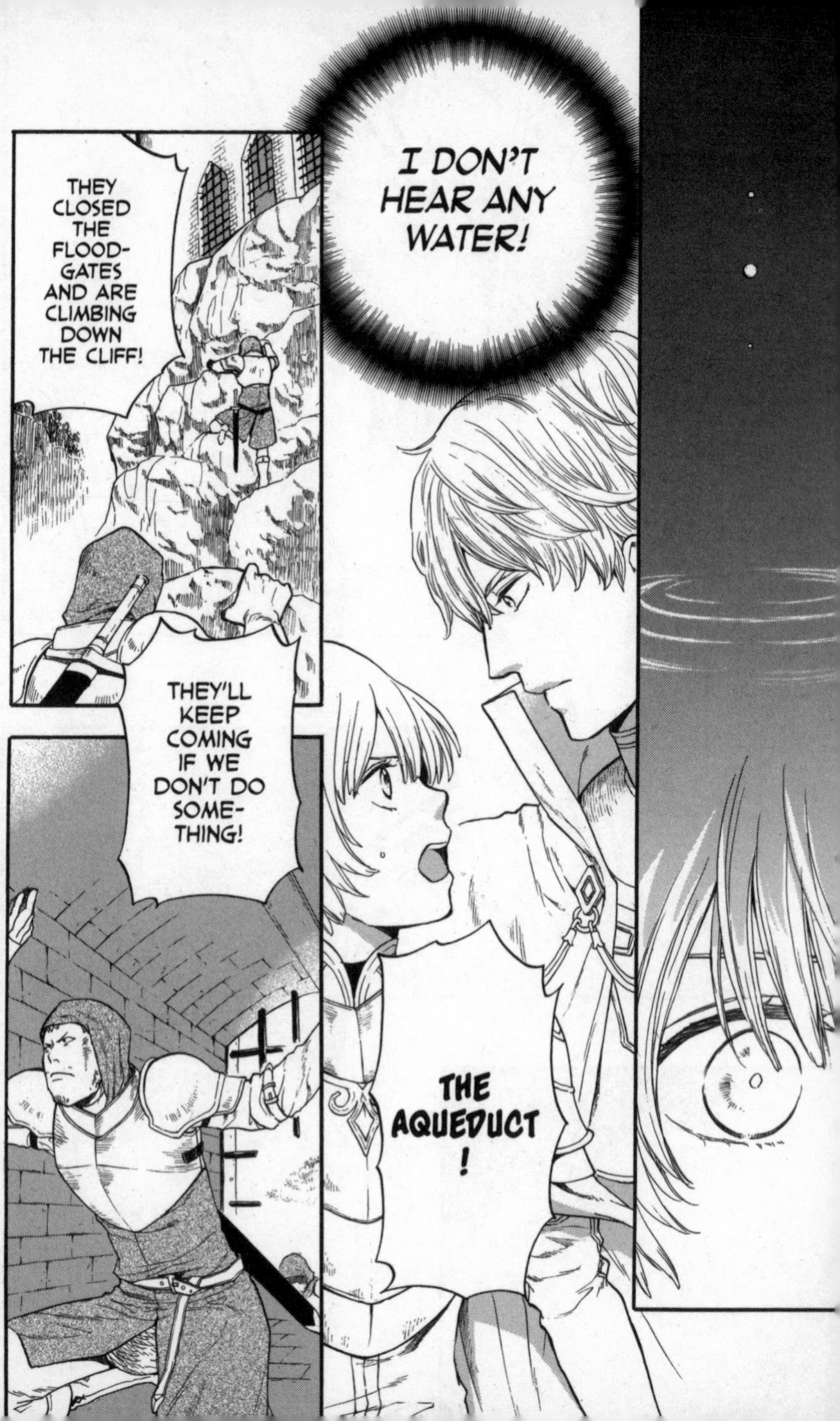
I DON'T HEAR ANY WATER!
THE AQUEDUCT!
THEY CLOSED THE FLOOD-GATES AND ARE CLIMBING DOWN THE CLIFF!
THEY'LL KEEP COMING IF WE DON'T DO SOME-THING!

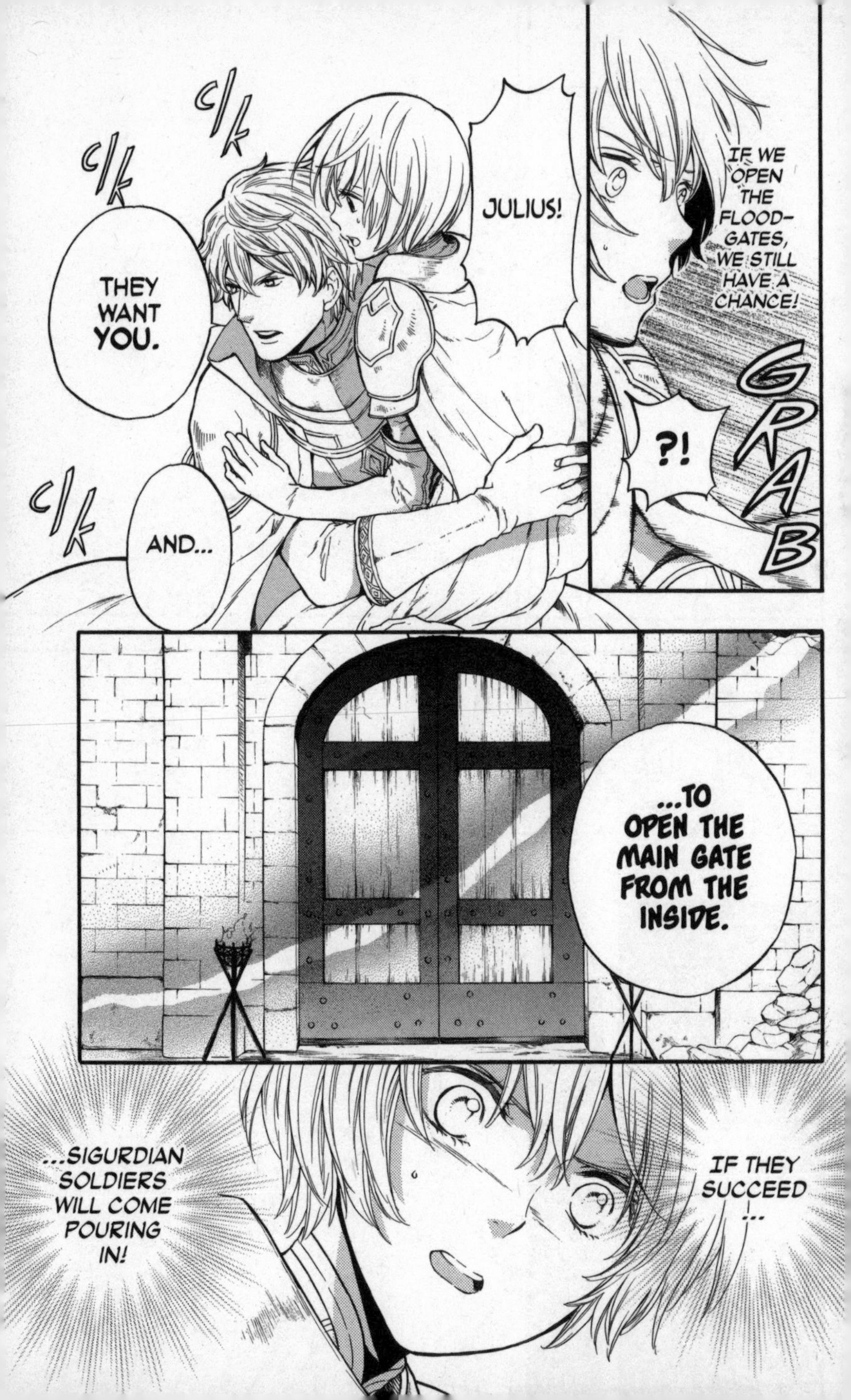
IF WE OPEN THE FLOOD-GATES, WE STILL HAVE A CHANCE!
GRAB
?!
JULIUS!
clk
clk
THEY WANT YOU.
clk
AND...
...TO OPEN THE MAIN GATE FROM THE INSIDE.
IF THEY SUCCEED!...
...SIGURDIAN SOLDIERS WILL COME POURING IN!

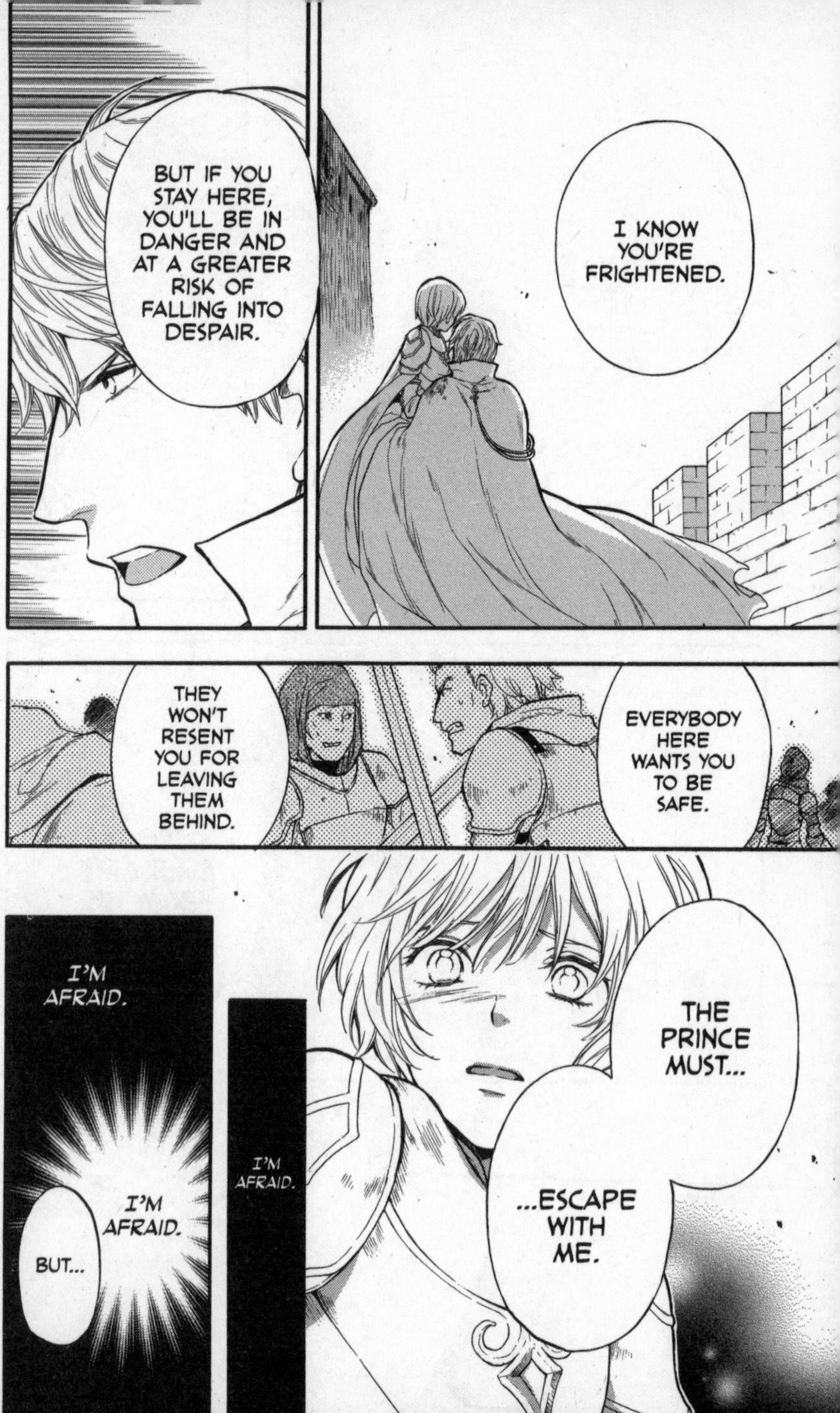
I KNOW YOU'RE FRIGHTENED.
BUT IF YOU STAY HERE, YOU'LL BE IN DANGER AND AT A GREATER RISK OF FALLING INTO DESPAIR.
EVERYBODY HERE WANTS YOU TO BE SAFE.
THEY WON'T RESENT YOU FOR LEAVING THEM BEHIND.
THE PRINCE MUST...
...ESCAPE WITH ME.
I'M AFRAID.
I'M AFRAID.
I'M AFRAID.
BUT...

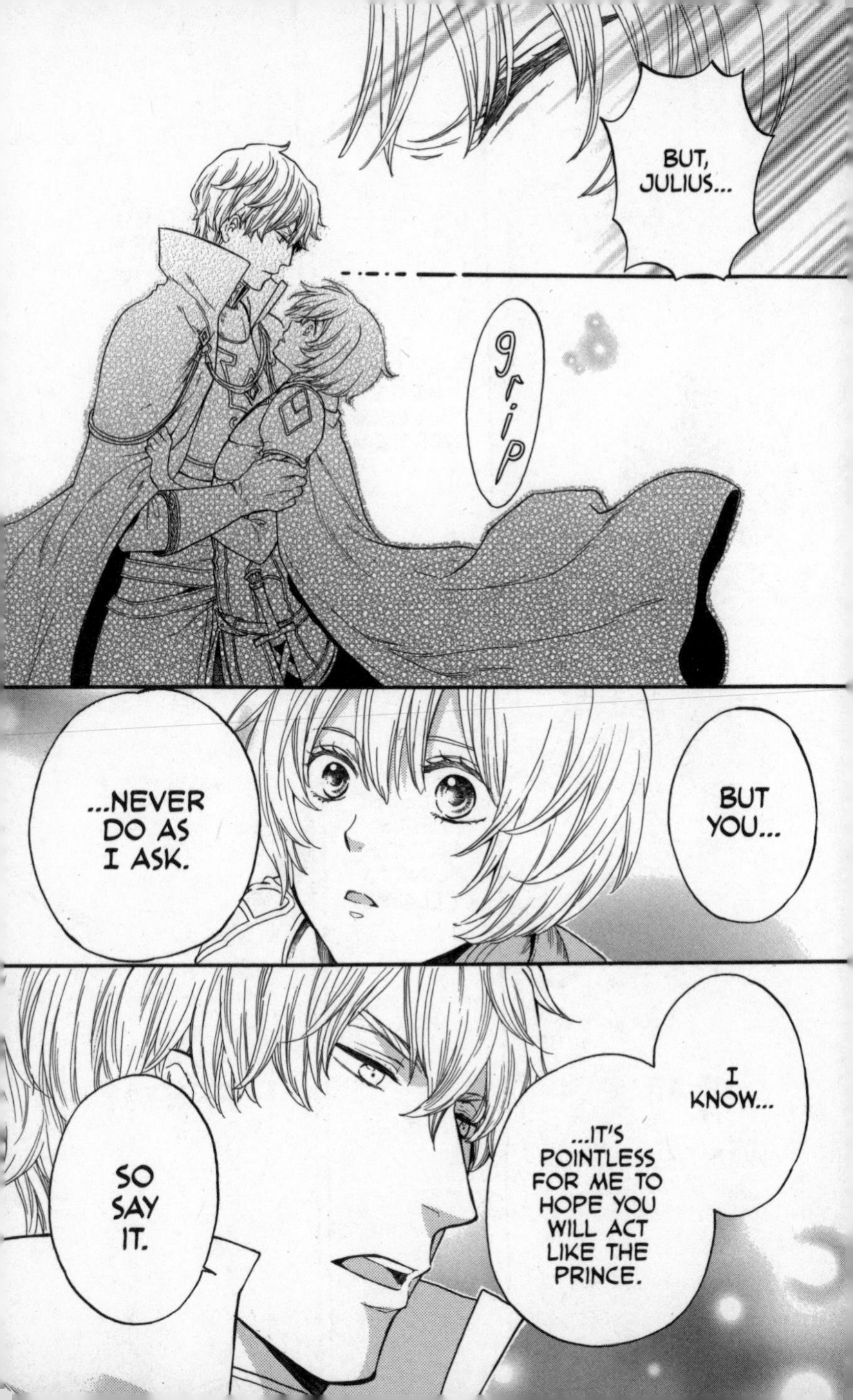
BUT, JULIUS...
grip
BUT YOU...
...NEVER DO AS I ASK.
I KNOW...
...IT'S POINTLESS FOR ME TO HOPE YOU WILL ACT LIKE THE PRINCE.
SO SAY IT.

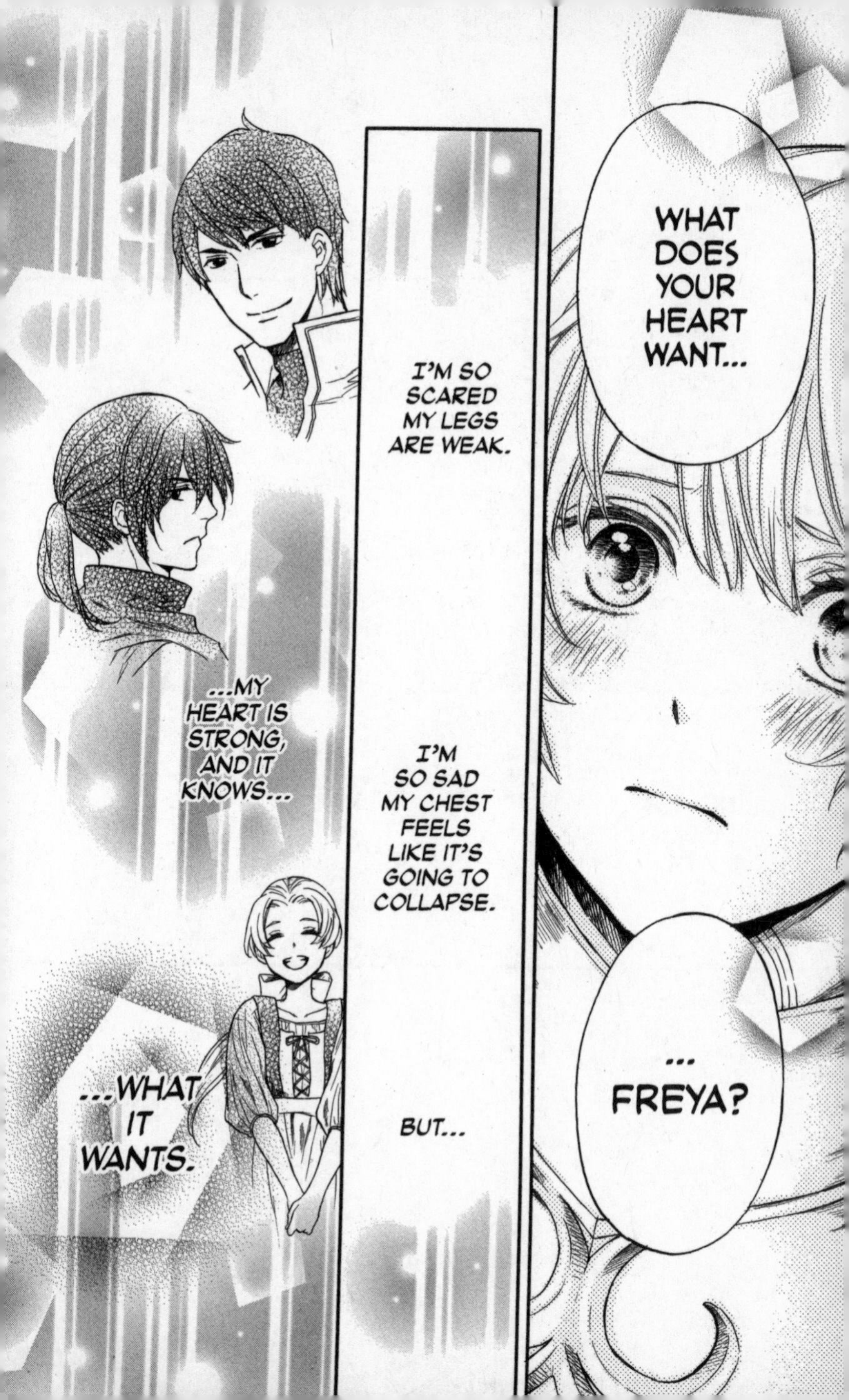
WHAT DOES YOUR HEART WANT...
...FREYA?
I'M SO SCARED MY LEGS ARE WEAK.
I'M SO SAD MY CHEST FEELS LIKE IT'S GOING TO COLLAPSE.
BUT...
...MY HEART IS STRONG, AND IT KNOWS...
...WHAT IT WANTS.

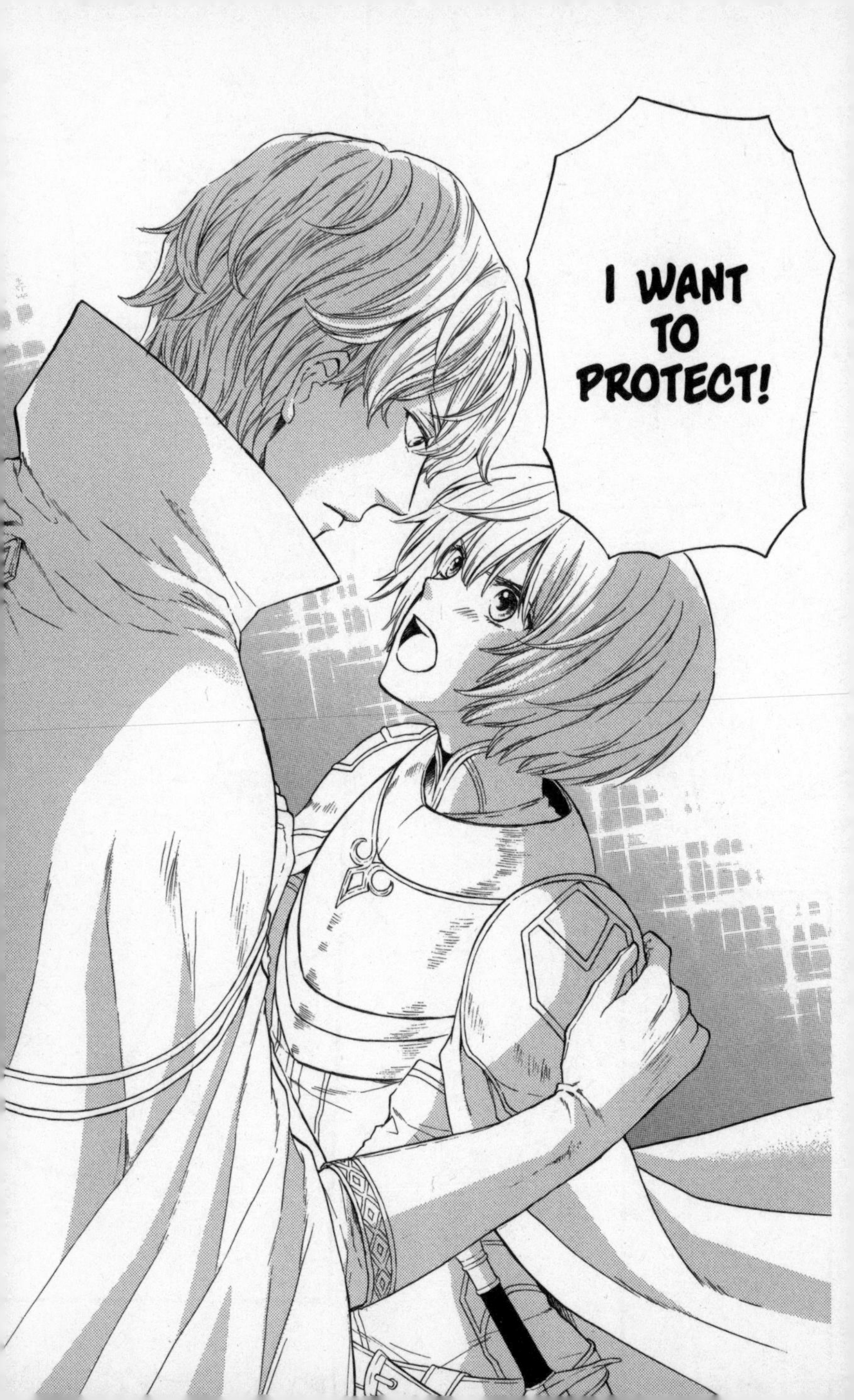
I WANT TO PROTECT!

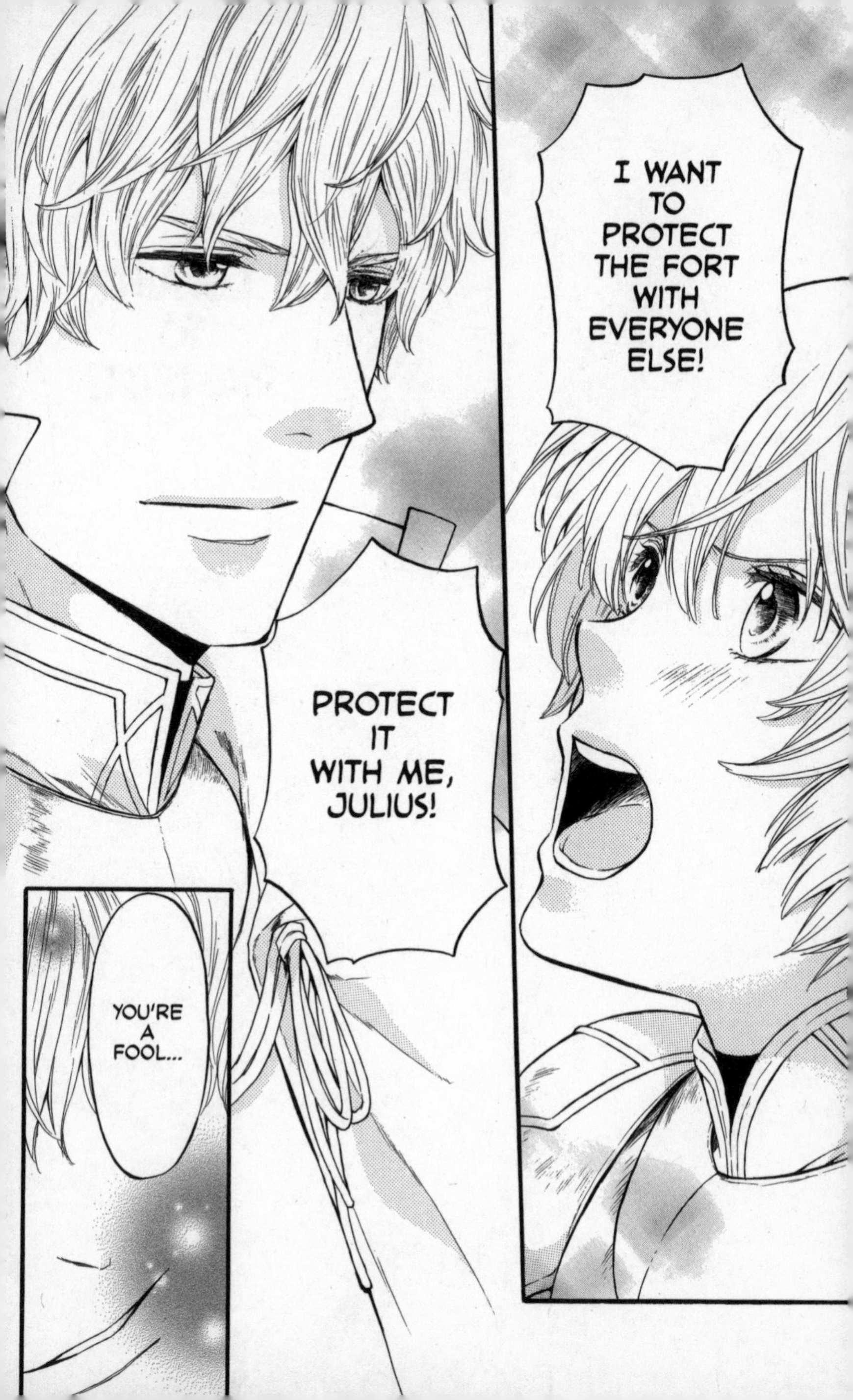
I WANT TO PROTECT THE FORT WITH EVERYONE ELSE!
PROTECT IT WITH ME, JULIUS!
YOU'RE A FOOL...

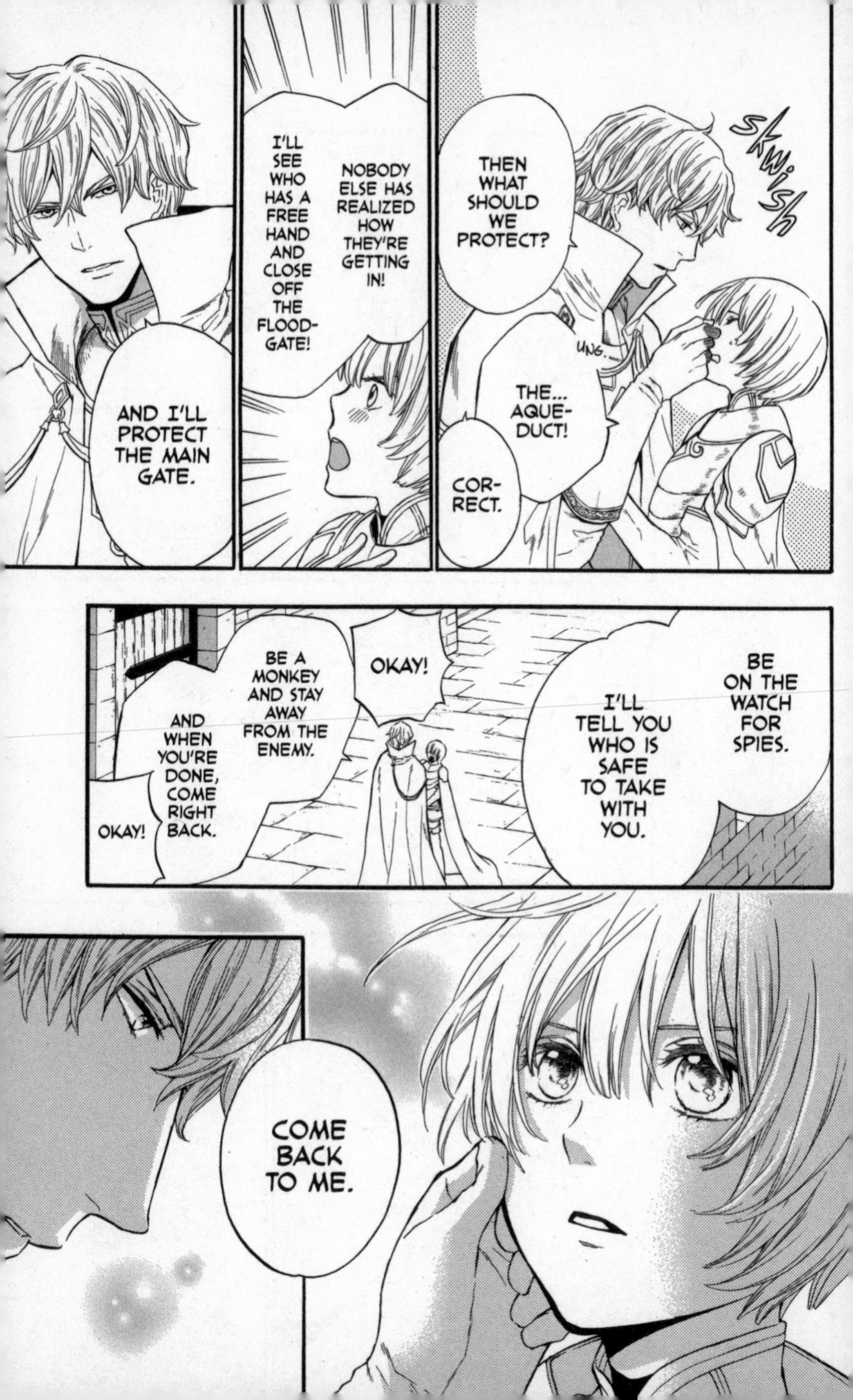
skwish
THEN WHAT SHOULD WE PROTECT?
UNG...
THE... AQUEDUCT!
CORRECT.
NOBODY ELSE HAS REALIZED HOW THEY'RE GETTING IN!
I'LL SEE WHO HAS A FREE HAND AND CLOSE OFF THE FLOODGATE!
AND I'LL PROTECT THE MAIN GATE.
BE ON THE WATCH FOR SPIES.
I'LL TELL YOU WHO IS SAFE TO TAKE WITH YOU.
OKAY!
BE A MONKEY AND STAY AWAY FROM THE ENEMY.
AND WHEN YOU'RE DONE, COME RIGHT BACK.
OKAY!
COME BACK TO ME.

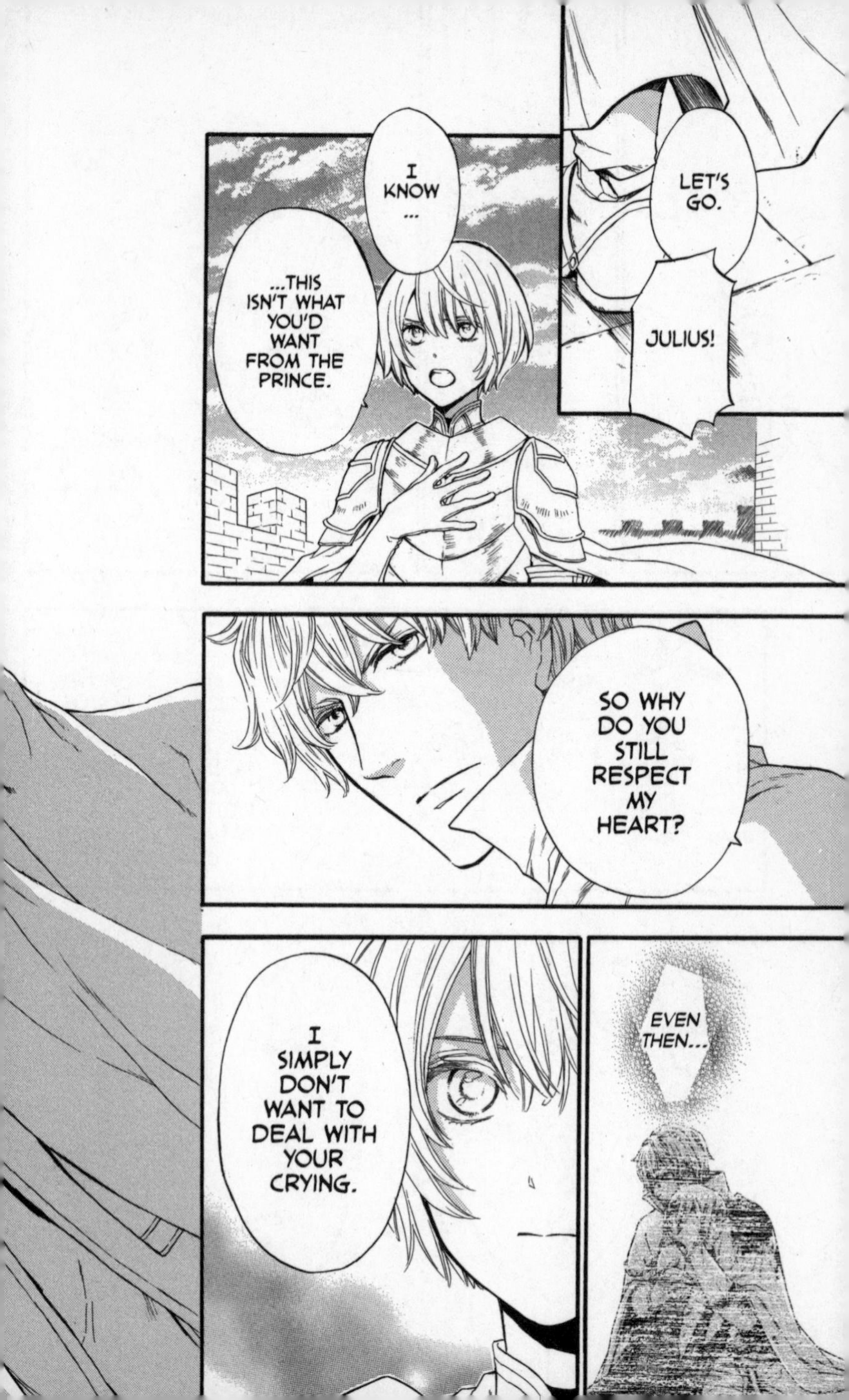
LET'S GO.
JULIUS!
I KNOW...
...THIS ISN'T WHAT YOU'D WANT FROM THE PRINCE.
SO WHY DO YOU STILL RESPECT MY HEART?
EVEN THEN...
I SIMPLY DON'T WANT TO DEAL WITH YOUR CRYING.

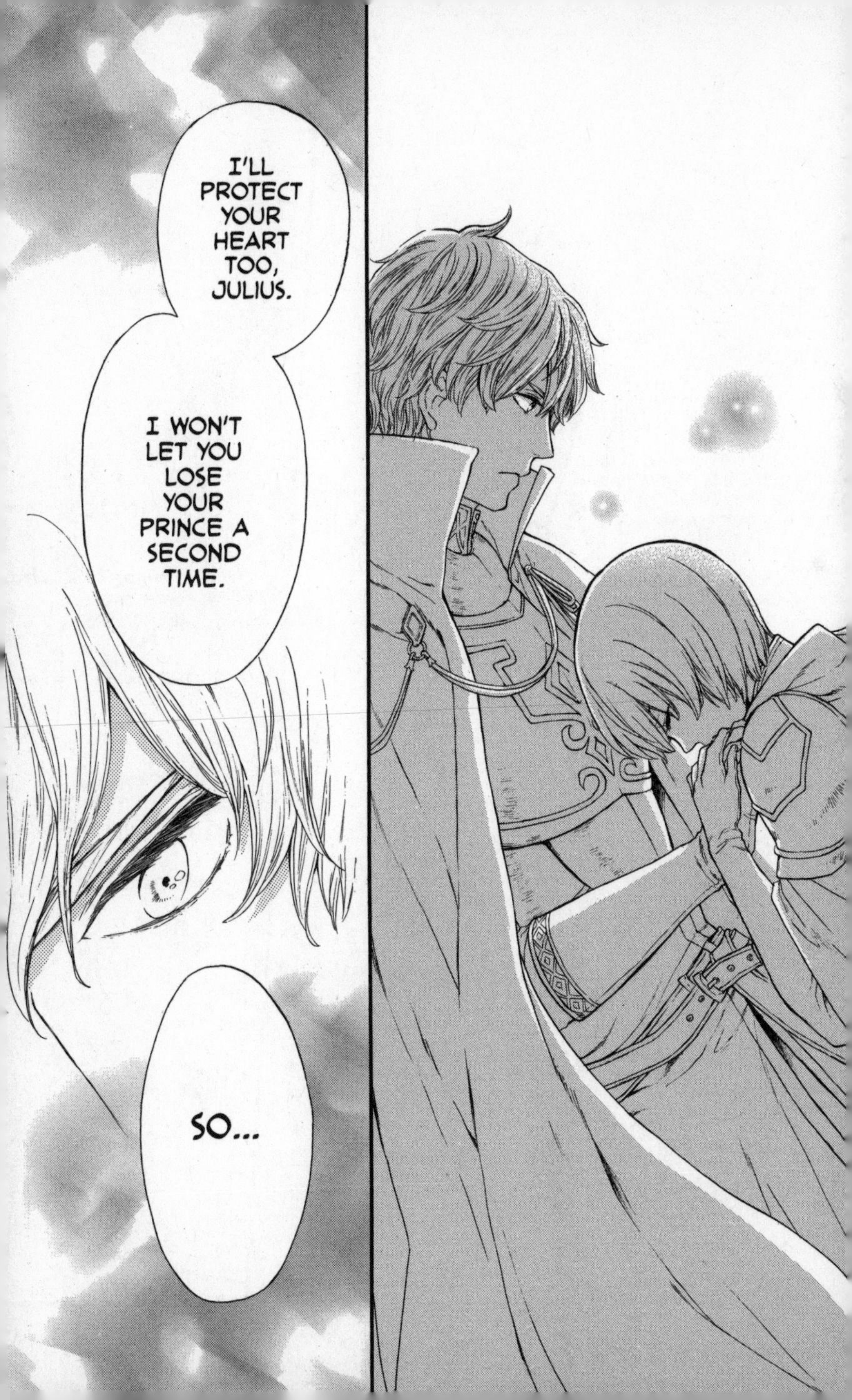
I'LL PROTECT YOUR HEART TOO, JULIUS.
I WON'T LET YOU LOSE YOUR PRINCE A SECOND TIME.
SO...

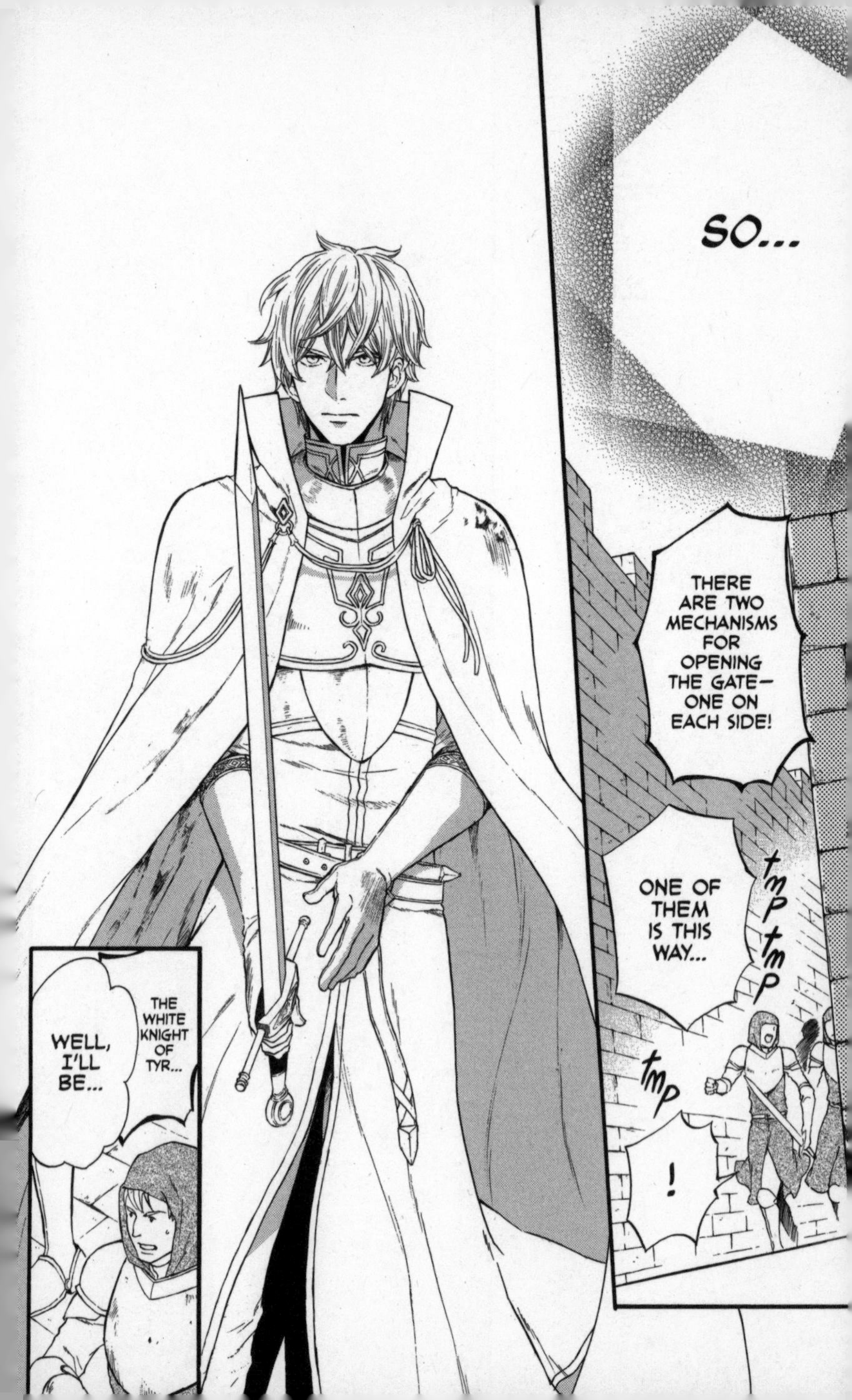
SO...
THERE ARE TWO MECHANISMS FOR OPENING THE GATE— ONE ON EACH SIDE!
ONE OF THEM IS THIS WAY...
tmp tmp
tmp
!
THE WHITE KNIGHT OF TYR...
WELL, I'LL BE...

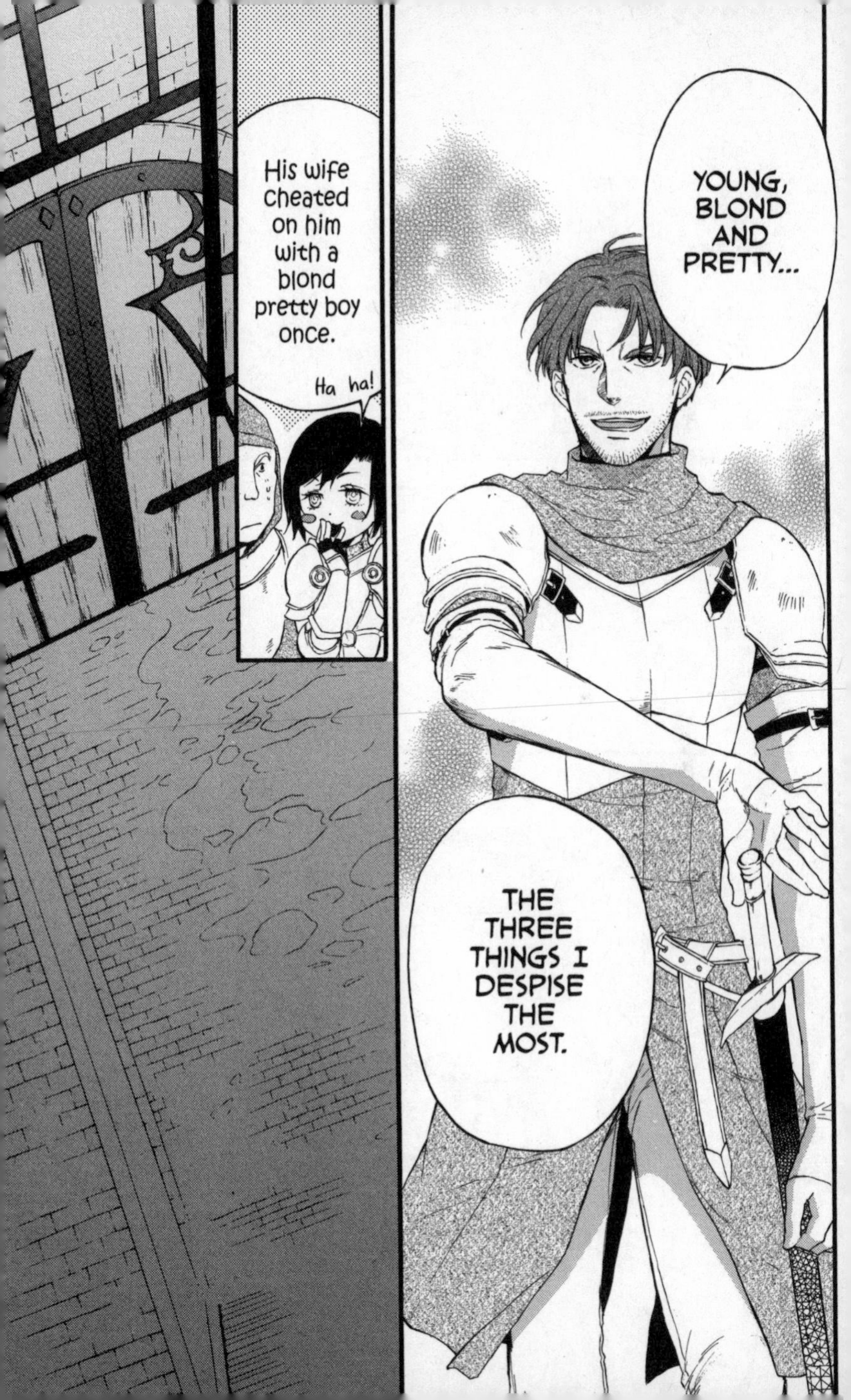
YOUNG, BLOND AND PRETTY...
THE THREE THINGS I DESPISE THE MOST.
His wife cheated on him with a blond pretty boy once.
Ha ha!

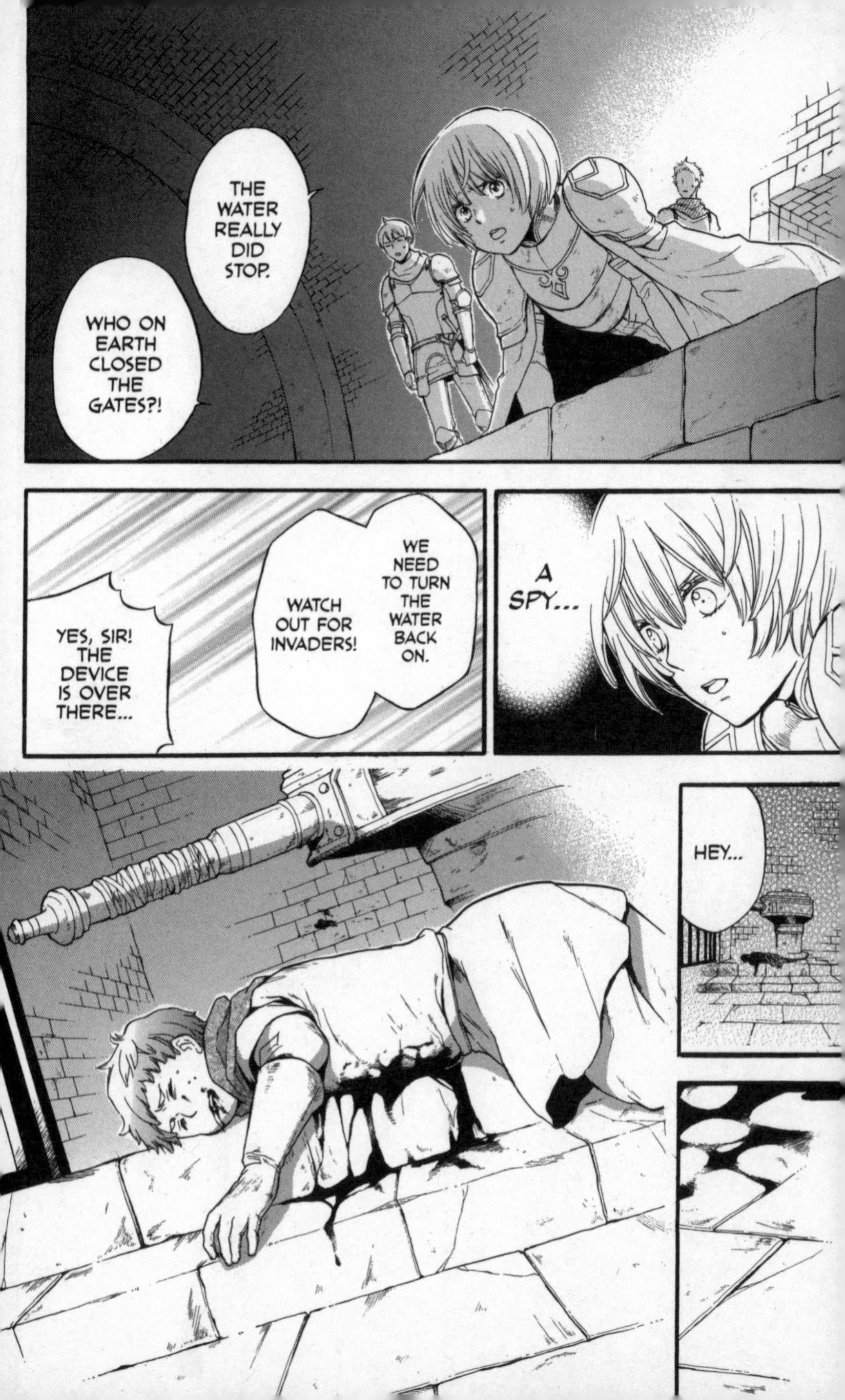
THE WATER REALLY DID STOP.
WHO ON EARTH CLOSED THE GATES?!
A SPY...
WE NEED TO TURN THE WATER BACK ON.
WATCH OUT FOR INVADERS!
YES, SIR! THE DEVICE IS OVER THERE...
HEY...

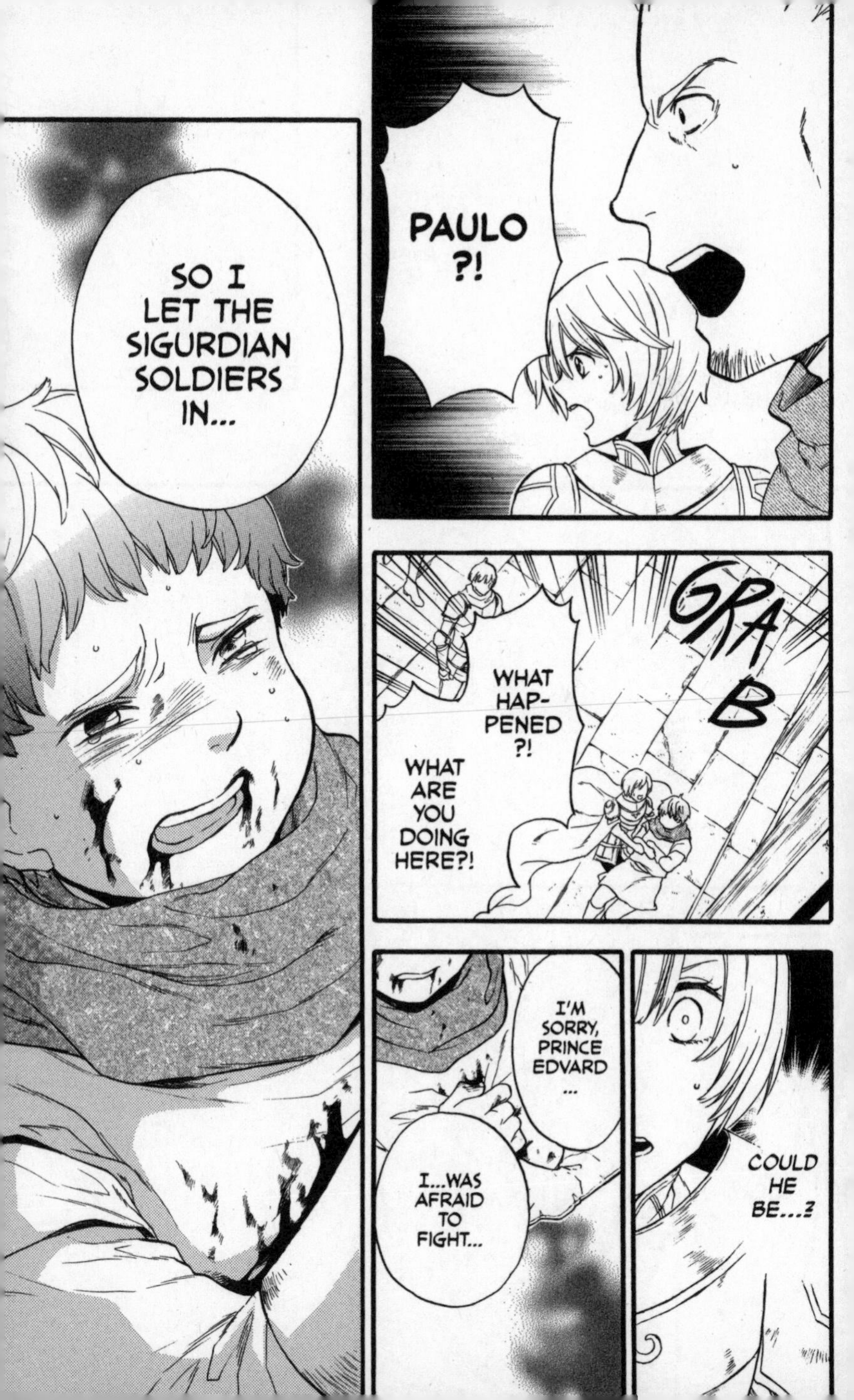
PAULO ?!
GRAB
WHAT HAPPENED ?!
WHAT ARE YOU DOING HERE?!
COULD HE BE...?
I'M SORRY, PRINCE EDVARD ...
I...WAS AFRAID TO FIGHT...
SO I LET THE SIGURDIAN SOLDIERS IN...

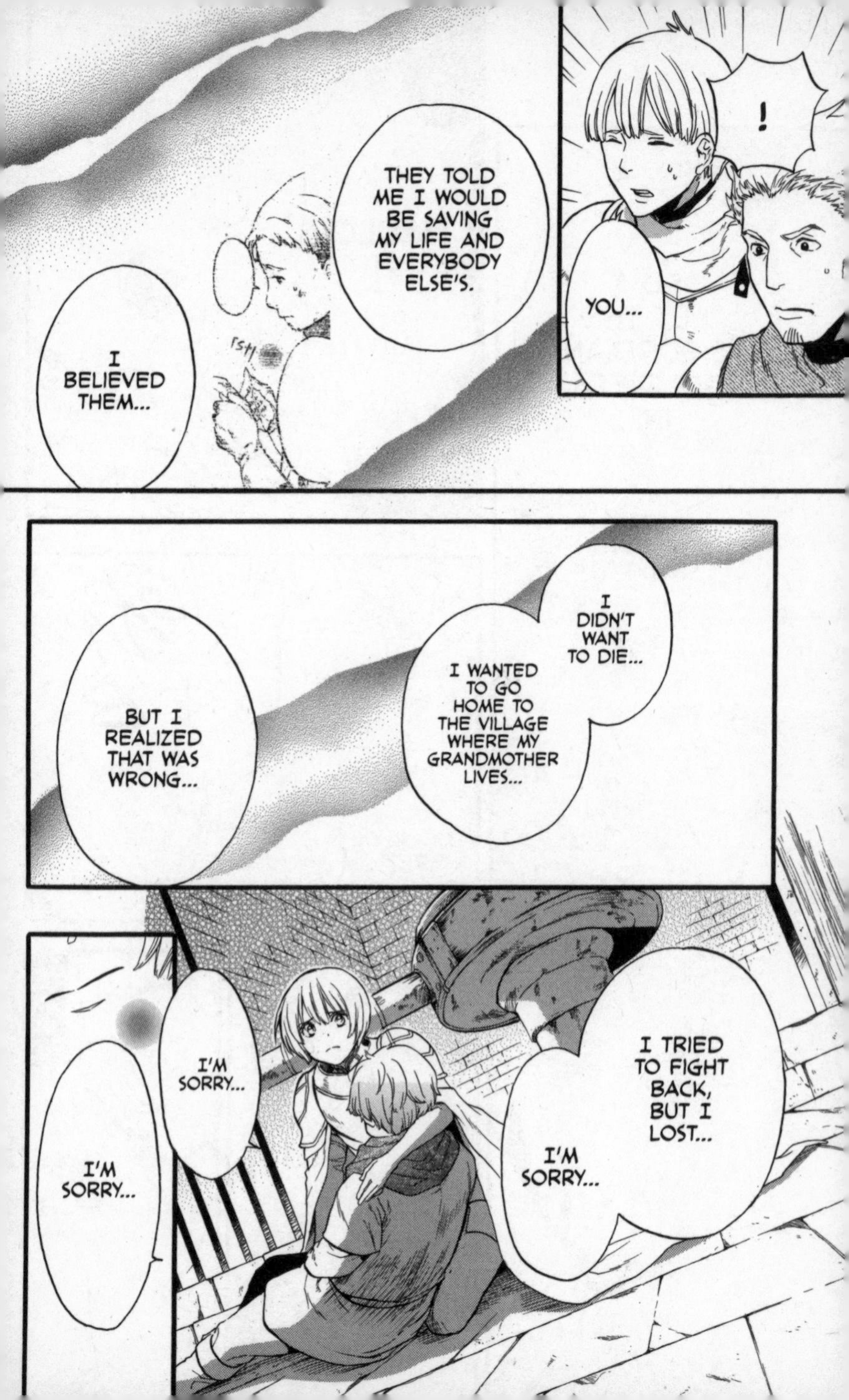
!
YOU...
THEY TOLD ME I WOULD BE SAVING MY LIFE AND EVERYBODY ELSE'S.
I BELIEVED THEM...
I DIDN'T WANT TO DIE...
I WANTED TO GO HOME TO THE VILLAGE WHERE MY GRANDMOTHER LIVES...
BUT I REALIZED THAT WAS WRONG...
I TRIED TO FIGHT BACK, BUT I LOST...
I'M SORRY...
I'M SORRY...
I'M SORRY...

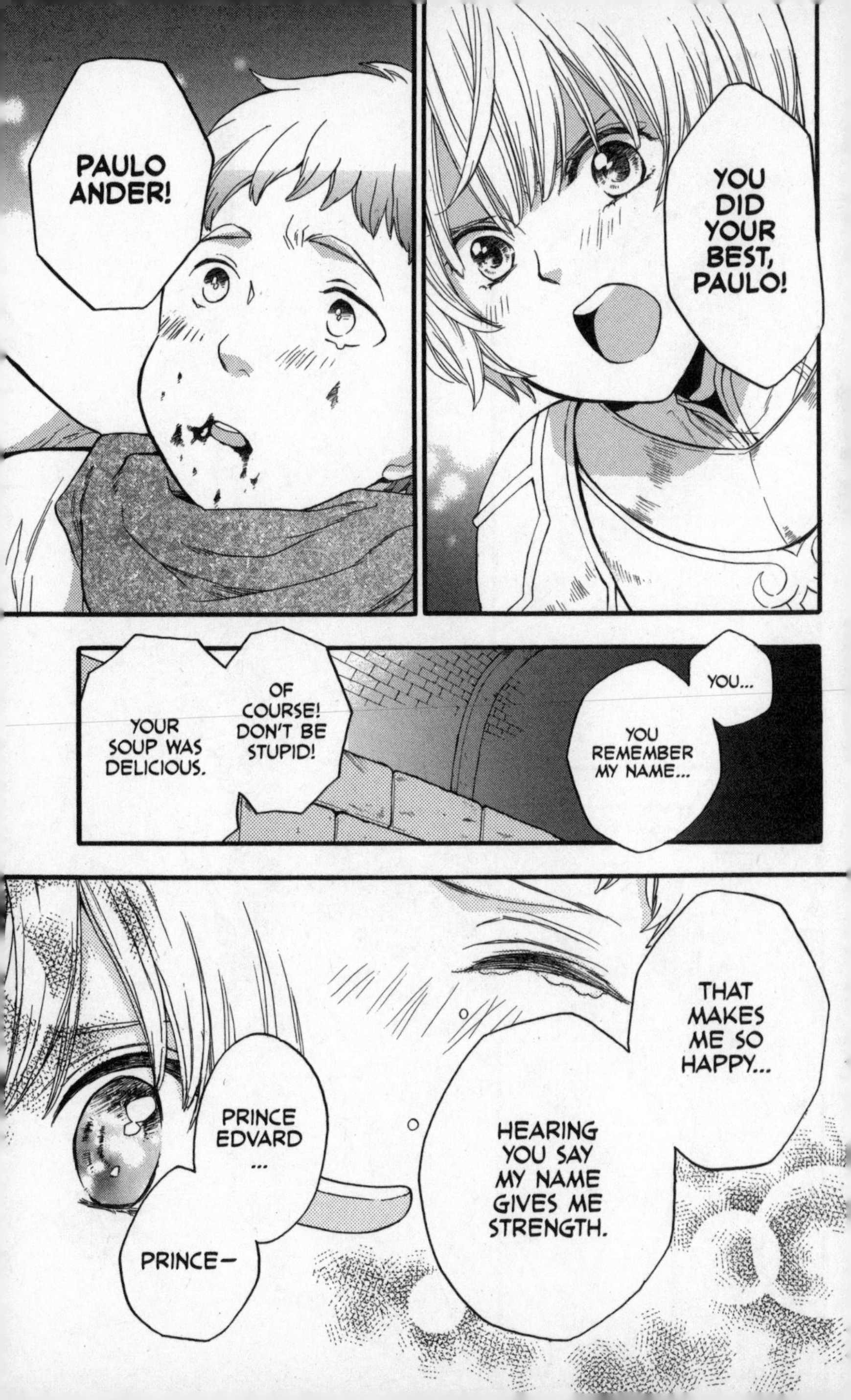
YOU DID YOUR BEST, PAULO!
PAULO ANDER!
YOU...
YOU REMEMBER MY NAME...
OF COURSE! DON'T BE STUPID!
YOUR SOUP WAS DELICIOUS.
THAT MAKES ME SO HAPPY...
HEARING YOU SAY MY NAME GIVES ME STRENGTH.
PRINCE EDVARD ...
PRINCE—

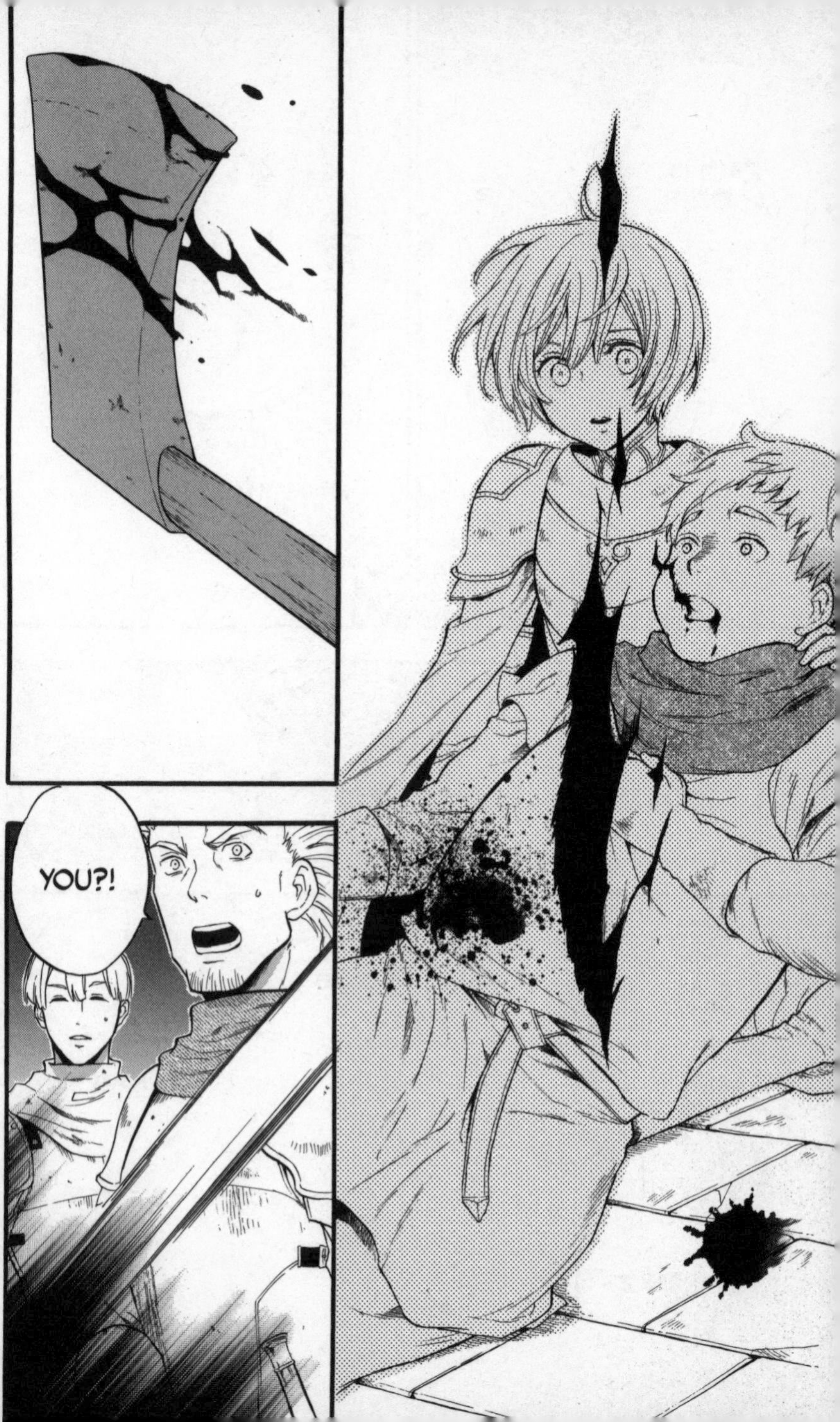
YOU?!

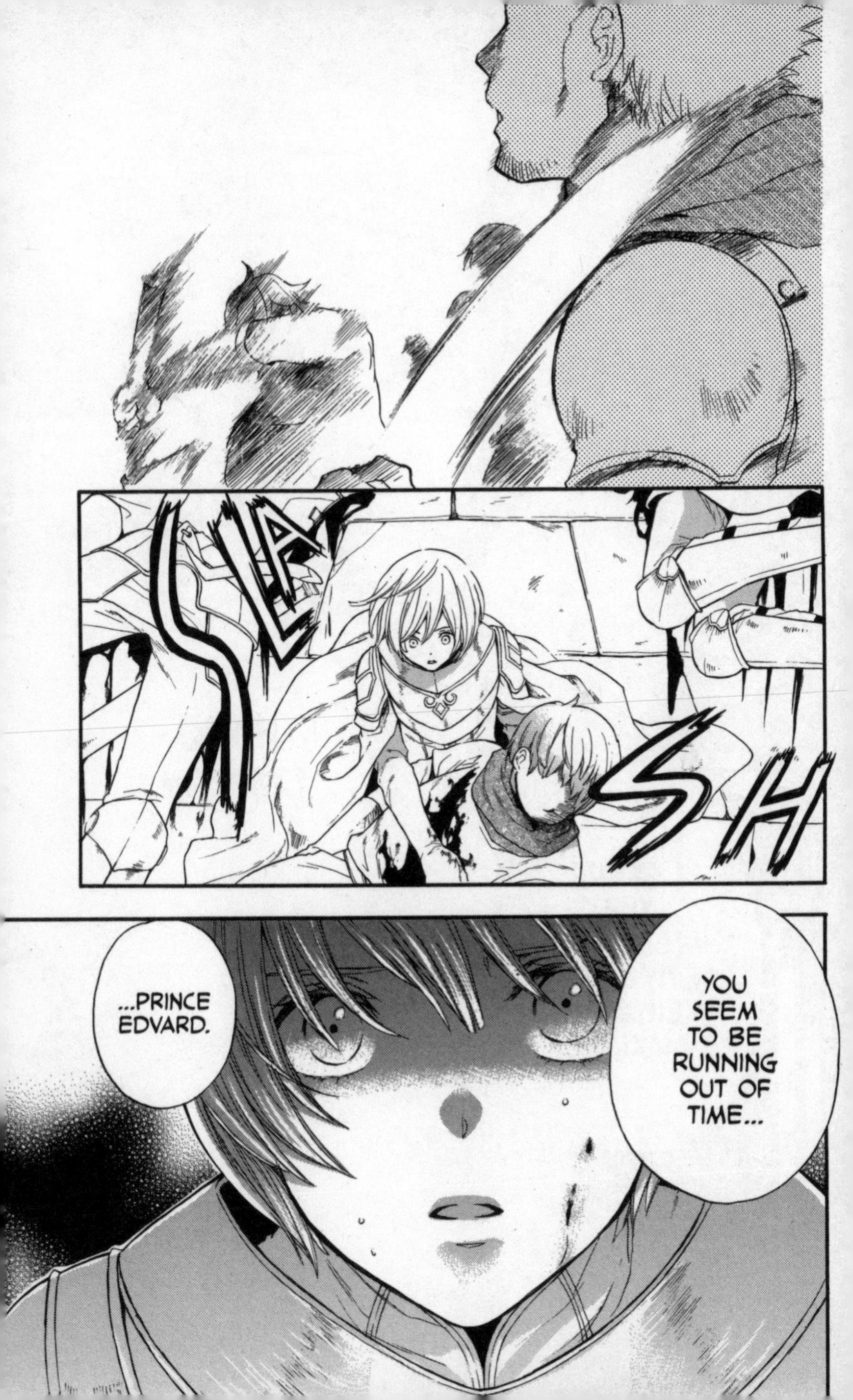
SLA
SH
YOU SEEM TO BE RUNNING OUT OF TIME...
...PRINCE EDVARD.

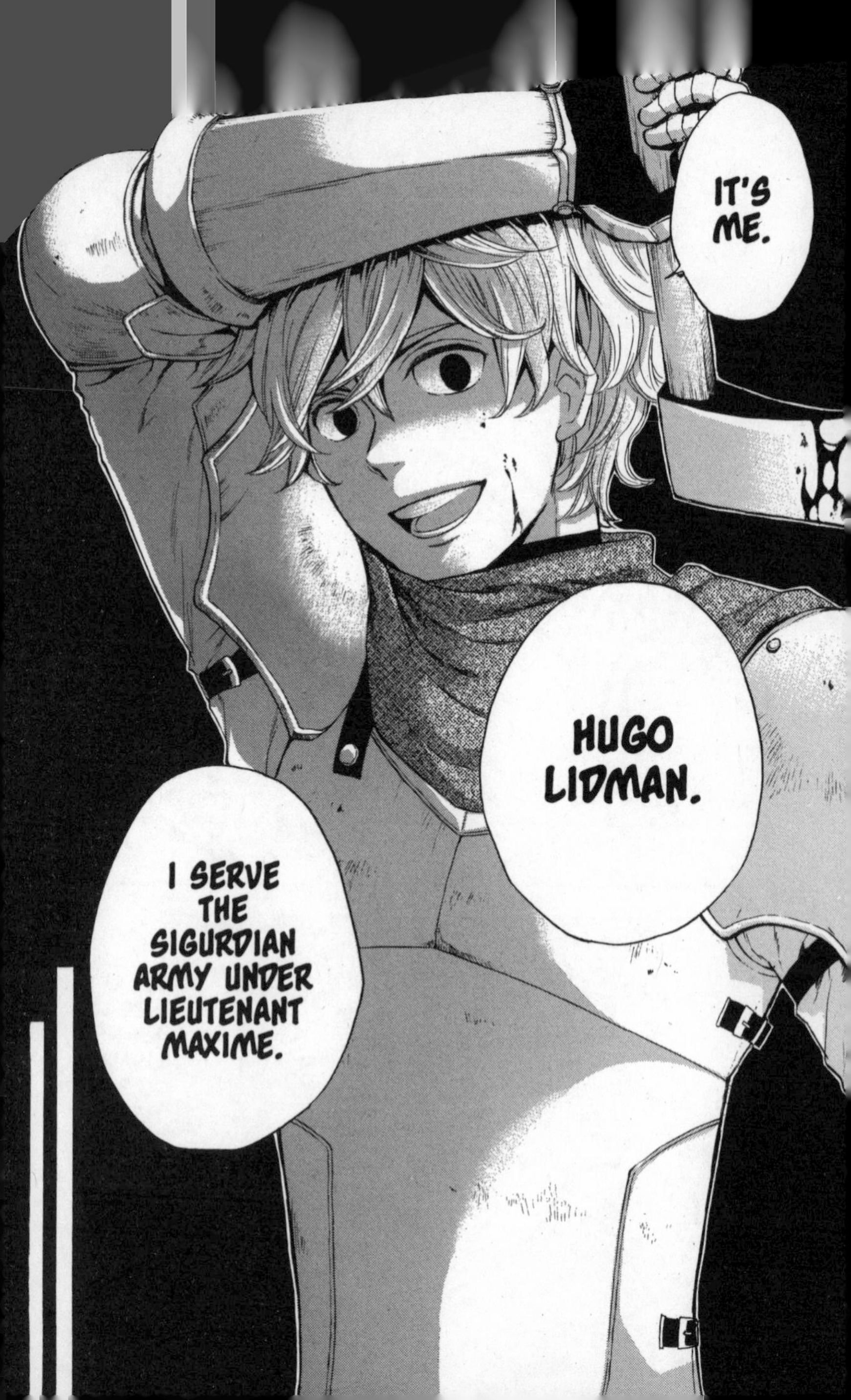
IT'S ME.
HUGO LIDMAN.
I SERVE THE SIGURDIAN ARMY UNDER LIEUTENANT MAXIME.

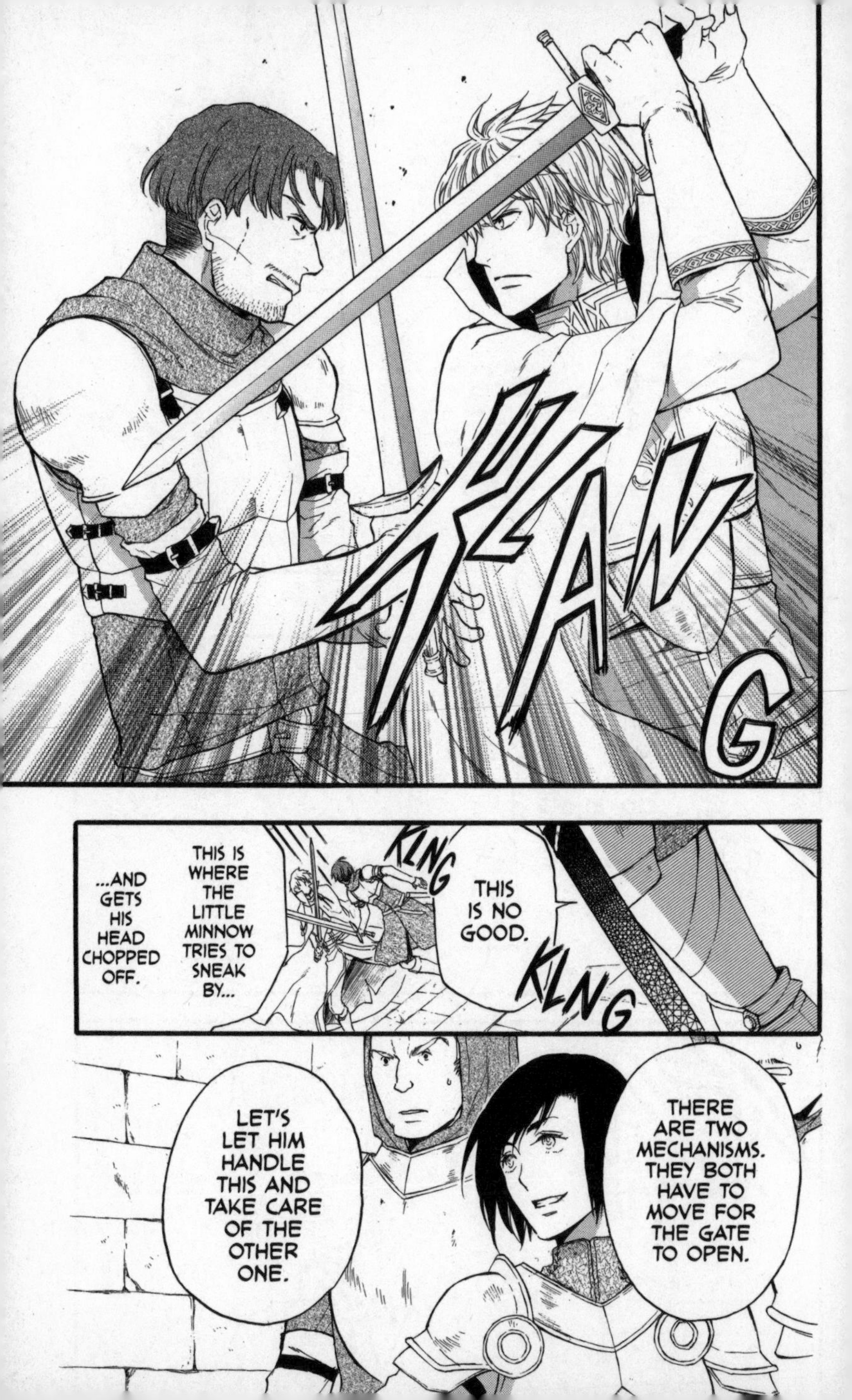
KLANG
KLNG
THIS IS NO GOOD.
KLNG
THIS IS WHERE THE LITTLE MINNOW TRIES TO SNEAK BY...
...AND GETS HIS HEAD CHOPPED OFF.
THERE ARE TWO MECHANISMS. THEY BOTH HAVE TO MOVE FOR THE GATE TO OPEN.
LET'S LET HIM HANDLE THIS AND TAKE CARE OF THE OTHER ONE.

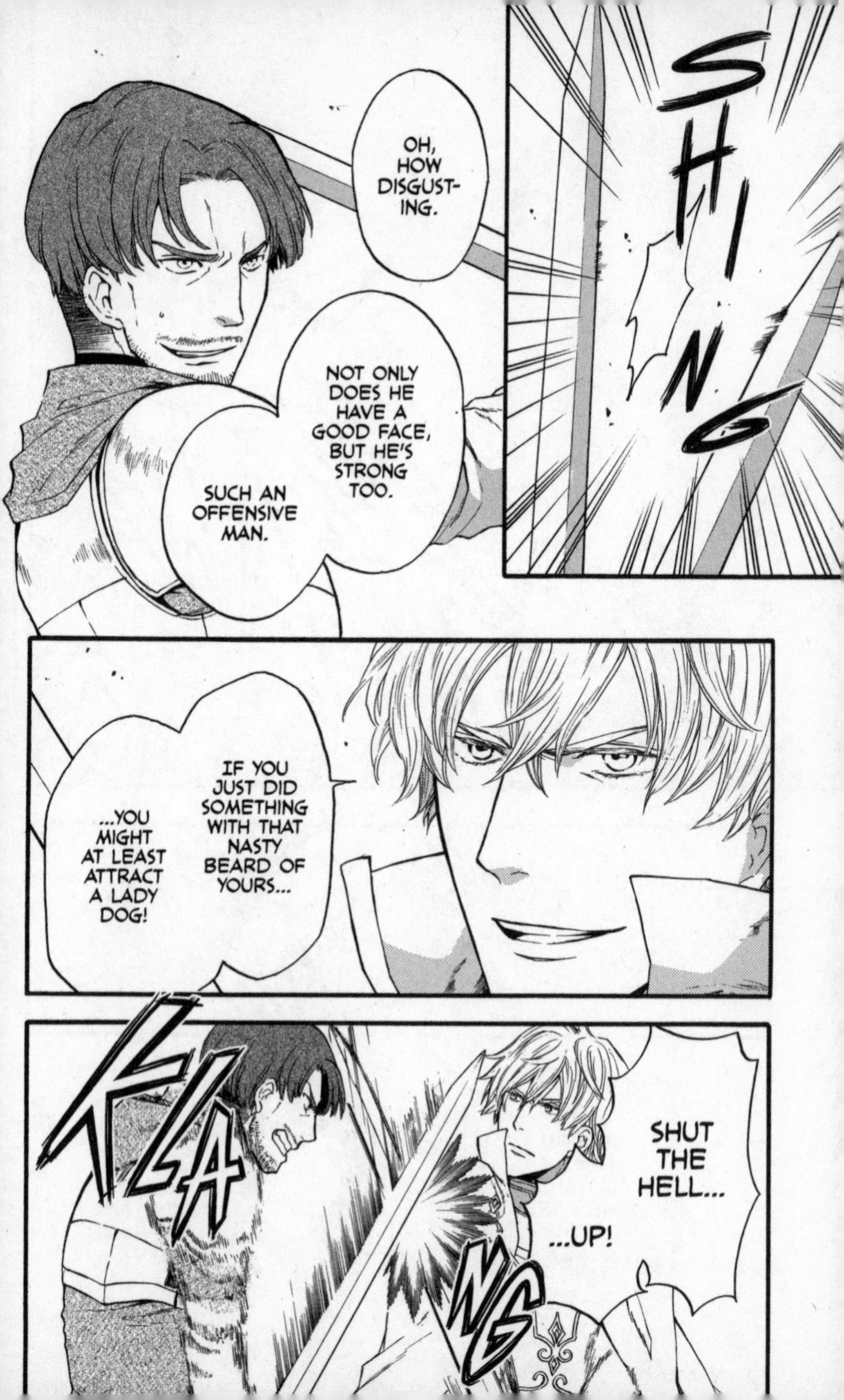
SHING
OH, HOW DISGUST-ING.
NOT ONLY DOES HE HAVE A GOOD FACE, BUT HE'S STRONG TOO.
SUCH AN OFFENSIVE MAN.
IF YOU JUST DID SOMETHING WITH THAT NASTY BEARD OF YOURS...
...YOU MIGHT AT LEAST ATTRACT A LADY DOG!
SHUT THE HELL...
...UP!
KLANG

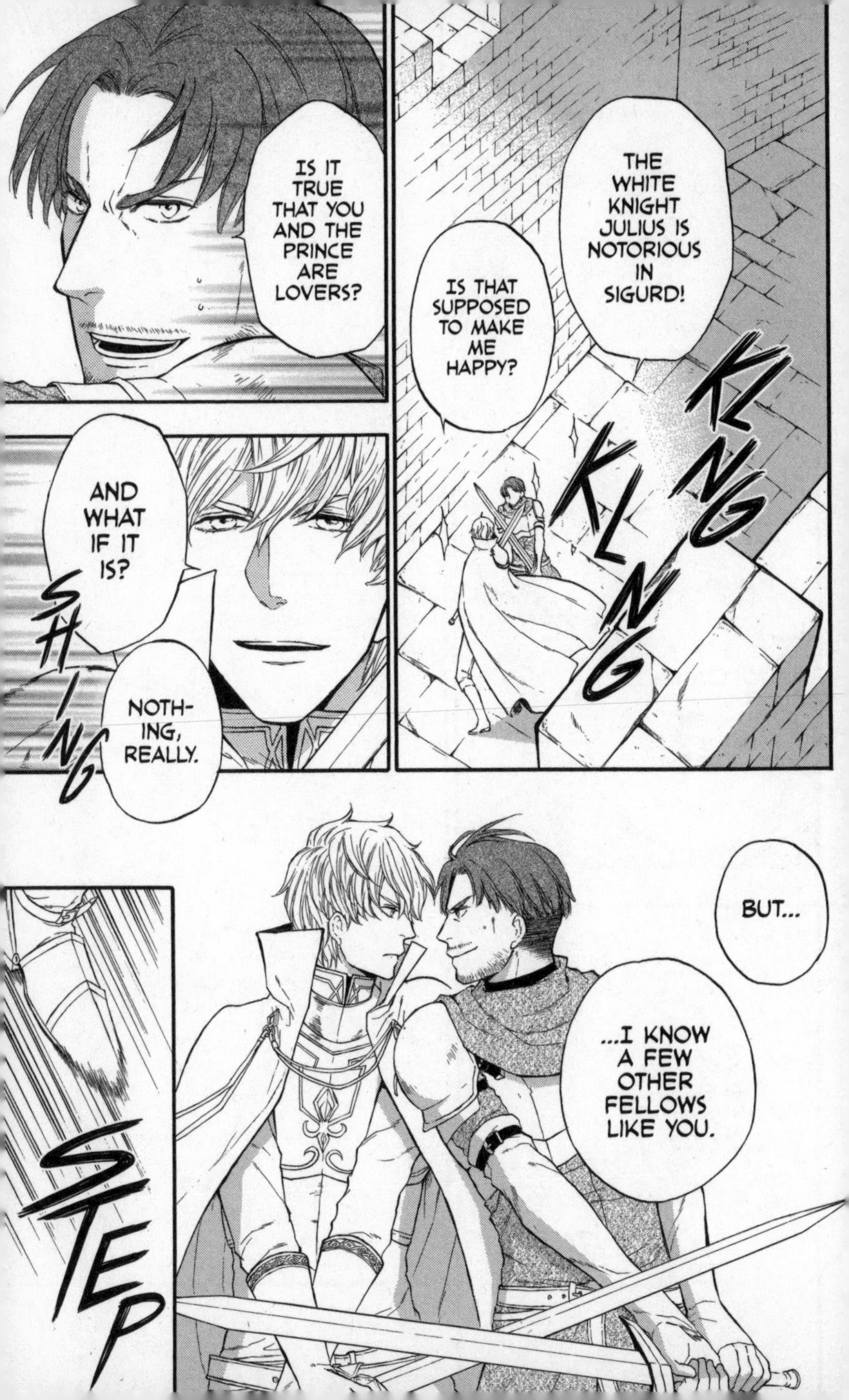
THE WHITE KNIGHT JULIUS IS NOTORIOUS IN SIGURD!
IS THAT SUPPOSED TO MAKE ME HAPPY?
KLNG KLNG
IS IT TRUE THAT YOU AND THE PRINCE ARE LOVERS?
AND WHAT IF IT IS?
NOTH-ING, REALLY.
SHING
BUT...
...I KNOW A FEW OTHER FELLOWS LIKE YOU.
STEP

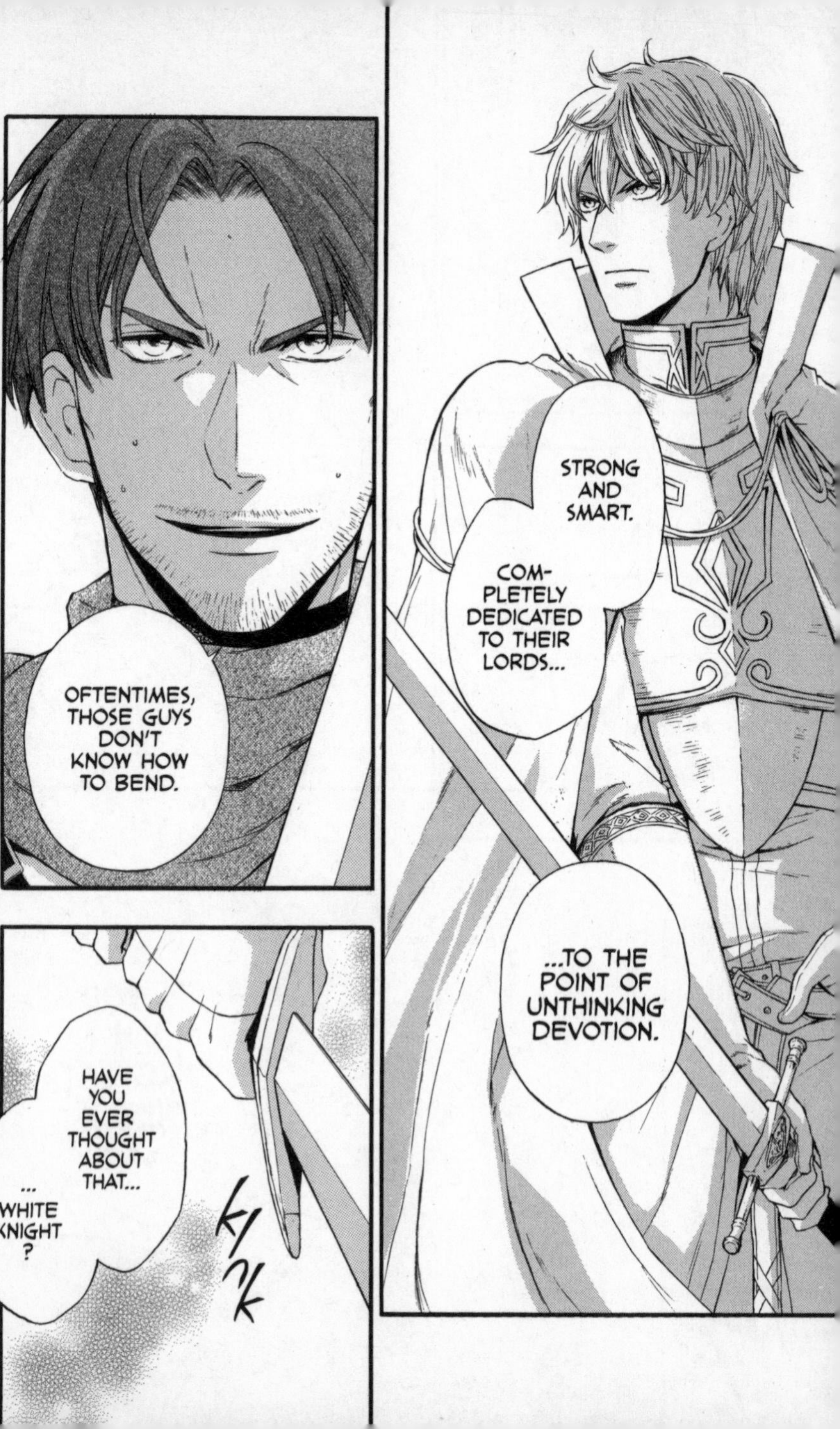
STRONG AND SMART.
COMPLETELY DEDICATED TO THEIR LORDS...
...TO THE POINT OF UNTHINKING DEVOTION.
OFTENTIMES, THOSE GUYS DON'T KNOW HOW TO BEND.
HAVE YOU EVER THOUGHT ABOUT THAT... ...WHITE KNIGHT?
KLNK

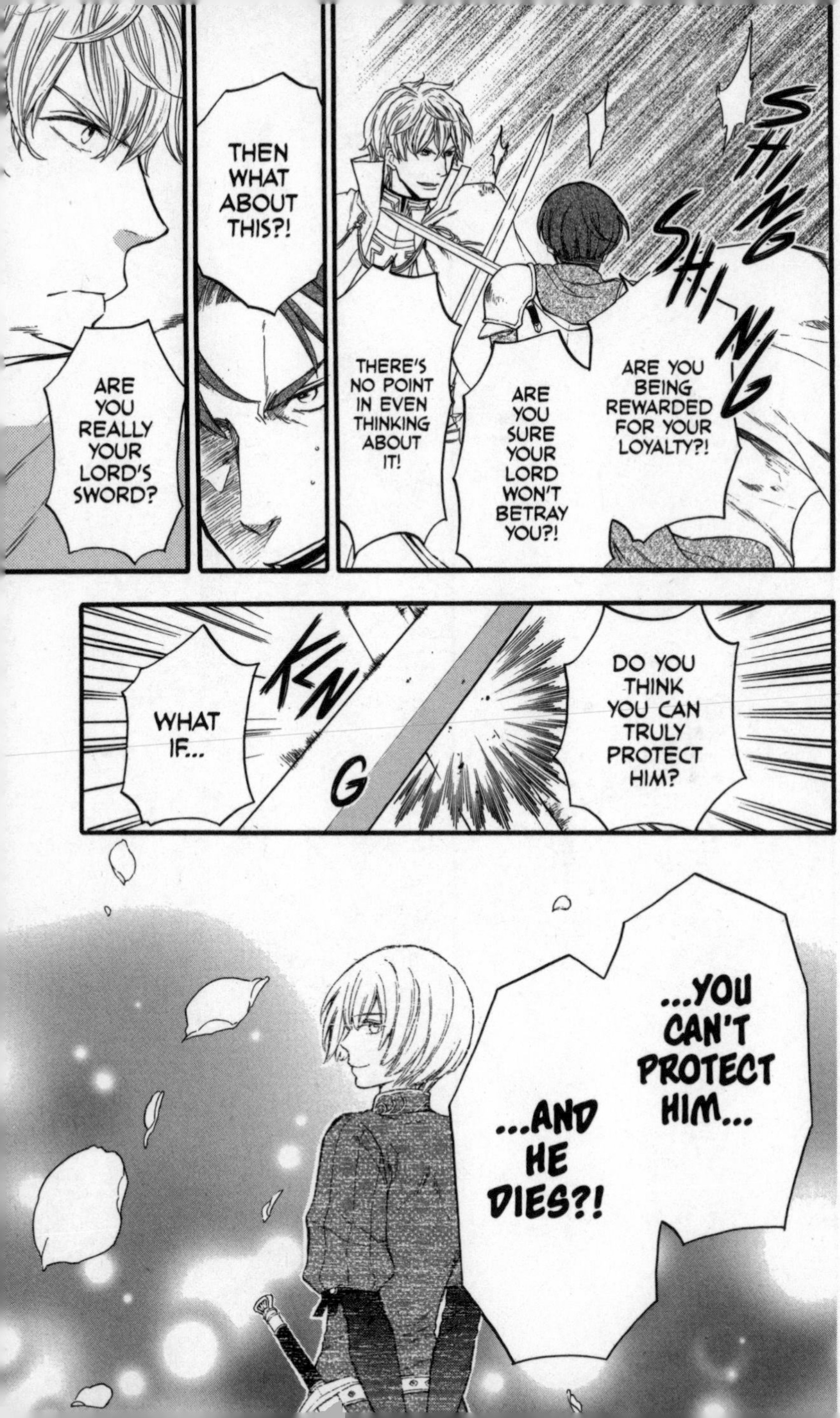
SHING
SHING
ARE YOU BEING REWARDED FOR YOUR LOYALTY?!
ARE YOU SURE YOUR LORD WON'T BETRAY YOU?!
THERE'S NO POINT IN EVEN THINKING ABOUT IT!
THEN WHAT ABOUT THIS?!
ARE YOU REALLY YOUR LORD'S SWORD?
DO YOU THINK YOU CAN TRULY PROTECT HIM?
KLNG
WHAT IF...
...YOU CAN'T PROTECT HIM...
...AND HE DIES?!

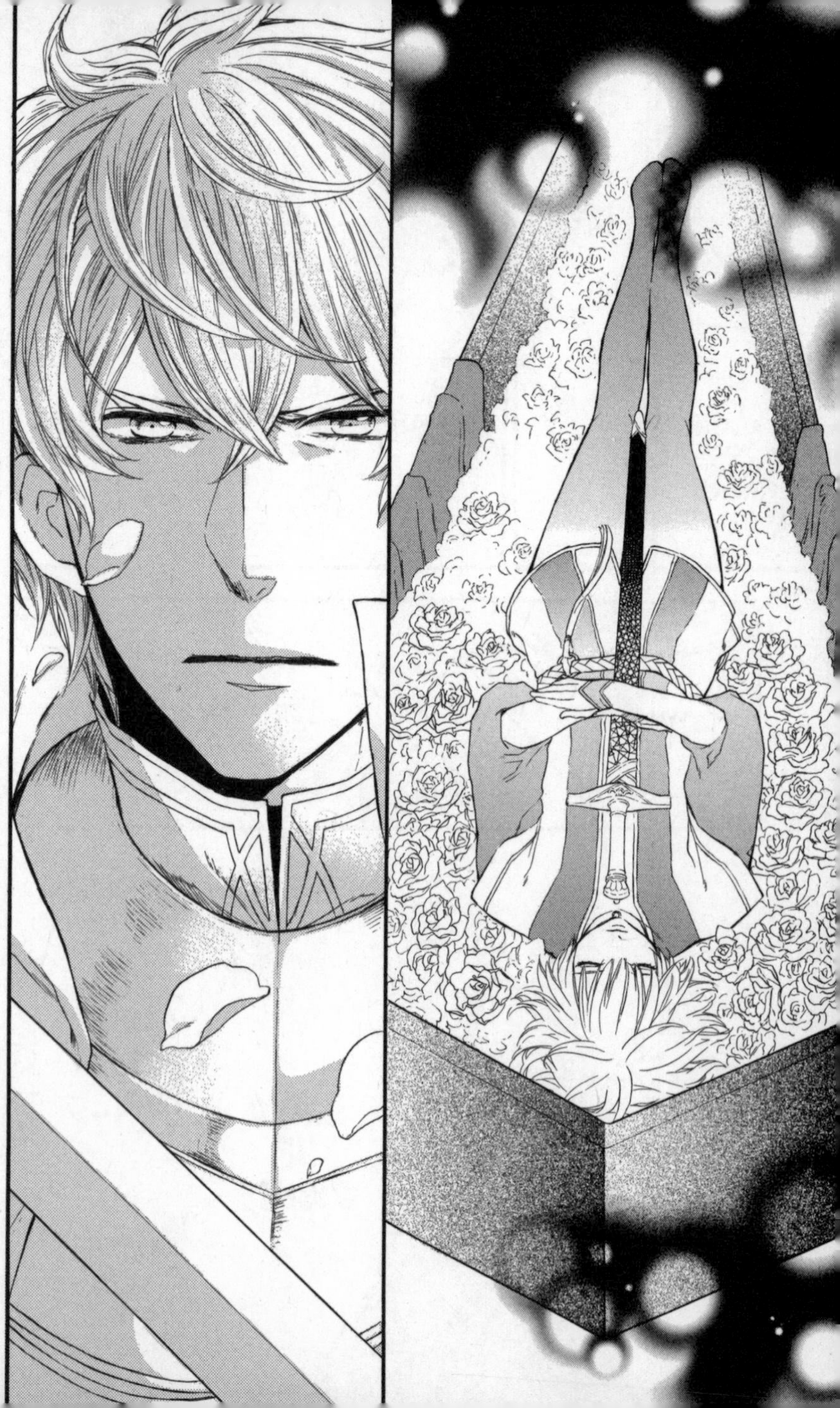

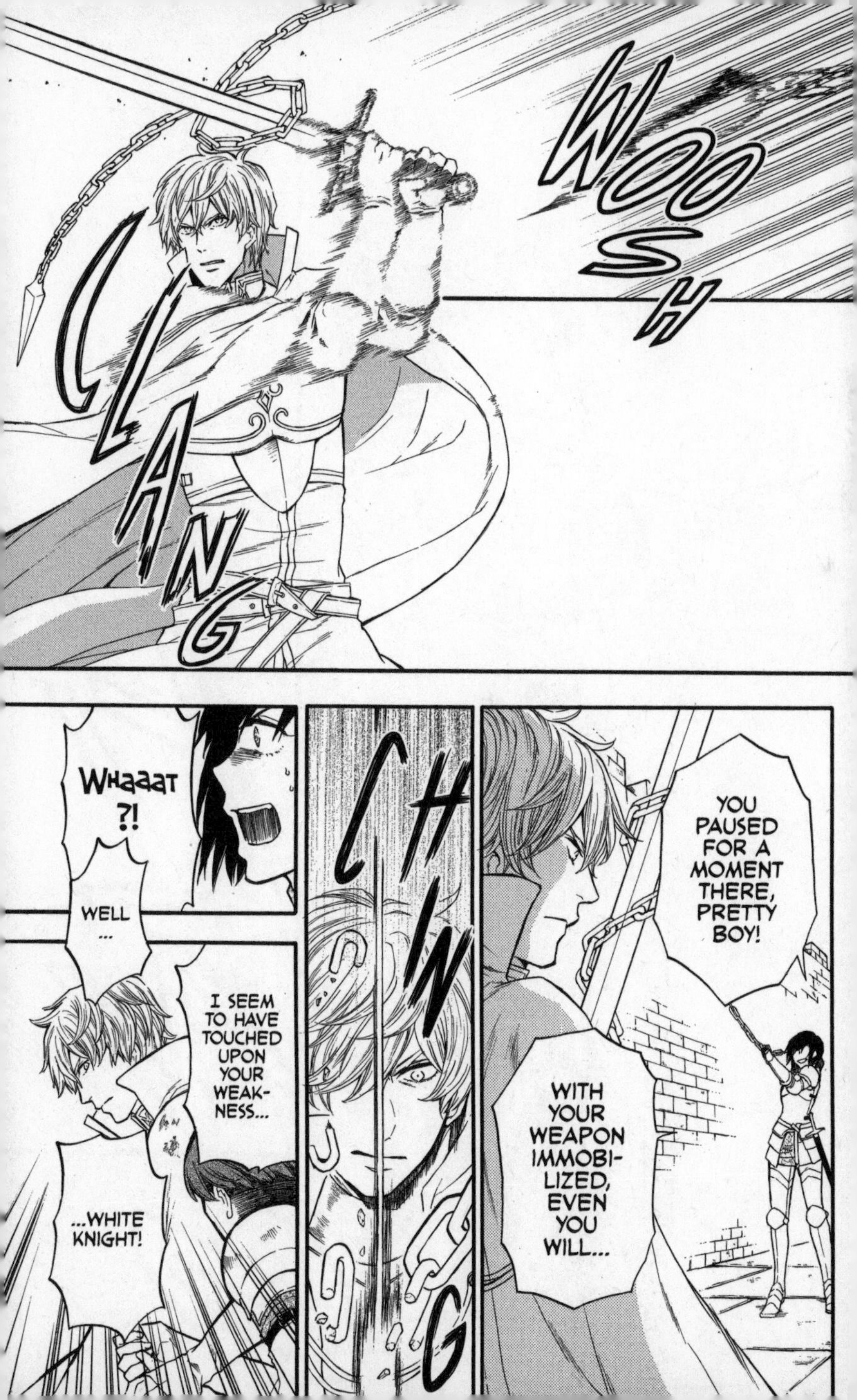
WOOSH
CLANG
YOU PAUSED FOR A MOMENT THERE, PRETTY BOY!
WITH YOUR WEAPON IMMOBILIZED, EVEN YOU WILL...
CHING
WHAAAT?!
WELL...
I SEEM TO HAVE TOUCHED UPON YOUR WEAKNESS...
...WHITE KNIGHT!

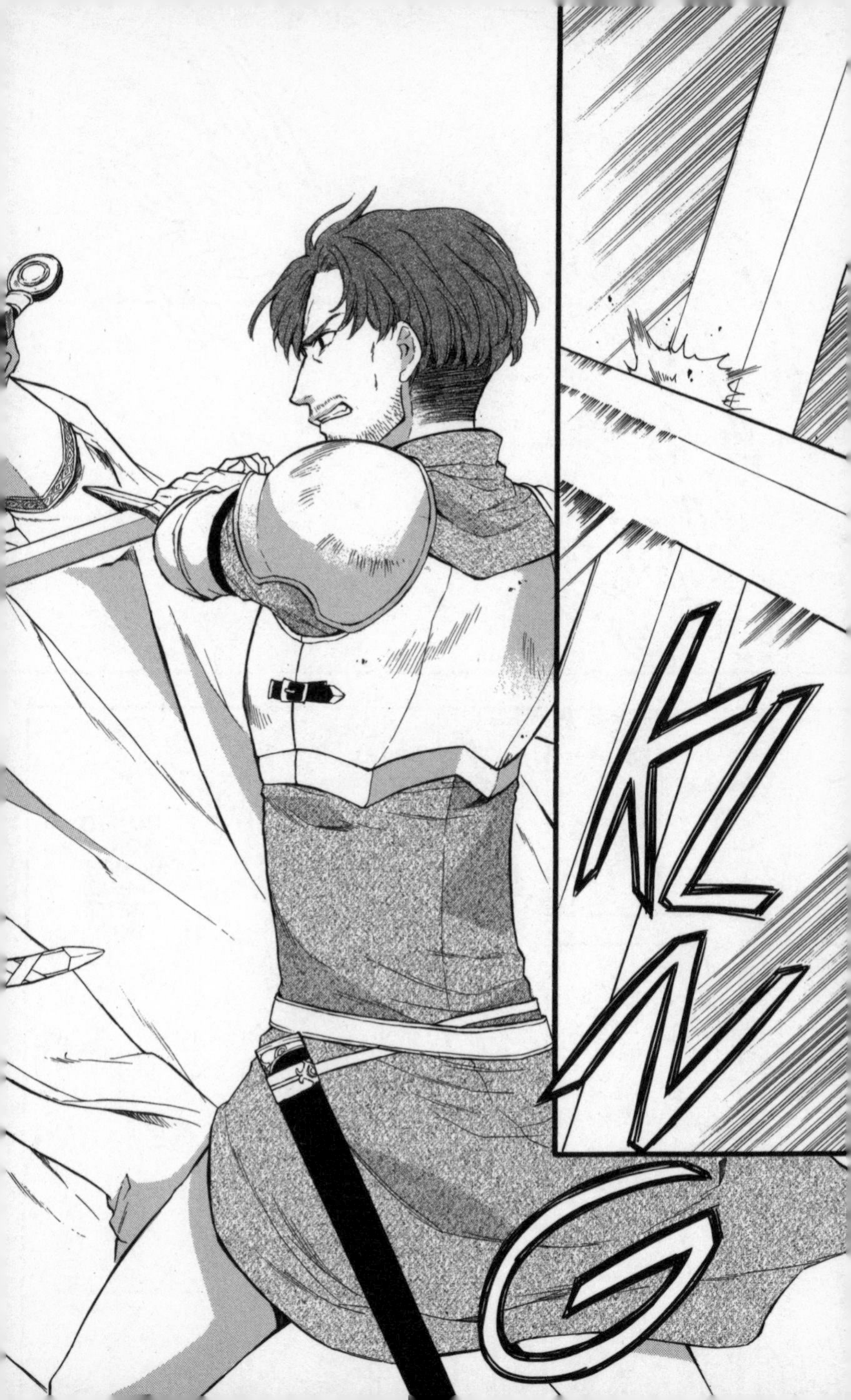
KLANG

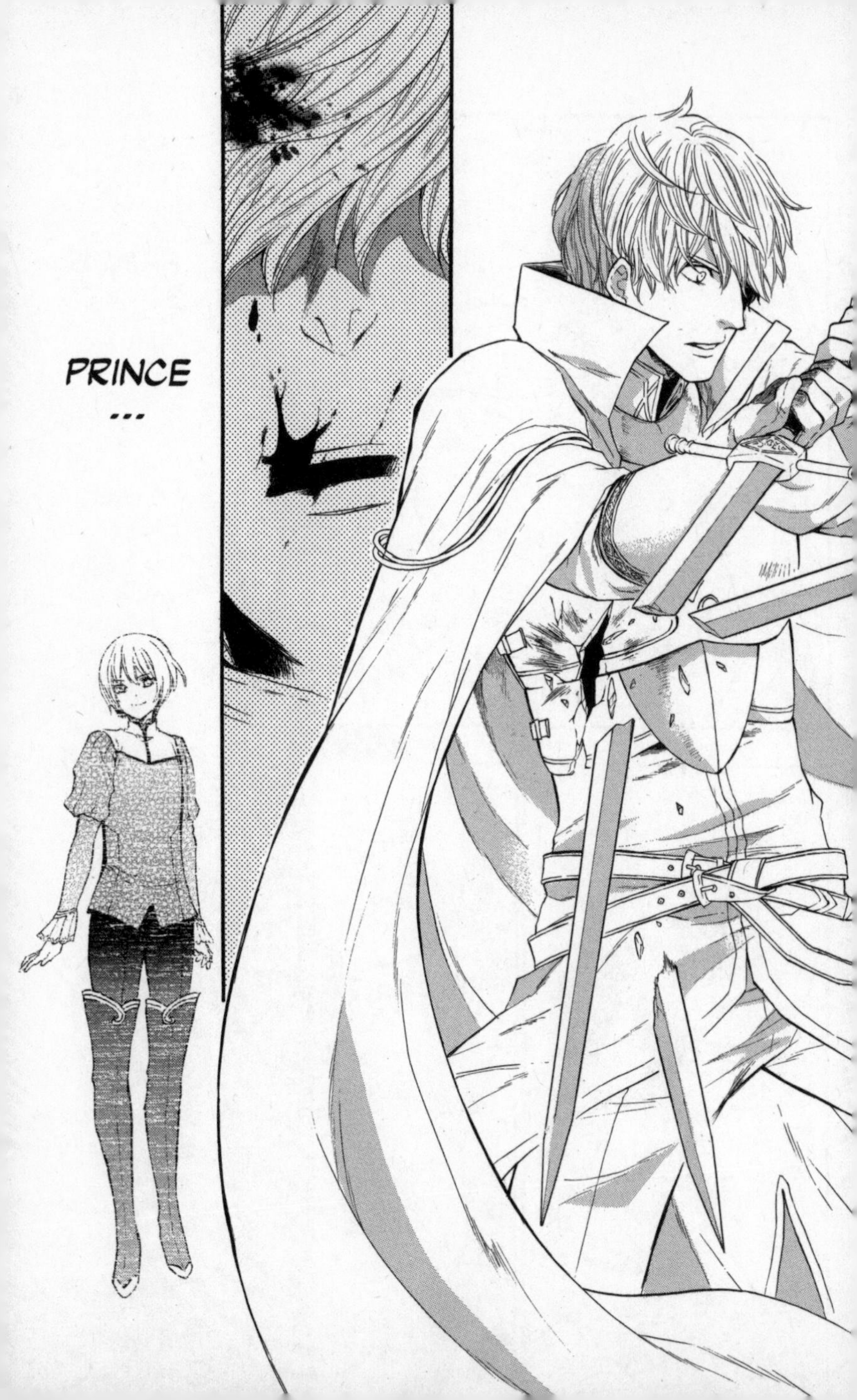
PRINCE
...

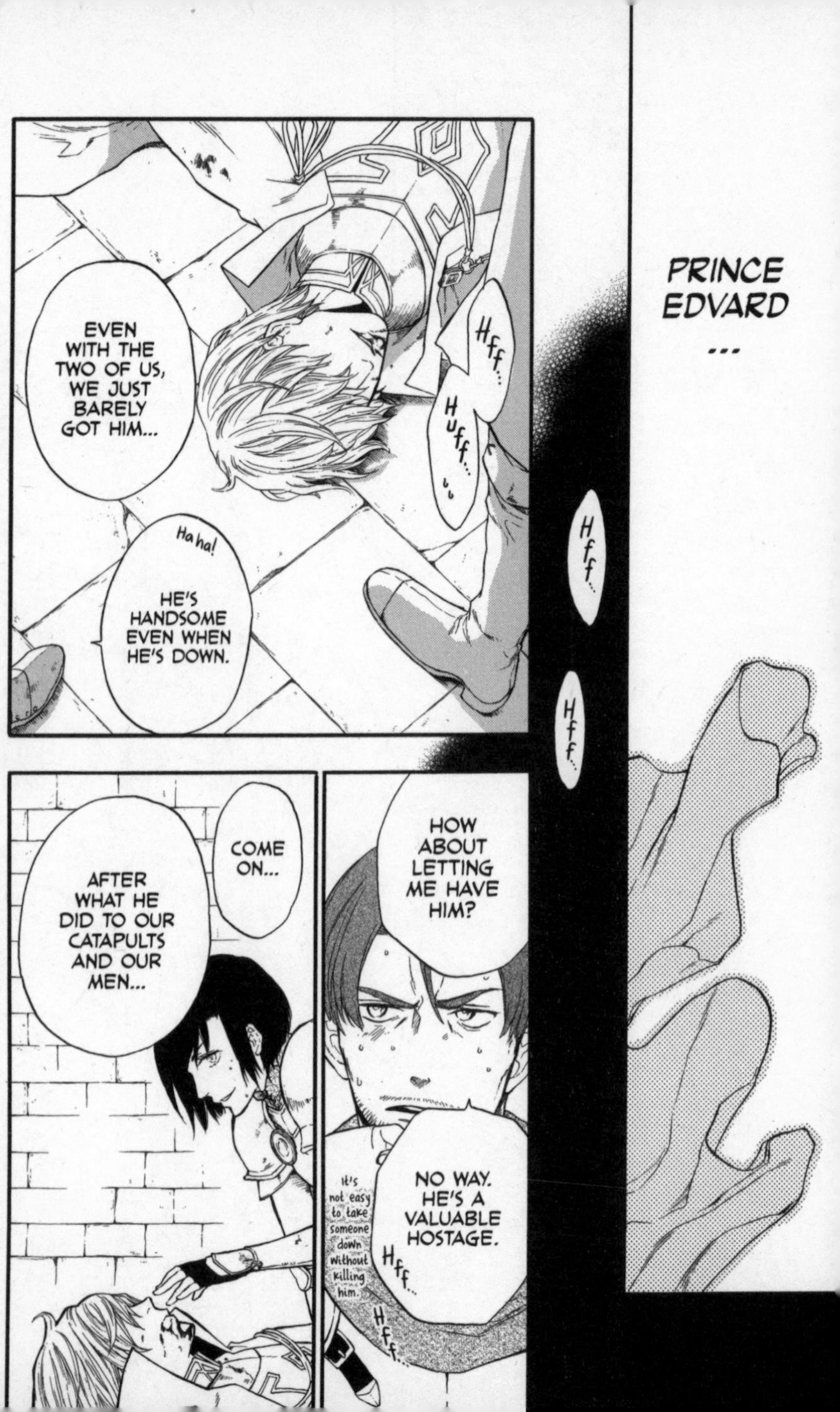
PRINCE EDVARD ...
Hff...
Hff...
Hff...
Huff...
EVEN WITH THE TWO OF US, WE JUST BARELY GOT HIM...
Ha ha!
HE'S HANDSOME EVEN WHEN HE'S DOWN.
HOW ABOUT LETTING ME HAVE HIM?
NO WAY. HE'S A VALUABLE HOSTAGE.
It's not easy to take someone down without killing him.
Hff...
Hff...
COME ON...
AFTER WHAT HE DID TO OUR CATAPULTS AND OUR MEN...

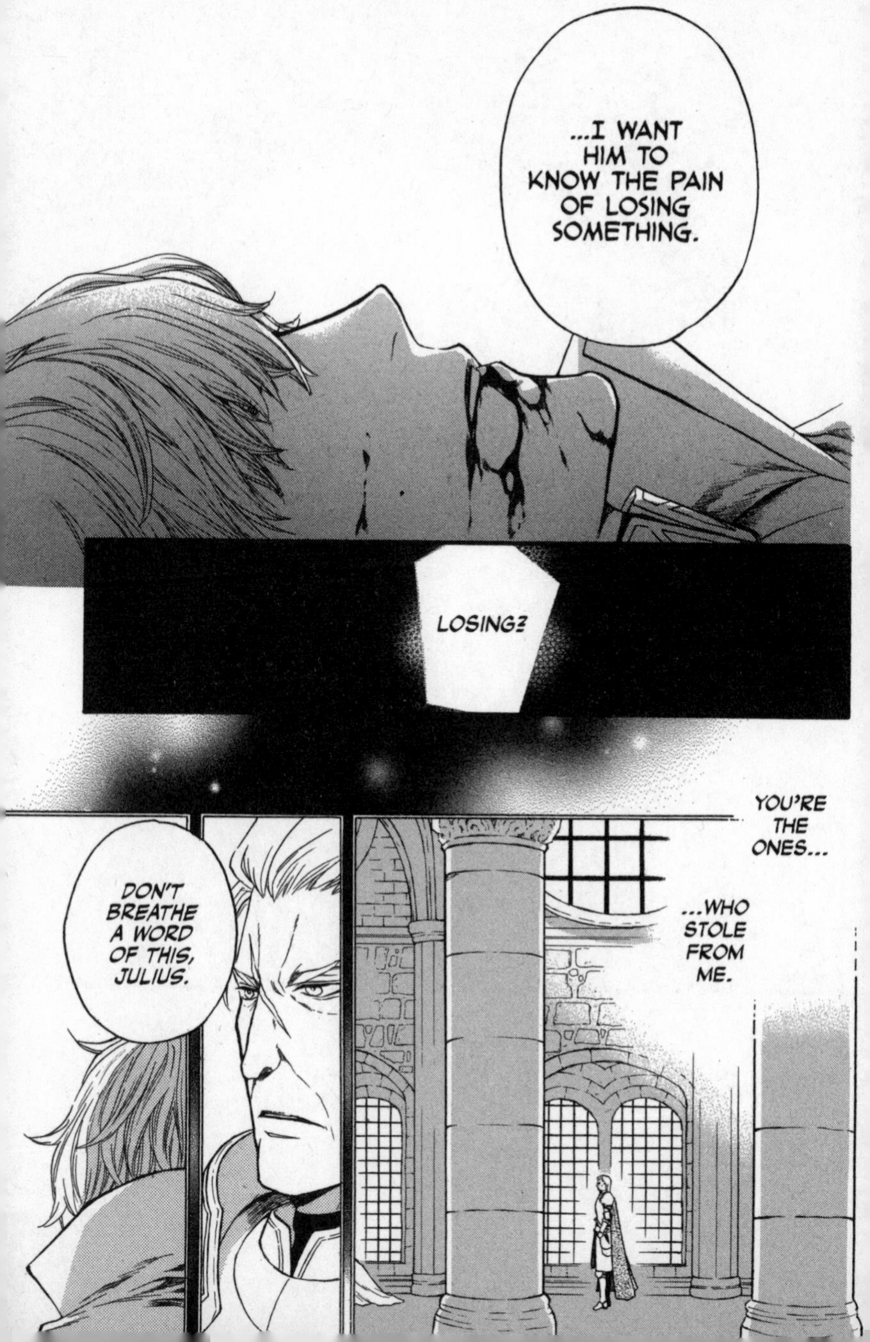
...I WANT HIM TO KNOW THE PAIN OF LOSING SOMETHING.
LOSING?
YOU'RE THE ONES...
...WHO STOLE FROM ME.
DON'T BREATHE A WORD OF THIS, JULIUS.

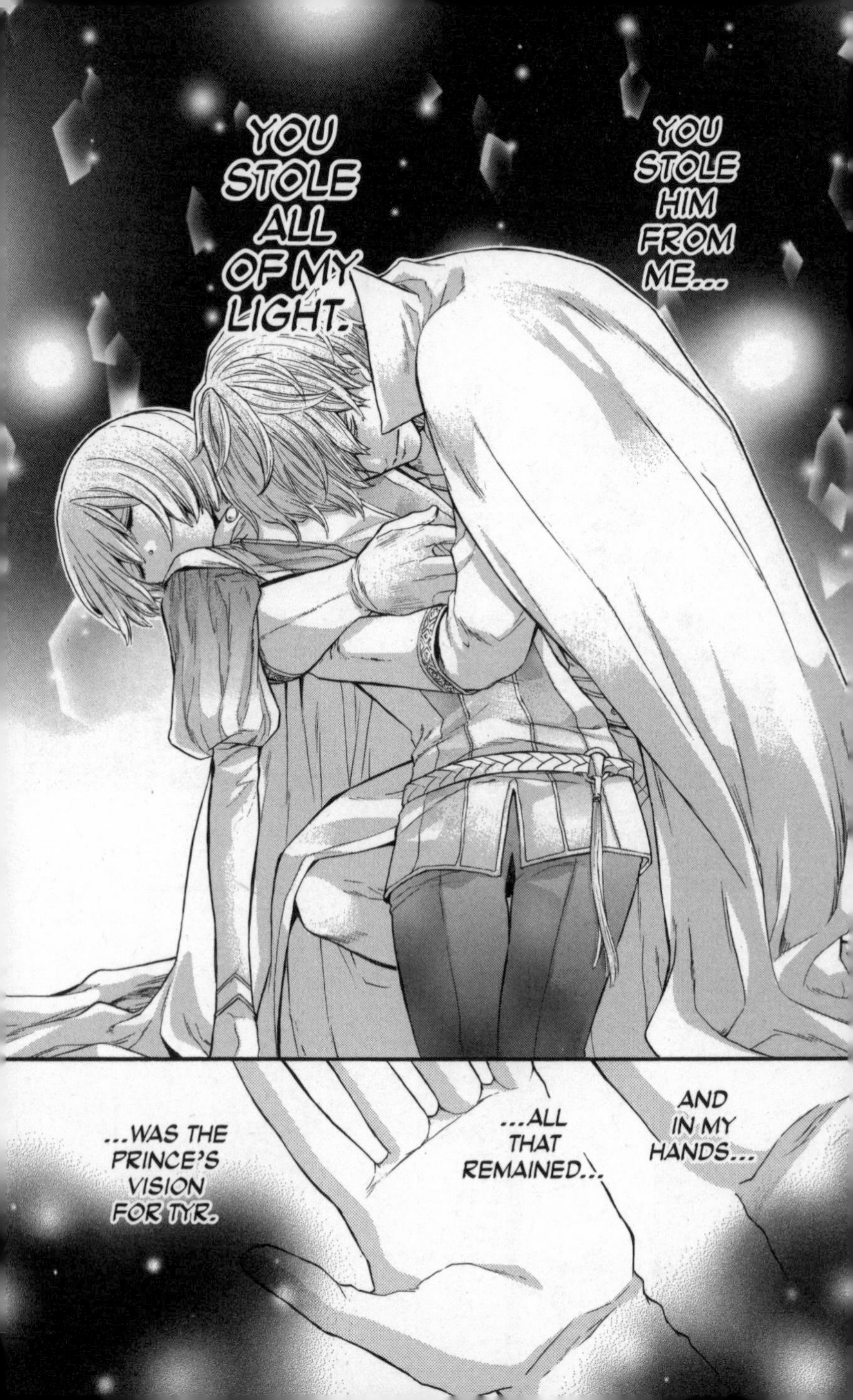
YOU STOLE HIM FROM ME...
YOU STOLE ALL OF MY LIGHT.
AND IN MY HANDS...
...ALL THAT REMAINED...
...WAS THE PRINCE'S VISION FOR TYR.

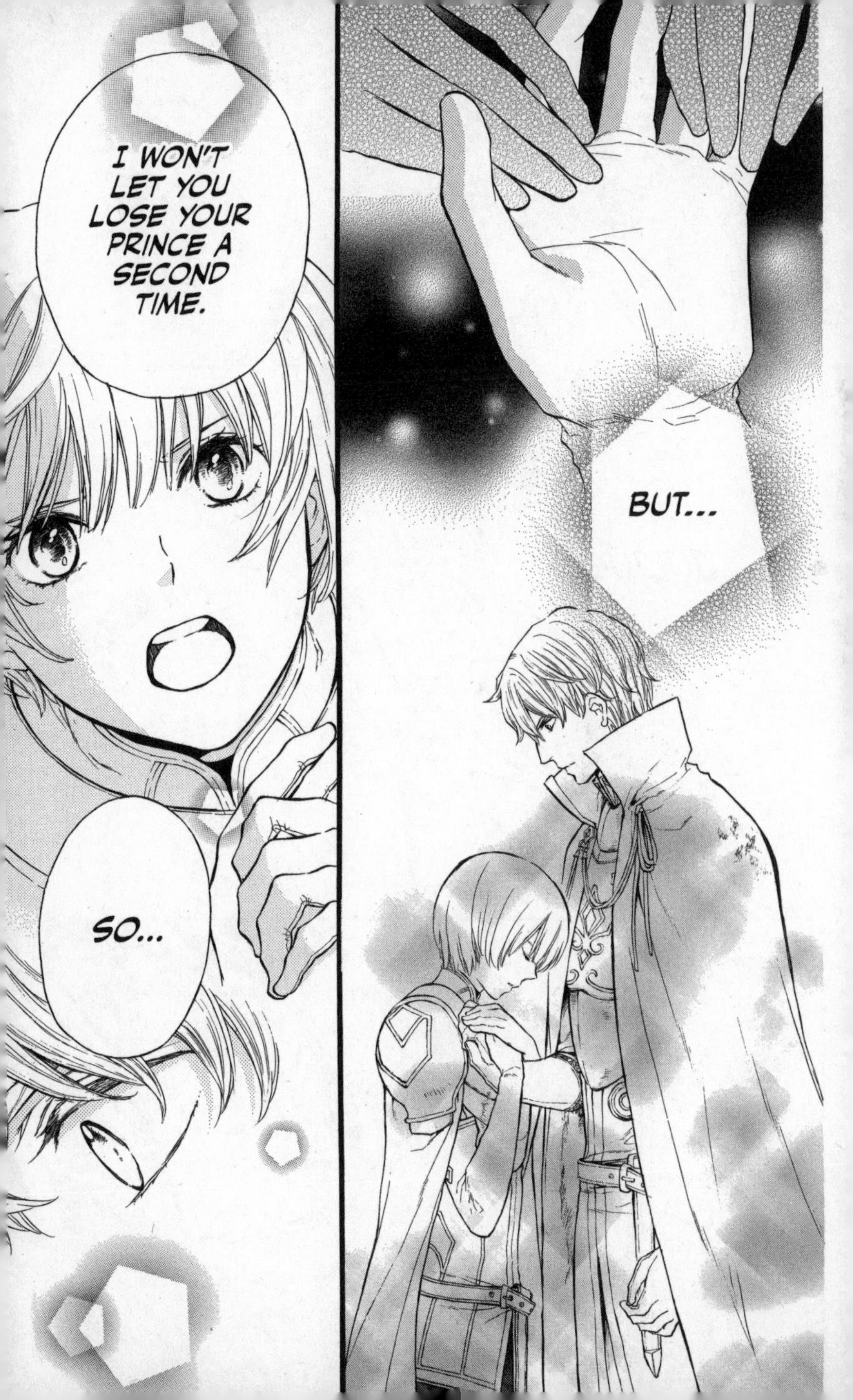
BUT...
I WON'T LET YOU LOSE YOUR PRINCE A SECOND TIME.
SO...

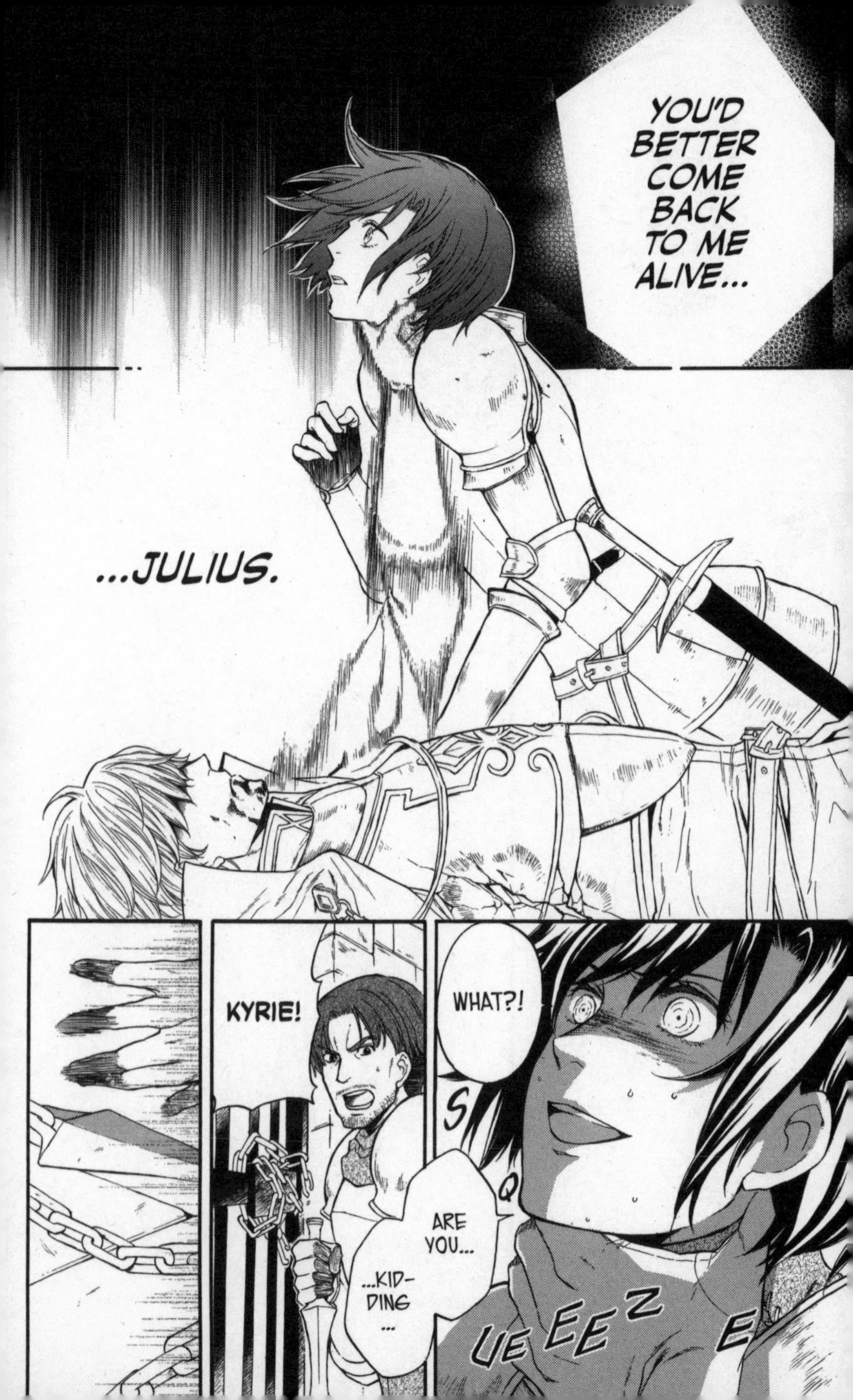
YOU'D BETTER COME BACK TO ME ALIVE...
...JULIUS.
WHAT?!
ARE YOU...
...KID-DING...
SQUEEEZE
KYRIE!

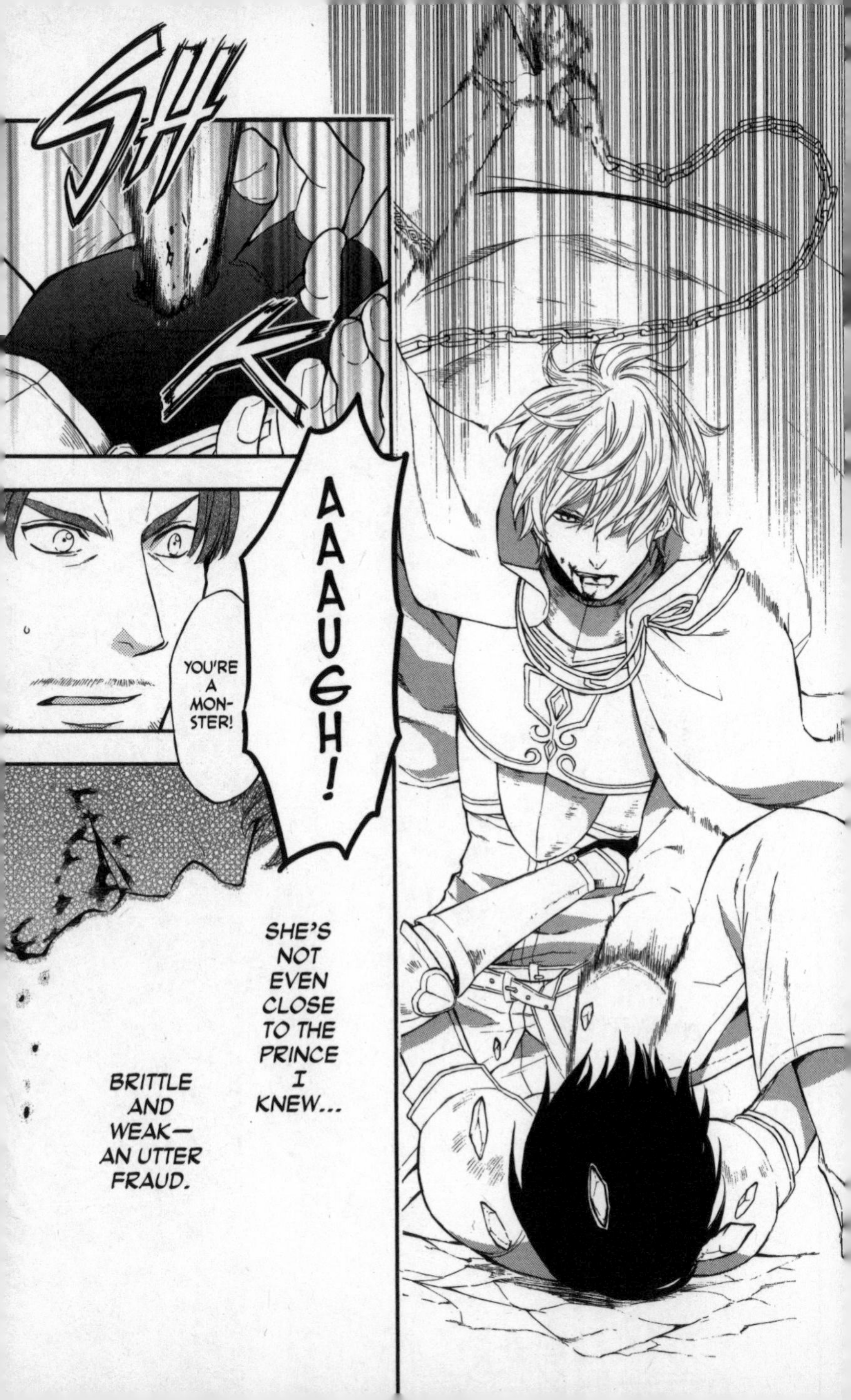
AAAUGH!
SHK
YOU'RE A MON-STER!
SHE'S NOT EVEN CLOSE TO THE PRINCE I KNEW...
BRITTLE AND WEAK—AN UTTER FRAUD.

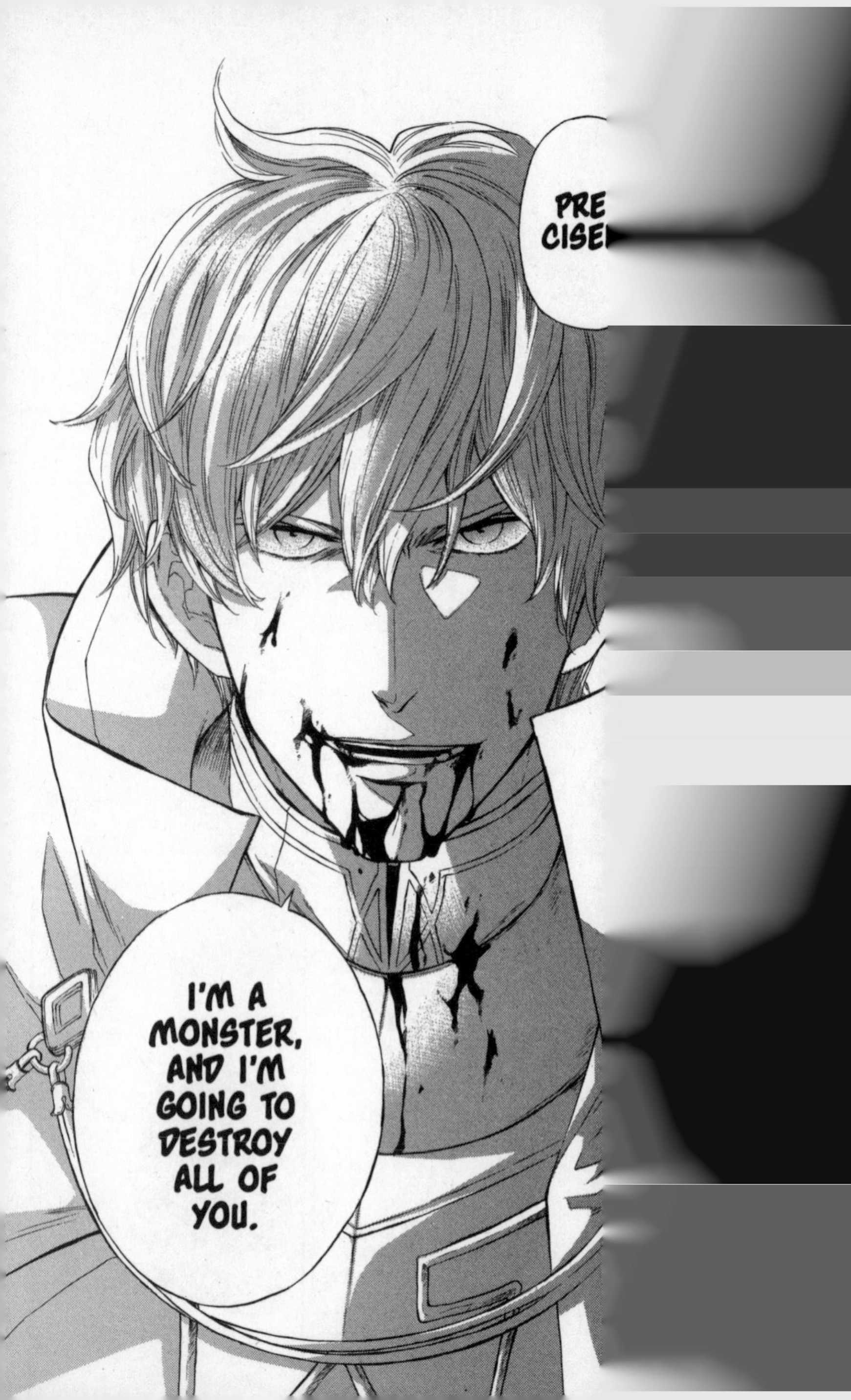
PRE CISE
I'M A MONSTER, AND I'M GOING TO DESTROY ALL OF YOU.

Chapter 9 The Shining Prince, Part 2

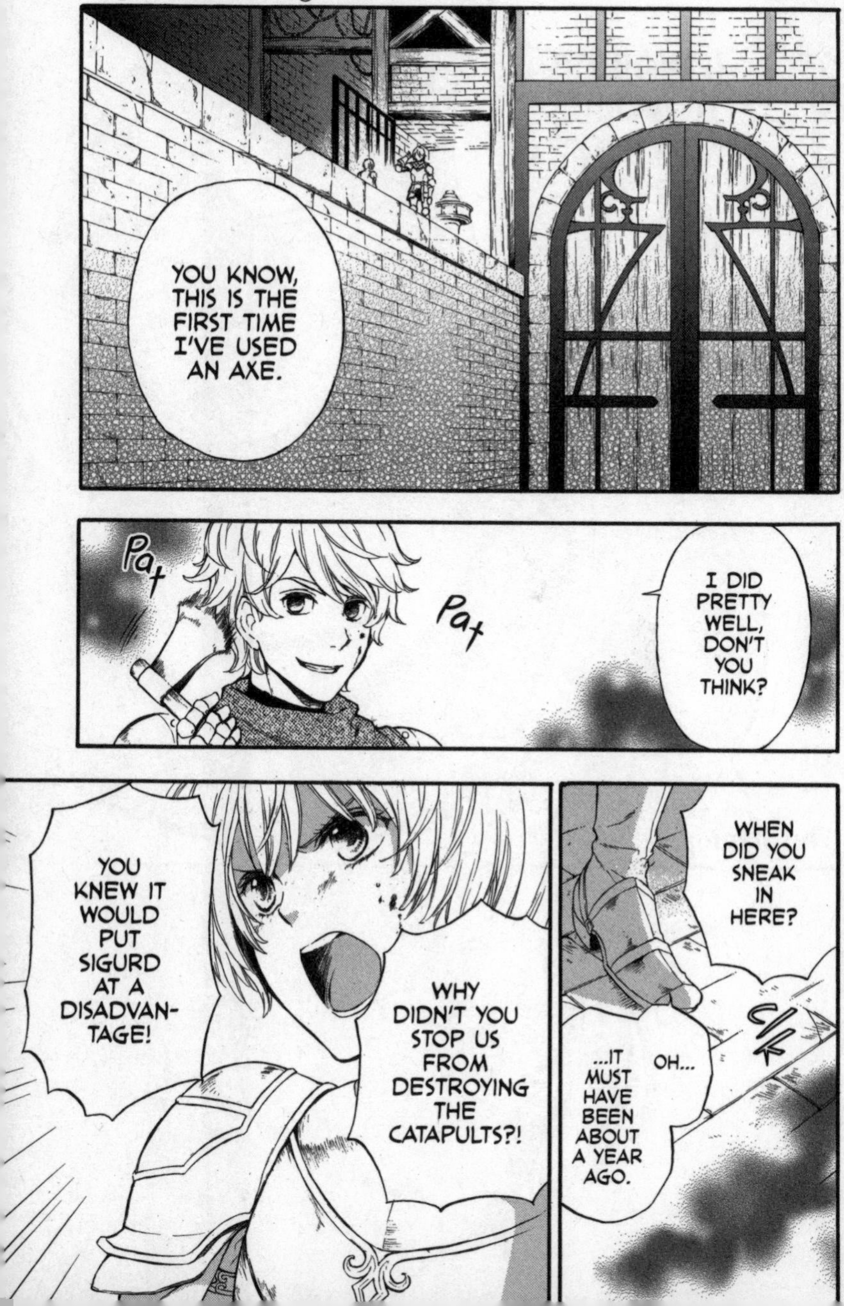
YOU KNOW, THIS IS THE FIRST TIME I'VE USED AN AXE.
I DID PRETTY WELL, DON'T YOU THINK?
Pat
Pat
WHEN DID YOU SNEAK IN HERE?
Clk
OH...
...IT MUST HAVE BEEN ABOUT A YEAR AGO.
WHY DIDN'T YOU STOP US FROM DESTROYING THE CATAPULTS?!
YOU KNEW IT WOULD PUT SIGURD AT A DISADVAN-TAGE!

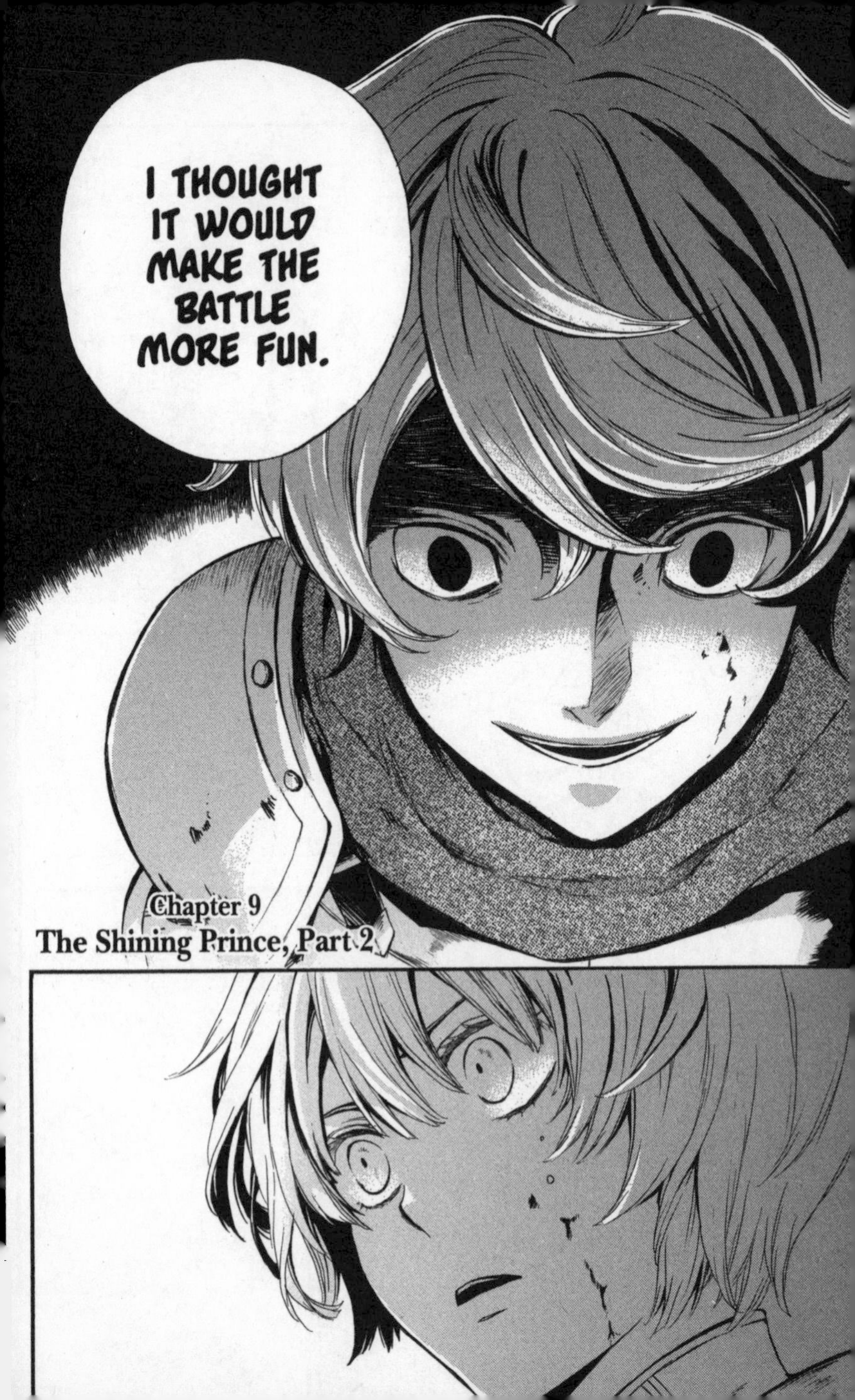
I THOUGHT IT WOULD MAKE THE BATTLE MORE FUN.

Chapter 9
The Shining Prince, Part 2

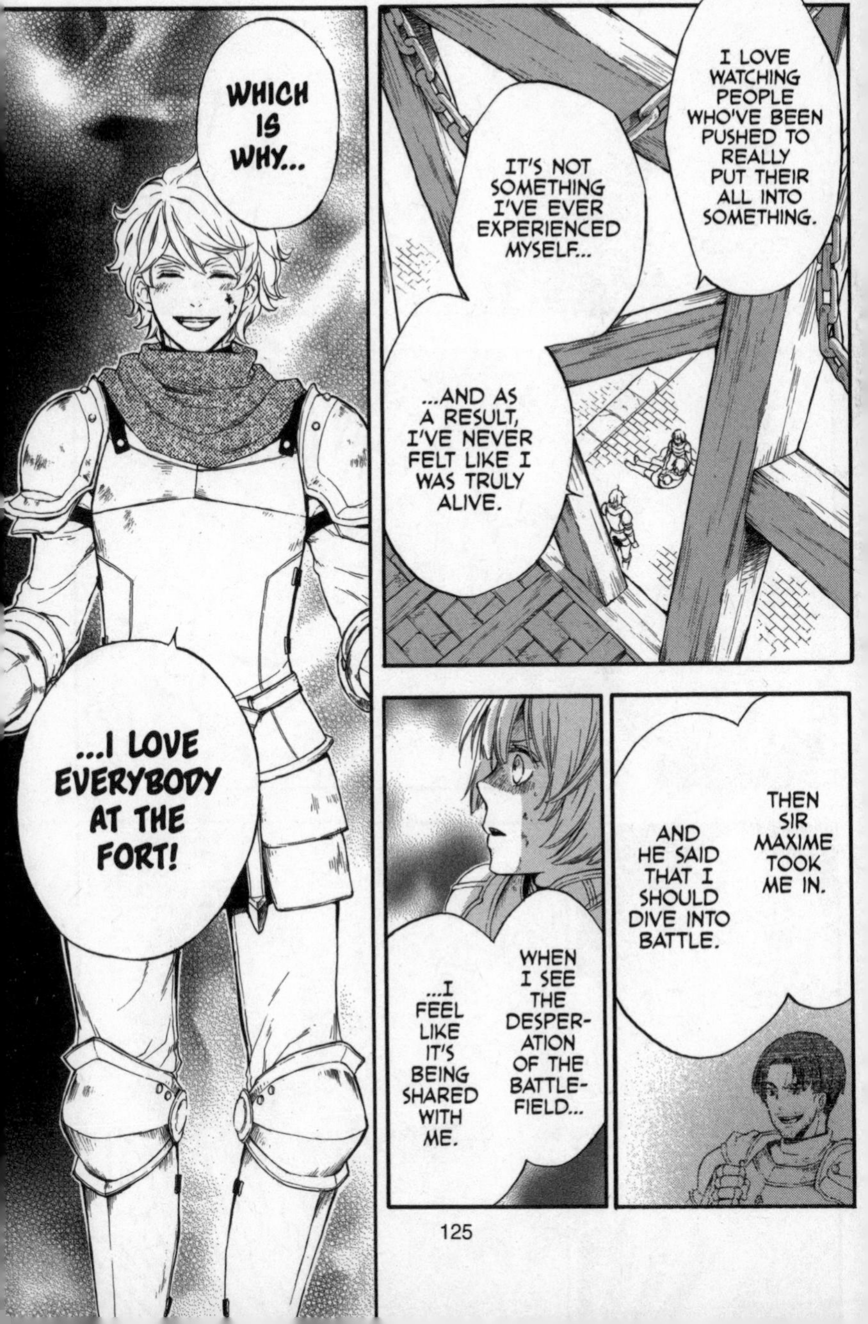
I LOVE WATCHING PEOPLE WHO'VE BEEN PUSHED TO REALLY PUT THEIR ALL INTO SOMETHING.
IT'S NOT SOMETHING I'VE EVER EXPERIENCED MYSELF...
...AND AS A RESULT, I'VE NEVER FELT LIKE I WAS TRULY ALIVE.
THEN SIR MAXIME TOOK ME IN.
AND HE SAID THAT I SHOULD DIVE INTO BATTLE.
WHEN I SEE THE DESPERATION OF THE BATTLEFIELD...
...I FEEL LIKE IT'S BEING SHARED WITH ME.
WHICH IS WHY...
...I LOVE EVERYBODY AT THE FORT!

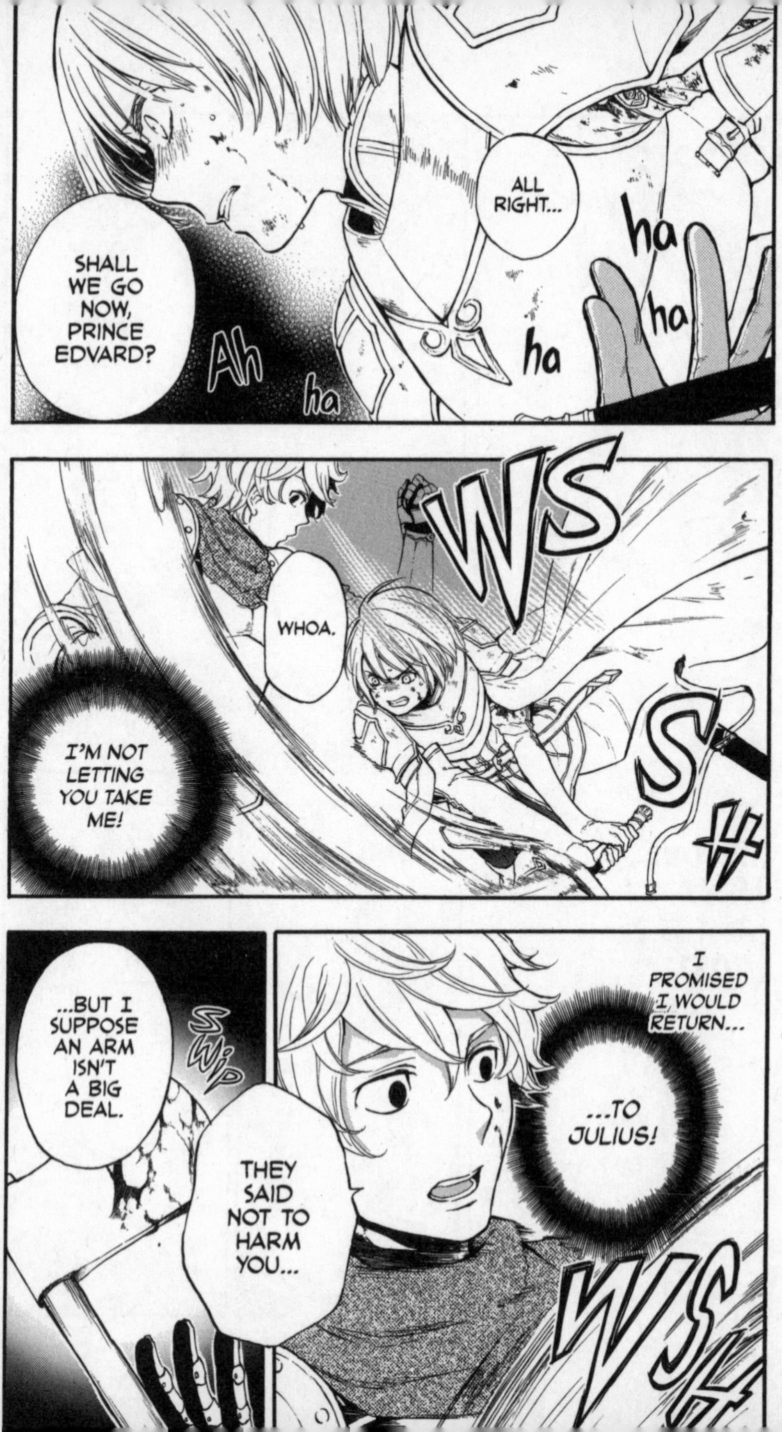
ALL RIGHT...
ha ha ha
SHALL WE GO NOW, PRINCE EDVARD?
Ah ha
WS
WHOA.
S
I'M NOT LETTING YOU TAKE ME!
I PROMISED I WOULD RETURN...
...TO JULIUS!
THEY SAID NOT TO HARM YOU...
WSH
...BUT I SUPPOSE AN ARM ISN'T A BIG DEAL.
SWIP

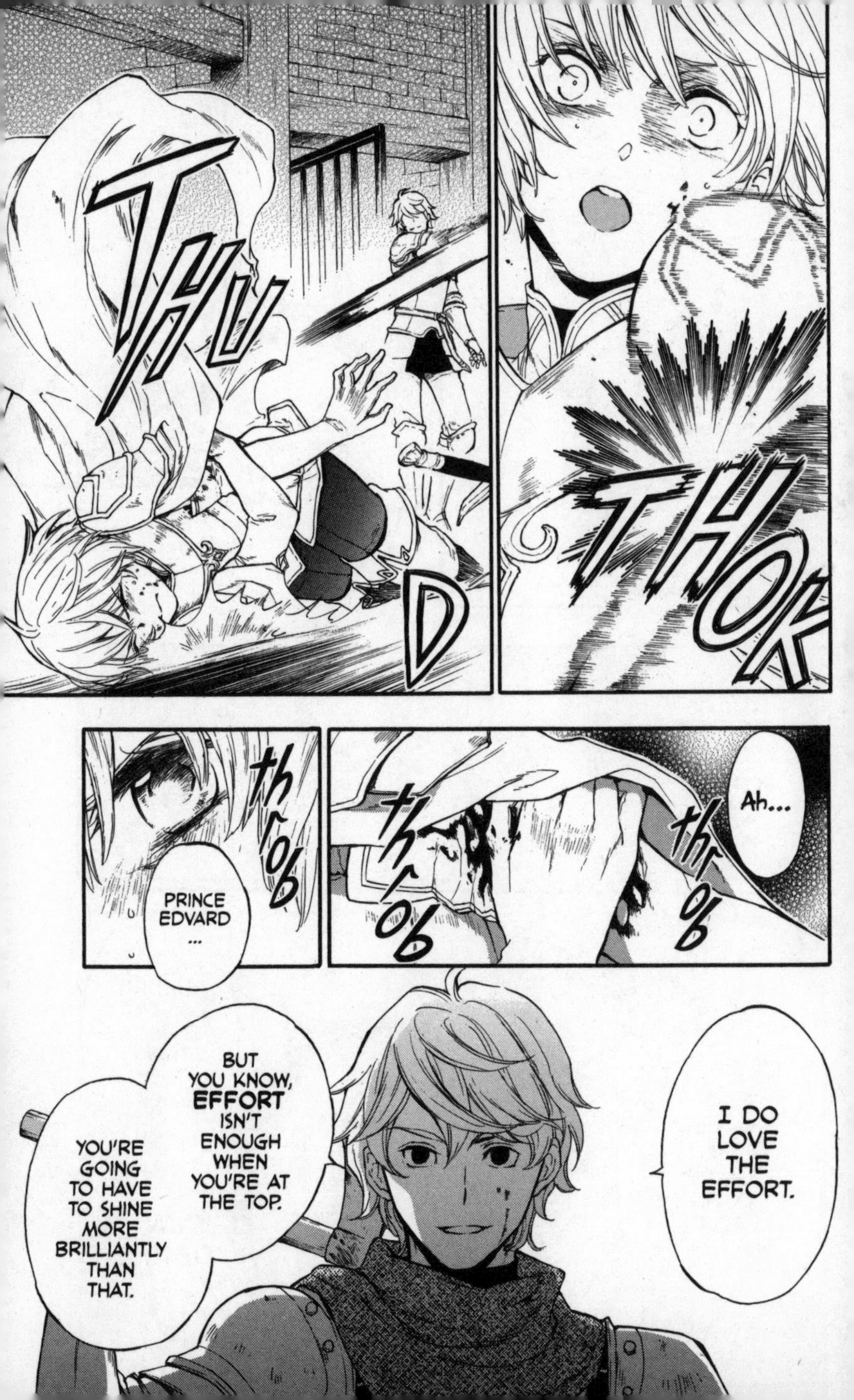
THOK
THUD
Ah...
throb
throb
throb
PRINCE EDVARD...
I DO LOVE THE EFFORT.
BUT YOU KNOW, EFFORT ISN'T ENOUGH WHEN YOU'RE AT THE TOP.
YOU'RE GOING TO HAVE TO SHINE MORE BRILLIANTLY THAN THAT.

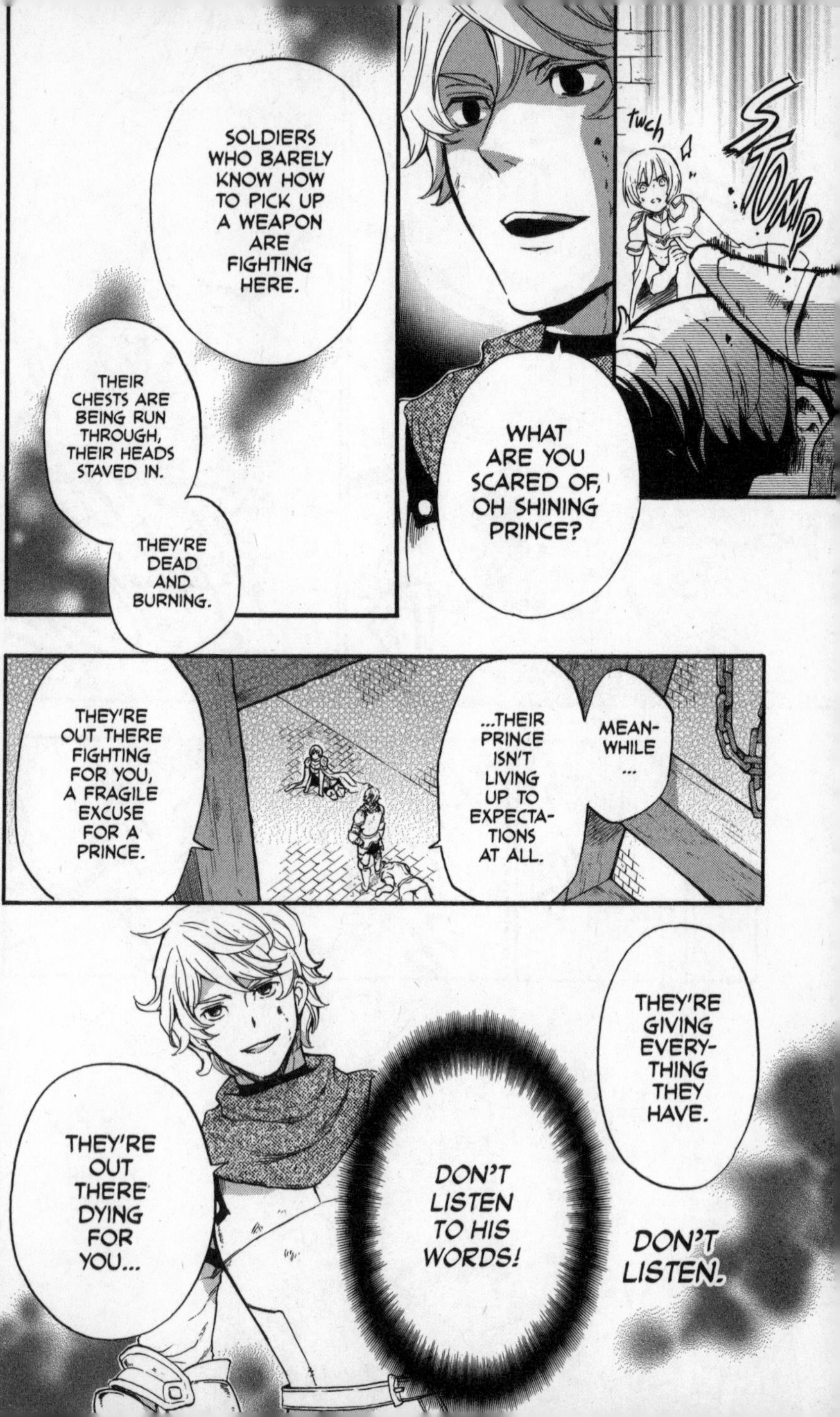
twch
STOMP
WHAT ARE YOU SCARED OF, OH SHINING PRINCE?
SOLDIERS WHO BARELY KNOW HOW TO PICK UP A WEAPON ARE FIGHTING HERE.
THEIR CHESTS ARE BEING RUN THROUGH, THEIR HEADS STAVED IN.
THEY'RE DEAD AND BURNING.
MEAN-WHILE...
...THEIR PRINCE ISN'T LIVING UP TO EXPECTA-TIONS AT ALL.
THEY'RE OUT THERE FIGHTING FOR YOU, A FRAGILE EXCUSE FOR A PRINCE.
THEY'RE GIVING EVERY-THING THEY HAVE.
THEY'RE OUT THERE DYING FOR YOU...
DON'T LISTEN TO HIS WORDS!
DON'T LISTEN.

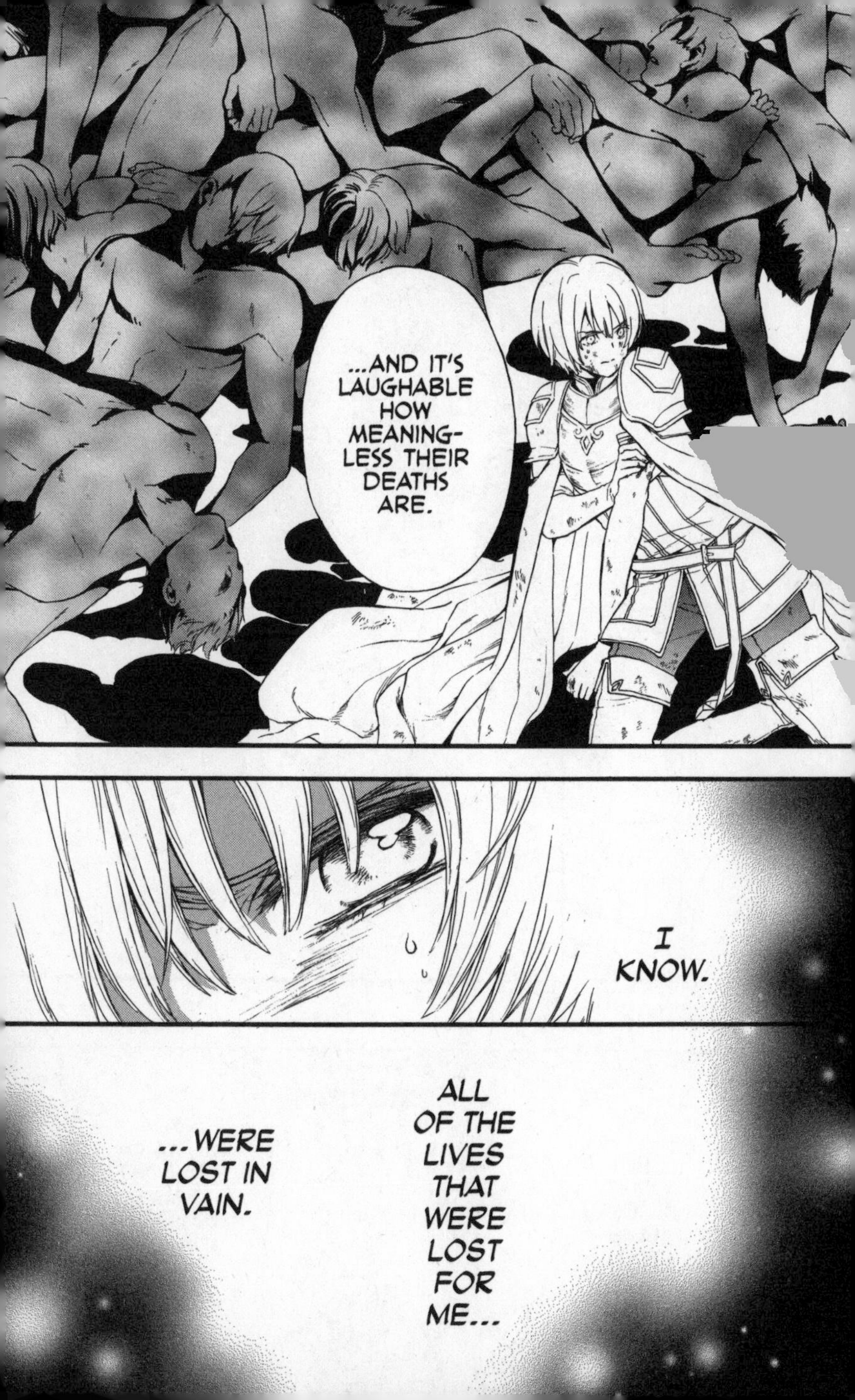
...AND IT'S LAUGHABLE HOW MEANINGLESS THEIR DEATHS ARE.
I KNOW.
ALL OF THE LIVES THAT WERE LOST FOR ME...
...WERE LOST IN VAIN.

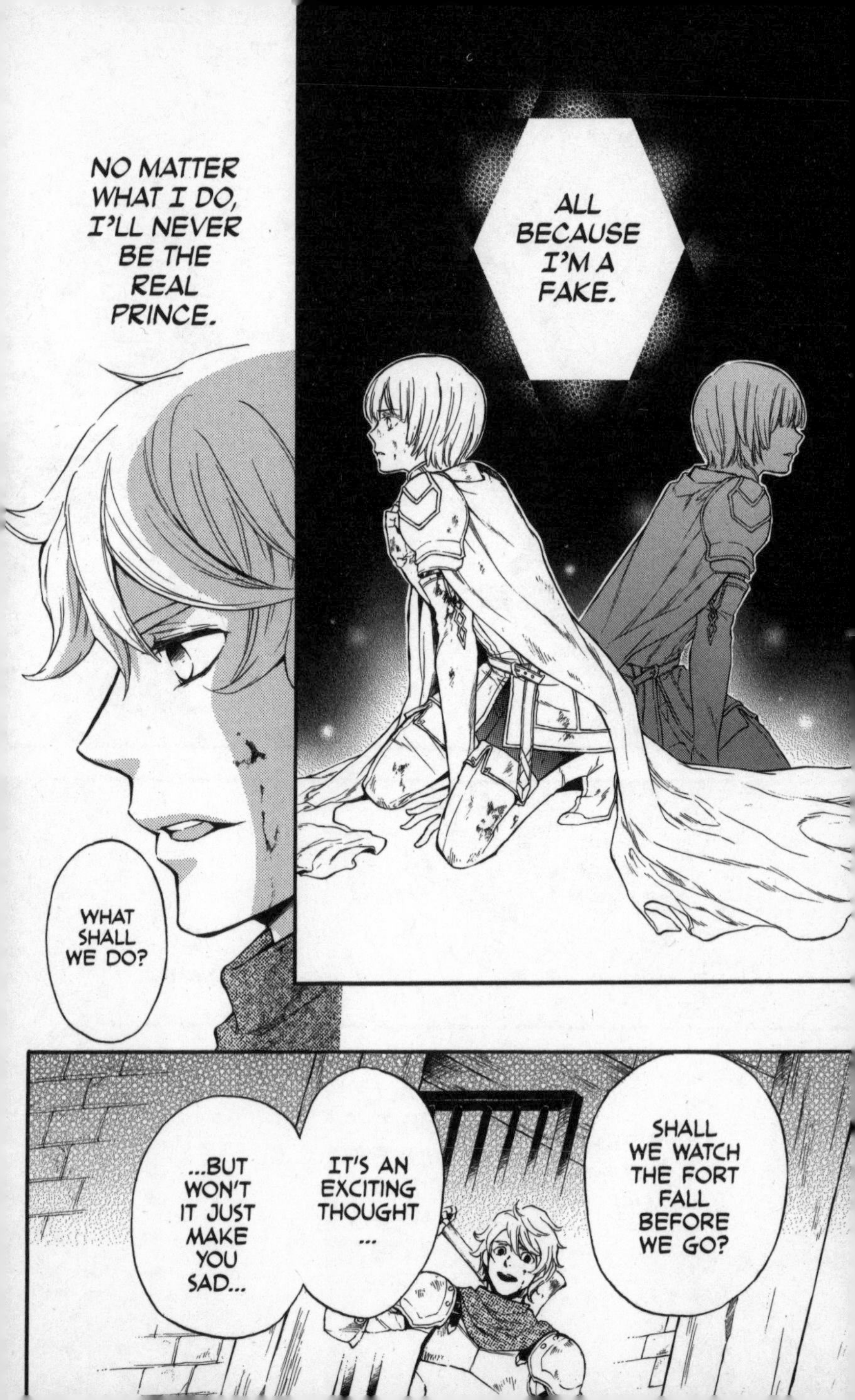
ALL BECAUSE I'M A FAKE.
NO MATTER WHAT I DO, I'LL NEVER BE THE REAL PRINCE.
WHAT SHALL WE DO?
SHALL WE WATCH THE FORT FALL BEFORE WE GO?
IT'S AN EXCITING THOUGHT...
...BUT WON'T IT JUST MAKE YOU SAD...

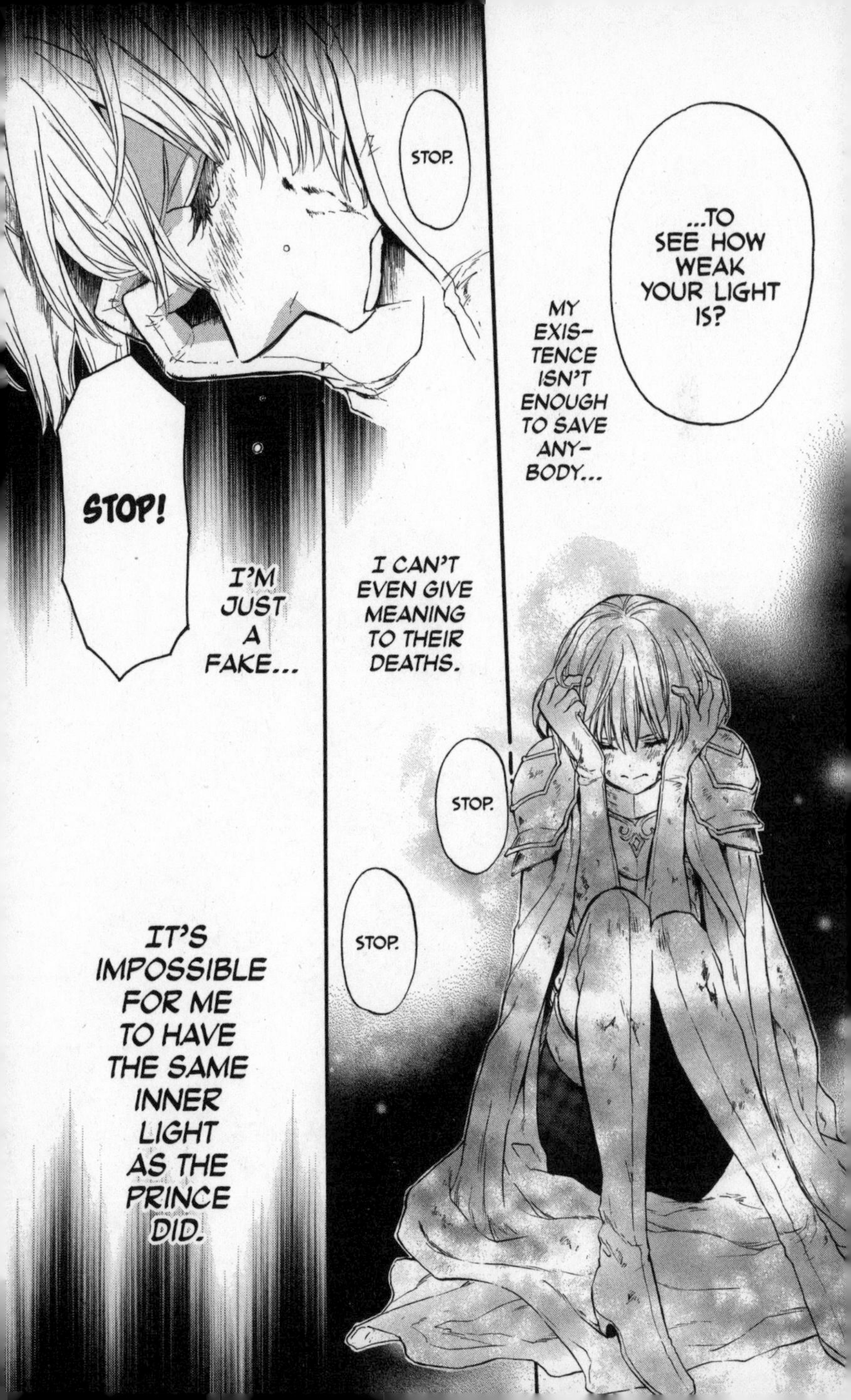
...TO SEE HOW WEAK YOUR LIGHT IS?
MY EXISTENCE ISN'T ENOUGH TO SAVE ANYBODY...
I CAN'T EVEN GIVE MEANING TO THEIR DEATHS.
STOP.
STOP.
STOP.
STOP!
I'M JUST A FAKE...
IT'S IMPOSSIBLE FOR ME TO HAVE THE SAME INNER LIGHT AS THE PRINCE DID.

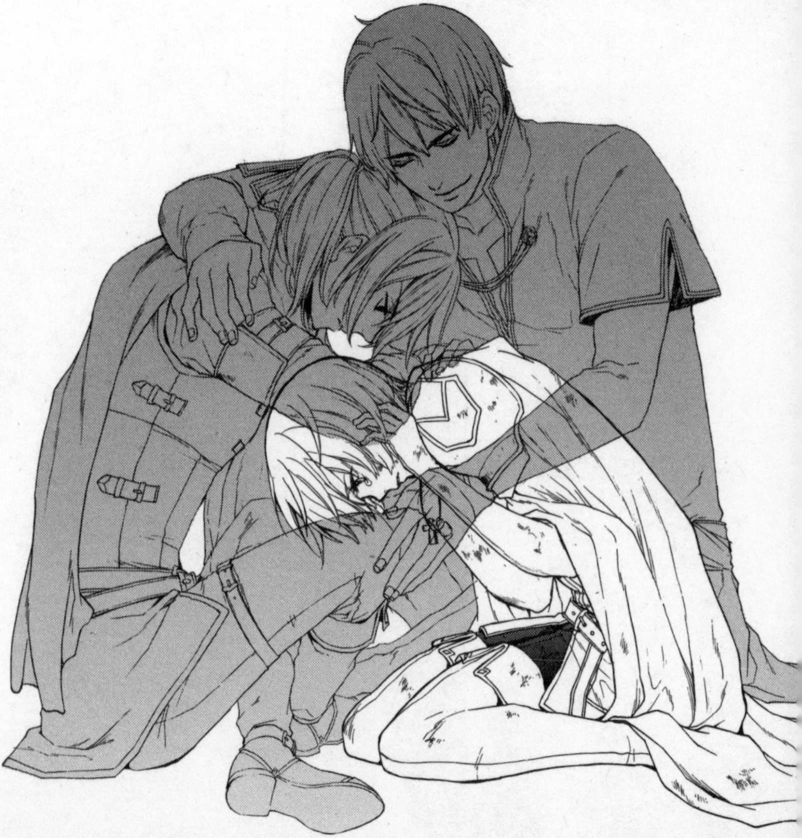

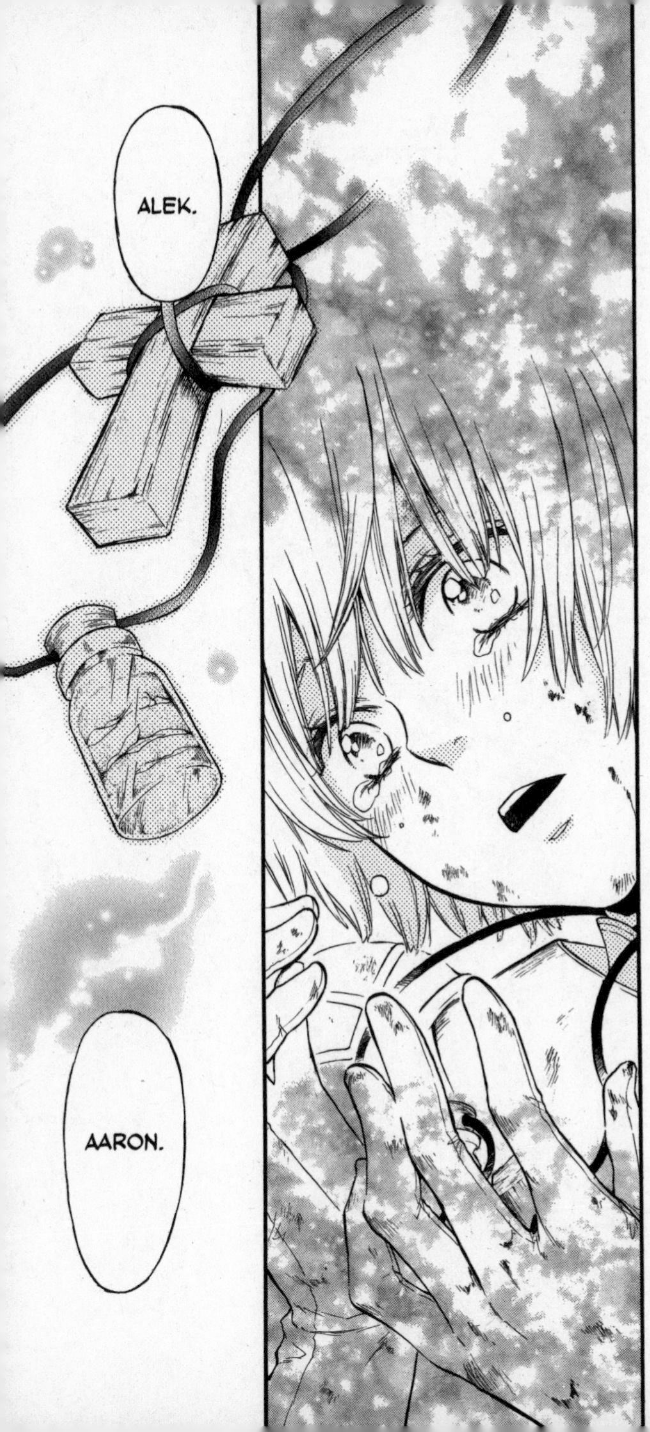
ALEK.
AARON.

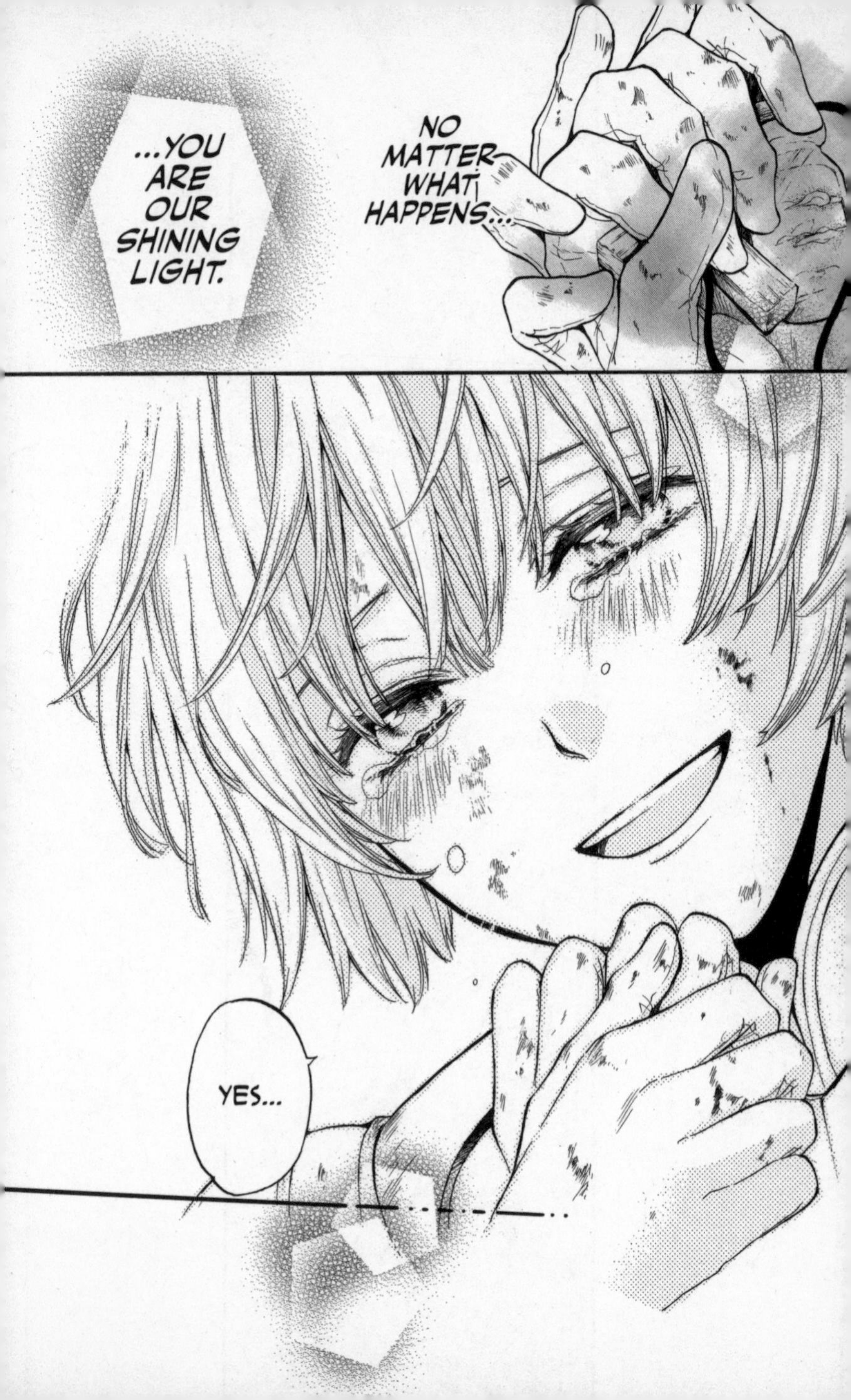
NO MATTER WHAT HAPPENS...
...YOU ARE OUR SHINING LIGHT.
YES...

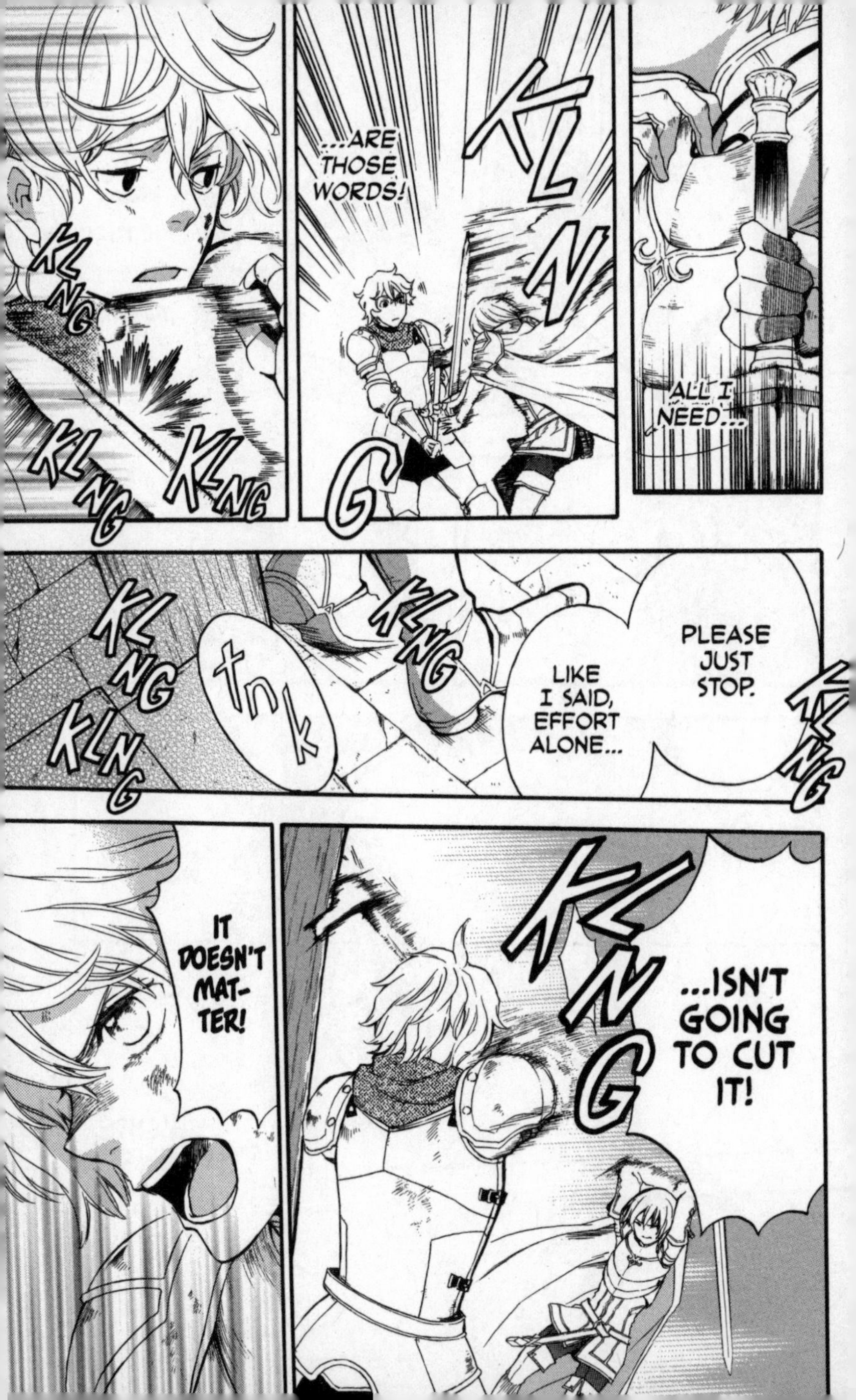
ALL I NEED...
...ARE THOSE WORDS!
KLNG
KLNG
KLNG
KLNG
KLNG
PLEASE JUST STOP.
LIKE I SAID, EFFORT ALONE...
KLNG
tnk
KLNG
KLNG
KLNG
...ISN'T GOING TO CUT IT!
IT DOESN'T MAT-TER!

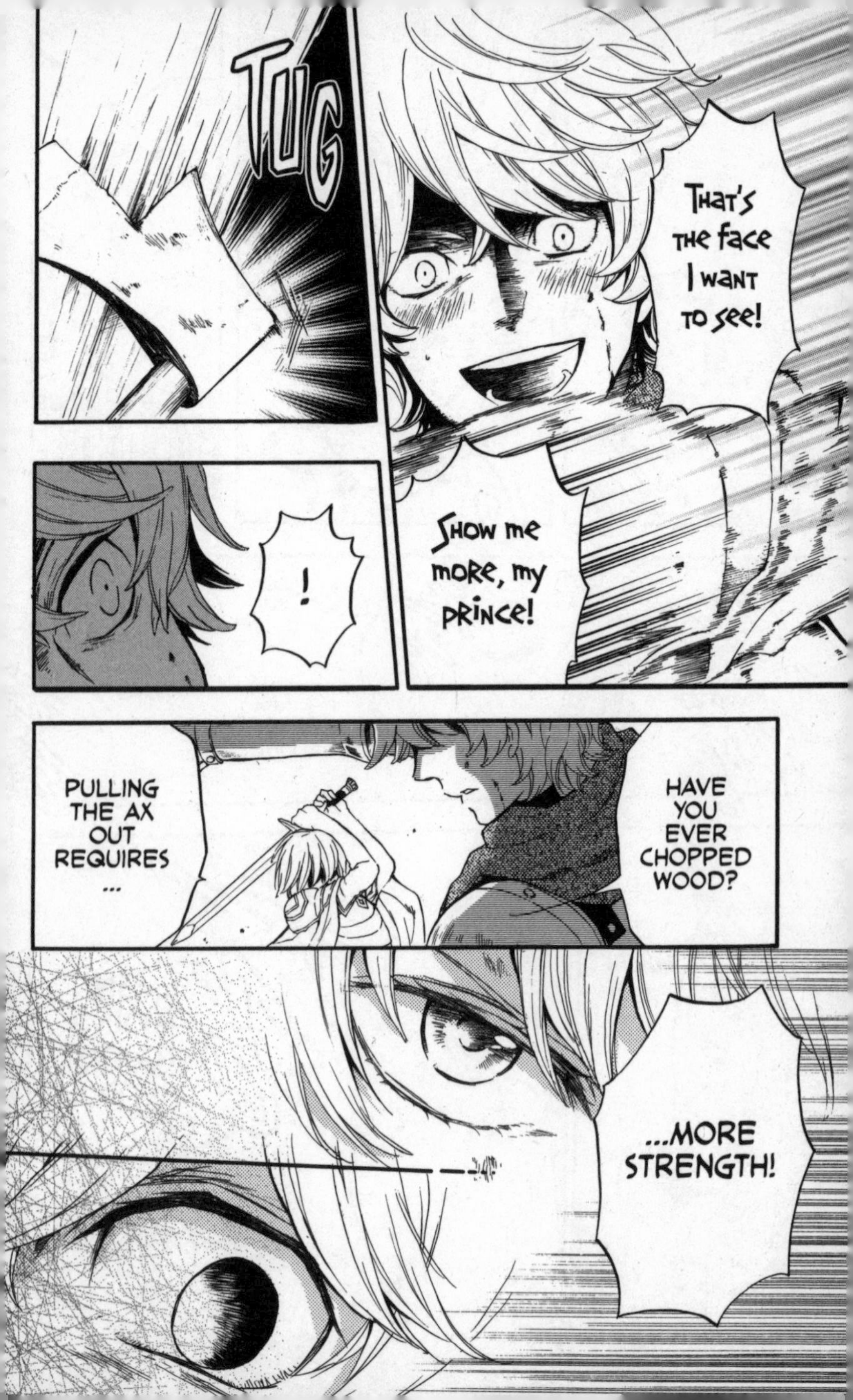
That's the face I want to see!
Show me more, my prince!
TUG
!
HAVE YOU EVER CHOPPED WOOD?
PULLING THE AX OUT REQUIRES ...
...MORE STRENGTH!

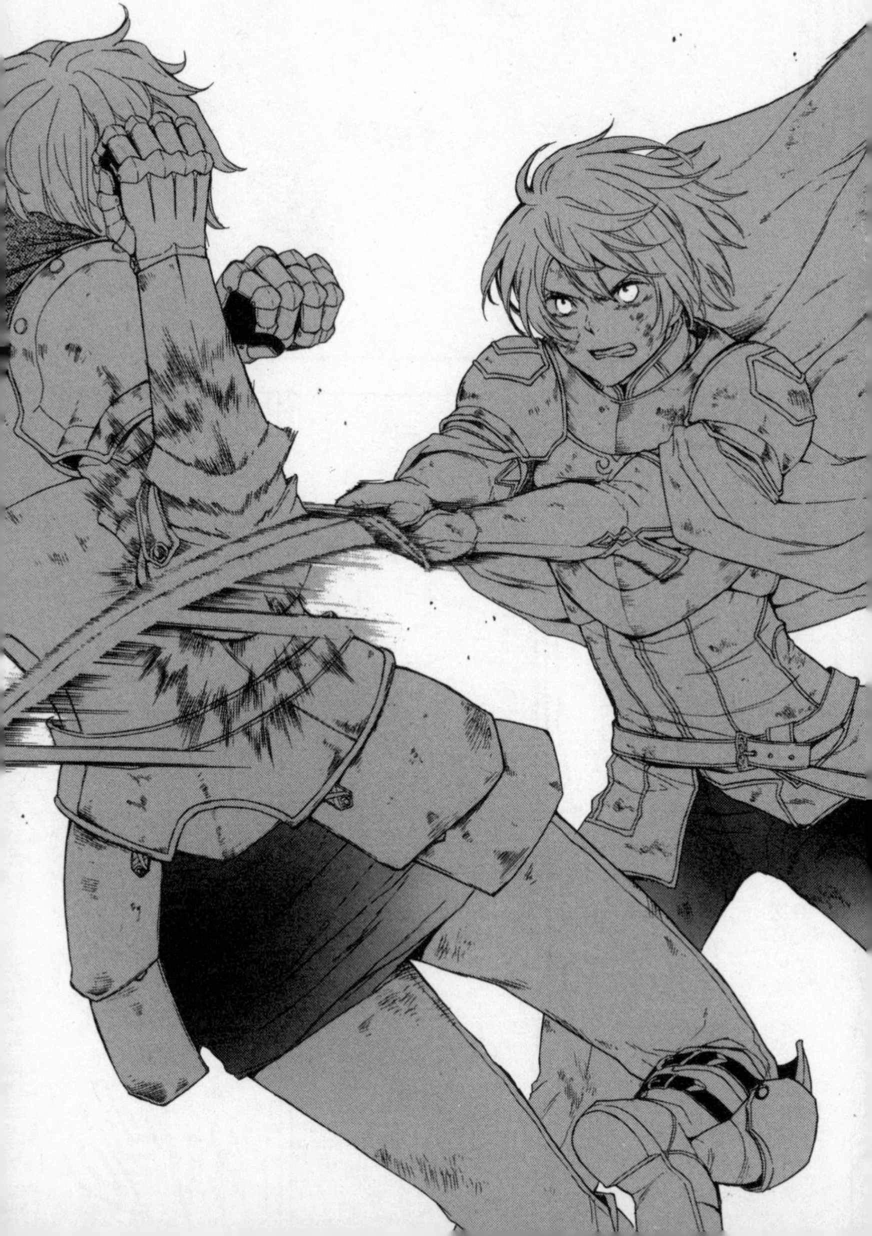

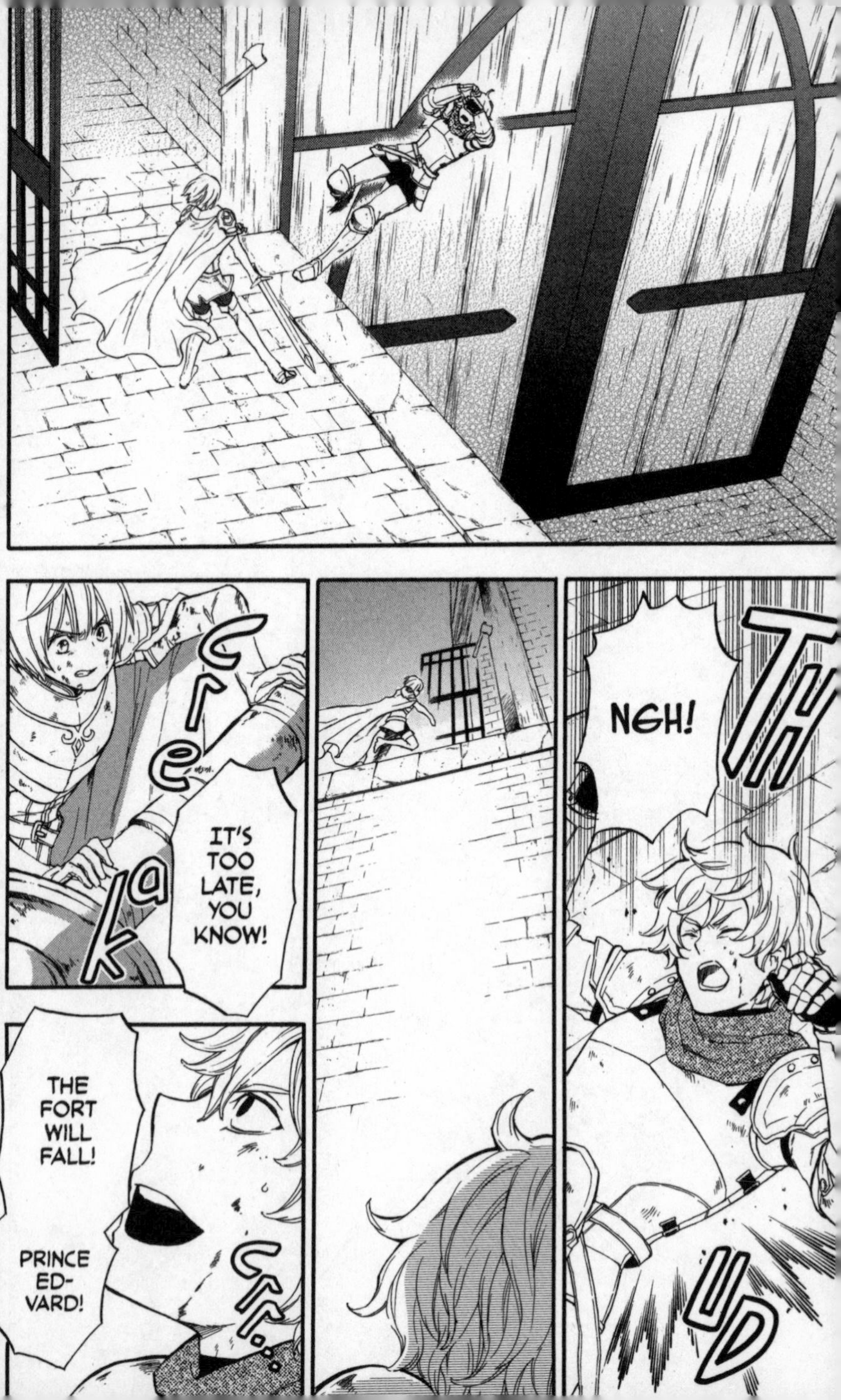
NGH!
THUD
Creak
IT'S TOO LATE, YOU KNOW!
THE FORT WILL FALL!
PRINCE ED-VARD!
Crr...

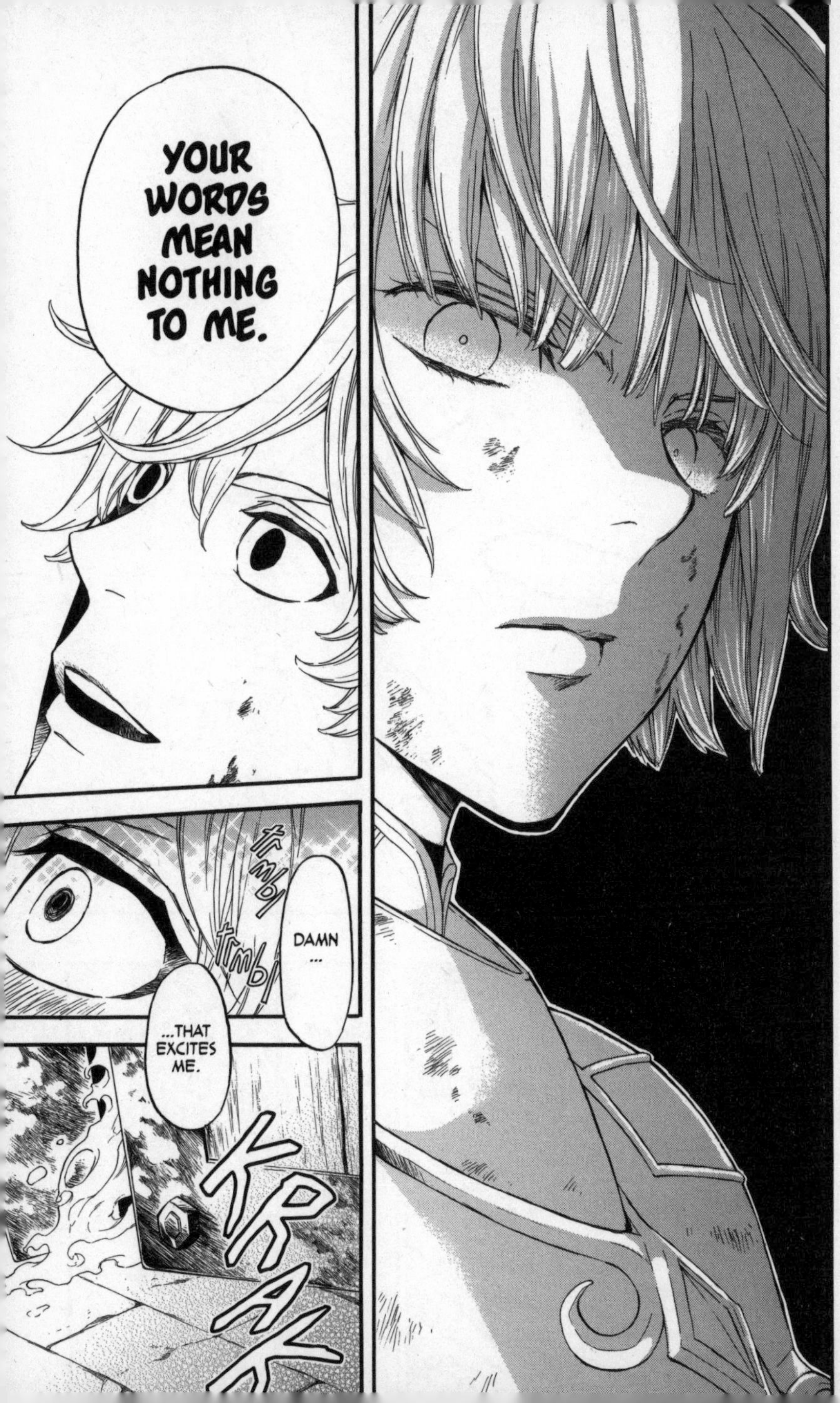
YOUR WORDS MEAN NOTHING TO ME.
trmbl
trmbl
DAMN...
...THAT EXCITES ME.
KRAK

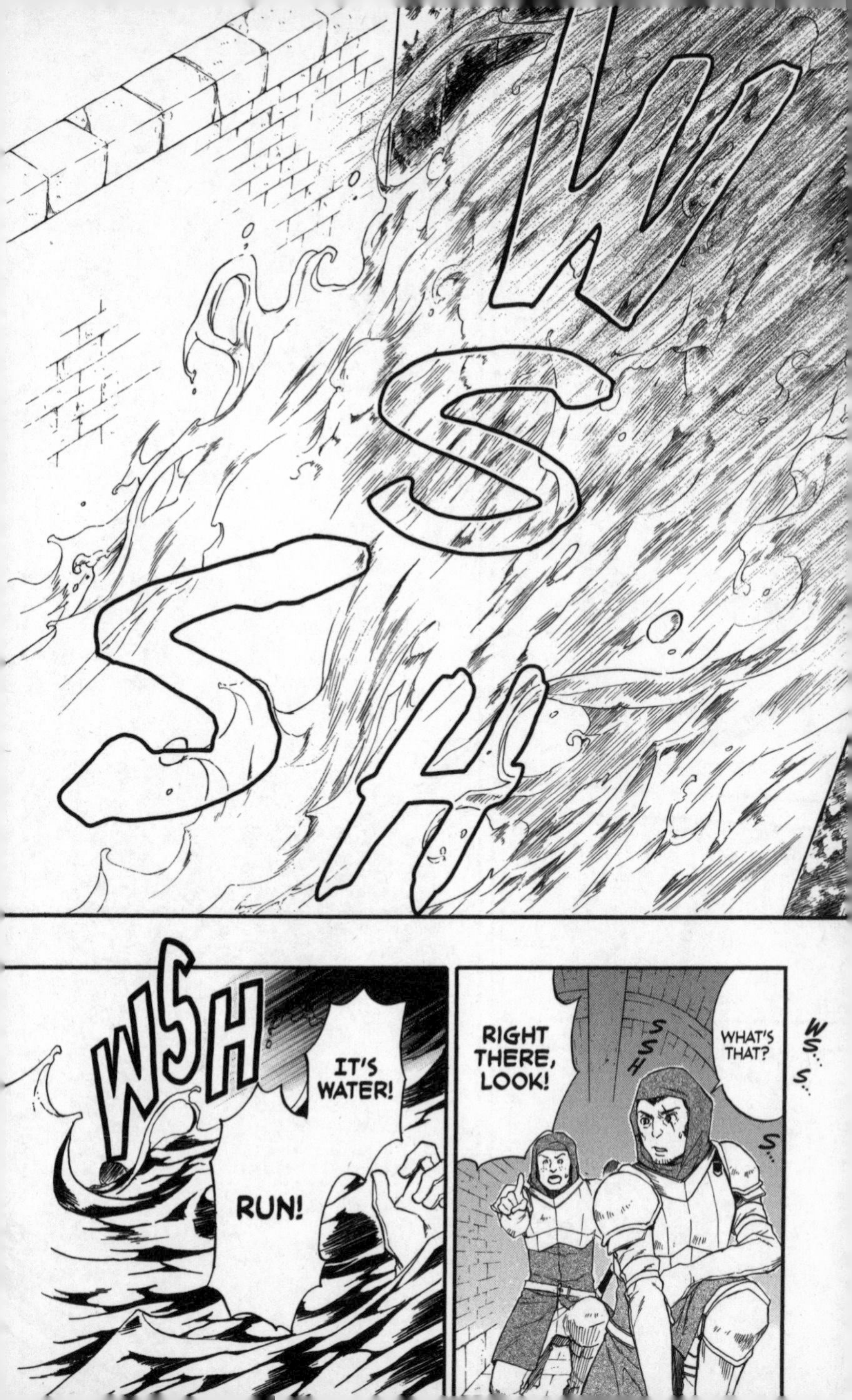
WSSH
WS... S...
WHAT'S THAT?
SSH
RIGHT THERE, LOOK!
S...
IT'S WATER!
RUN!
WSH

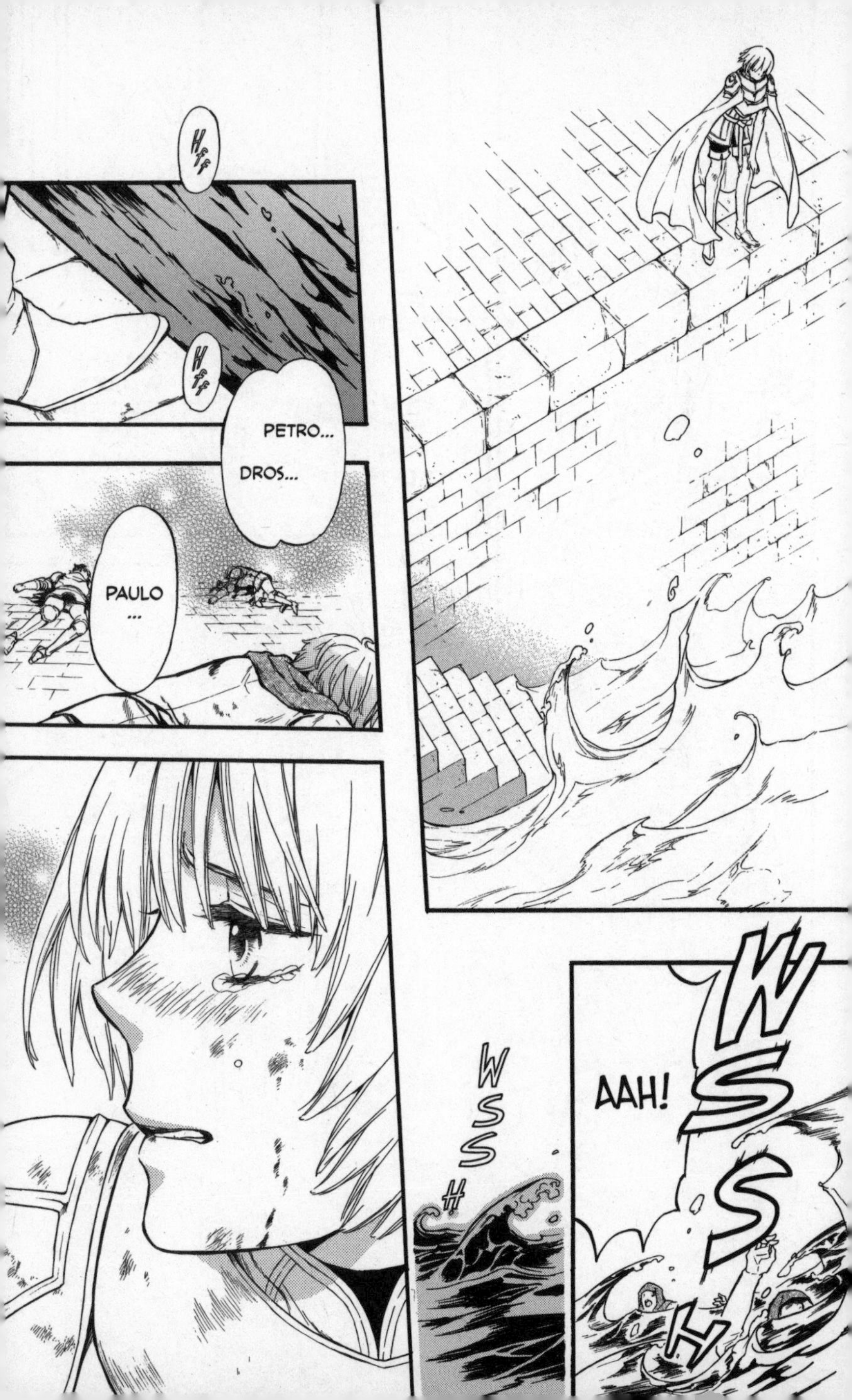
Hff
Hff
PETRO... DROS...
PAULO ...
WSSH
AAH!
WSSH

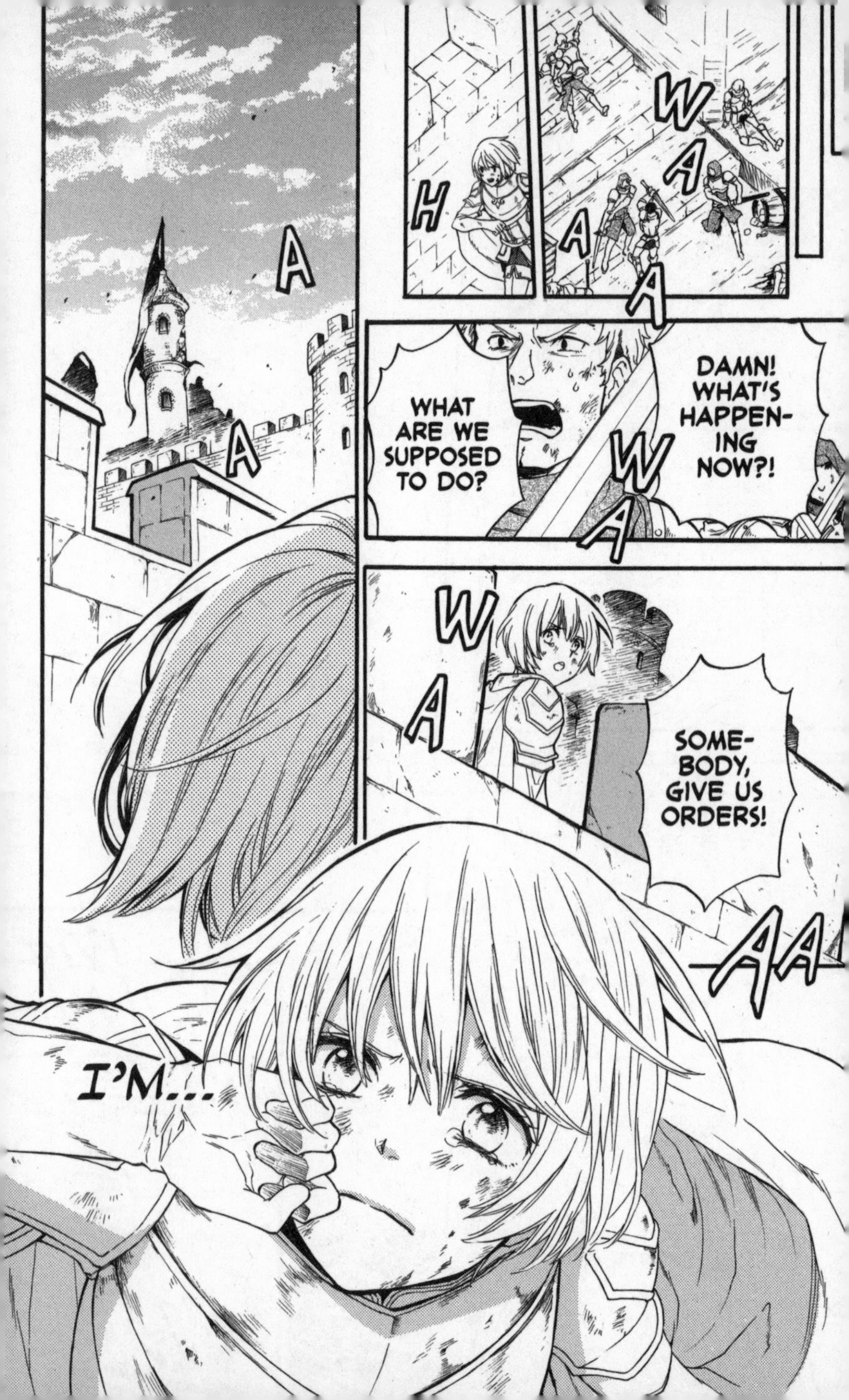
WA
HA
A
DAMN! WHAT'S HAPPEN-ING NOW?!
WHAT ARE WE SUPPOSED TO DO?
WA
WA
A
SOME-BODY, GIVE US ORDERS!
A
A
AA
I'M...

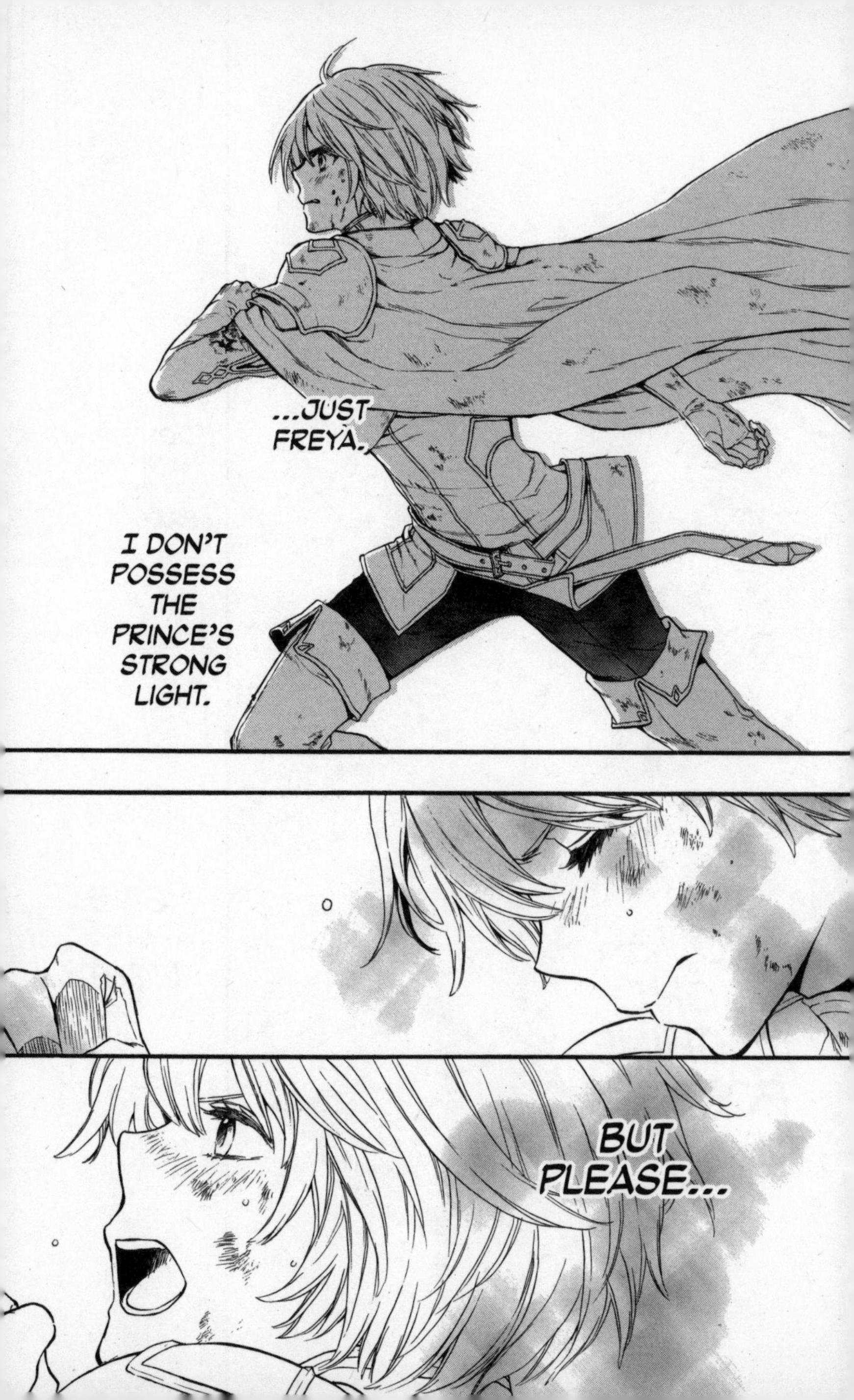
...JUST FREYA...
I DON'T POSSESS THE PRINCE'S STRONG LIGHT.
BUT PLEASE...

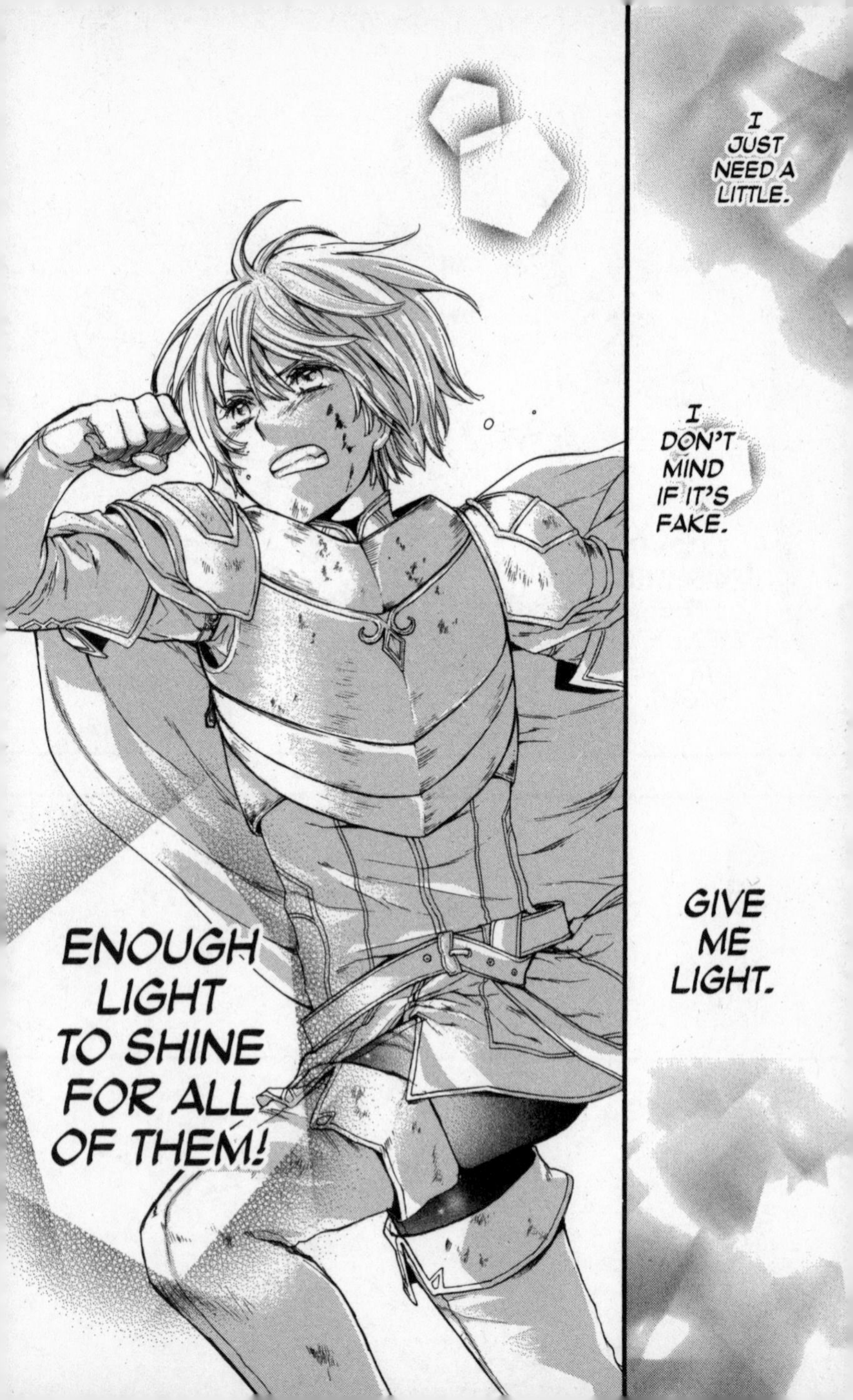
I JUST NEED A LITTLE.
I DON'T MIND IF IT'S FAKE.
GIVE ME LIGHT.
ENOUGH LIGHT TO SHINE FOR ALL OF THEM!

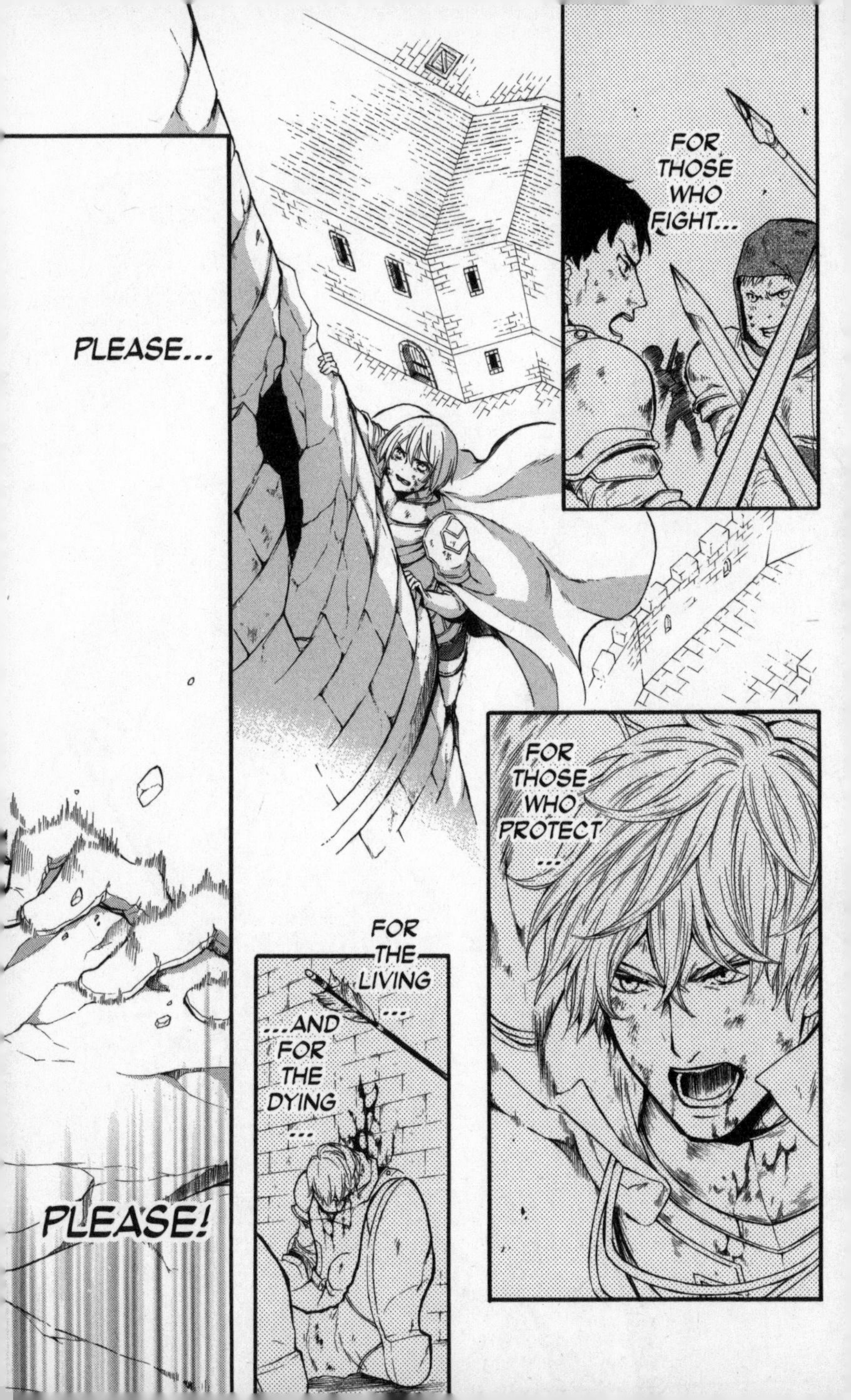
FOR THOSE WHO FIGHT...
FOR THOSE WHO PROTECT...
FOR THE LIVING...
...AND FOR THE DYING...
PLEASE...
PLEASE!

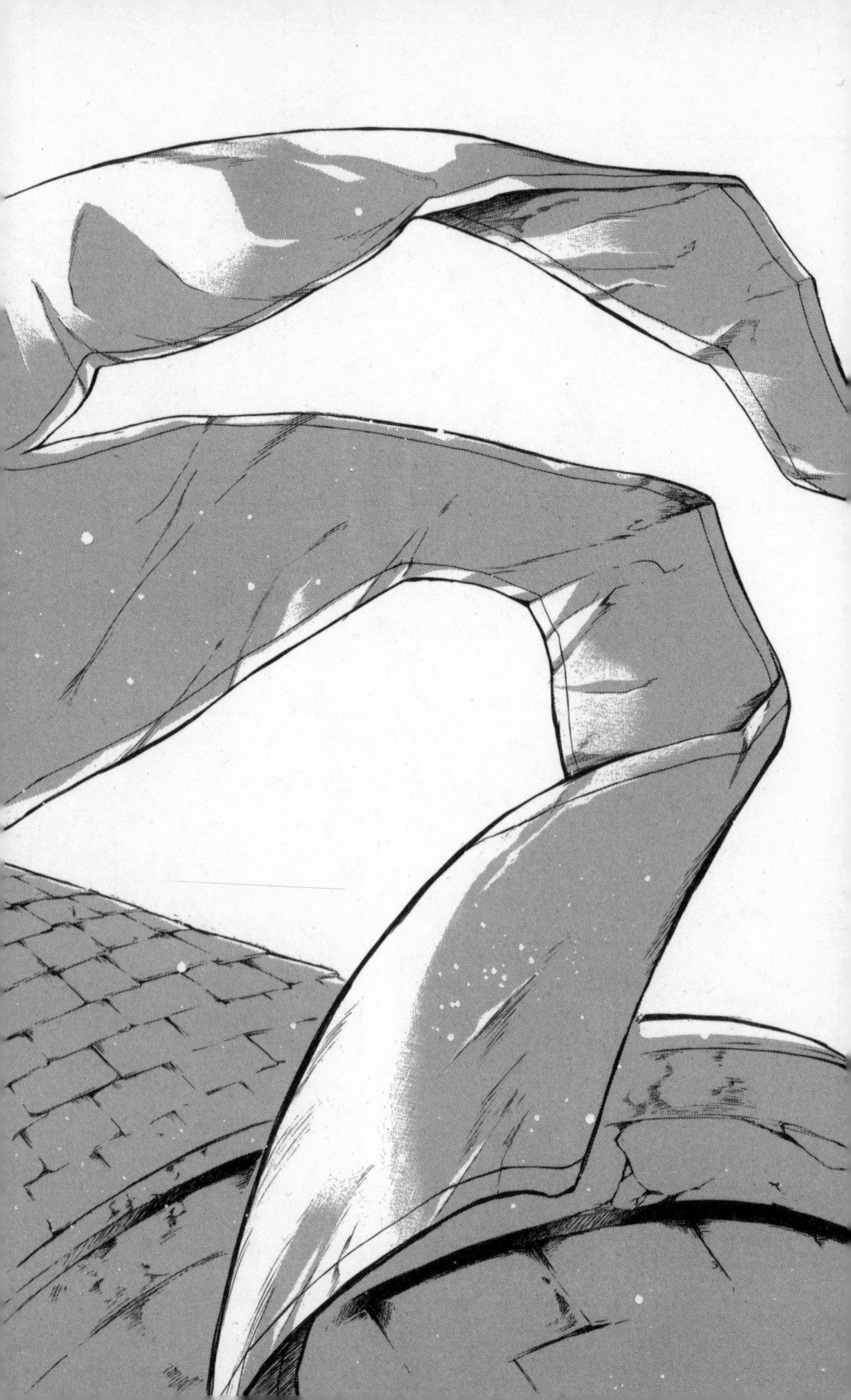

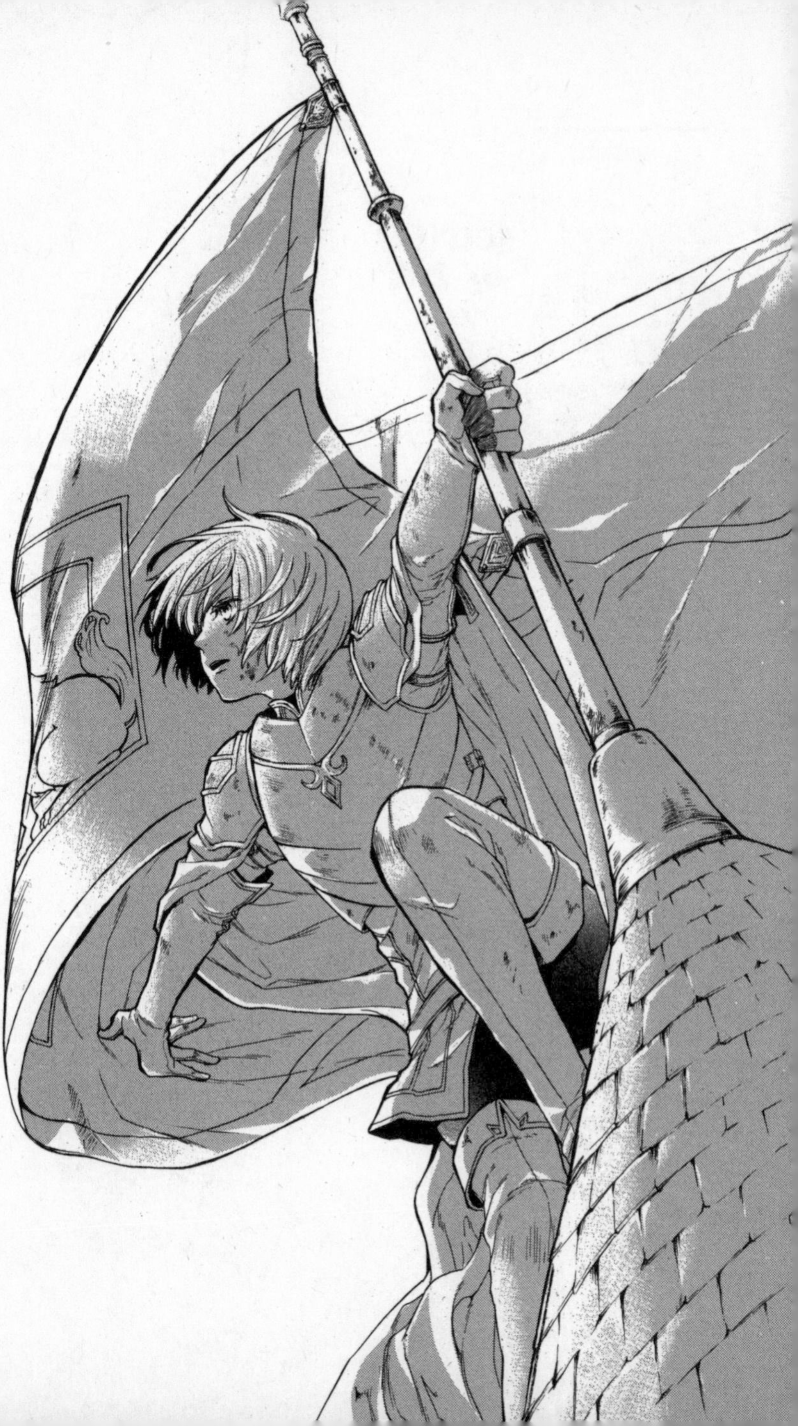

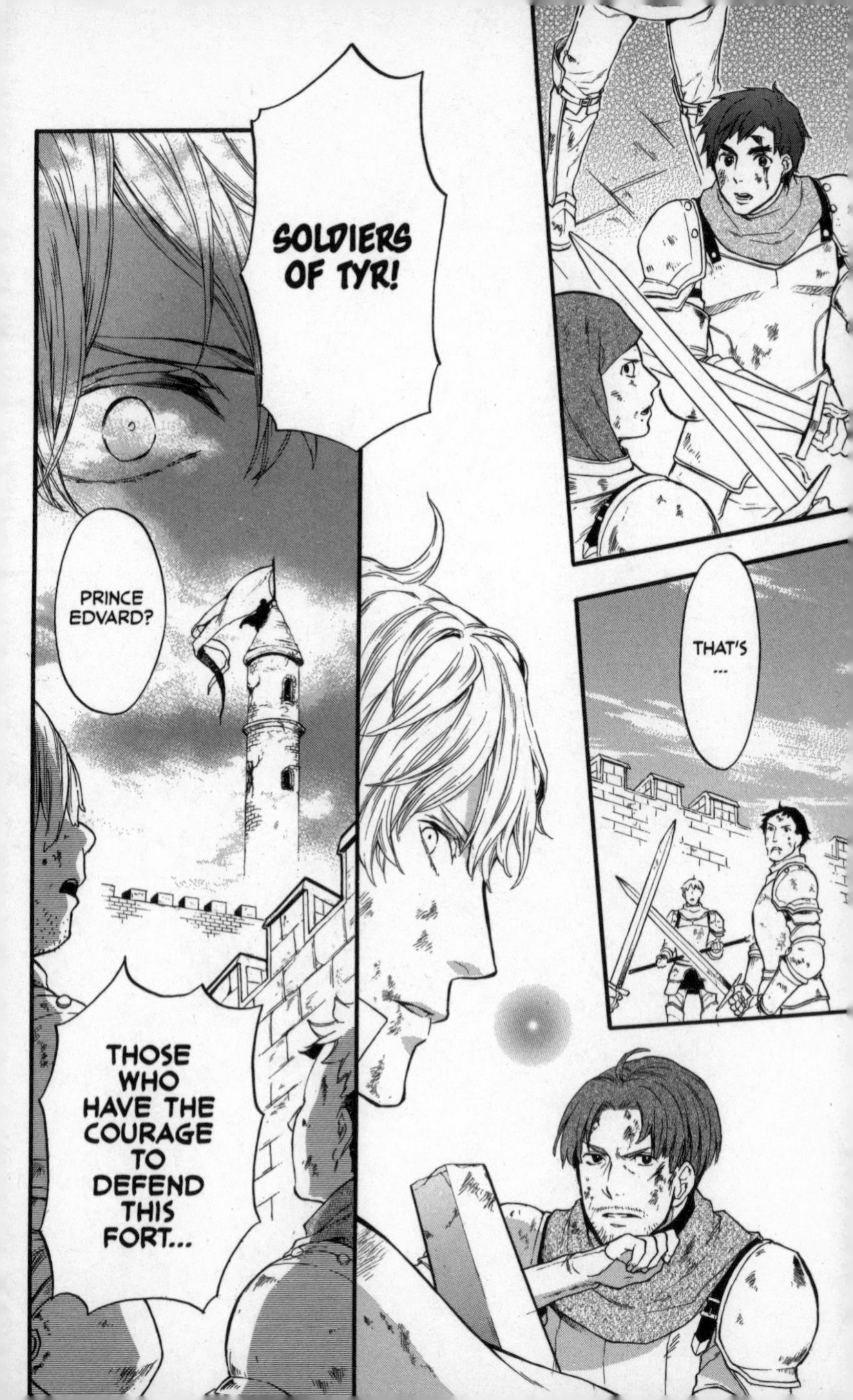
THAT'S ...
SOLDIERS OF TYR!
PRINCE EDVARD?
THOSE WHO HAVE THE COURAGE TO DEFEND THIS FORT...

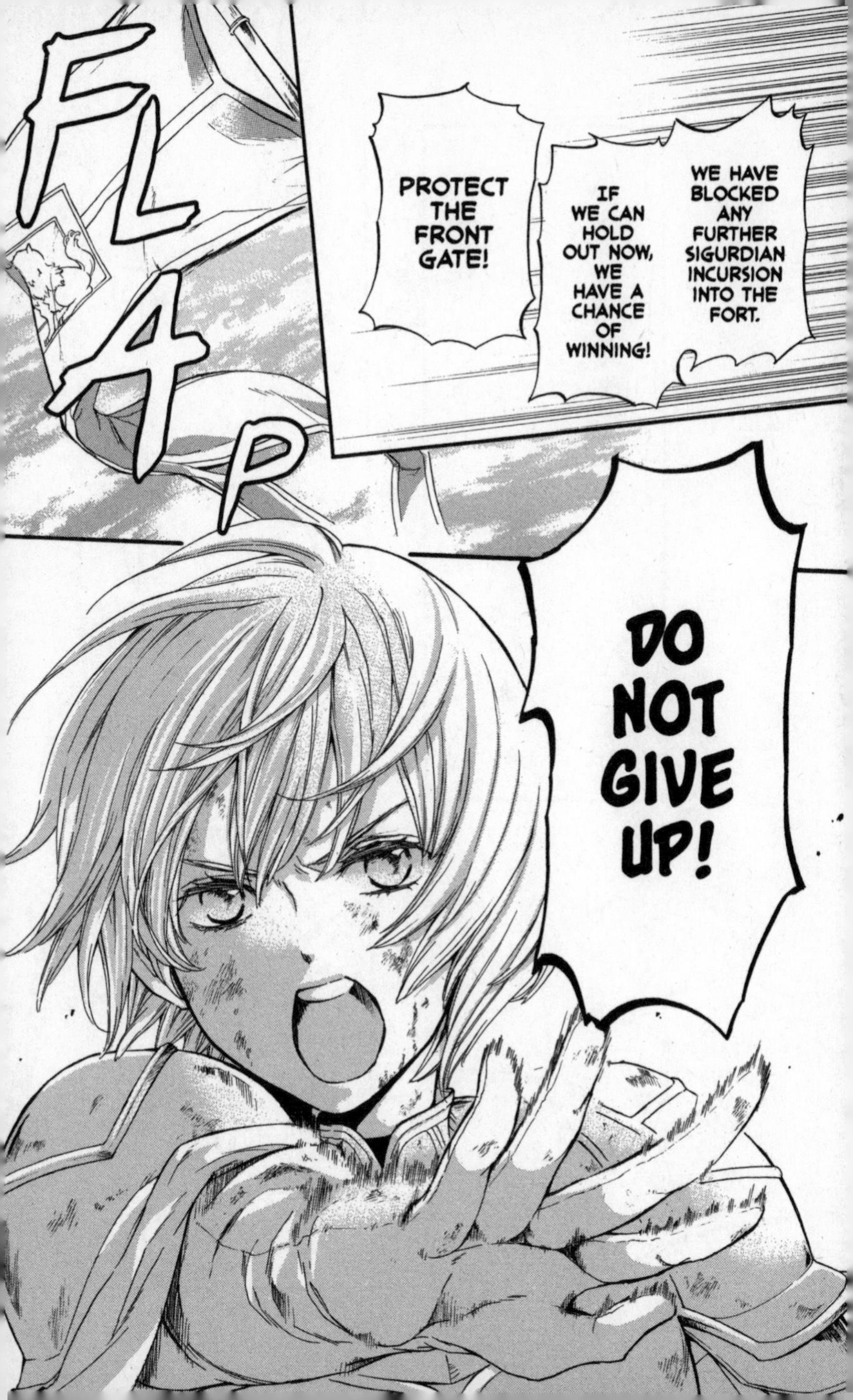
WE HAVE BLOCKED ANY FURTHER SIGURDIAN INCURSION INTO THE FORT.
IF WE CAN HOLD OUT NOW, WE HAVE A CHANCE OF WINNING!
PROTECT THE FRONT GATE!
FLAP
DO NOT GIVE UP!

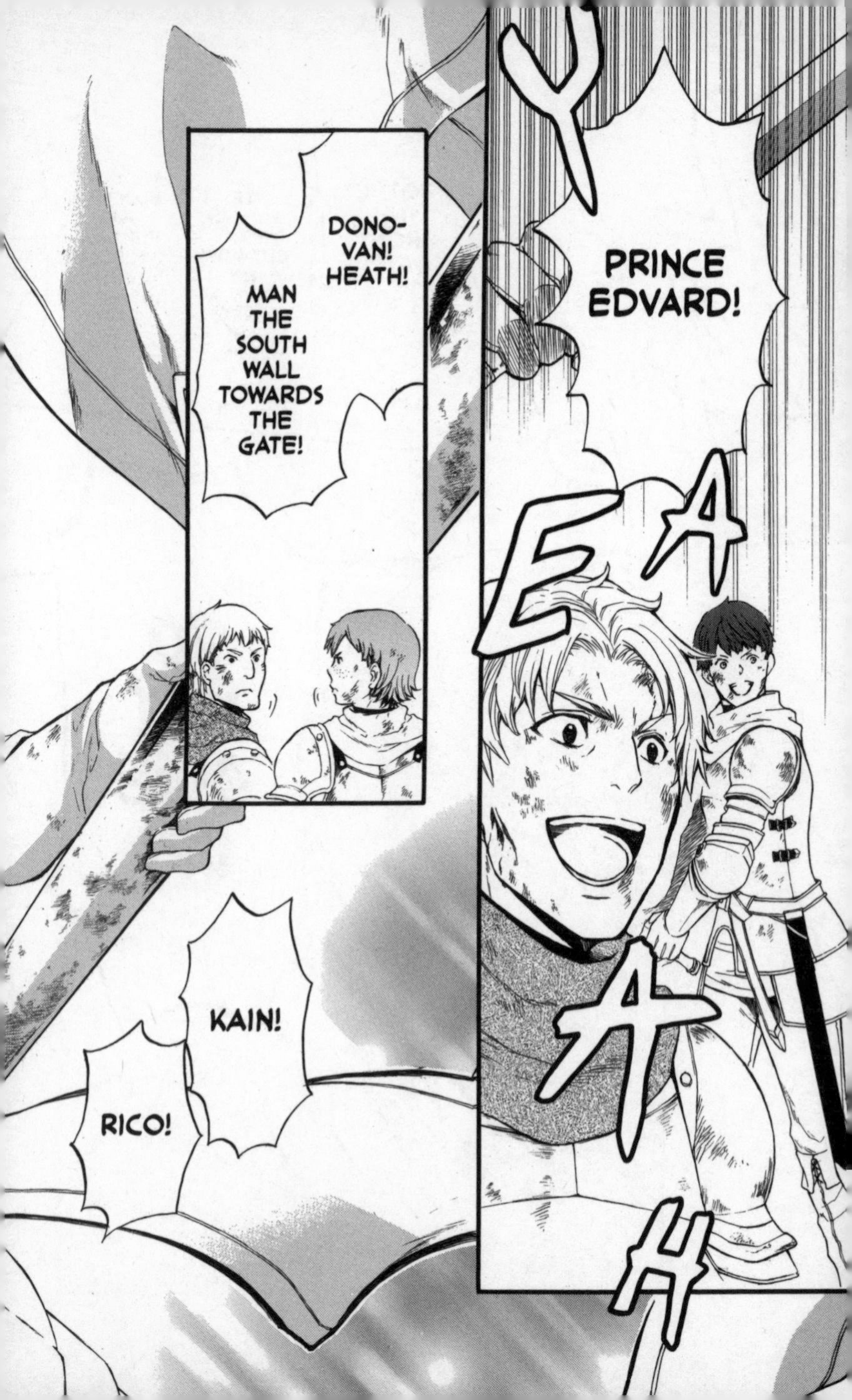
PRINCE EDVARD!
YEAAH
DONO-VAN! HEATH!
MAN THE SOUTH WALL TOWARDS THE GATE!
KAIN!
RICO!

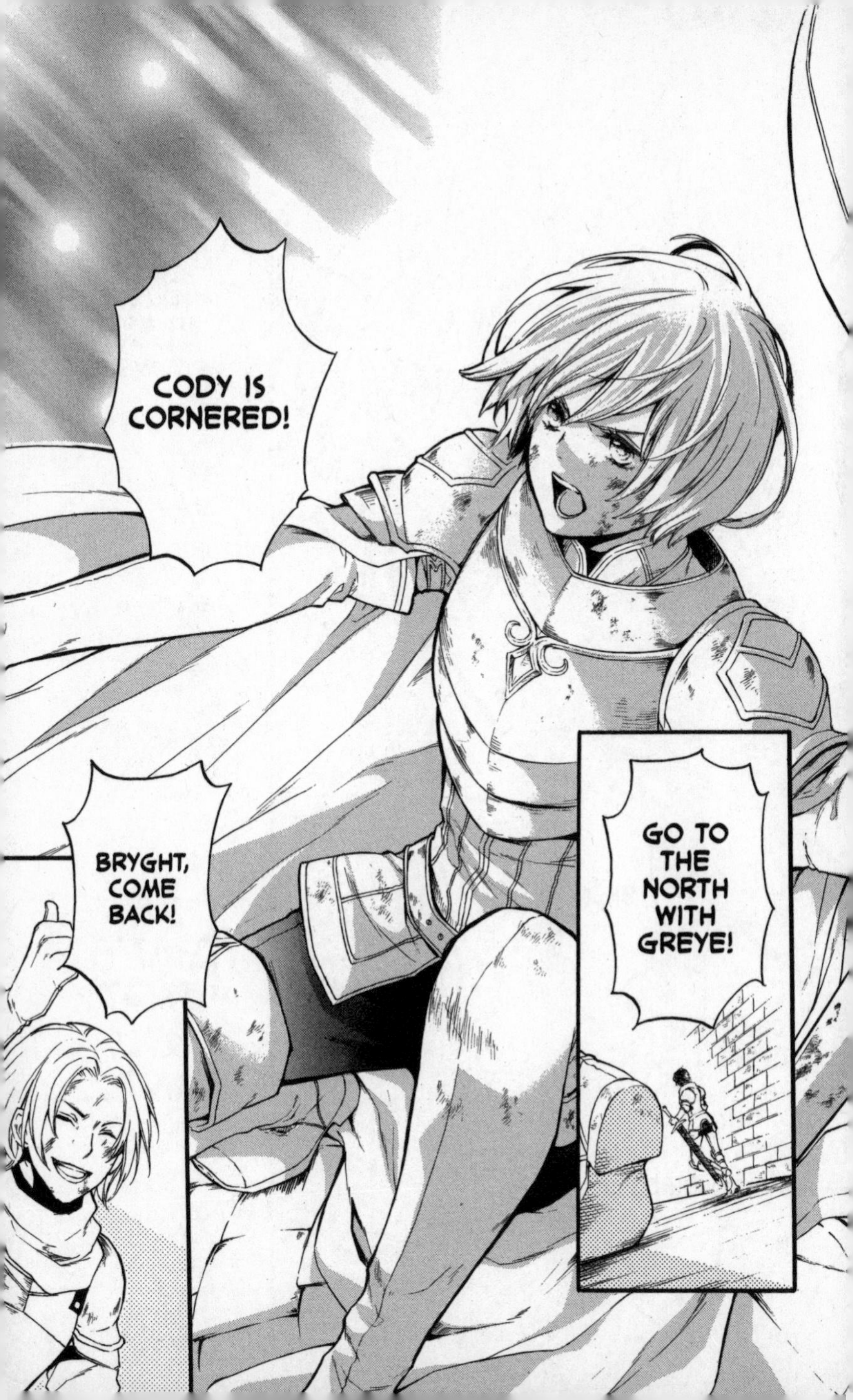
CODY IS CORNERED!
GO TO THE NORTH WITH GREYE!
BRYGHT, COME BACK!

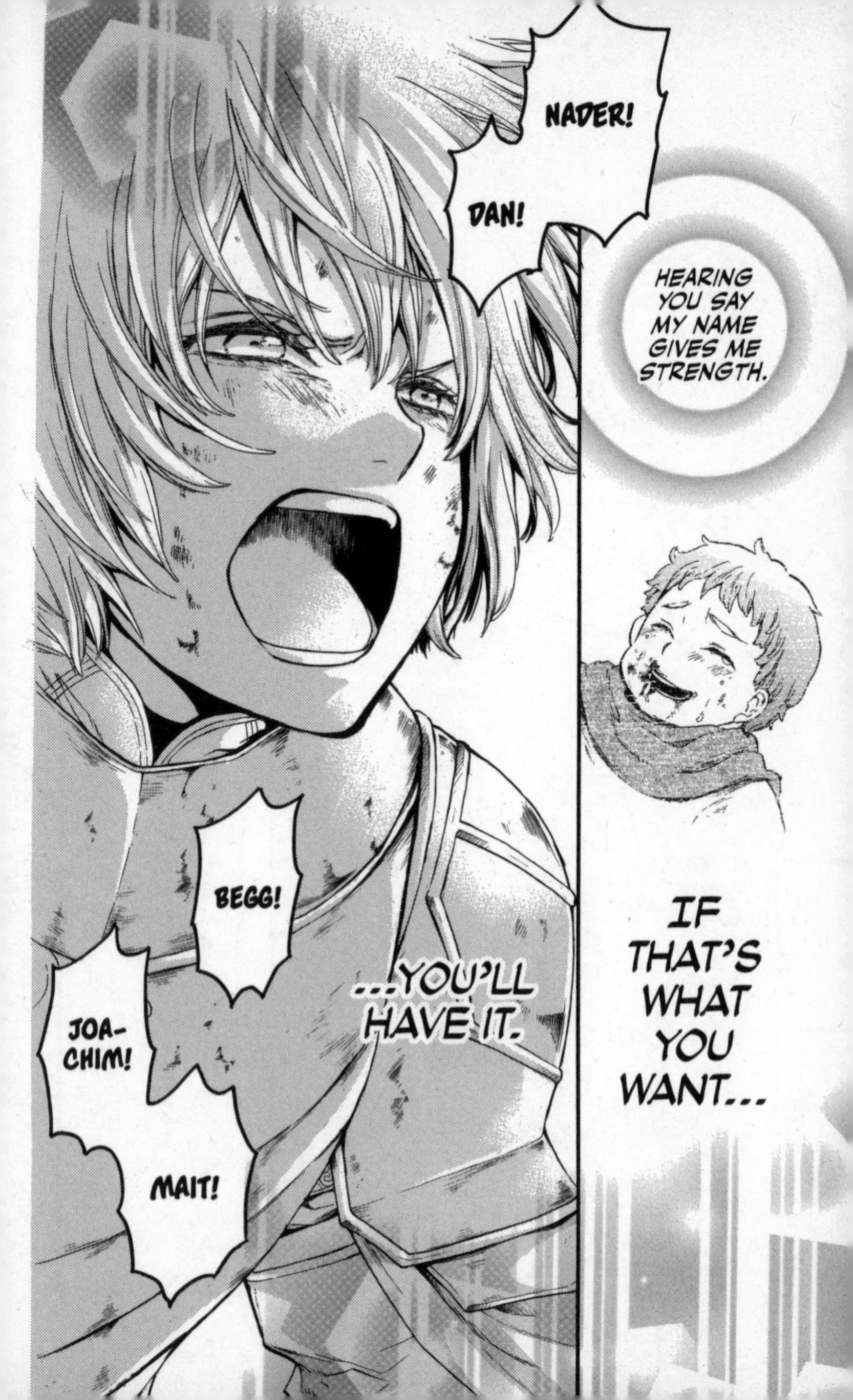
HEARING YOU SAY MY NAME GIVES ME STRENGTH.
IF THAT'S WHAT YOU WANT...
NADER!
DAN!
BEGG!
...YOU'LL HAVE IT.
JOA-CHIM!
MAIT!

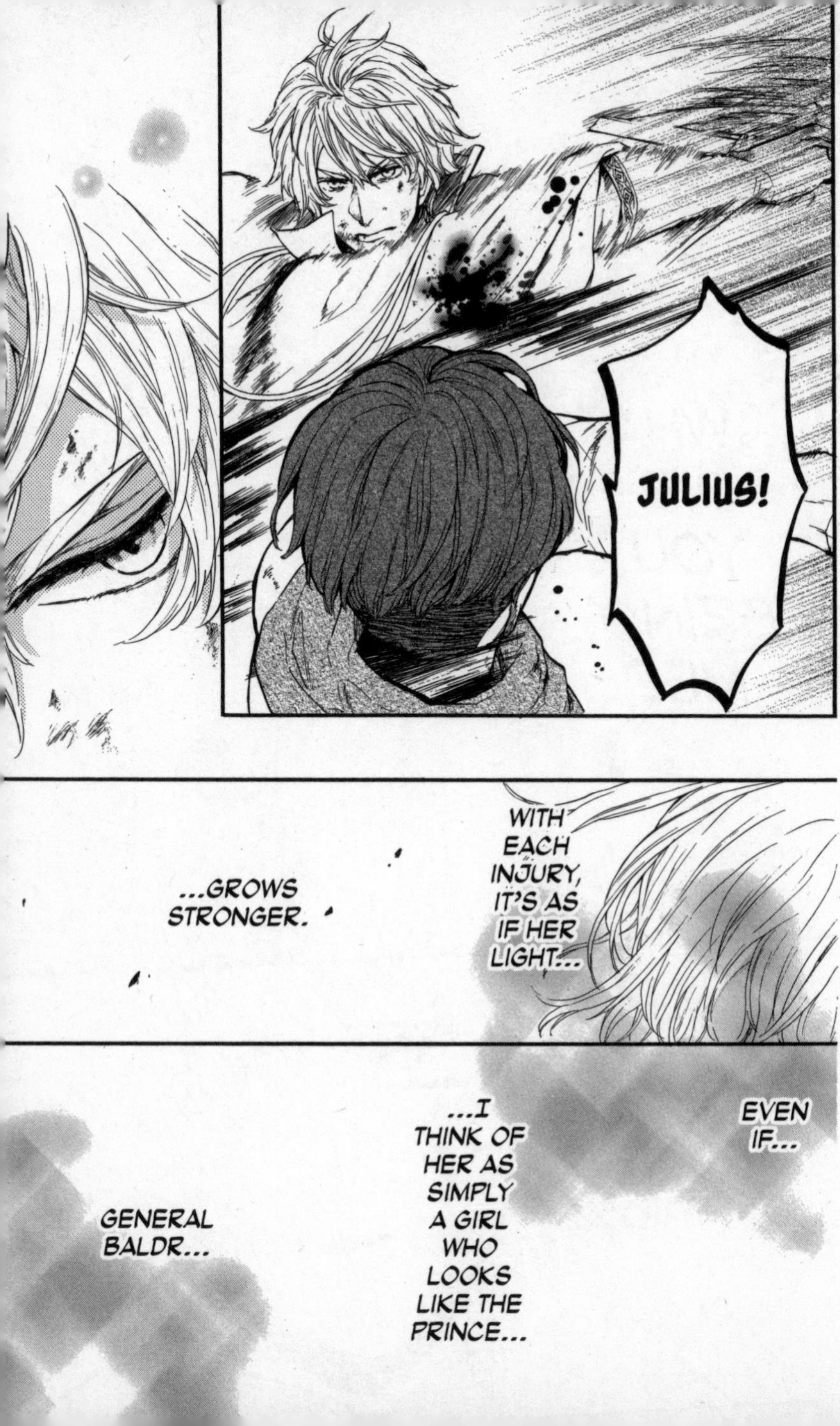
JULIUS!
WITH EACH INJURY, IT'S AS IF HER LIGHT...
...GROWS STRONGER.
EVEN IF...
...I THINK OF HER AS SIMPLY A GIRL WHO LOOKS LIKE THE PRINCE...
GENERAL BALDR...

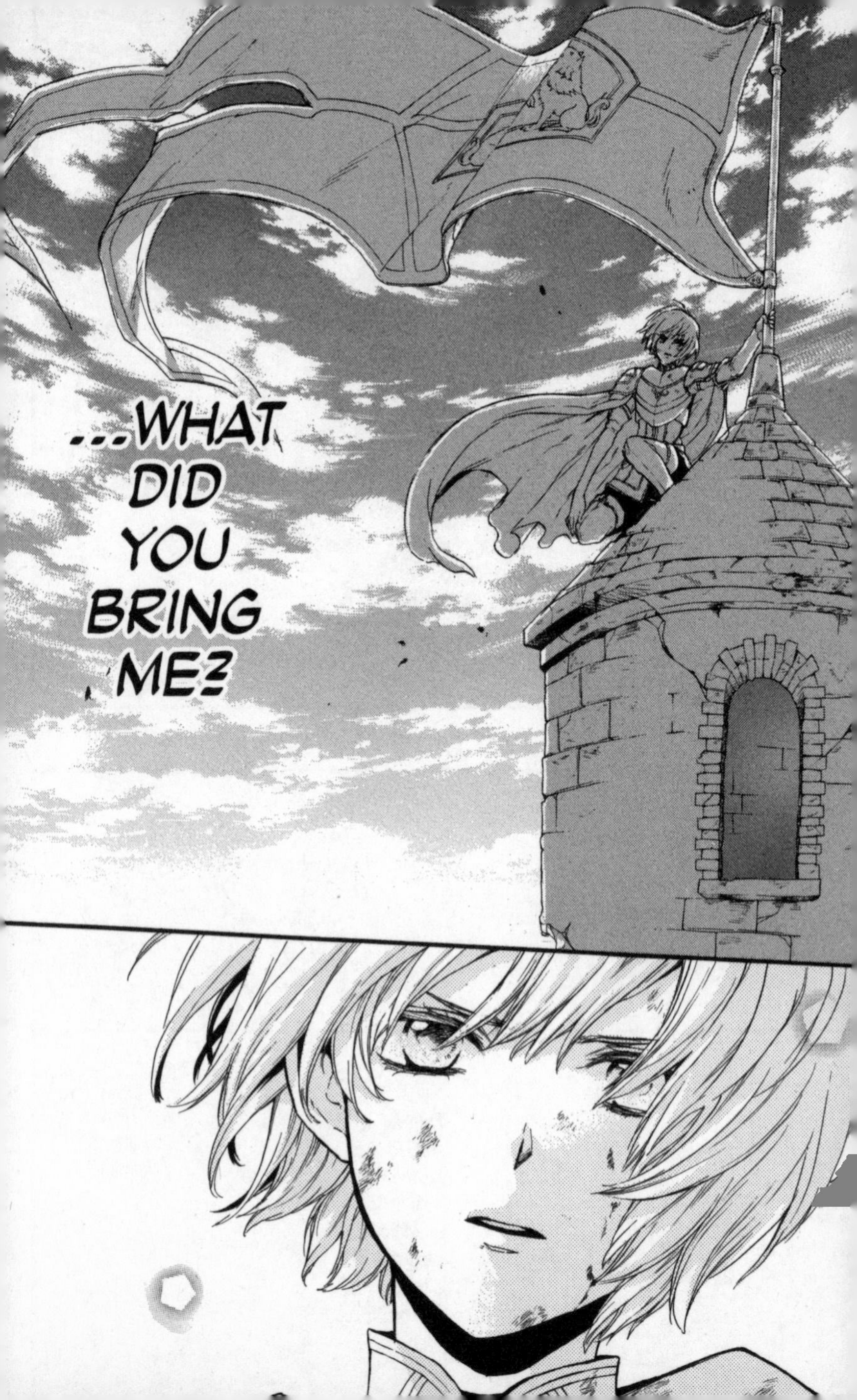
...WHAT DID YOU BRING ME?

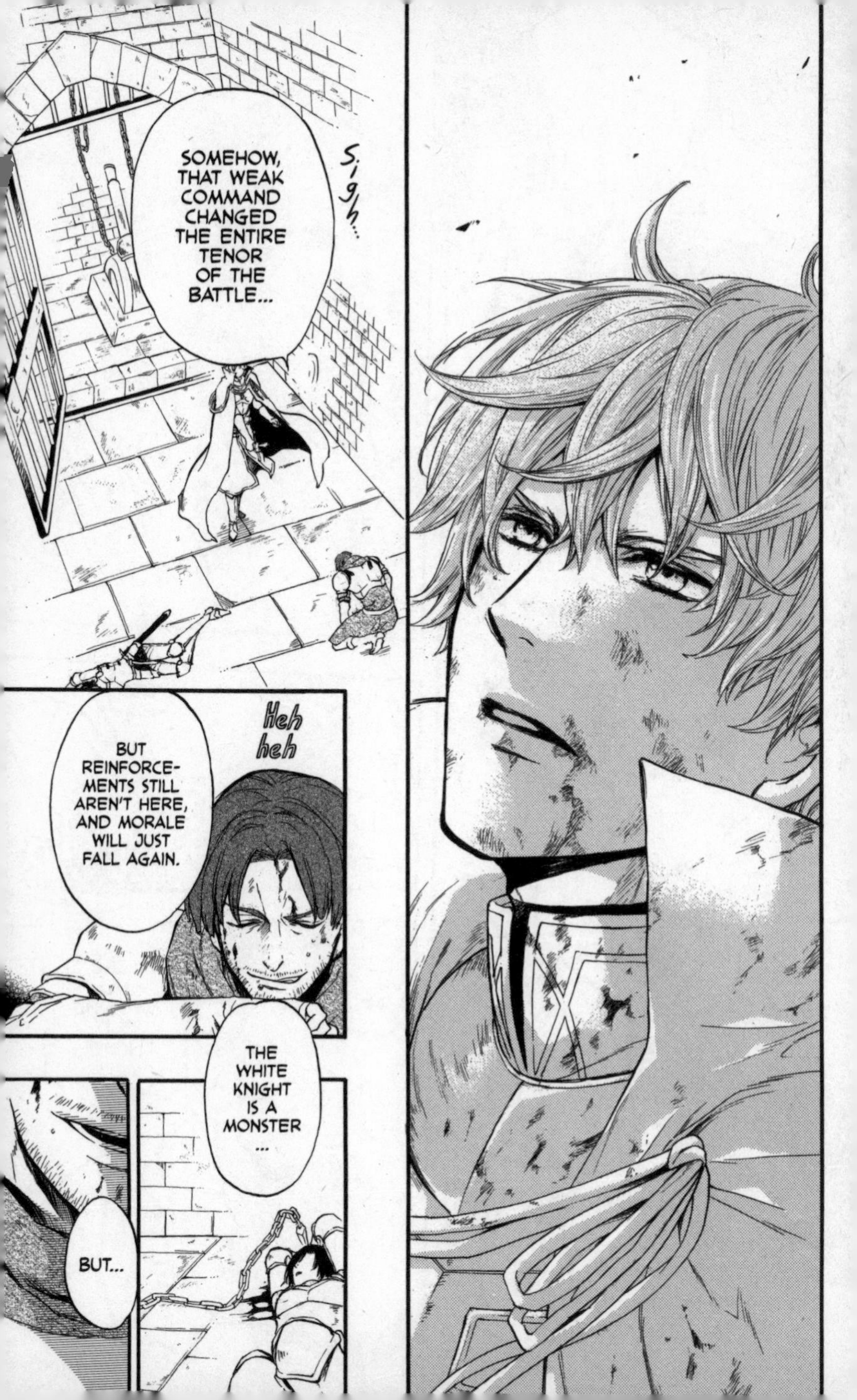
Sigh...
SOMEHOW, THAT WEAK COMMAND CHANGED THE ENTIRE TENOR OF THE BATTLE...
Heh heh
BUT REINFORCEMENTS STILL AREN'T HERE, AND MORALE WILL JUST FALL AGAIN.
THE WHITE KNIGHT IS A MONSTER...
BUT...

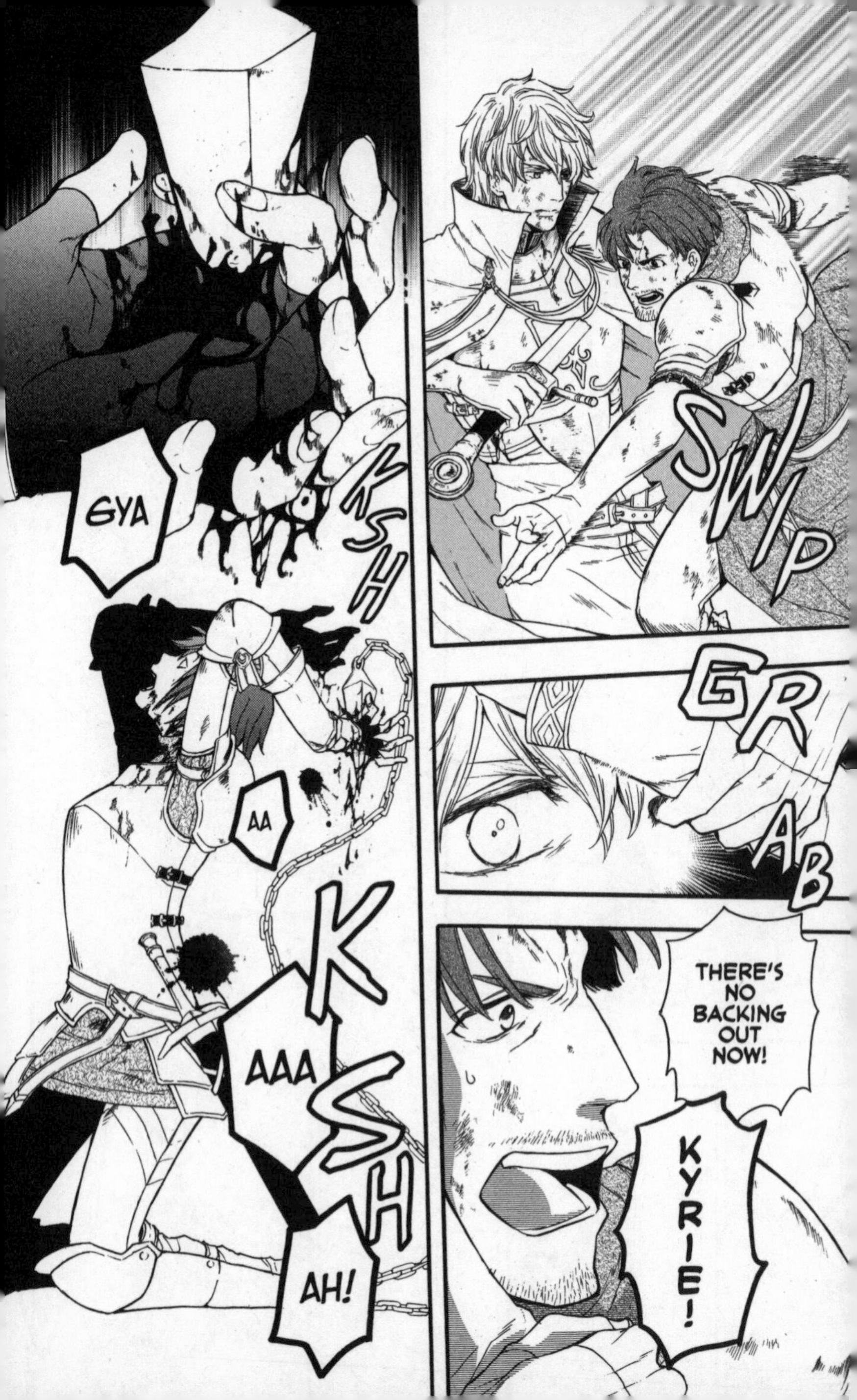

SWIP
GRAB
THERE'S NO BACKING OUT NOW!
KYRIE!
KSH
GYA
AA
KSH
AAA
AH!

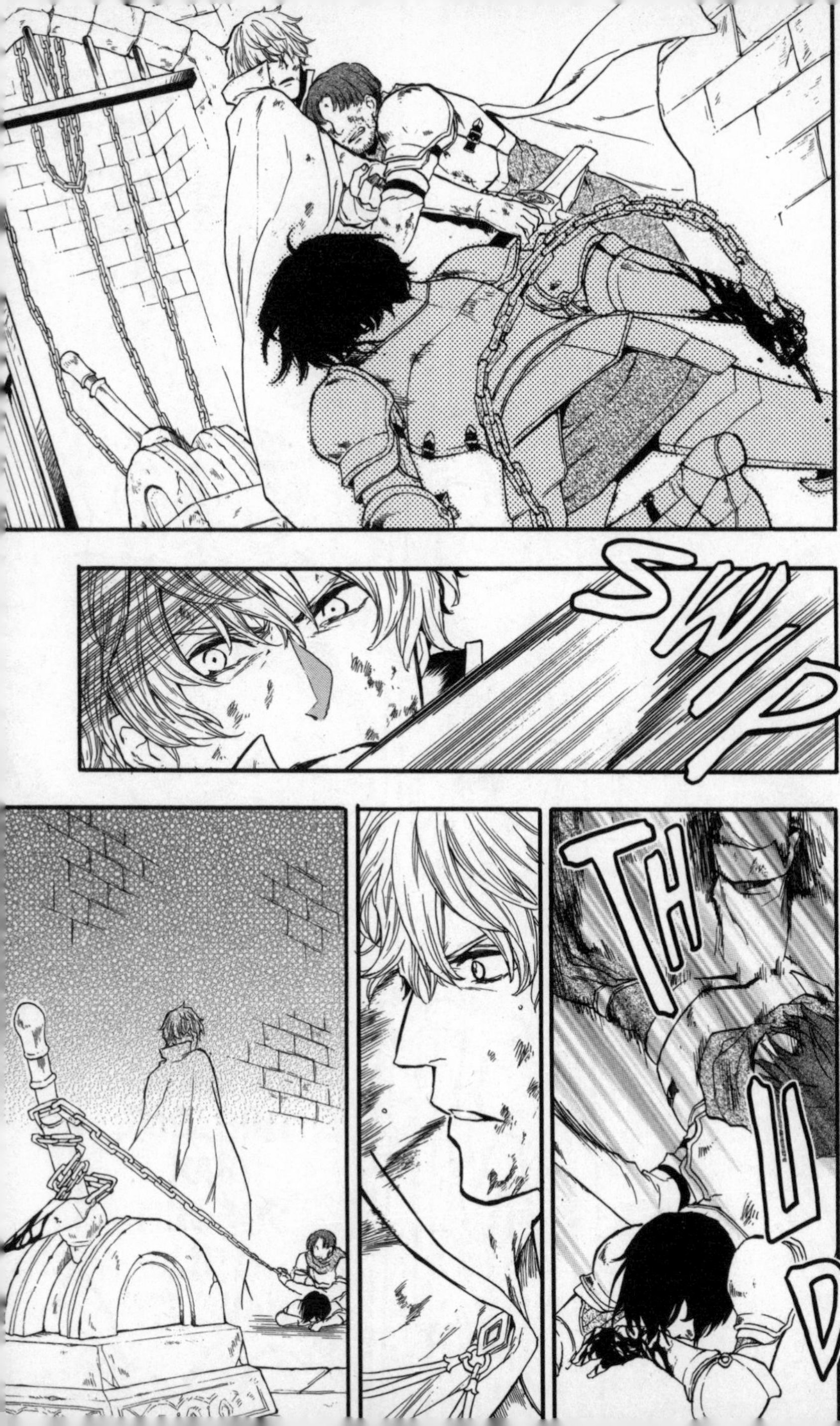
SWIP
THUD

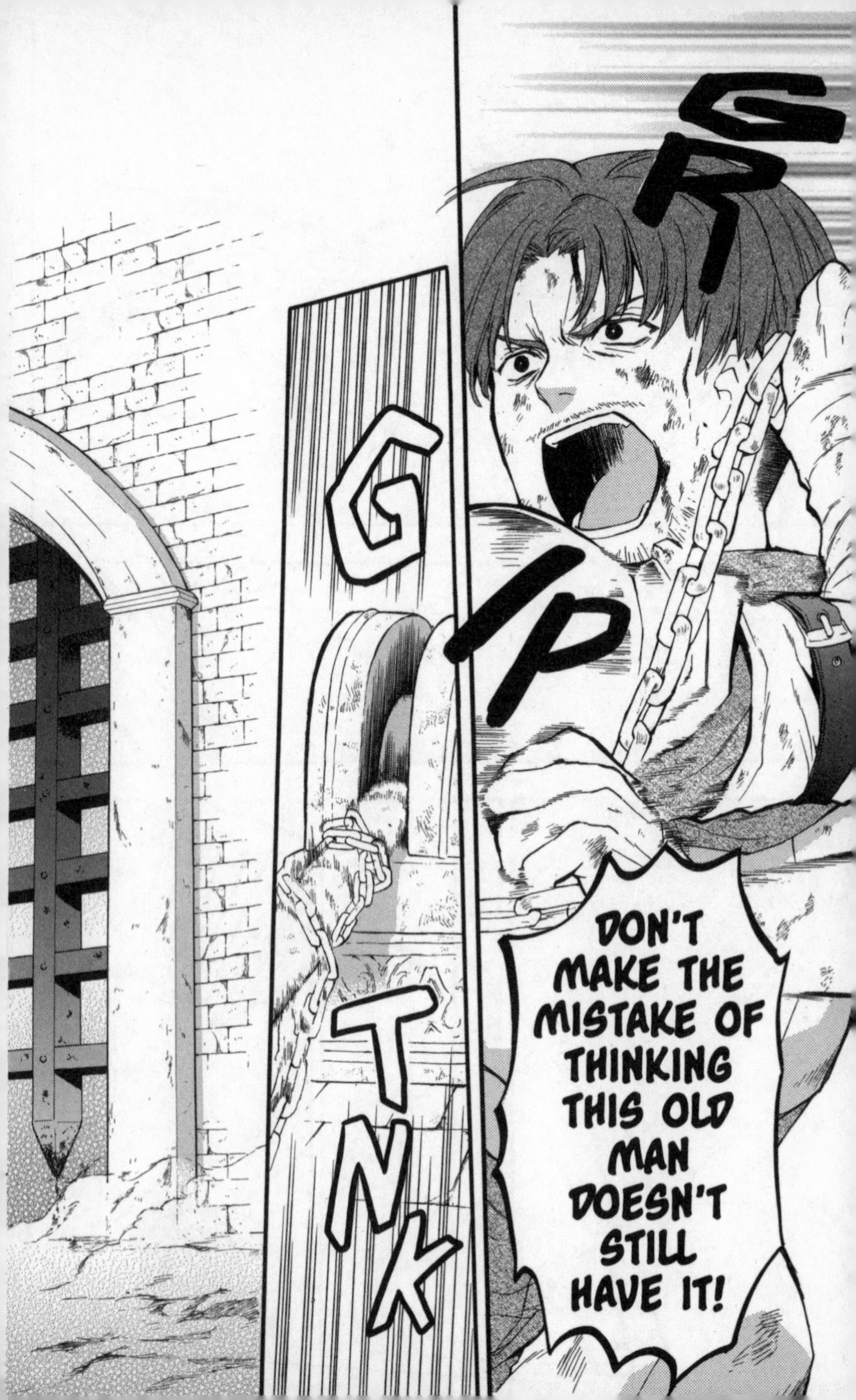
GRIP
DON'T MAKE THE MISTAKE OF THINKING THIS OLD MAN DOESN'T STILL HAVE IT!
GTNK

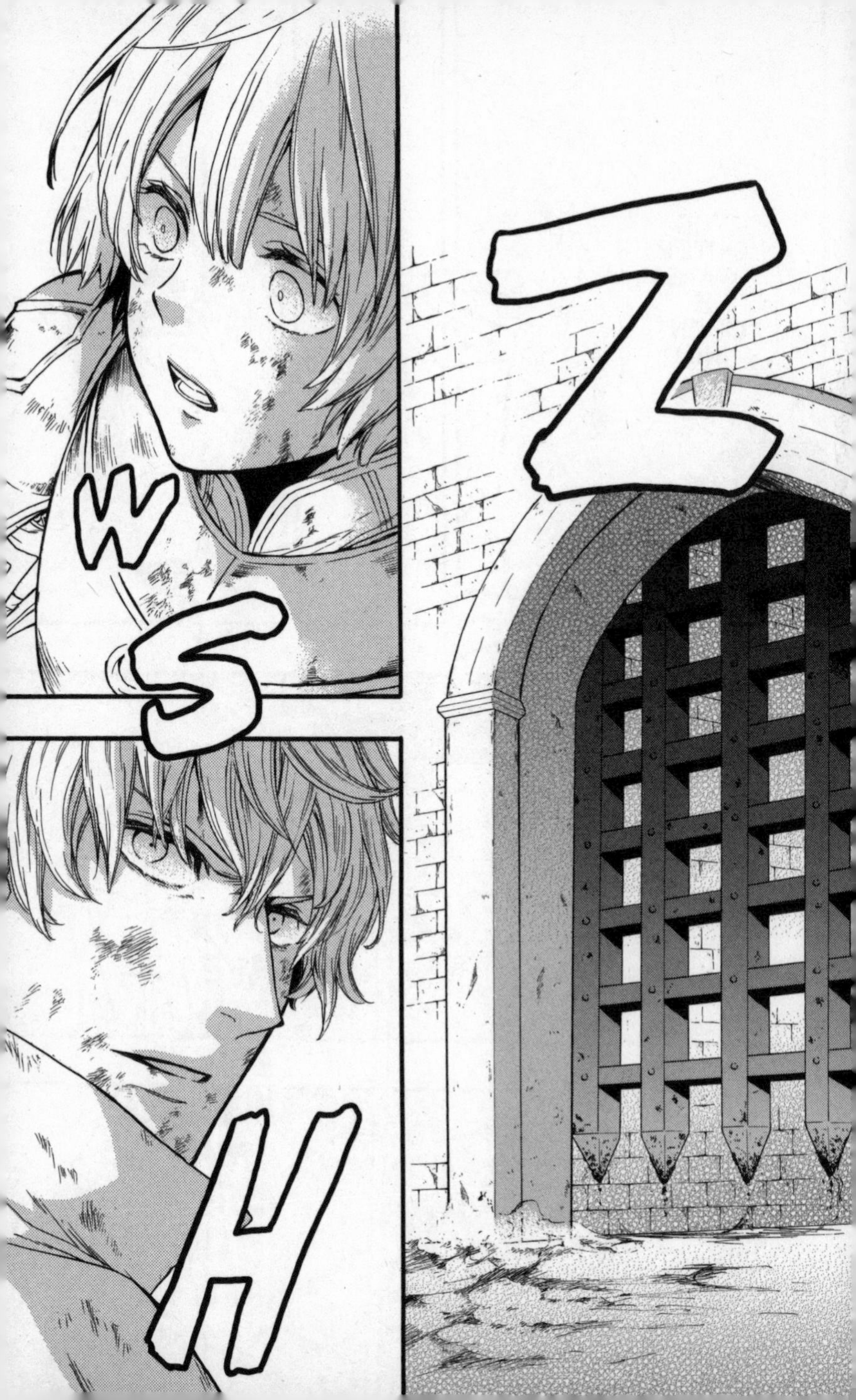
ZWSH

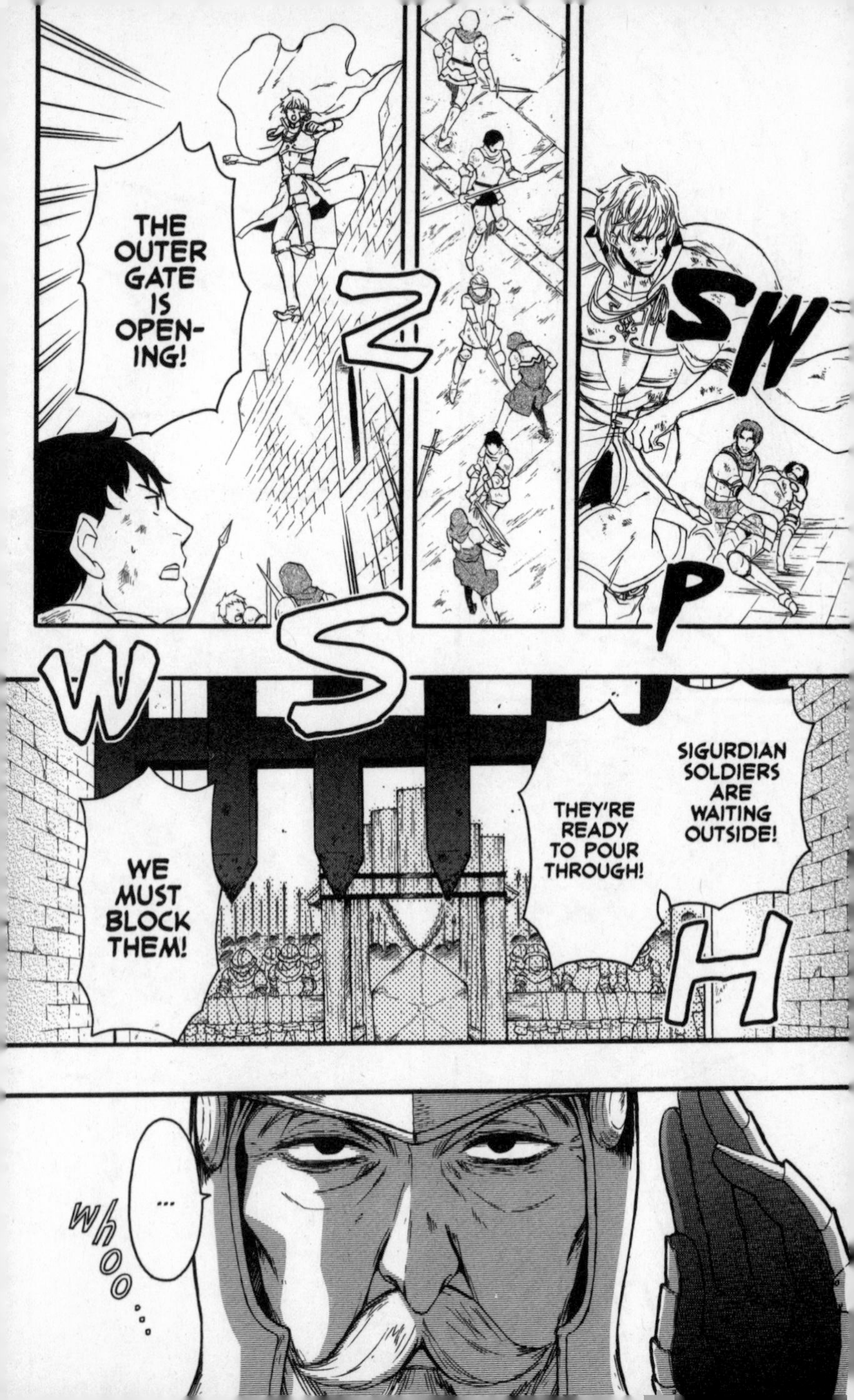

SW
P
THE OUTER GATE IS OPEN-ING!
Z
S
W
SIGURDIAN SOLDIERS ARE WAITING OUTSIDE!
THEY'RE READY TO POUR THROUGH!
WE MUST BLOCK THEM!
H
...
whoo...

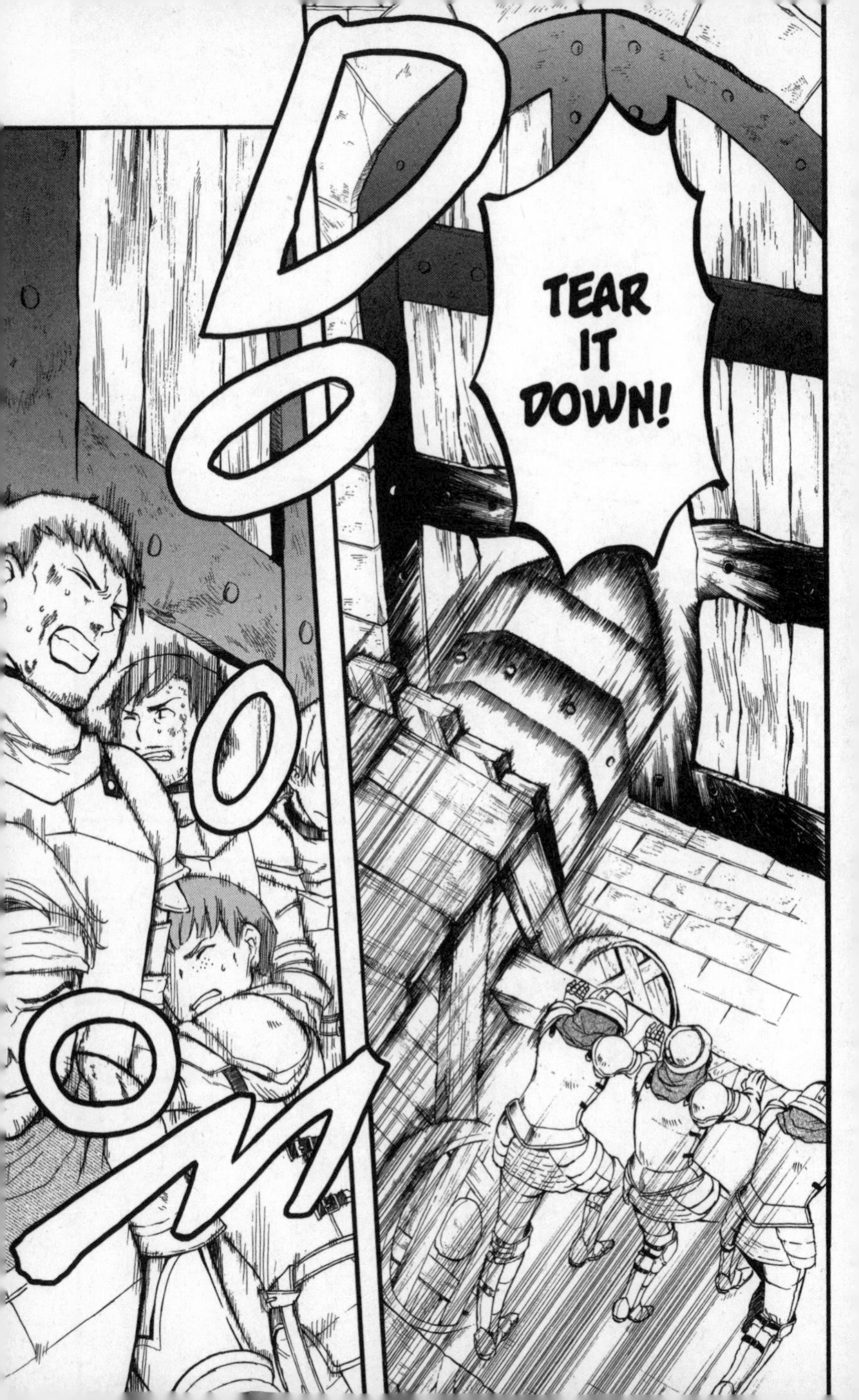
TEAR IT DOWN!
DOOOM

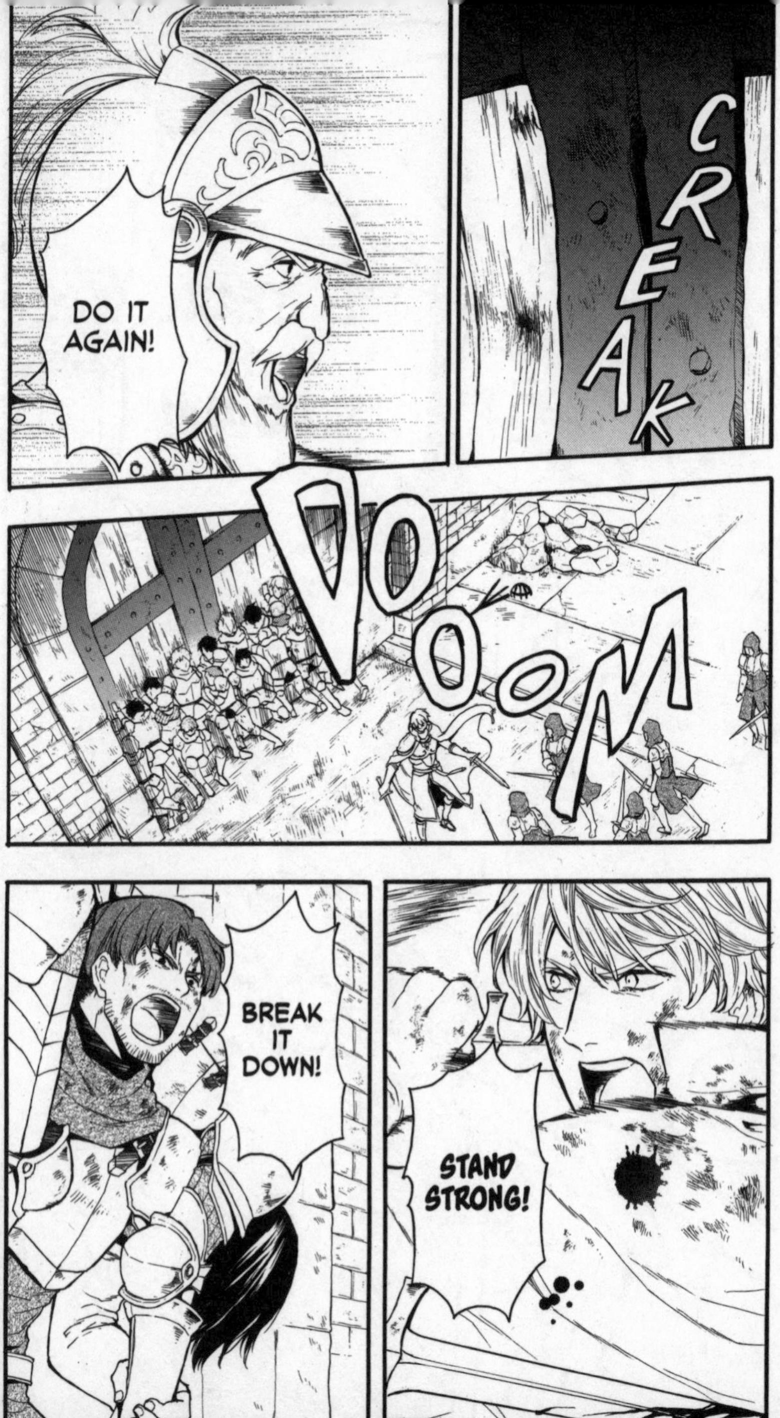
CREAK
DO IT AGAIN!
DOOOM
STAND STRONG!
BREAK IT DOWN!

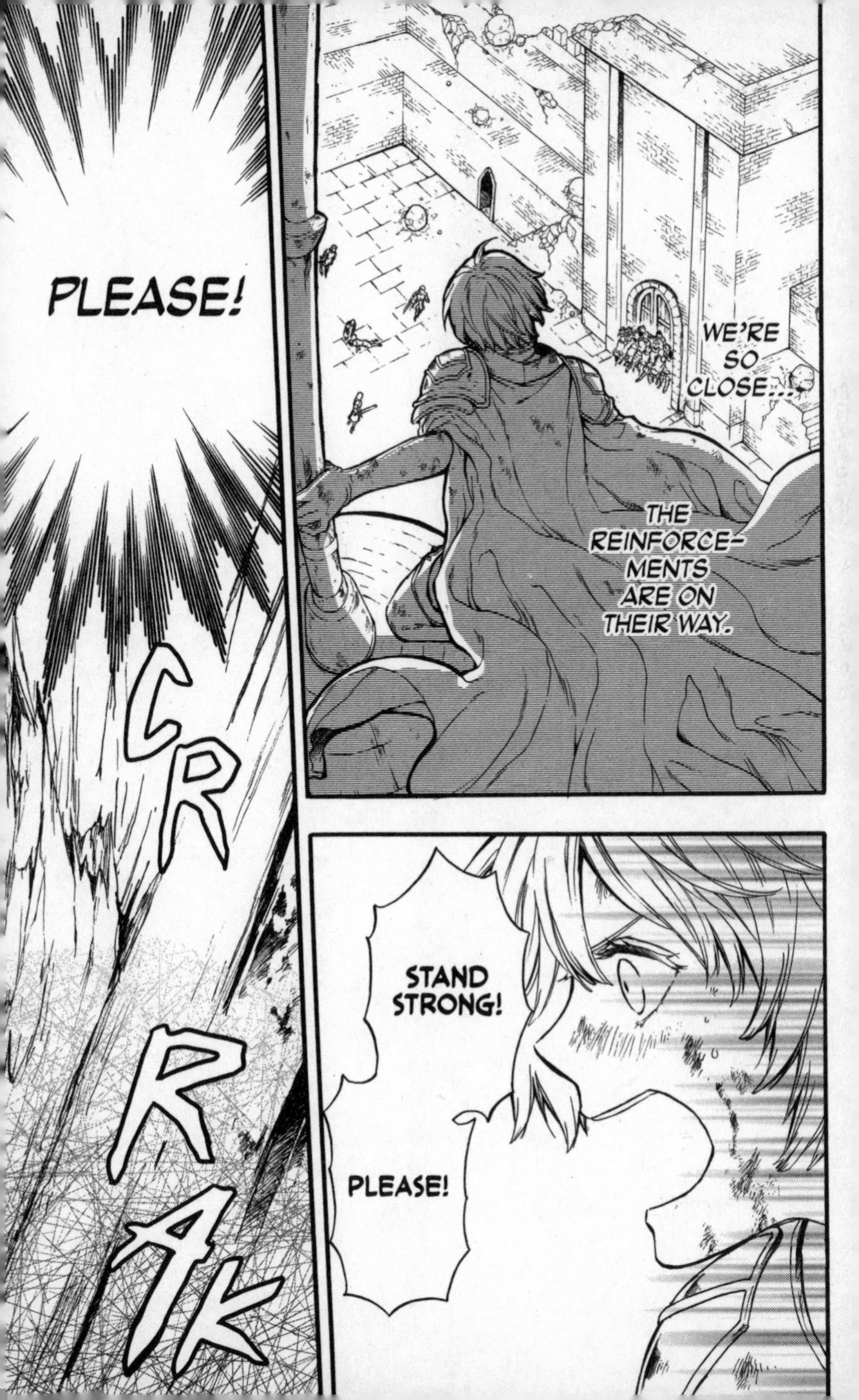
WE'RE SO CLOSE...
THE REINFORCE-MENTS ARE ON THEIR WAY.
STAND STRONG!
PLEASE!
PLEASE!
CRRAK

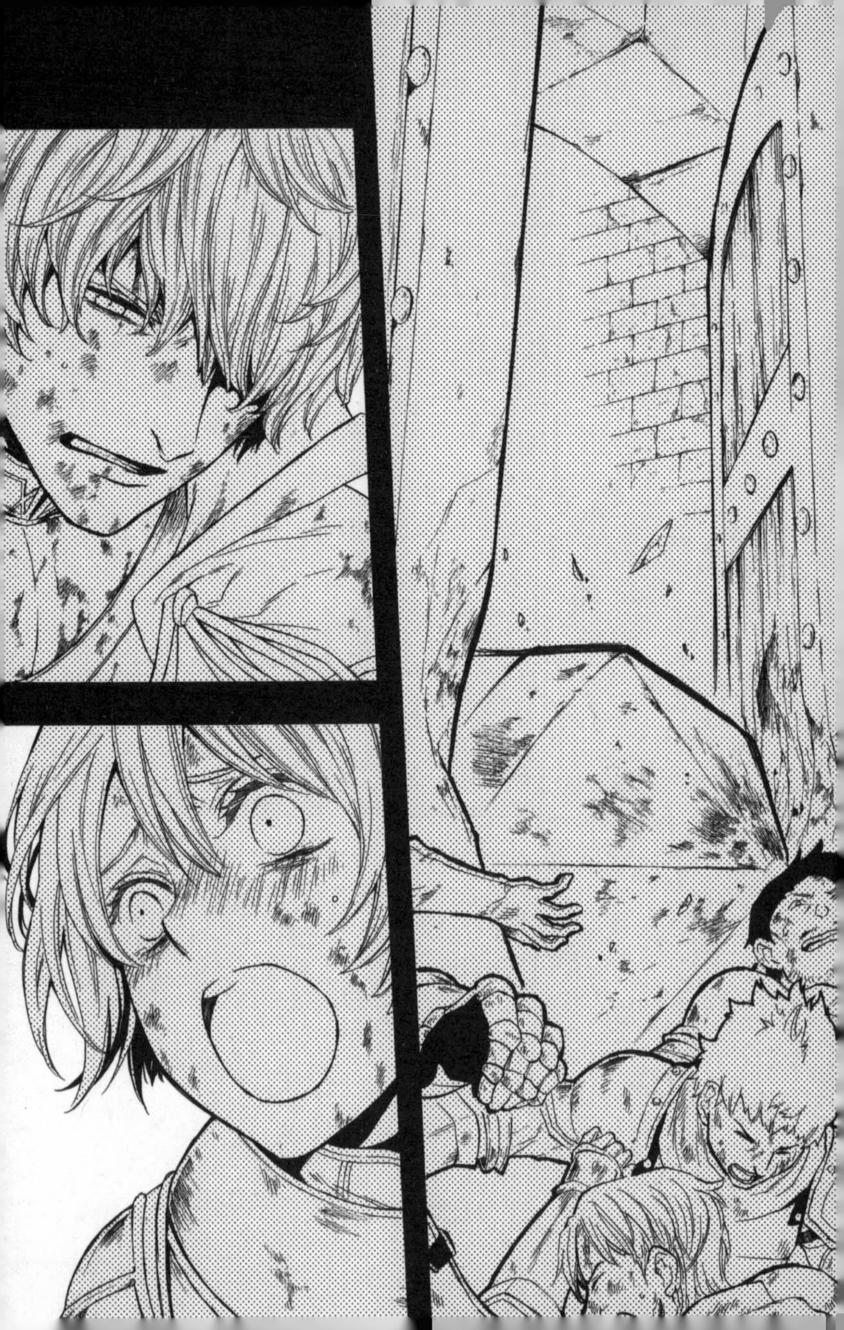

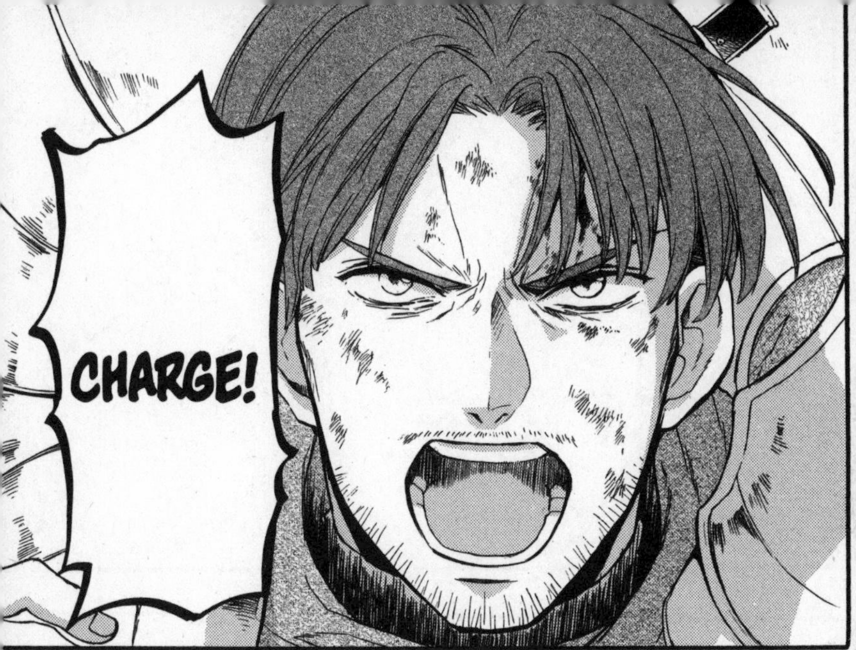
CHARGE!

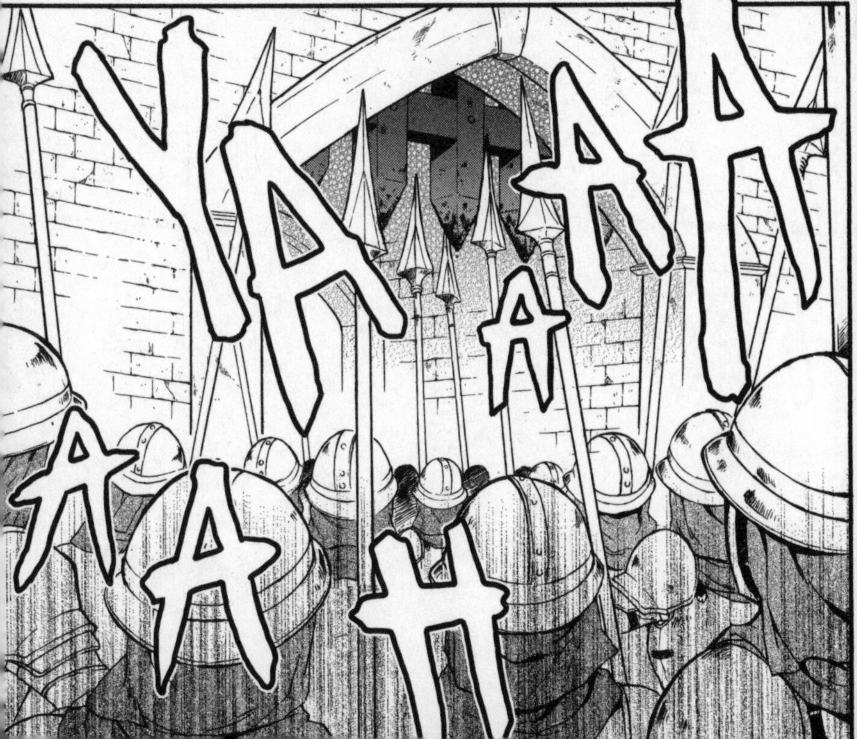
YAAAAAAH

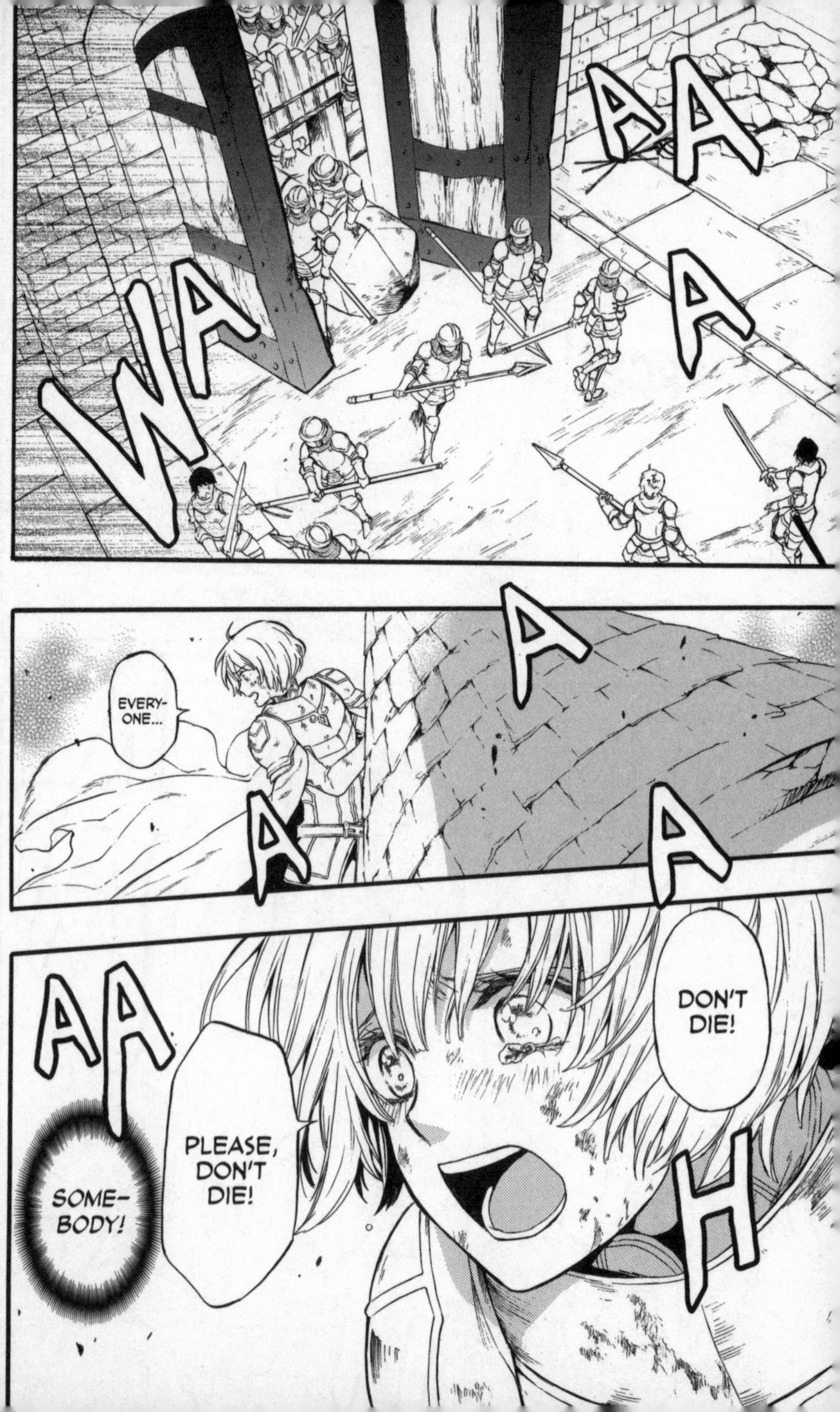
WA
AA
A
EVERY-ONE...
A
A
A
DON'T DIE!
PLEASE, DON'T DIE!
SOME-BODY!
AA
H

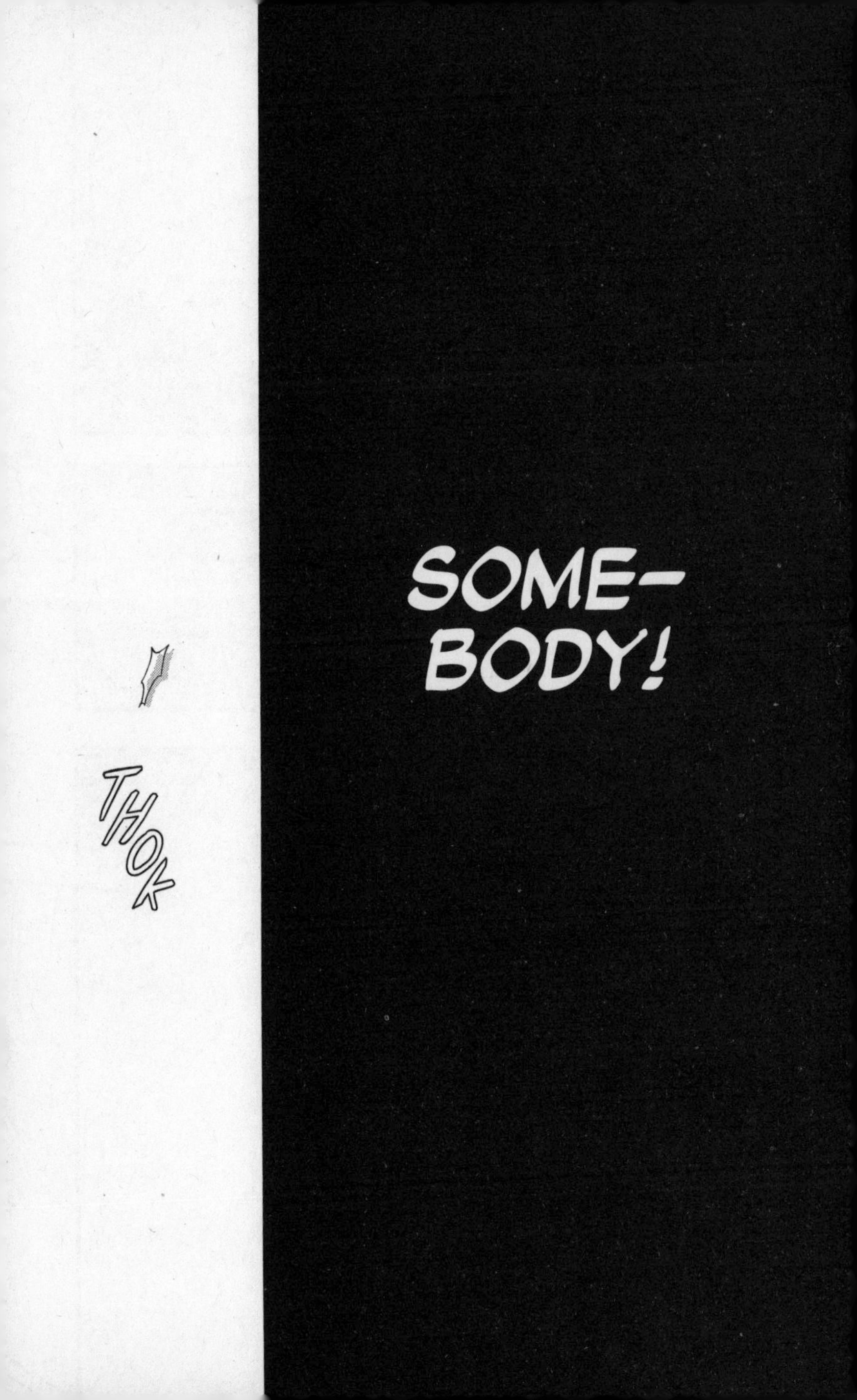
SOME-
BODY!
THOK

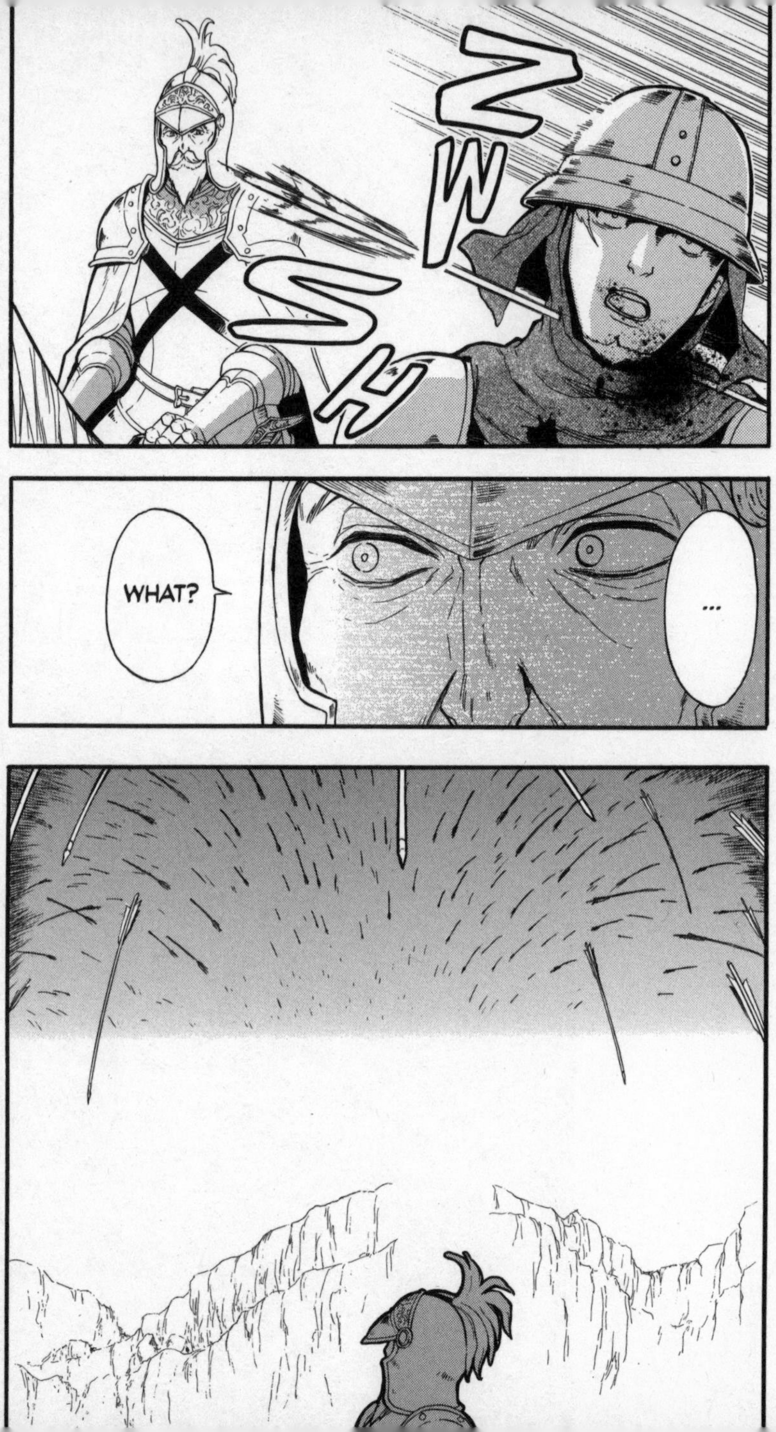
SWISH
...
WHAT?

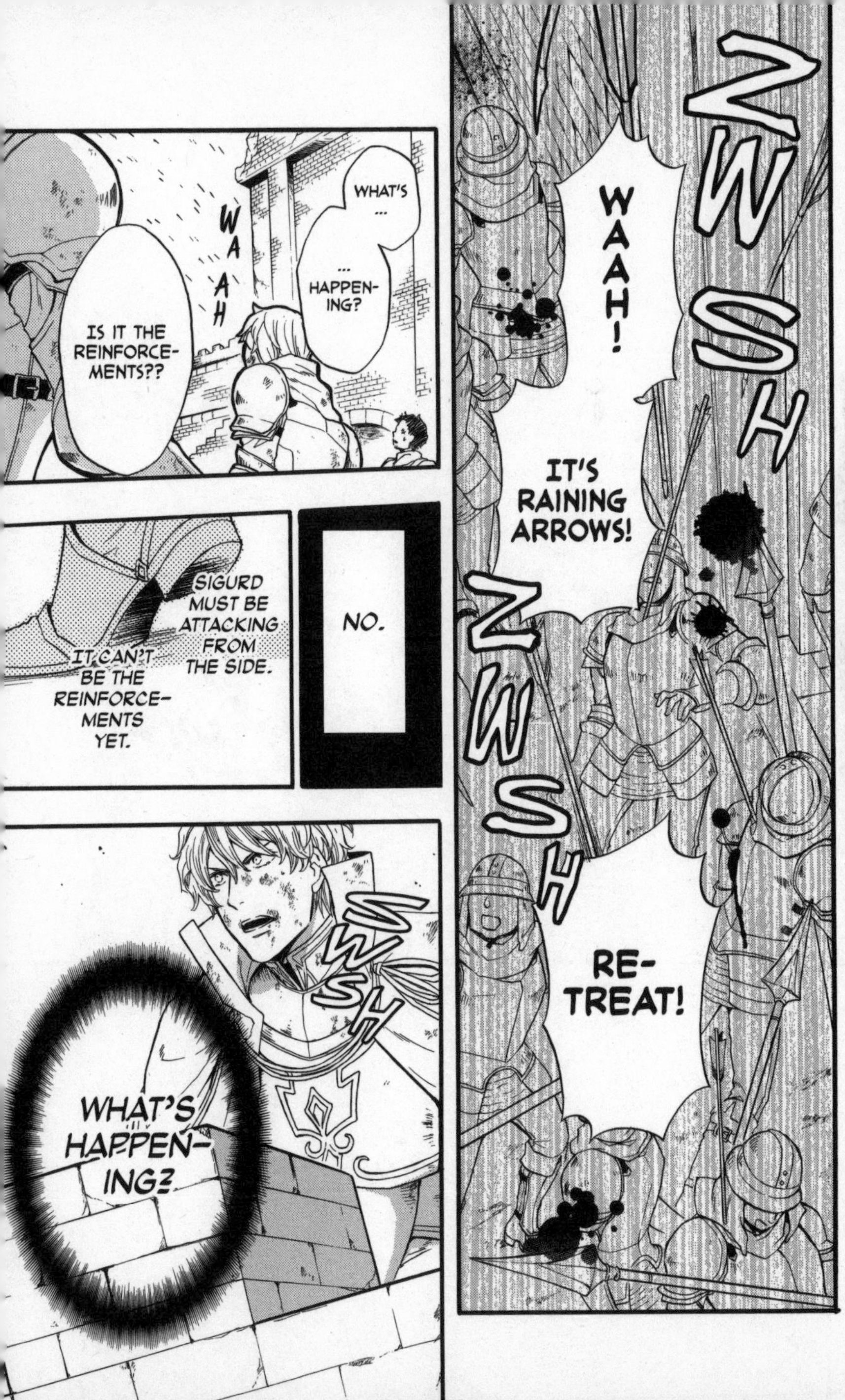
ZWSH
WAAAH!
IT'S RAINING ARROWS!
ZWSH
RE-TREAT!
WHAT'S ...
... HAPPEN-ING?
WAAH
IS IT THE REINFORCE-MENTS??
NO.
SIGURD MUST BE ATTACKING FROM THE SIDE.
IT CAN'T BE THE REINFORCE-MENTS YET.
SWSH
WHAT'S HAPPEN-ING?

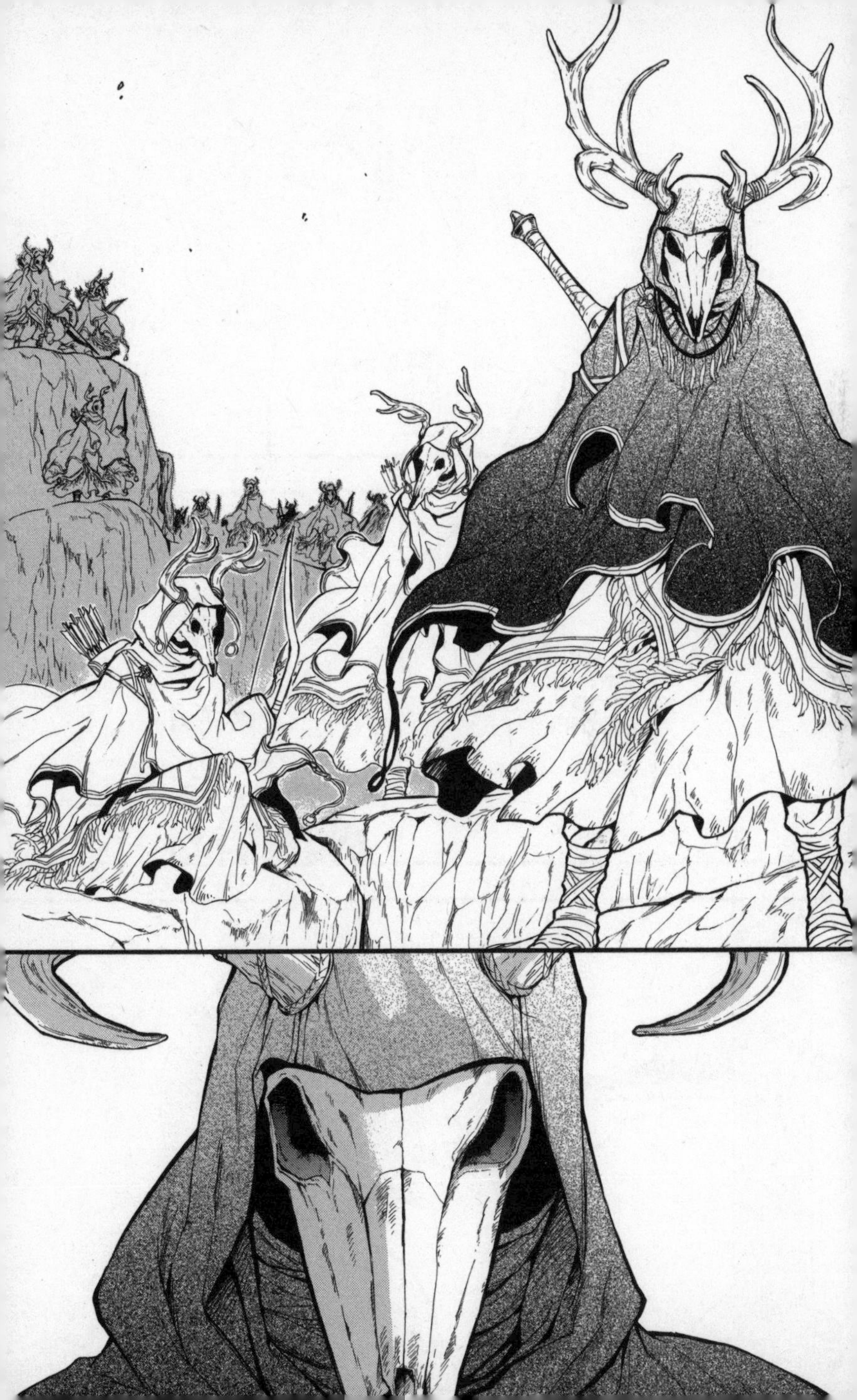

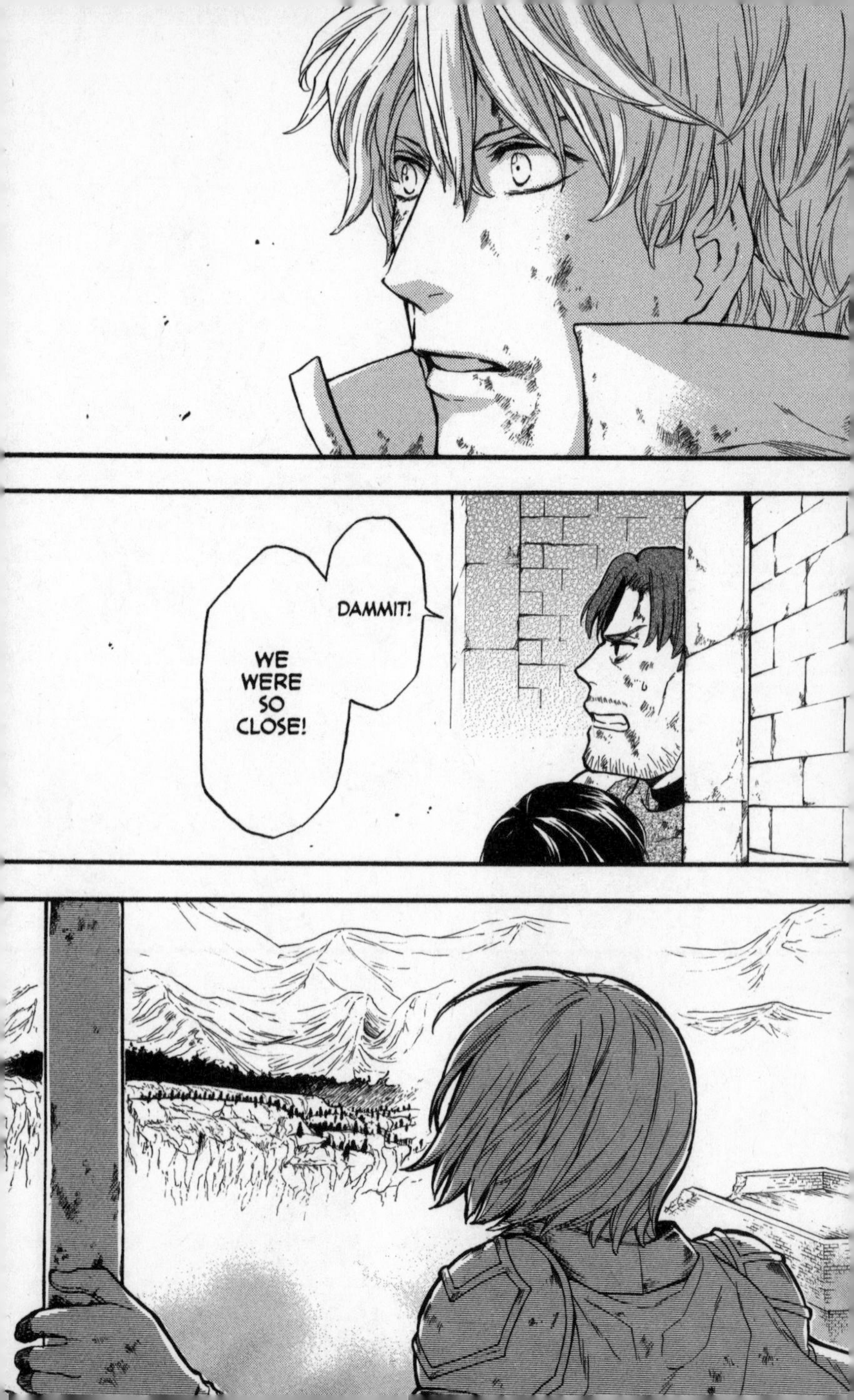
DAMMIT!
WE WERE SO CLOSE!

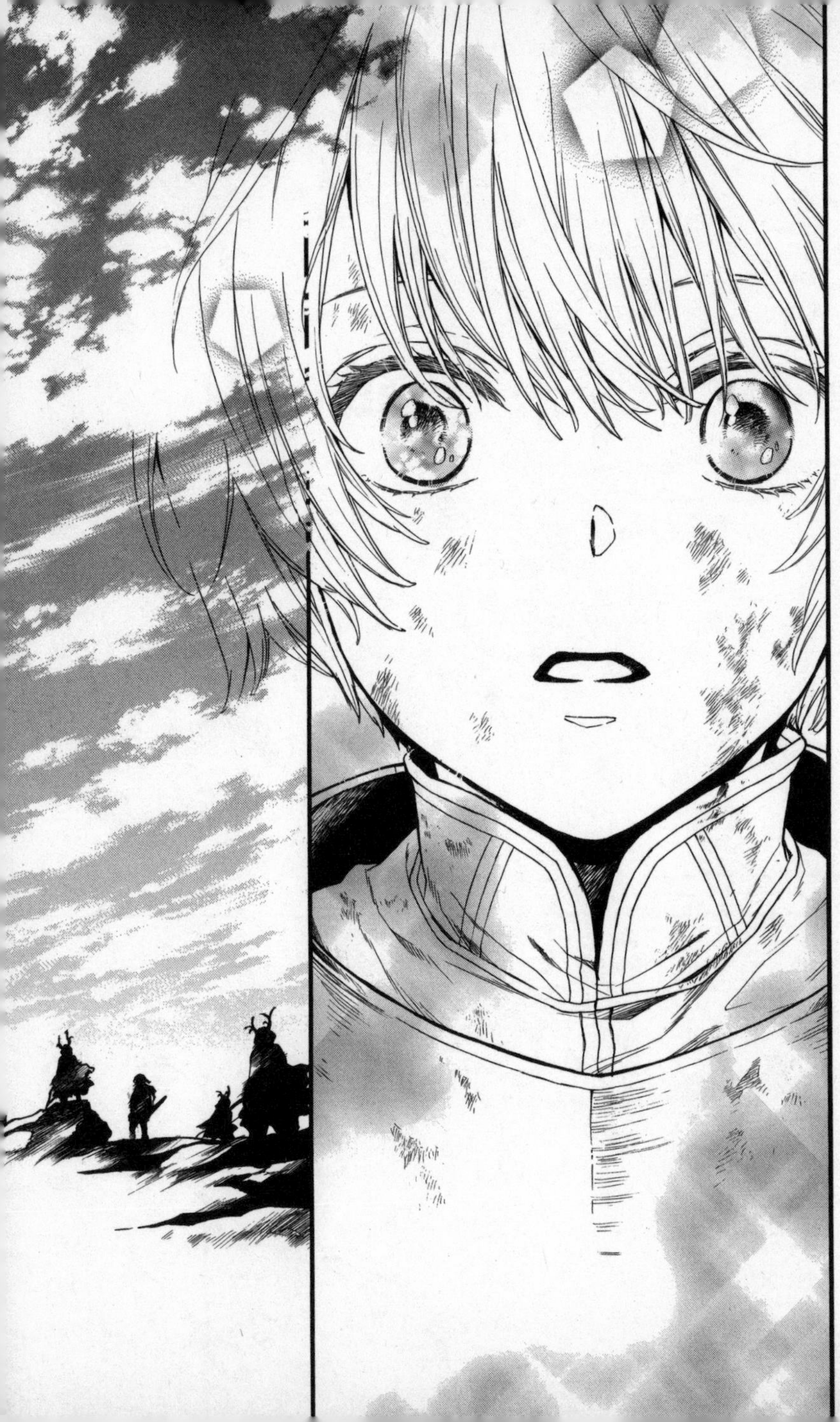

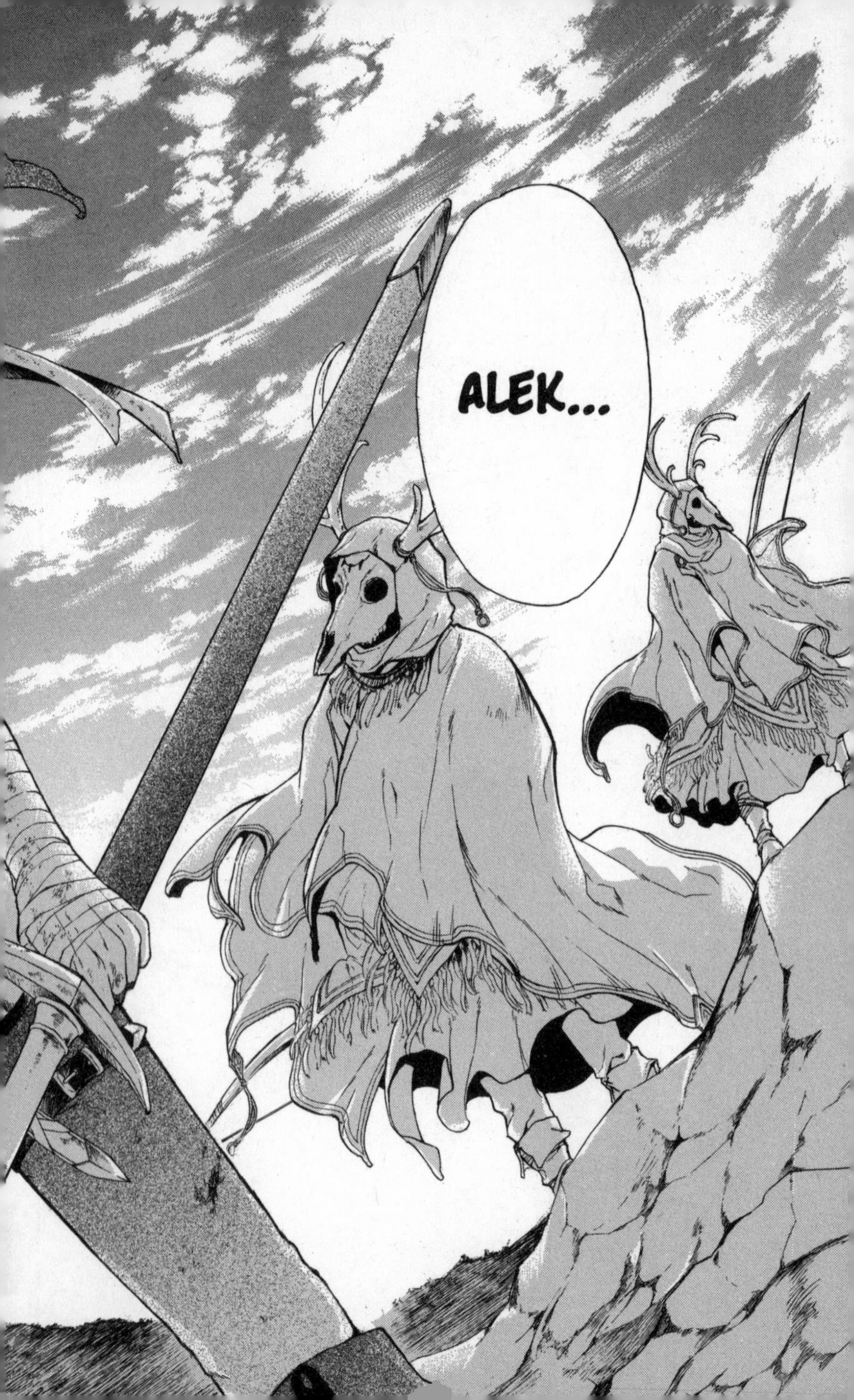
ALEK...

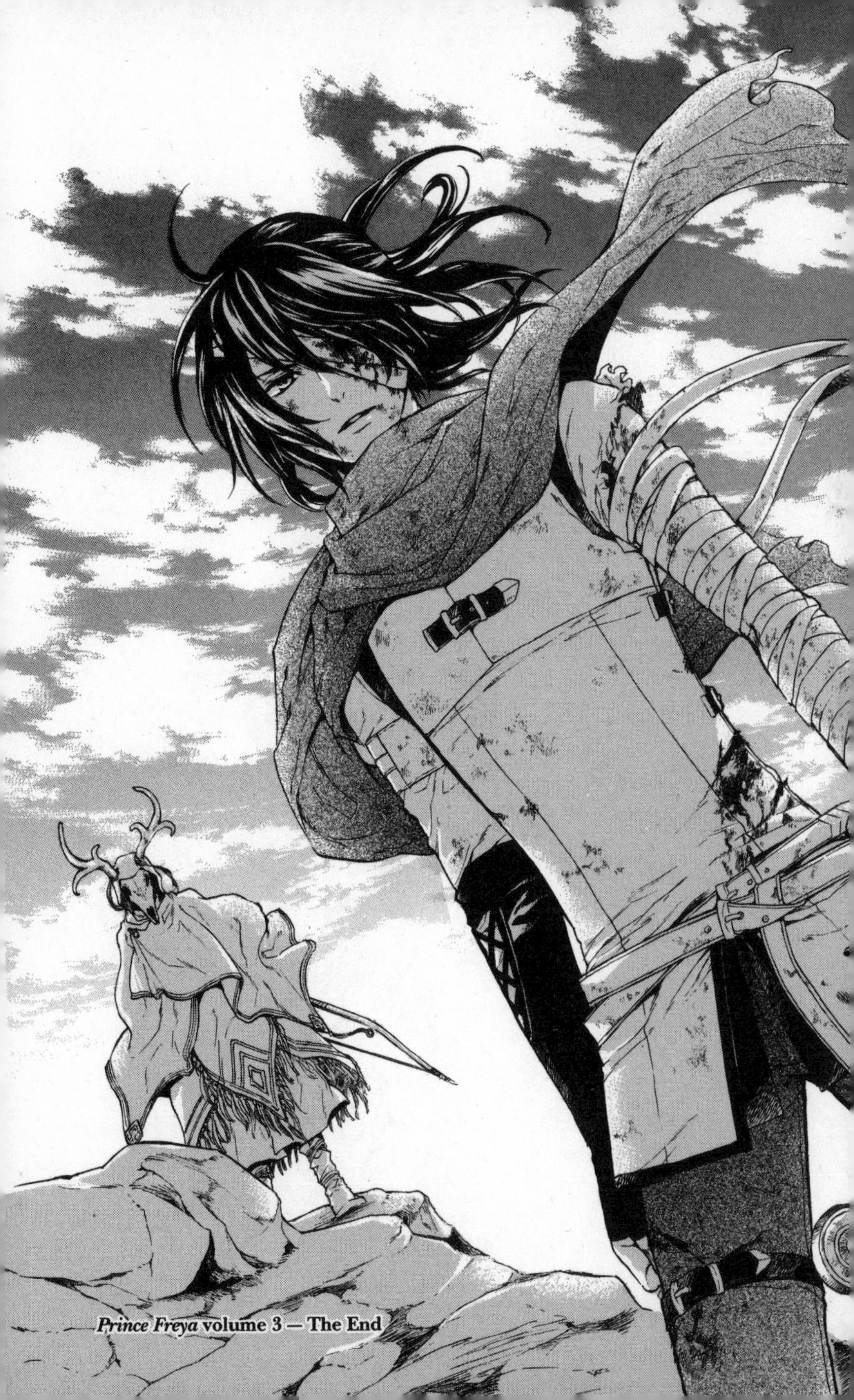
Prince Freya volume 3 — The End

Bonus Chapter
Knights from the Past

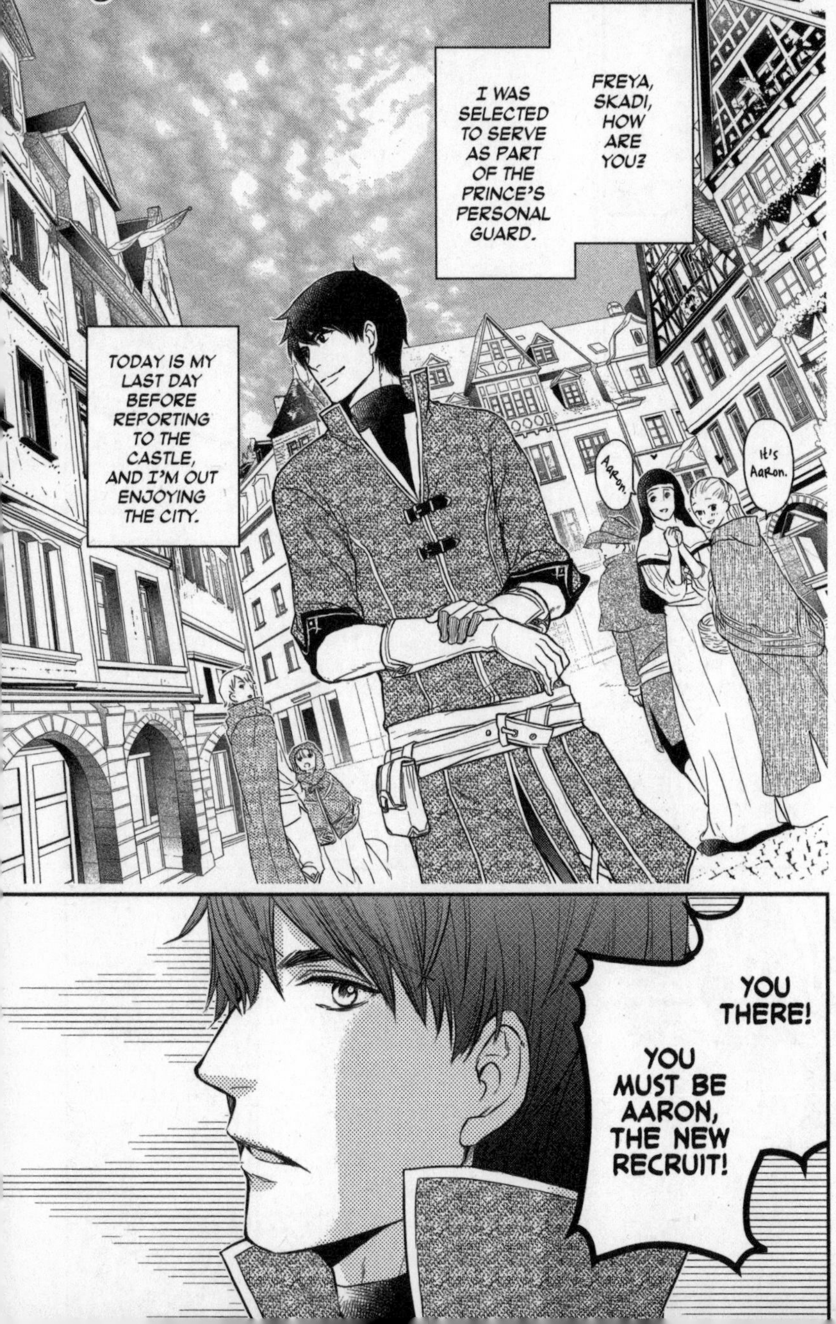
FREYA, SKADI, HOW ARE YOU?
I WAS SELECTED TO SERVE AS PART OF THE PRINCE'S PERSONAL GUARD.
TODAY IS MY LAST DAY BEFORE REPORTING TO THE CASTLE, AND I'M OUT ENJOYING THE CITY.
It's Aaron.
Aaron.
YOU THERE!
YOU MUST BE AARON, THE NEW RECRUIT!

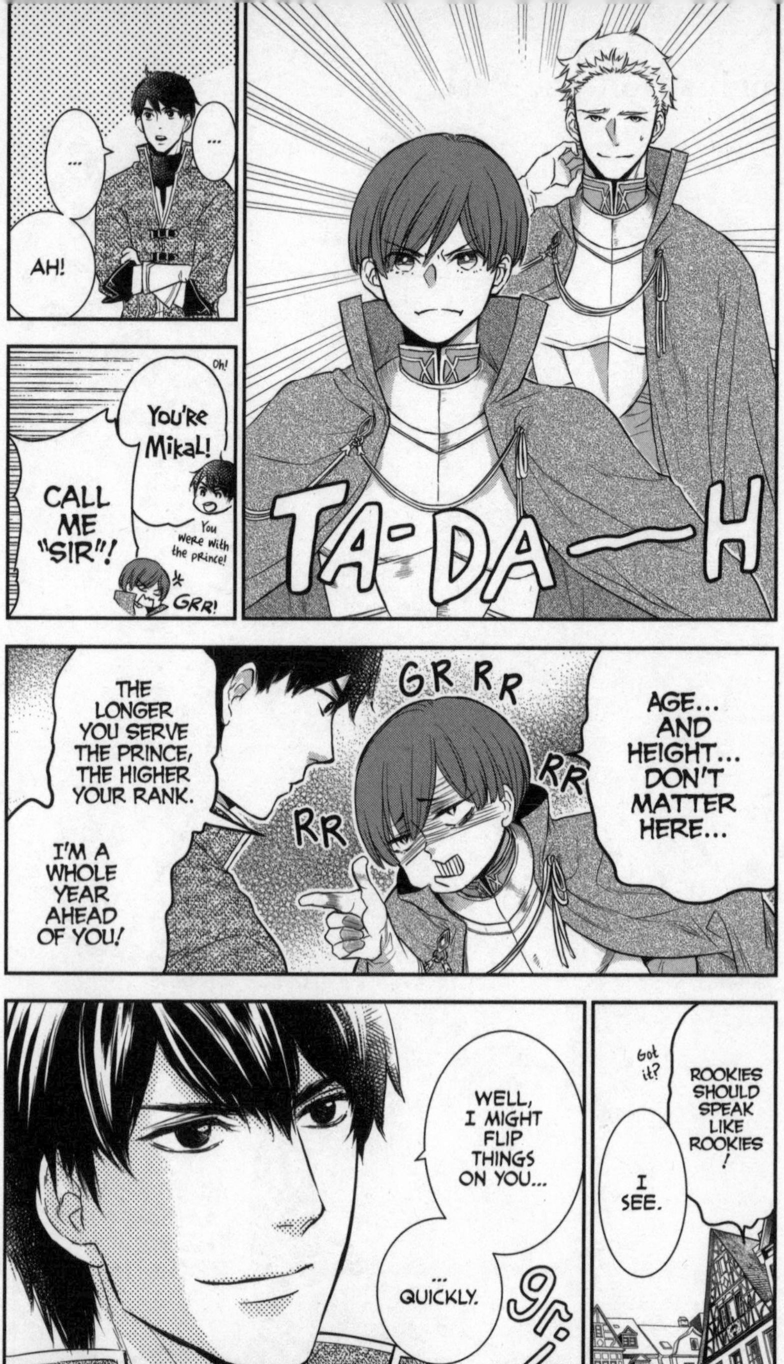
TA-DA—H
...
...
AH!
Oh!
You're Mikal!
You were with the prince!
CALL ME "SIR"!
GRR!
AGE... AND HEIGHT... DON'T MATTER HERE...
GRRRRRRRR
THE LONGER YOU SERVE THE PRINCE, THE HIGHER YOUR RANK.
I'M A WHOLE YEAR AHEAD OF YOU!
ROOKIES SHOULD SPEAK LIKE ROOKIES!
Got it?
I SEE.
WELL, I MIGHT FLIP THINGS ON YOU...
... QUICKLY.
grin

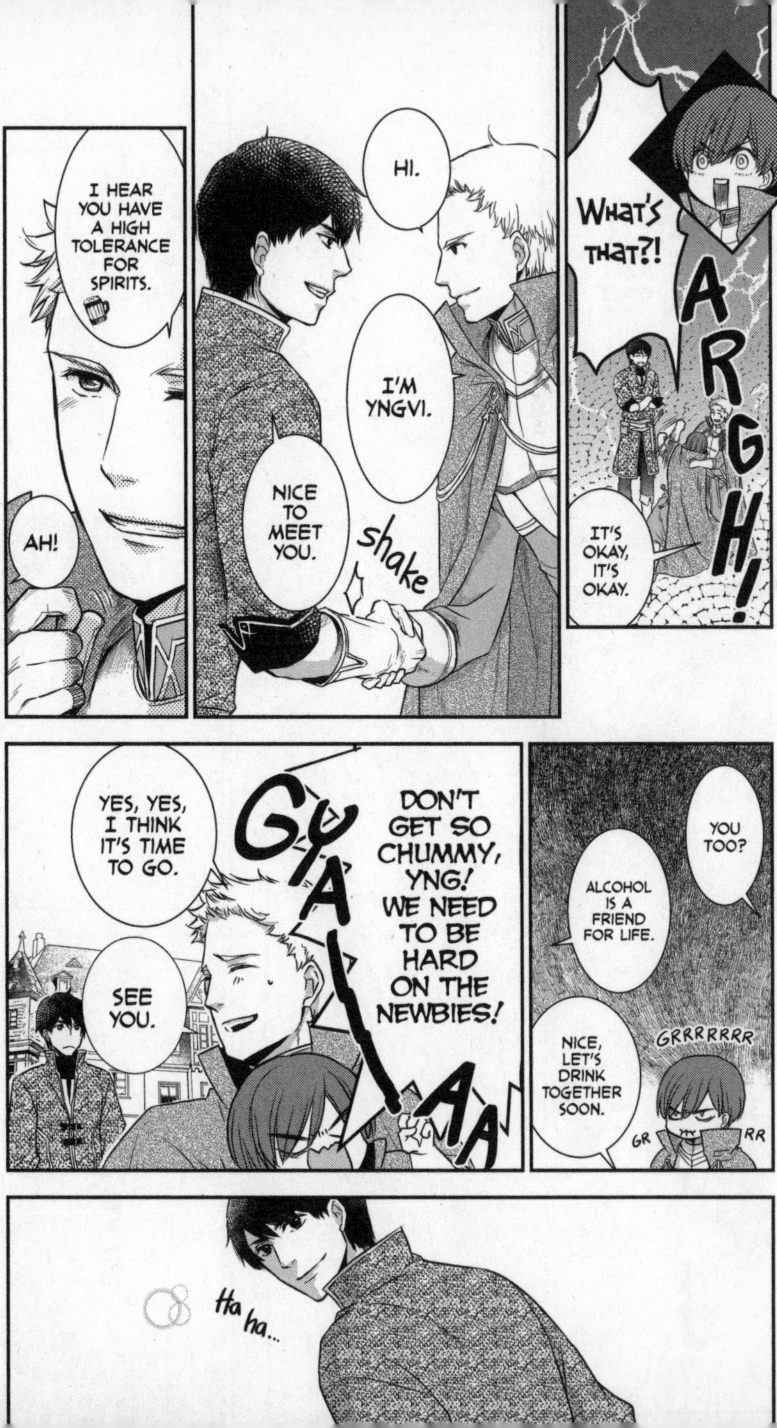
WHAT'S THAT?!
ARGH!
IT'S OKAY, IT'S OKAY.
HI.
I'M YNGVI.
NICE TO MEET YOU.
shake
I HEAR YOU HAVE A HIGH TOLERANCE FOR SPIRITS.
AH!
YOU TOO?
ALCOHOL IS A FRIEND FOR LIFE.
NICE, LET'S DRINK TOGETHER SOON.
GRRRRRRR
GR
RR
DON'T GET SO CHUMMY, YNG! WE NEED TO BE HARD ON THE NEWBIES!
GYAAA
YES, YES, I THINK IT'S TIME TO GO.
SEE YOU.
Ha ha...

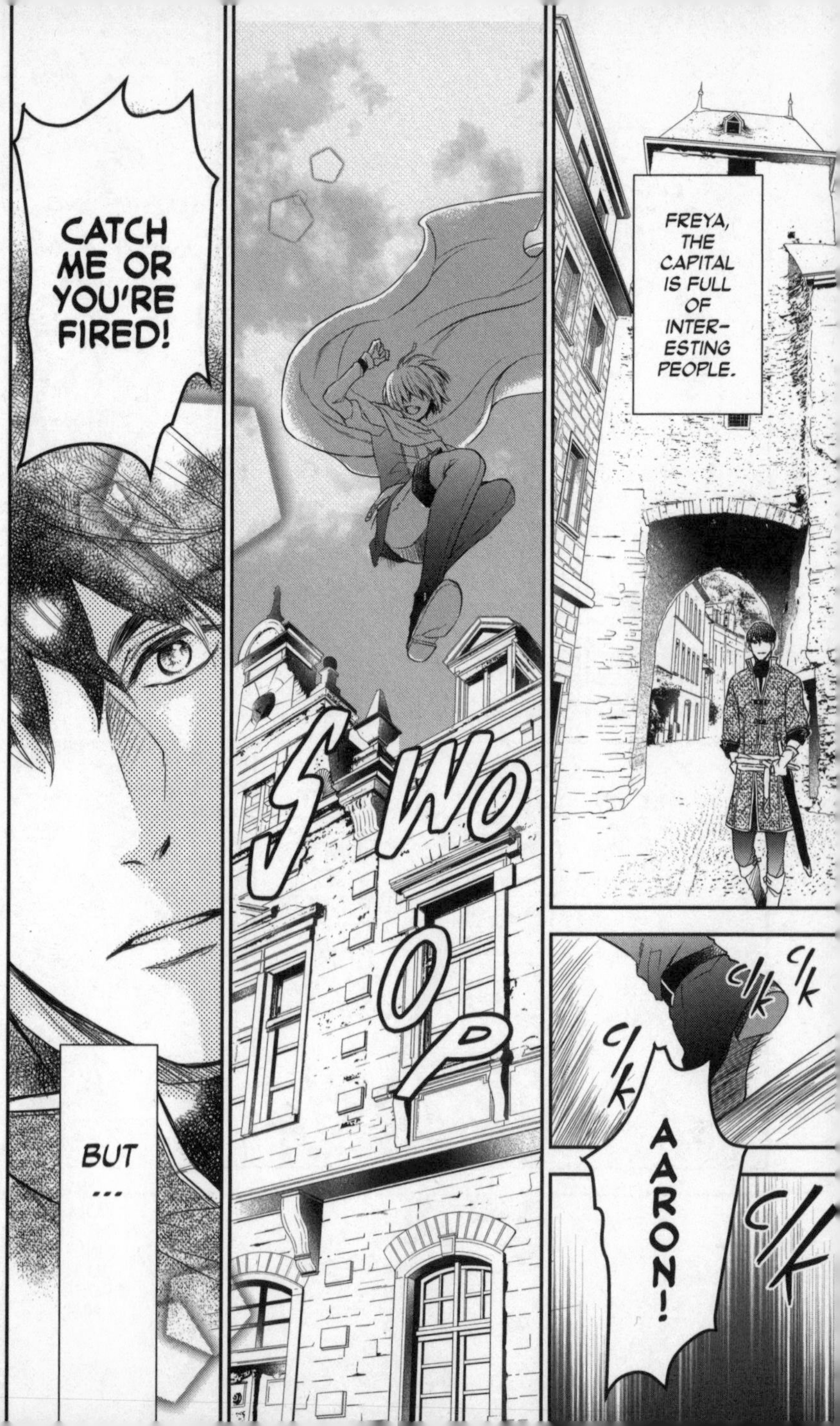
FREYA, THE CAPITAL IS FULL OF INTER-ESTING PEOPLE.
C/K C/K
C/K
C/K
AARON!
C/K
SWOOP
CATCH ME OR YOU'RE FIRED!
BUT ...

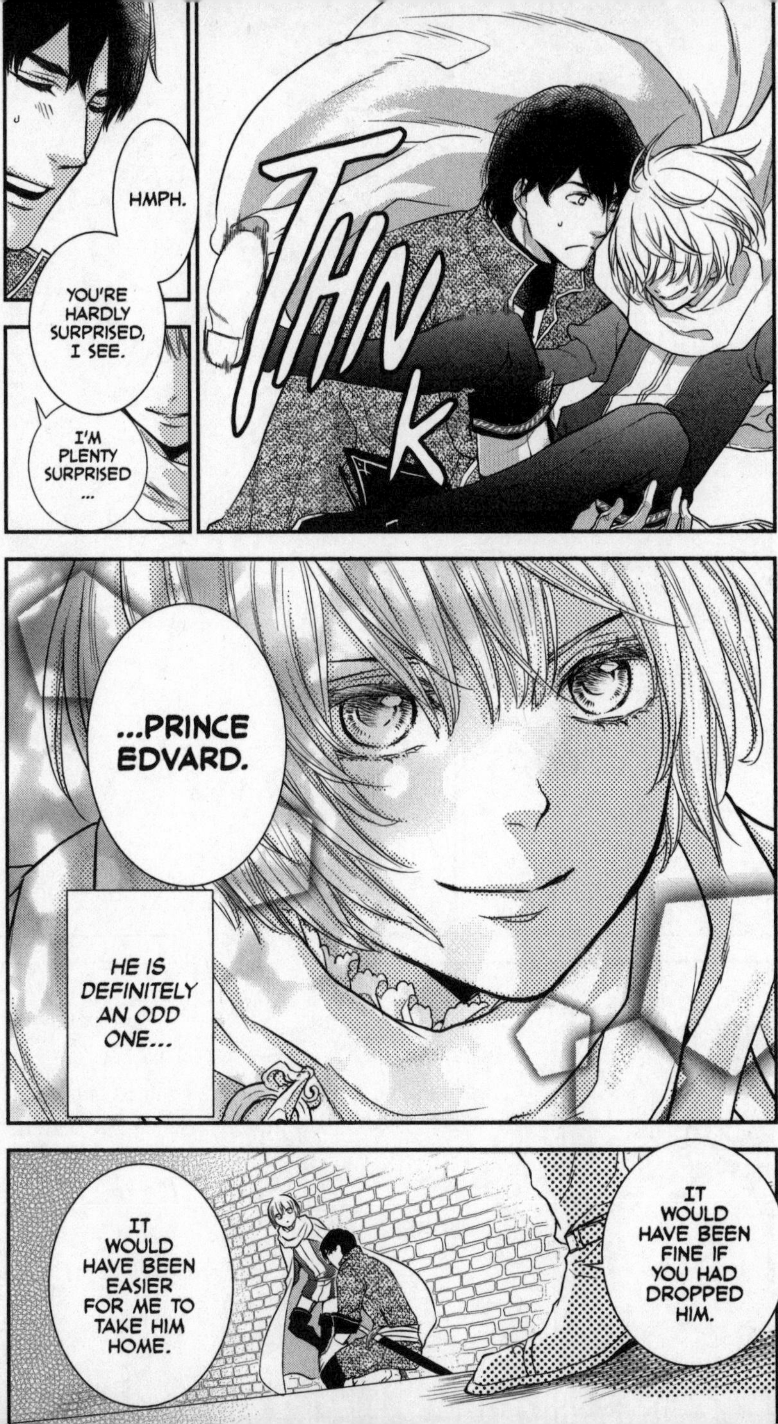
THNK
HMPH.
YOU'RE HARDLY SURPRISED, I SEE.
I'M PLENTY SURPRISED ...
...PRINCE EDVARD.
HE IS DEFINITELY AN ODD ONE...
IT WOULD HAVE BEEN FINE IF YOU HAD DROPPED HIM.
IT WOULD HAVE BEEN EASIER FOR ME TO TAKE HIM HOME.

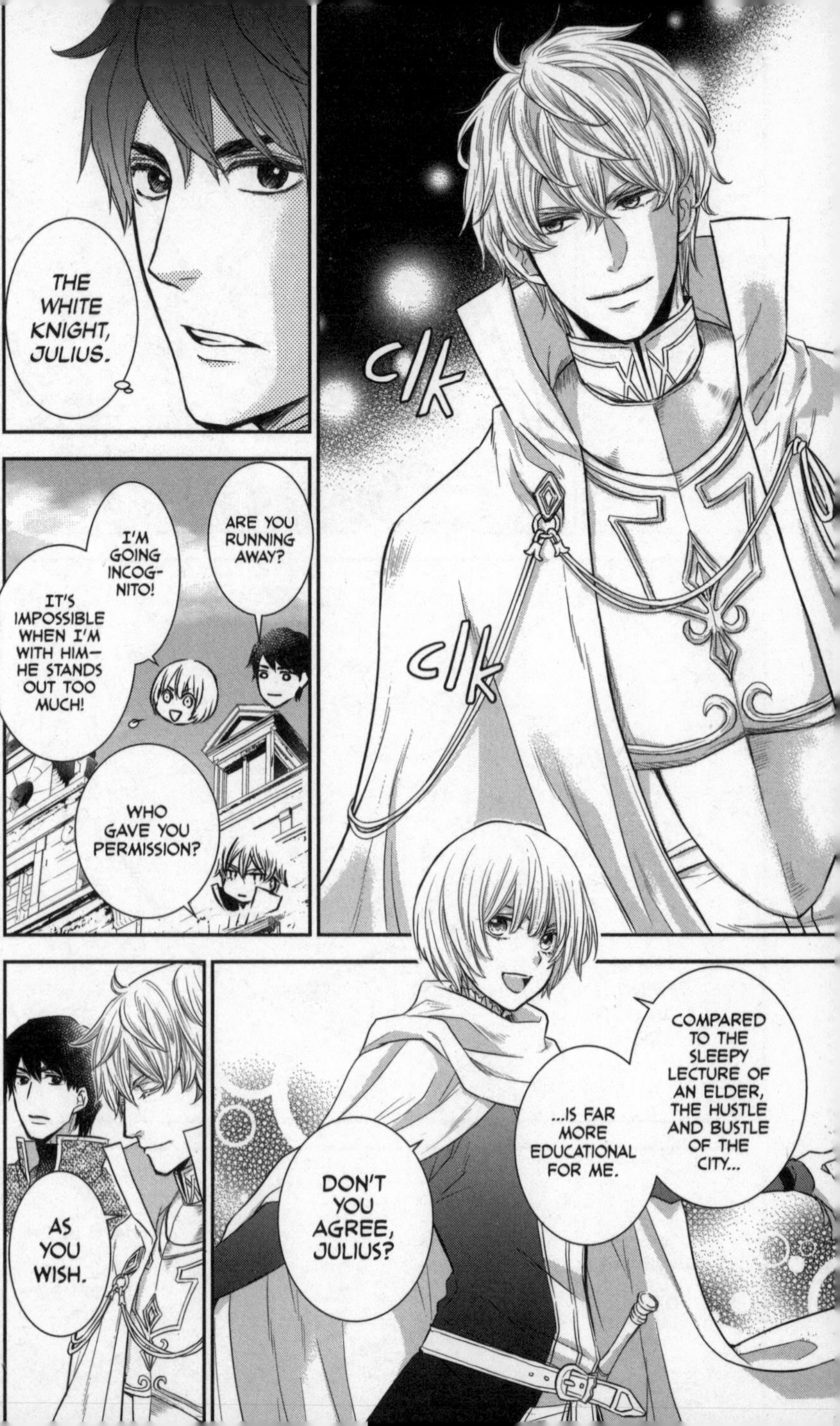
CLK
CLK
THE WHITE KNIGHT, JULIUS.
ARE YOU RUNNING AWAY?
I'M GOING INCOG-NITO!
IT'S IMPOSSIBLE WHEN I'M WITH HIM—HE STANDS OUT TOO MUCH!
WHO GAVE YOU PERMISSION?
COMPARED TO THE SLEEPY LECTURE OF AN ELDER, THE HUSTLE AND BUSTLE OF THE CITY...
...IS FAR MORE EDUCATIONAL FOR ME.
DON'T YOU AGREE, JULIUS?
AS YOU WISH.

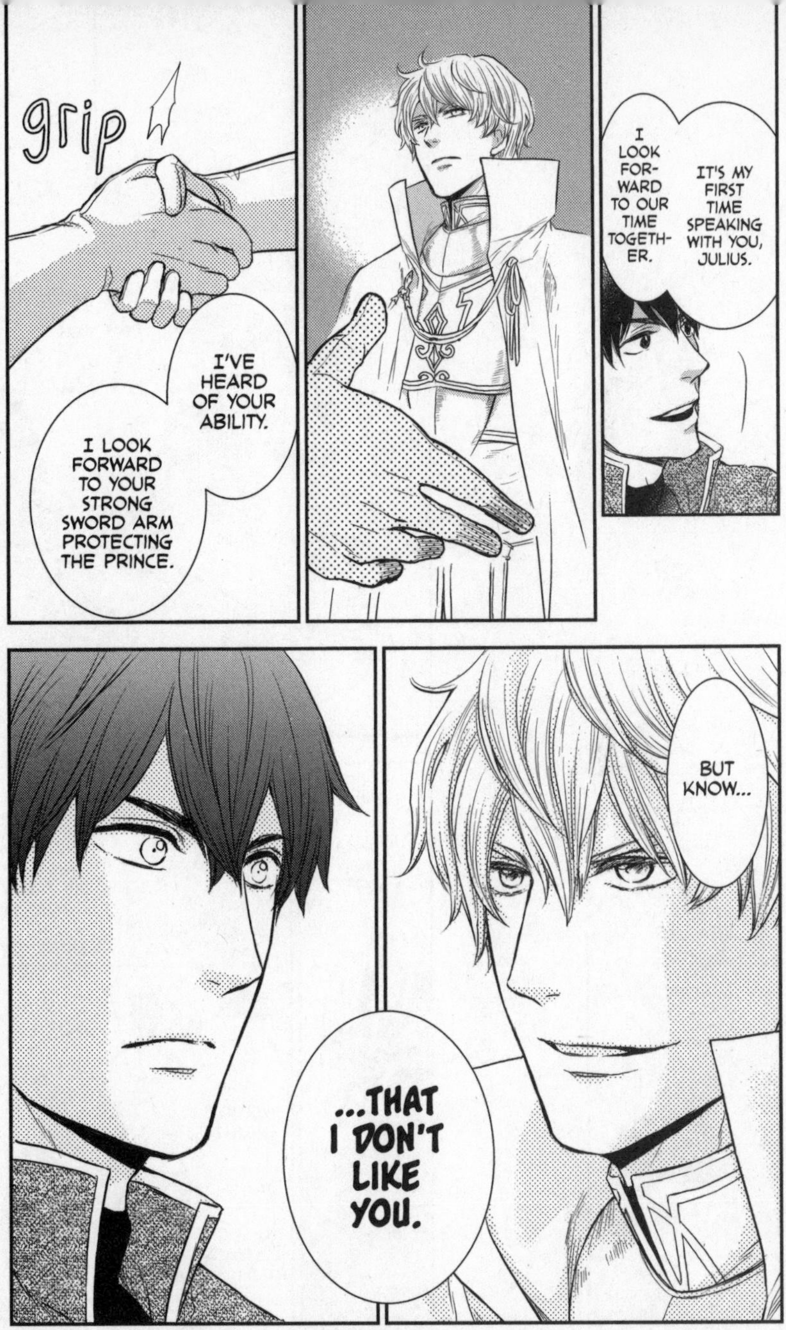
IT'S MY FIRST TIME SPEAKING WITH YOU, JULIUS.
I LOOK FOR-WARD TO OUR TIME TOGETH-ER.
grip
I'VE HEARD OF YOUR ABILITY.
I LOOK FORWARD TO YOUR STRONG SWORD ARM PROTECTING THE PRINCE.
BUT KNOW...
...THAT I DON'T LIKE YOU.

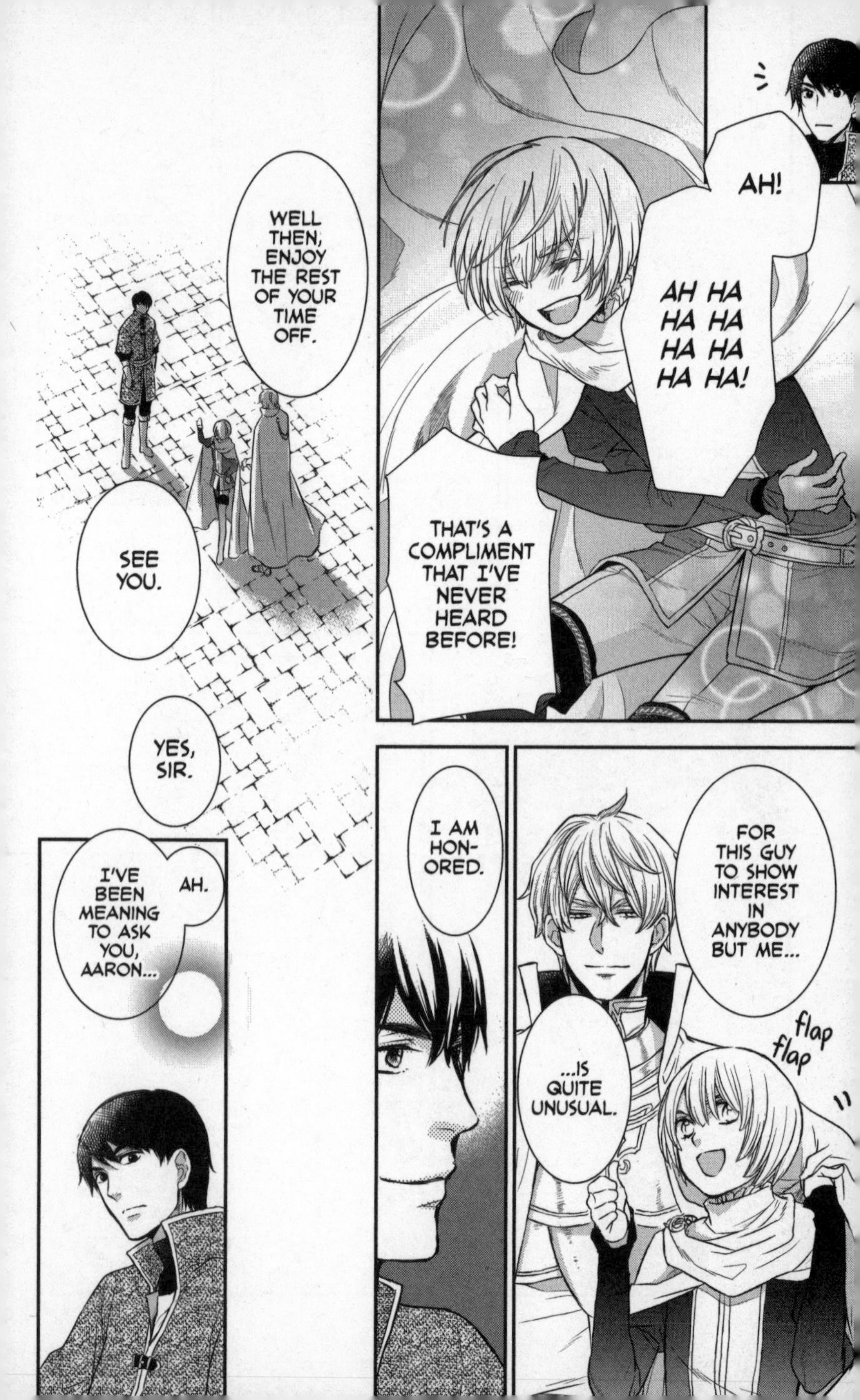
AH!
AH HA HA HA HA HA HA HA!
THAT'S A COMPLIMENT THAT I'VE NEVER HEARD BEFORE!
FOR THIS GUY TO SHOW INTEREST IN ANYBODY BUT ME...
...IS QUITE UNUSUAL.
flap flap
I AM HON-ORED.
WELL THEN, ENJOY THE REST OF YOUR TIME OFF.
SEE YOU.
YES, SIR.
AH.
I'VE BEEN MEANING TO ASK YOU, AARON...

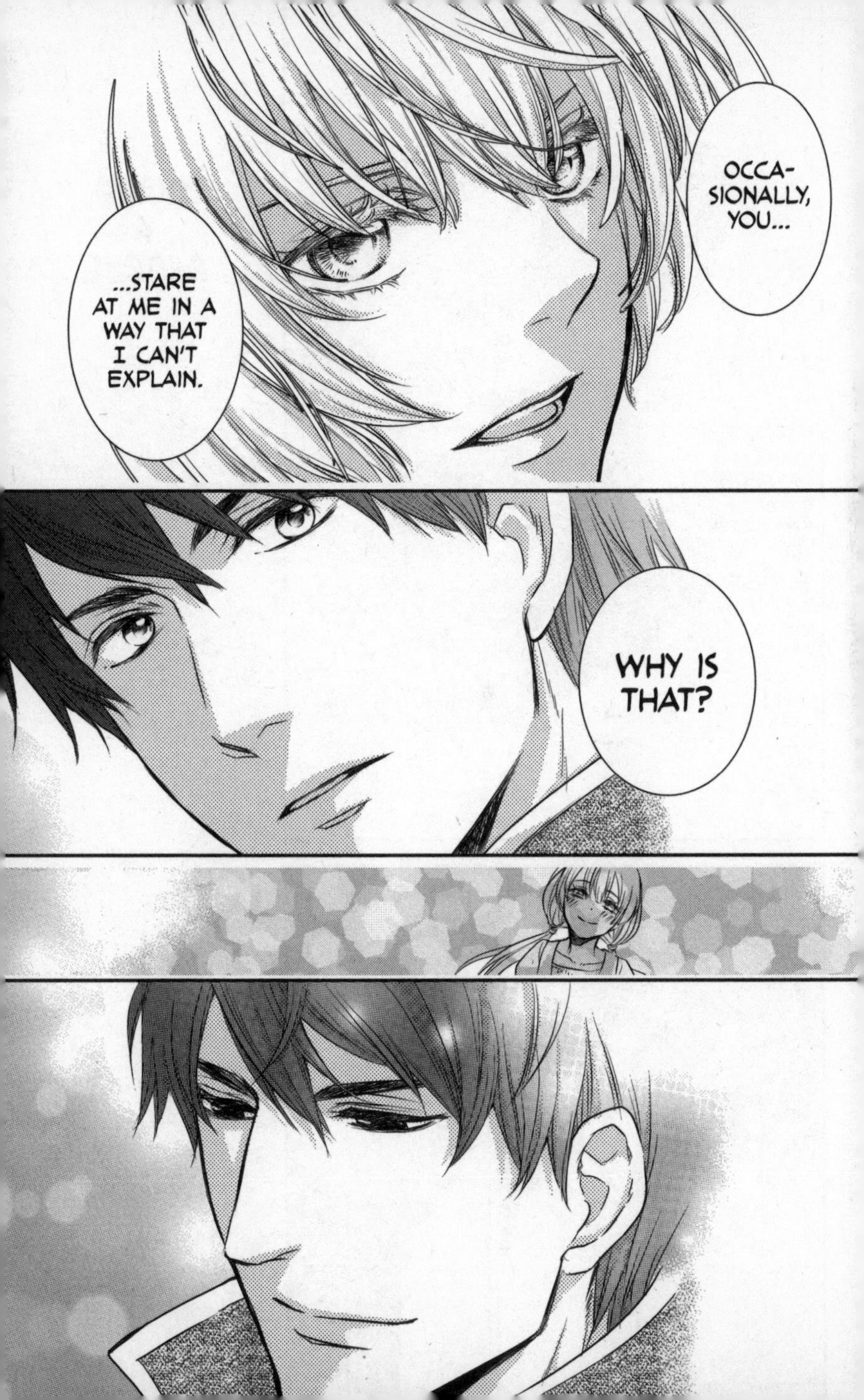
OCCA-SIONALLY, YOU...
...STARE AT ME IN A WAY THAT I CAN'T EXPLAIN.
WHY IS THAT?

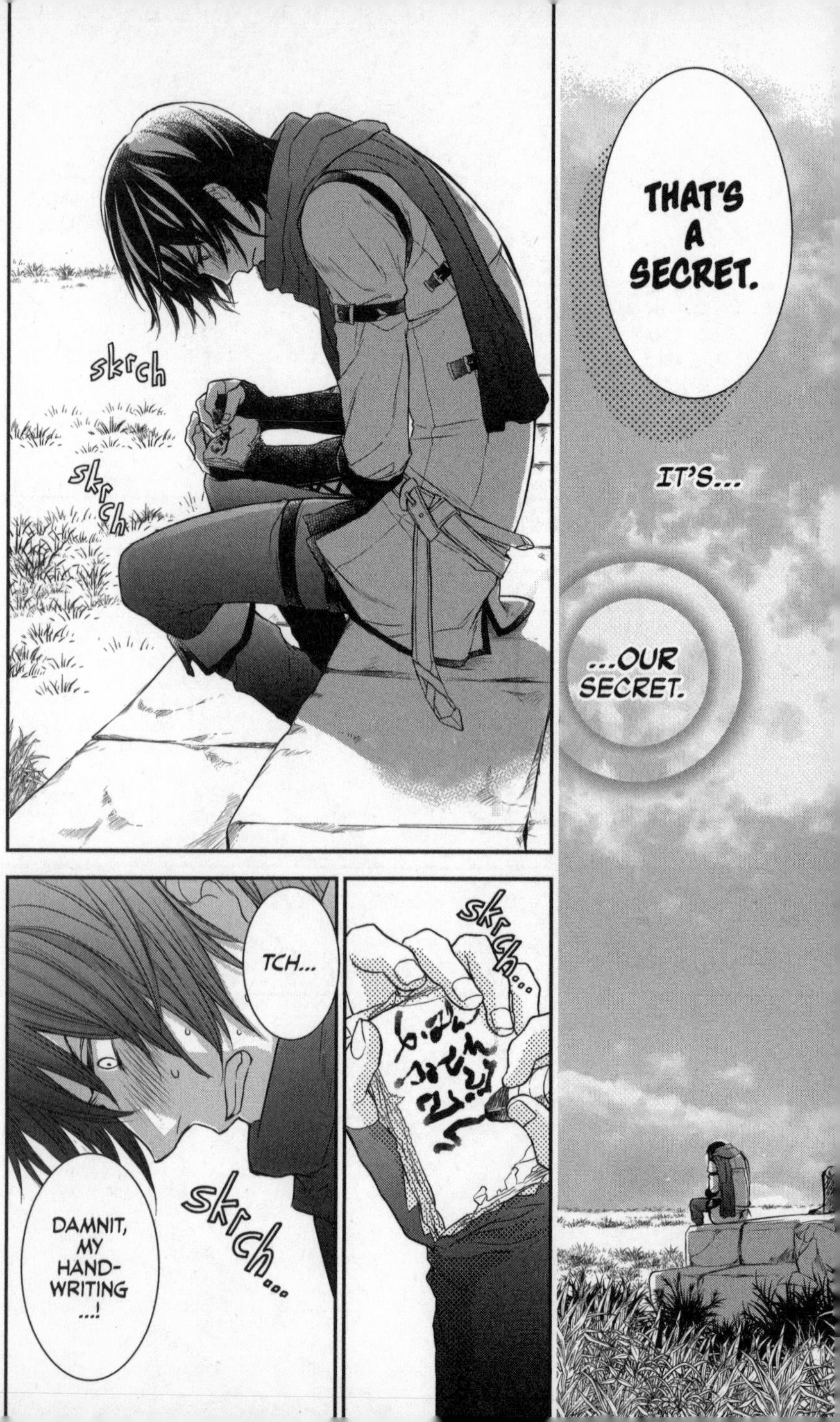
THAT'S A SECRET.
IT'S...
...OUR SECRET.
skrch
skrch
skrch...
TCH...
skrch...
DAMNIT, MY HAND-WRITING ...!

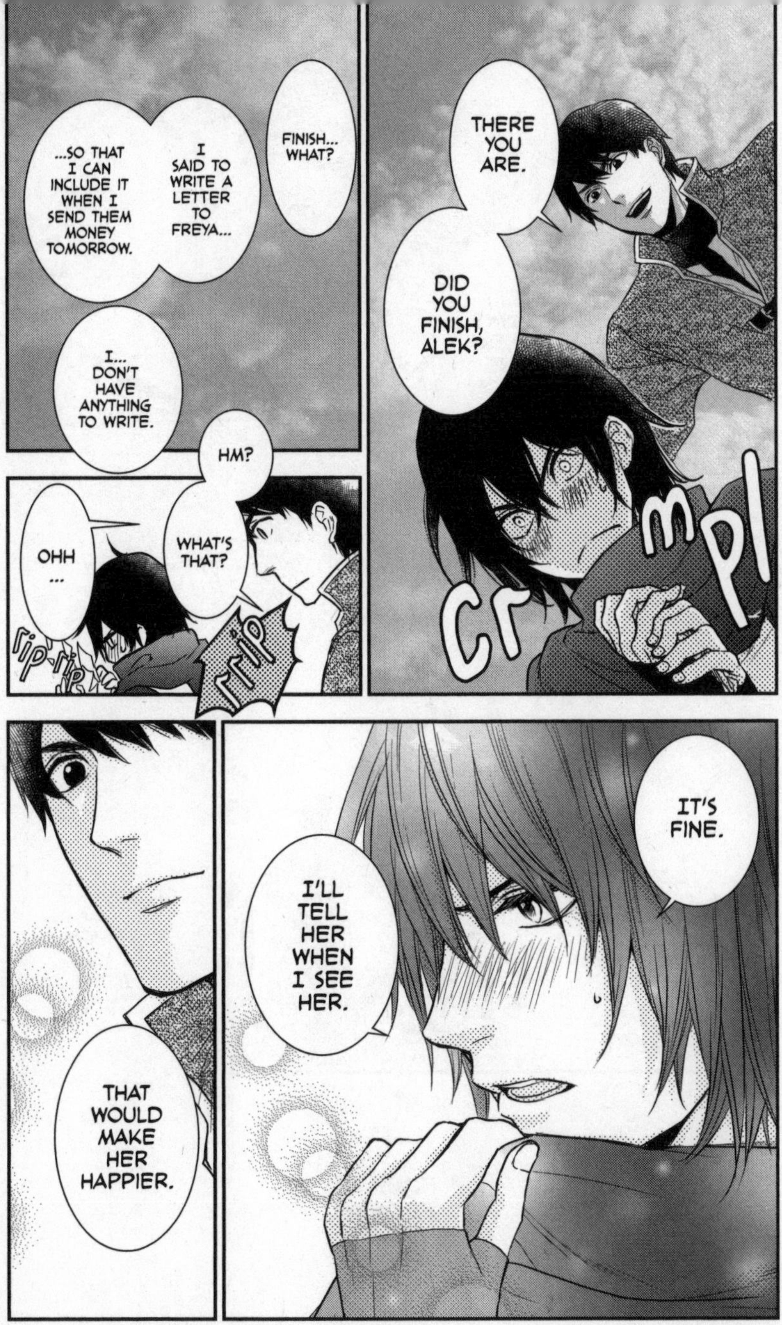
THERE YOU ARE.
DID YOU FINISH, ALEK?
crmpl
FINISH... WHAT?
I SAID TO WRITE A LETTER TO FREYA...
...SO THAT I CAN INCLUDE IT WHEN I SEND THEM MONEY TOMORROW.
I... DON'T HAVE ANYTHING TO WRITE.
HM?
WHAT'S THAT?
OHH...
rrip
rip-rip
IT'S FINE.
I'LL TELL HER WHEN I SEE HER.
THAT WOULD MAKE HER HAPPIER.

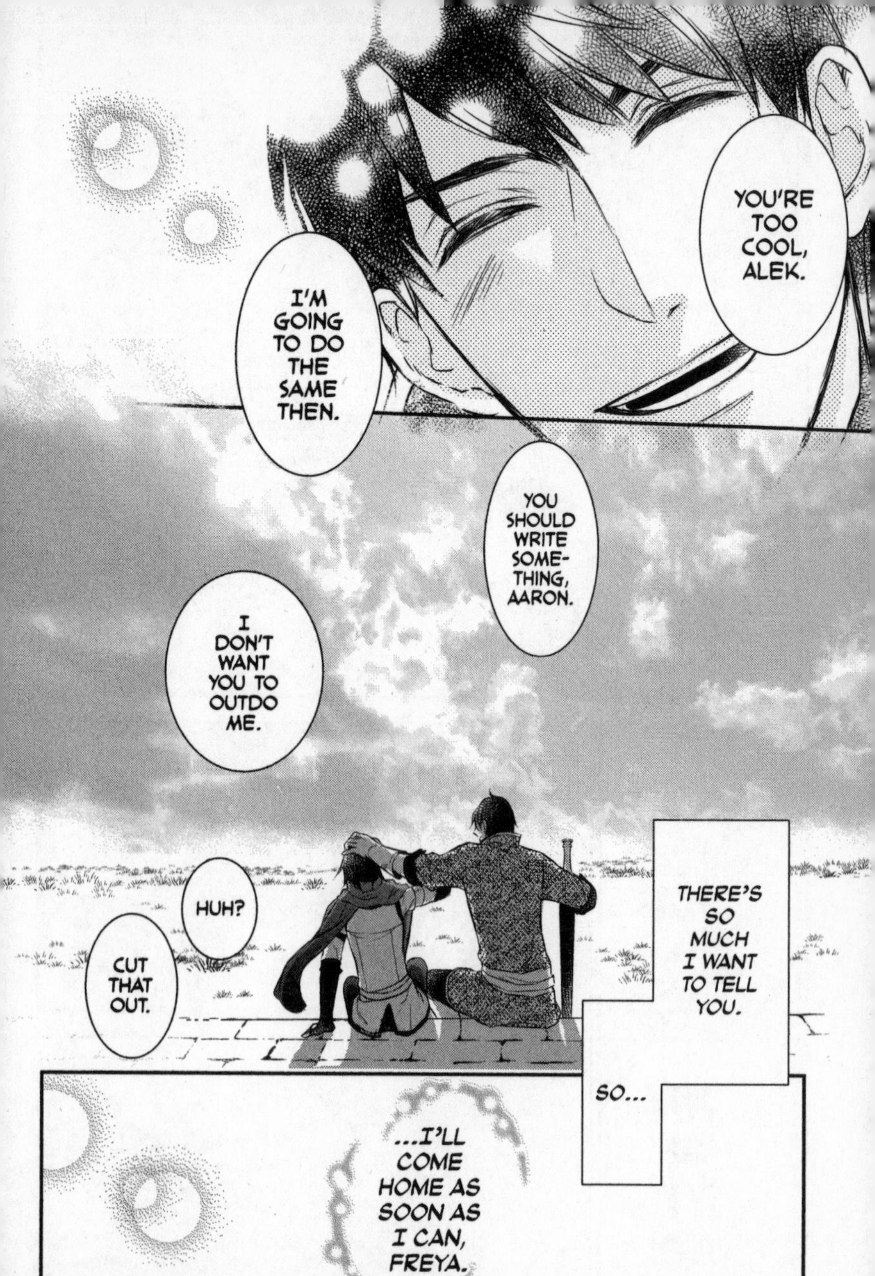
YOU'RE TOO COOL, ALEK.
I'M GOING TO DO THE SAME THEN.
YOU SHOULD WRITE SOMETHING, AARON.
I DON'T WANT YOU TO OUTDO ME.
THERE'S SO MUCH I WANT TO TELL YOU.
HUH?
CUT THAT OUT.
SO...
...I'LL COME HOME AS SOON AS I CAN, FREYA.

Bonus Chapter — The End

Afterword

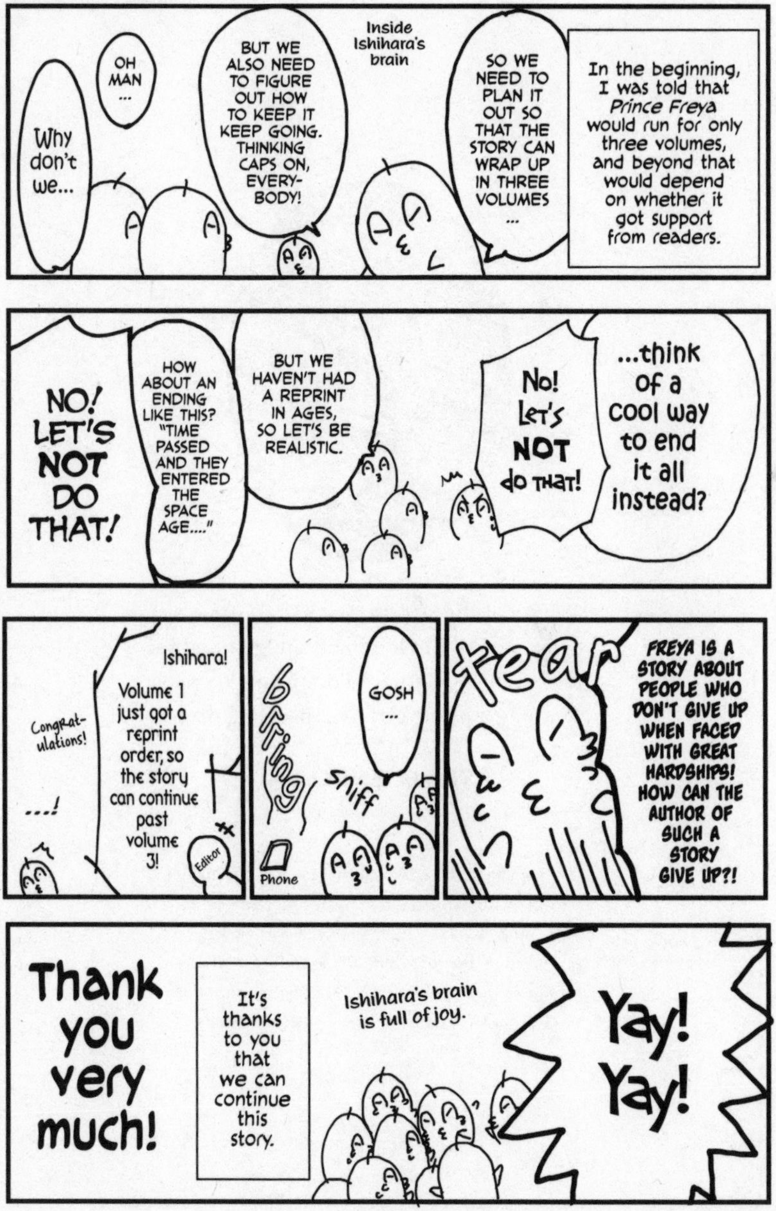

In the beginning, I was told that *Prince Freya* would run for only three volumes, and beyond that would depend on whether it got support from readers.
SO WE NEED TO PLAN IT OUT SO THAT THE STORY CAN WRAP UP IN THREE VOLUMES...
Inside Ishihara's brain
BUT WE ALSO NEED TO FIGURE OUT HOW TO KEEP IT KEEP GOING. THINKING CAPS ON, EVERYBODY!
OH MAN...
Why don't we...
...think of a cool way to end it all instead?
No! Let's NOT do that!
BUT WE HAVEN'T HAD A REPRINT IN AGES, SO LET'S BE REALISTIC.
HOW ABOUT AN ENDING LIKE THIS? "TIME PASSED AND THEY ENTERED THE SPACE AGE...."
NO! LET'S NOT DO THAT!
tear
FREYA IS A STORY ABOUT PEOPLE WHO DON'T GIVE UP WHEN FACED WITH GREAT HARDSHIPS! HOW CAN THE AUTHOR OF SUCH A STORY GIVE UP?!
GOSH...
sniff
brring
Phone
Ishihara!
Volume 1 just got a reprint order, so the story can continue past volume 3!
Congratulations!
...!
Editor
Yay! Yay!
Ishihara's brain is full of joy.
It's thanks to you that we can continue this story.
Thank you very much!

I've spent the last two years or so drawing
men soaked in blood and sludge…and I
love it! But sometimes I do think I'd enjoy
drawing a pretty girl in a sparkling dress.

KEIKO ISHIHARA

Born on April 14, Keiko Ishihara began her manga
career with *Keisan Desu Kara* (It's All Calculated).
Her other works include *Strange Dragon*, which was
serialized in the magazine *LaLa*, and *The Heiress and
the Chauffeur*, published by VIZ Media. Ishihara
is from Hyogo Prefecture, and she loves cats.

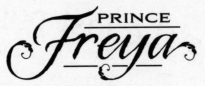

PRINCE Freya

VOLUME 3 · SHOJO BEAT EDITION

STORY AND ART BY
KEIKO ISHIHARA

ENGLISH TRANSLATION & ADAPTATION Emi Louie-Nishikawa
TOUCH-UP ART & LETTERING Sabrina Heep
DESIGN Shawn Carrico
EDITOR Pancha Diaz

Itsuwari no Freya by Keiko Ishihara

First published in Japan in 2019 by HAKUSENSHA, Inc., Tokyo.
English language translation rights
arranged with HAKUSENSHA, Inc., Tokyo.

Printed in the U.S.A.

Published by VIZ Media, LLC
P.O. Box 77010
San Francisco, CA 94107

10 9 8 7 6 5 4 3 2 1
First printing, October 2020

ratings.viz.com RATED T+ OLDER TEEN

PARENTAL ADVISORY
PRINCE FREYA is rated T+ for Older Teen and is recommended for ages 16 and up. This volume contains death and violence.

VIZ MEDIA
viz.com

Shojo Beat
shojobeat.com

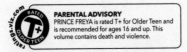

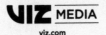

This is the last page.

In keeping with the original Japanese comic format, this book reads from right to left— so action, sound effects, and word balloons are completely reversed. This preserves the orientation of the original artwork—plus, it's fun! Check out the diagram shown here to get the hang of things, and then turn to the other side of the book to get started!

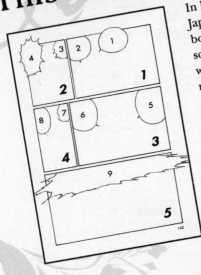